Madam PRESIDENT

Madam
PRESIDENT

Women Blazing
the Leadership Trail

BY ELEANOR CLIFT
AND TOM BRAZAITIS

Routledge
NEW YORK LONDON

Published in 2003 by
Routledge
29 West 35th Street
New York, NY 10001
www.routledge-ny.com

Routledge is an imprint of the Taylor & Francis Group.
Printed in the United States of America on acid-free paper.

First published in hardcover in 2000 by Scribner, and reprinted by
arrangement with Scribner. First Routledge paperback edition 2003.

10 9 8 7 6 5 4 3 2 1

Library of Congress Cataloging-in-Publication Data

Clift, Eleanor.
   Madam president : women blazing the leadership trail / Eleanor
Clift and Tom Brazaitis.
      p. cm.
Includes bibliographical references and index.
      ISBN 0-415-93432-X
   1. Women presidents—United States. 2. Women political
candidates—United States. 3. Women in politics—United States.
4. United States—Politics and government—20th century.
I. Brazaitis, Tom. II. Title.

Contents

———— ∿ ————

Why Not a Woman?

Marie Wilson is a card-carrying feminist. She's the kind of woman who would never buy her daughter a Barbie doll for fear of forever stunting her career ambitions and imbuing her with the vision of an unattainable body type. So, it is with a mixture of embarrassment and pride that Wilson claims parentage of President 2000 Barbie, the Mattel Corporation's "inspirational doll of the year" in 2000. "I never thought I'd be in bed with Barbie," says Wilson, who organized the popular "Take Our Daughters to Work Day,"[1] and whose offhand suggestion to a Mattel executive spurred the doll's creation. "But you know what? My grandchildren play with those dolls, and I'd rather have them playing with this one."

Whether it's President Barbie or the actress Glenn Close as a vice president standing up to terrorists in the movie *Air Force One*, or Lisa Simpson growing up to become president on "The Simpsons," cultural symbols prepare the way for real-life women to pursue the highest office in the land. In 1936, when George Gallup first asked people whether they would "vote for a woman for president if she qualified in every other respect," 65 percent said they would not. Women were only slightly more open to the idea than men. A recent poll by the National Opinion Research Center found that 90 percent of American voters could support a woman for president, with men and women equally eager to witness history being made in their lifetime.

The 1990s ushered in an extraordinary period of peace and prosperity. National security concerns and military spending took a back seat to the so-called soft issues like education, health, and gun control.

---

[1] The idea for "Take Our Daughters to Work Day" originated in 1993 with Nell Merlino, a consultant for the Ms. Foundation.

Suburban women, dubbed "soccer moms," were the most sought-after voters, and their home-and-hearth priorities set the national agenda. President Clinton's ill-advised fling with a young White House intern was a parody of testosterone-driven politics, and prompted some analysts to conclude it was time to give the other hormone a chance. The receptivity to women candidates underwent such a transformation that the wives of the two presidential candidates in the 1996 election—Hillary Clinton and Elizabeth Dole—looked forward to political futures of their own while their husbands exited elected office. The possibility exists, at least theoretically, that Clinton, elected to the U.S. Senate from New York in 2000, and Dole, who won a seat in the Senate in her native North Carolina in 2002, could take the next step and face off against each other for the presidency.

A woman taking on the same career challenges as men has become commonplace, yet the election of a woman as president still seems remote. Elizabeth Dole running for president in 2000 faded into the shadow of Texas governor George W. Bush's overwhelming lead, where she was pegged more as a potential running mate for him than an eventual victor. Jokes about her cautious campaign and her lacquered look took their toll, and the rival campaigns could scarcely contain their snickers when Dole's strongest support in an early test in Iowa came from her sorority sisters. "In a way, we have a country that is more ready than we are," says Wilson, a co-founder of the White House Project, an effort to promote the idea of a woman president. The Project's goal is to create a more welcoming climate for women seeking the presidency so that by 2008, not one, but several women will be competing for the presidency. When a women candidate is no longer a novelty, the thinking goes, success becomes more likely.

As the twentieth century drew to a close, anything seemed possible. California Rep. Nancy Pelosi launched her campaign to become Democratic Whip a full two years before the election was held in the fall of 2001. It was an audacious move, and it paid off. Pelosi's gender was an advantage. Democrats like to brag they're the more diverse of the two parties, but they had never had a woman in a top leadership post. Pelosi became the first woman elected from outside the Democratic Party's good ol' boy leadership structure, and the first woman in either party to win a high leadership post. Pelosi was sworn in on February 6, 2002. She had barely uttered the words of her oath before people were predicting she could be the first female House Speaker if the Democrats regained the majority. The drama of her achievement was highlighted at a luncheon she hosted before her swearing-in for all the former and current female members of Congress. Out of about 12,000 members, only 209 have been women; and 117 of those are still living. Many joined Pelosi for a celebratory meal served at the Library of Congress.

Congressional Democrats installed women as the heads of the campaign committees in both the House and Senate, another first in the heavily male environment on Capitol Hill. Privately, some women lawmakers wondered if this was an honor, or if they were being set up as scapegoats. When the appointments were announced, George W. Bush had just been declared president after a long and contentious vote recount, and the two parties were vying for control in a bitterly divided Congress. Washington State Senator Patty Murray at the helm of the Senate Campaign Committee and New York's Rep. Nita Lowey heading up the Congressional Campaign Committee knew that sniping and second-guessing came with the territory, and that they ultimately would be judged by how well Democrats did in the 2002 elections.

The biggest problem Washington faced in the spring of 2001 was how to spend a burgeoning budget surplus after more than two decades of deficits. A record number of women were preparing to run for Congress, their chances boosted by a higher number of open seats created by the congressional redistricting that takes place after the census every ten years. It's easier to win if you don't have to defeat an entrenched incumbent.

That heady period came to an abrupt end with the terrorist attacks on New York and Washington on September 11, 2001. With the country suddenly focused on war preparedness, the once bright prospects for women seeking elective office dimmed. Some women dropped out; others saw their chances diminish in the polls. Campaigns designed around domestic priorities were overtaken by a new set of voter concerns centered on security and safety. Women had to face the hard reality that voters may not trust them to lead the country in a time of war.

What we set out to do in this book is chart the efforts to get a woman on the presidential ticket, beginning with the 1984 campaign when Representative Geraldine Ferraro (D., N.Y.) became the first woman vice presidential candidate on a major party ticket. The Democratic nominee, Walter Mondale, was far behind President Reagan in the polls, and needed to do something dramatic to shake up the electorate. In hindsight, Mondale probably would have lost to Reagan no matter who was his running mate. Women did not rally behind Mondale even though he had picked one of their own. Male candidates since then have shied away from using gender as a ticket-balancer, and four presidential campaigns have passed without another woman as a vice presidential candidate. The experience made women realize that there are no Cinderellas in politics, and that getting women elected to high office requires hard work. We document that work, starting with the creation of Emily's List, which stands for Early Money Is Like Yeast—that is, it makes the dough rise.

The impact of Ferraro's candidacy is still debated. Did it advance or set back women's aspirations? The scrutiny of her husband's tangled finances was such an emotionally searing experience for Ferraro and her family that she recounts in her memoir how she called home several times a day to check on her husband, fearing he might be suicidal. The promise of her candidacy was not fulfilled, yet two years later, in 1986, inspired by Ferraro, the number of women candidates for state office and for Congress mushroomed. That year, a record fifty-four women ran for the House, nine for governor, eleven for lieutenant governor, and six for the Senate. The Democrats elected their first woman to the Senate, Maryland's Barbara Mikulski, who is the longest-serving woman in the Senate today.

Women continued to make incremental gains in numbers until 1998, when, for the first time, fewer women ran for public office than in the previous election. The falloff was puzzling because running for office had gotten easier for women. Many of the barriers had fallen. A study done by the National Women's Political Caucus (NWPC) showed that women, when they ran, won as often as men did. Raising money was still a challenge, but women running for Congress had reached parity with men in the money race. There was simply no way to sugarcoat the fact that fewer women chose to run. Personal issues like privacy, how to keep your family intact, and the scrutiny that politicians must endure loomed as deterrents to women who could have rewarding careers without the hassle of public life. "Women say, is it really worth it?" says Anita Perez Ferguson, former head of the NWPC.

In evaluating women who could be taken seriously as a potential president, we looked to the traditional feeder systems: statehouses, the Senate, and the House. Four of the last five presidents are former governors, which suggests that voters value executive experience more highly than a legislative record. Yet there are only six elected women governors out of fifty, a dearth that women must address before they can move up to national office. The numbers elsewhere are not much better. At the start of the new millennium, there were 13 women among the 100 senators, and 62 women among 435 members of the House. At the current rate, it will be 250 years before the number of women reaches parity with the number of men in the Congress.

Why worry about the percentage of women? What can a woman bring to the process of governing that men cannot? We don't know for sure because we've never tried it. The closest we've come is in Arizona, where women for a time occupied the top five positions in the executive branch, and in the state of Washington, where women hold the balance of power in the legislative branch. We assess how they're doing in the chapter titled "Go West, Young Woman."

Women don't need to apologize for wanting a fair share of the seats at the table of political power; after all, they are more than half the population. There is evidence at every level where women have played a role in governing that their politics overall tend toward the progressive side. Research by the Rutgers Center for the American Woman and Politics shows that a conservative woman is more likely to favor somewhat more progressive social policies than her conservative male counterpart. If only women's votes counted in Congress, the Family Leave Act and other family-friendly legislation would have passed years earlier. Senator Ted Stevens (R., Alaska), chairman of the Senate Appropriations Committee, complained in July 1999 that women don't support military spending because "there's all these touchy-feely things that they want to spend money on." He said women constantly ask him, "Why do you want to spend more money on the military? Don't they have enough?" After the 9/11 terrorist attacks, women's concern about security and safety overtook for the time being any reluctance to spend more on the military. Polls showed no gender gap in attitudes toward President Bush's war on terrorism, which drew strong support from the American people, at least in its opening stages.

Political analysts believe the first woman president will be a "Sister Mister," having the body of a woman with the character traits of a man. More than likely she will come from the moderate-to-conservative segment of the ideological spectrum. Women are presumed to be compassionate. To succeed in politics, they must prove their toughness. When we appeared on a radio show to discuss this book, a male caller said he worried that an "estrogen-driven social policy" would carry compassion too far. He needn't worry. Democratic women typically go to great lengths to avoid being pegged as liberal, a label that began losing favor more than two decades ago when Ronald Reagan won the presidency. Women frequently go too far in proving their toughness. Seeking credibility, they cater to men's issues—military defense and the economy—sometimes at the expense of losing touch with their natural constituency of women.

The most hopeful trend for women in politics is taking place outside the Washington Beltway, in state government. Women hold more than a fourth of administrative positions in state government and more than a fifth of the seats in state legislatures. The number of women serving in state legislatures has increased more than fivefold since 1969, when only 4 percent of all state legislators were women.

Recognizing the need to showcase women in high office, seventeen governors have chosen women as their lieutenant governors. Nine of the female lieutenant governors are Republicans, testimony to the GOP's concern about the gender gap—the split between how men and women vote—that has tended to work to the advantage of Democrats. Gail Manning, director of the National Conference of Lieutenant Governors, describes the states as laboratories for women in politics. The model of a male-female tandem at the top of the ticket is becoming the norm in the states, she says. The same configuration on a national level cannot be far off.

When it comes to winning the presidency, however, few women get taken seriously as potential candidates. Even among the top tier of women in office—the six governors and thirteen senators—it is easy to disqualify this one or that because she comes from too small a state, or is too young or too old or divorced. Men often get away with being one or more of these things, but the admission standards for women into the highest echelon of politics are higher. If Oprah decided to change careers and become a politician, would she be credible? Reagan was. Try to imagine the female political equivalent of, say, Steve Forbes, the wealthy publisher who decided to run for president. If Hillary Clinton had been governor of Arkansas instead of her husband, would she have made it to the White House, or would party leaders have dismissed her as coming from an inconsequential state? If Kathleen Kennedy Townsend, Maryland's lieutenant governor, were a male, with her praiseworthy record in politics and unblemished character, would she inherit the Kennedy legacy and vault to the top of everybody's list of presidential prospects?

On the afternoon in late February 2000 when we interviewed Hillary Clinton, she had just returned from a fund-raising lunch hosted by the women Democratic senators. The event was closed to the press, so the women felt freer to vent their frustration about the campaign trail. They shared war stories and got each other laughing about the particular burdens women bear in the American political scene. Hillary recalled Arkansas senator Blanche Lincoln's remark that "it doesn't matter what I say about an issue. If I have a run in my panty hose, that's all anybody will talk about." Dianne Feinstein, the senior senator from California, who has proven herself many times over, cautioned the assemblage of women politicos, "It doesn't matter how good you are on the issues, you're still judged differently. And you can be absolutely a person of incredible integrity and credibility, but it is still a harder sell."

A mid-January poll by Hillary's pollster, Mark Penn, confirmed the attitudinal hurdle that confronts women seeking elective office. "Across the board, including women, the public is more likely to vote for a male candidate," says Penn. "There is a net ten-point edge that a woman candidate has to overcome." Women have an edge on honesty and caring, but on the qualities that matter most, leadership and the ability to be decisive, men rule. Among those polled, including women, 9 percent declared they were "against women in political of-fices," and 7 percent thought women are "not capable of doing the job." Penn believes the real numbers are several times higher. "You've got to figure a lot of people are hiding what they think. Women have the opportunity to run but we shouldn't kid ourselves. There's an electoral hurdle to overcome."

Candidates in the end are judged by the picture they paint of them-selves, and overcoming gender bias is like dealing with any other disadvantage going into a competitive race. The difference is that women do not have as broad a canvas to work with as male candi-dates. "The stylistic range seems to be more limited as to what is or is not appropriate for a woman to do, or say, or appear," says Hillary Clinton. Imagine any woman, she adds, even an accomplished office-holder like Feinstein, saying some of the things that leading presiden-tial candidates—Vice President Gore, Senator Bradley, Governor Bush, and Senator McCain—have said in the course of their cam-paigns. "She couldn't be as tough, or as whiney, or sanctimonious, or self-righteous," Hillary said. "It wouldn't work coming out of a woman's mouth."

The former First Lady says being a candidate is like being in a courtroom, an environment she knows something about, having practiced law for twenty years before coming to Washington. "You can be who you are but you just have to be very conscious that you're given no benefit of the doubt as a woman."

Women have not yet reached the point where they can get away with being mediocre. Conventional wisdom says voters want the American version of Margaret Thatcher, a woman who won't go wobbly in a crisis. Women are still new enough on the political scene that their mere presence signals change. Yet too much change scares voters. So the perfect female candidate is a political moderate who projects traditional values, and who can reassure voters that when they wake up the day after voting for her, the world won't be all that different. "Margaret Thatcher did a great thing for women because of the Falklands war," says Kathleen Hall Jamieson, dean of the Annenberg School for Communication at the University of Pennsylvania. "When people say women can't be tough, you say, 'Oh, yeah, what about Margaret Thatcher?' She's the example that confronts the stereotype head-on."

Party professionals talked about putting a woman on the ticket in 2000, but it didn't happen. The prospect of a woman on the ticket doesn't have the shock value it once did. Women have risen to the top in business, medicine, and the law. Why not politics?

Our book examines the changing political landscape and the women who will be leaders in the new century: who they are, what drew them to politics, what sacrifices they have had to make, and how politics will be different because of them.

The Clinton sex scandal piqued public interest in electing women on the theory that women can better control their sexual impulses. In itself this is quite a shift, since the female hormone and the unpredictability it causes has been cited as a reason not to put women in high leadership positions. ABC commentator Cokie Roberts suggested women run on the slogan "I won't embarrass you in front of your children." Women may be better able to control their hormones, but placing women on a pedestal only makes their fall more precipitous when their flaws are exposed. Women get tripped up by some of the same things as men—financial improprieties, ethical lapses—but for women, one mistake can be fatal. Could any woman in politics survive a sex scandal with an intern the way Clinton did? When have you ever heard anyone say girls will be girls?

Sex aside, Clinton deserves credit for making the presence of women in government seem routine. Seeing Janet Reno as the first woman attorney general and Madeleine Albright as secretary of state made it easier for voters to imagine a woman as president. Neither woman lacks toughness. Reno stood up to critics on the right and the left to become the longest-serving attorney general of the century, despite a worsening case of Parkinson's disease. Albright successfully prosecuted a bombing campaign of the Serbian province of Kosovo despite widespread jitters in the administration and in the media about U.S. intervention in the Balkans. At the same time, she openly displays her femininity by wearing colorful scarves, pins, and hats. Negotiating with Serbian leaders, she hummed a Serbian lullaby she remembered from her childhood in Europe. She described her role in Middle East peace talks as that of a "handmaiden."

President Bush continued the gains for women, naming Russian scholar and Stanford professor Condoleezza Rice the nation's first female national security advisor. Skepticism about whether Rice, a soft-spoken African American, the first in her family to attend college, could hold her own among the high-powered egos quickly gave way to news stories about her influence on policy, and her close relationship with Bush. Frequently, she was the only senior official invited to spend the weekend at Camp David with the first family. Her prominence as a member of Bush's War Cabinet led to speculation that Bush might make her his running mate in 2004, opening the door for the first woman and first black to hold the office. Bush also relied to an extraordinary degree on his communications advisor, Karen Hughes, a former television reporter in Texas who had been with him as governor. Hughes is the first woman anybody can remember who is truly a member of the White House inner circle. She is said to know Bush so well that she can finish his thoughts. Even after she returned to Texas, little happened in the White House without her input.

Signals of societal change hint that acceptance of a woman president is not far off. One such signal appeared in December 1998 when *USA Today* reported that a female navy carrier pilot participated in the opening wave of air strikes ordered against Iraq. Proof that a female combat pilot is no longer a novelty was the fact that the story ran on page eighteen. This kind of shift in thinking is another milestone in women's march to the White House.

Women's success in sports offers another clue. A male spectator at the 1989 Women's World Cup Soccer games, asked by National Public Radio why he was there, replied, "Their passes are sharper, they play with more finesse, they aren't greedy with the ball, and they're more of a team." The image of these gutsy women winning the world championship captured the country's imagination. Elizabeth Dole hired a plane to fly over the Rose Bowl, where the championship game was played, with the message "Go Team USA! Make History!" President Clinton's Health and Human Services secretary Donna Shalala exulted, "They've broken every glass ceiling."

Celebrating after the game, a fan held up a sign that read "Thank You Title IX." The 1972 federal civil rights law requires colleges and universities to provide equal opportunity for men and women to participate in intercollegiate sports. Former labor secretary Lynn Martin says the importance of this law should not be underestimated. "The girls are now playing competitive sports, and that has had a whole different effect. I'm not talking about sports as a career. I'm talking about learning to win and lose, to work together as a team. If you ask my kids to name a half dozen of their best friends, each of them would name at least one of the opposite sex. That didn't occur before, and it's an enormous change in terms of working together and getting rid of some of the sludge that's still out there."

Former New Jersey governor Christine Todd Whitman, whose tomboy childhood conditioned her for the rough and tumble of politics, echoes the praise for Title IX. Her daughter Kate played varsity ice hockey and lacrosse at Wesleyan. "You can see the difference in her," says Whitman. "You see a lot of women coming out as leaders in sport, and sport teaches you a lot. It's good to see."

The idea of a female president has been talked about, more or less seriously, for half a century. In 1956, John F. Kennedy, then a U.S. senator, ruminated about the attributes the first woman elected president would have to possess. The ideal woman, he wrote in *Everywoman's Magazine*, would have the wisdom of Eleanor Roosevelt, the leadership of Joan of Arc, the compassion of Queen Victoria, the cleverness of Clare Booth Luce, the determination of polio nurse Sister Kenny, and the courage of Helen Keller. He might have added that it wouldn't hurt if she could walk on water.

These days, most voters know they'll never find perfection in a political candidate, male or female. In 1986, two years after Ferraro's unsuccessful bid for the vice presidency, a *U.S. News & World Report* poll found that more than a third of voters would not vote for a female president. In 1988, Ronald Reagan, whose conservative candidacy produced the first clear manifestation of the gender gap, told a group of students that the idea of a woman president would take "a little getting used to on the part of some people. But I think it's inevitable that in this country there will be a woman president because they've come up in so many different fields." By 1997, a survey conducted by the

Sara Lee Corp. found that nearly two-thirds of the public believes that a woman will be elected president by the year 2016.

A poll conducted by the accounting firm Deloitte & Touche and released in January 2000 deflated the rosy prospects. It found that three-quarters of Americans don't expect a female president in the next decade, and a third of the public believe that "there are general characteristics about women that make them less qualified to serve as president." The poll documented greater gains for women in the business world than in politics. "The climate for women in the board-room is somewhat warmer than for women in the White House," said pollster Holly Heline. Women are seen as less capable on foreign policy, law-and-order issues, and the economy. And they score significantly lower on the ability to lead during a crisis and the ability to make difficult decisions. Lynn Martin, who served in Congress and is a consultant with the firm, introduced the findings at a press conference in Washington. "In 1980, when I was first running on the national level, I said there would be a woman president by 2000, and so did everybody else who was trying to be cool," Martin said. "These are not the results I would have wished for or predicted. There are doubts about every single woman."

One in ten Americans thinks the United States will never elect a female president, and more women hold that view than men. Some of the most ardent feminists are the most pessimistic. They joke darkly that when the first woman president stands on the stage to be sworn in, her hand on a Bible held by her husband, her mother will nudge the person seated beside her in the audience and declare, "You see that woman up there? Her brother is a doctor."

Laura Liswood knows what to do when she hears women say they don't expect to see a female president in their lifetime. Liswood, founder and vice chair of the Council of Women World Leaders at the Kennedy School of Government at Harvard University, shows them a videotape she has compiled with highlights of interviews she conducted with female presidents and prime ministers of countries around the world. Liswood says the reaction she gets from American women is surprise, quickly followed by anger. Why should the United States lag behind foreign nations in recognizing women's ability to wield power?

Liswood's answer starts with the structural barrier of the U.S. winner-take-all system of politics. In countries with parliamentary systems, like England, the head of a political party takes office if the party wins a plurality of the vote in a national election. That's how

Thatcher became prime minister. It is harder for an outsider to break into the fifty-plus-one American system that puts the emphasis on candidates, not parties. When Marjorie Margolies Mezvinsky, then head of the Women's Campaign Fund and a former member of Congress, complained that the year of the woman lasted only 365 days, she was more than literally right. The record gains that women made in 1992 were less the result of a sea change in voter attitudes than the availability of open seats—congressional districts where there is no incumbent. Every ten years, the census creates open seats because districts are redrawn to accommodate the new demographics. Following this logic, the next "year of the woman" should have been 2002, the first national election after the 2000 census. But the 9/11 terrorist attacks stalled women's progress. Women held their own, but just barely. The overall number of women in Congress remained the same. Republican women gained a handful of seats while Democratic women lost ground, a reflection of the national trend toward the GOP in the aftermath of 9/11.

Another factor is the relatively small number of women in the pool from which presidential candidates are drawn. "How many three-star generals and above do we have that are women?" Liswood asks. "If we have even five of them and you need a thousand people to get one willing to run, five are not nearly enough." For most offices, women who challenge an incumbent or run to fill a vacancy are successful as often as men are. The problem is that fewer women choose to run at all, which increases the odds against a woman rising to the highest level.

Then there is the problem of raising enough money to run for president. In foreign countries, it doesn't take anywhere near the $25 million required to be a credible presidential candidate in the United States. Female candidates, more than men, depend on female contributors. A study by the National Women's Political Caucus shows that women typically write checks for $100 or less, whereas men contribute $500 or more. When Elizabeth Dole announced her interest in the presidency, she was taken seriously because it was assumed that she could raise the necessary money. Unfortunately for her, the Republican establishment had already coalesced behind Texas governor George W. Bush, who seemed more electable. Shut out from the party's biggest donors, Dole sought contributions from female executives who had not previously participated in politics. She had only modest success. Women normally comprise a quarter of the contributors to Republican campaigns. Slightly more than half of

Dole's donors were women, and they were responsible for almost half the money she raised. But the dollar disparity with Bush was too great. In the scramble for cash, Dole aides sold the table centerpieces at fund-raising events for $5 apiece to the party faithful. Dole's effort fell short, but her mailing list could prove invaluable to any GOP nominee seeking to reach out to women.

Conflicts between professional and personal responsibilities weigh heavier on women. Building a political career takes time. Many women, at least those who marry and have children, postpone the start of their career and are never able to catch up. It is easier for an American man to fit an all-consuming focus into his life than it is for a woman. "By freeing up men's time, women subsidize men," says Liswood. Shortly before she was elected lieutenant governor of Massachusetts in 1998, Republican Jane Swift observed that a male candidate who rose to that office at a young age would spark speculation about his bright political future. But Swift, thirty-four and pregnant with her first child, was the subject of different speculation. Who would take care of the baby? Could she maintain her passion for public service? Why groom this young woman, however talented she might be, when there is no guarantee that she will still be in politics ten years from now? When we caught up with Swift again in the spring of 1999, she said that leaving her infant daughter was hard, and that when she was out of town she sometimes awoke in the middle of the night in a hotel room gripped by irrational worry about the child. These fears are familiar to any mother, and they breed ambivalence in women pursuing a career in politics.

Swift remains at the center of an ongoing debate about career and motherhood. Soon after she was elevated to governor in April 2001, her doctor ordered her to bed rest to await the birth of twin daughters. She said she would conduct the state's business by speakerphone. A political rival, sensing an opportunity, questioned the legality of meetings held under those terms. The ensuing controversy rallied the public to Swift's side, and for a time it appeared as though the voters were ready to judge Swift on her record as opposed to her child-care arrangements. But Swift never overcame early impressions that she was distracted by family concerns and not up to the job of running a state. The situation worsened after 9/11, and in March 2002, Swift ended her race for reelection, pressured by her own party to make way for a more popular candidate. In a tearful press conference, she tried to put a happy face on the media attention she had gotten, telling reporters, "I'm thinner, better dressed and better made up, thanks to you."

Perhaps the most perverse obstacle to a woman becoming president is that no woman has ever been president. There is no one for girls growing up to emulate. Elizabeth Dole's exploration of a run, which ended before she officially entered the race, was praised as an example to future generations of women. Even an abortive run was lifted to the level of role model, showing how desperate the need. Boys grow up with the image of the warrior going out into the world, conquering and returning to claim the princess in the castle. The basic myth for girls, on the other hand, is Cinderella, whose most significant conversations are with mice, says Liswood. Until recently, women have been portrayed in books and in the mass media primarily as caretakers and nurturers, not leaders. There is no mirror for American women to gaze into and imagine someone who looks like them becoming president. Images can be powerful. Iceland's Vigdis Finnbogadottir said that after she had been president for eight years, she realized that there were children in her country who thought that only a woman could hold that office. But when American voters picture a president, he's not wearing a skirt.

Stereotypes are hard to shake. The American media fret about whether to call a female president's spouse the First Man, whether he should keep his day job, and what he knows about planning a menu. Bob Dole, always quick with a quip, entertained as a guest on the late-night talk shows by wisecracking about how he would adjust if his wife were elected president. All he would need, he said, was a car, a driver, and a cell phone, just in case he got left behind. That wouldn't get a laugh in many foreign countries where the class system allows women born into a political dynasty to rise to the top despite their gender. India's Indira Gandhi, Pakistan's Benazir Bhutto, and the Philippines' Corazon Aquino all are examples of dynastic rule. Each of them achieved their office after the assassination of a father or a husband. Had their male relative not been murdered they might never have run for office. In countries where they have a sitting queen, people are accustomed to seeing men in the consort role.

Many women do not long for one of their own in high office. Liswood chose the British actress Glenda Jackson to narrate her film about female world leaders, but Jackson turned out not to have her heart in it. Asked to say something into a microphone about women and leadership, the actress intoned in her melodious voice, "Well, I'm bitterly, bitterly disappointed that the first woman prime minister of England was Margaret Thatcher, who has single-handedly destroyed the fabric of British society." CNN's Judy Woodruff did the sound track instead.

Women will not throw over a male candidate whose policies they support for a woman who shares their chromosomes but does not represent their views. "I'd rather vote for a white guy from the South who is pro-choice than somebody wearing a skirt," says Farai Chideya, a young African-American woman who recently started her own media company on the Internet after serving as a political analyst for CNN and ABC. "There are a lot of different ways to care about women other than electing someone with boobs."

Women are often hard on other women running for office. They don't want to be embarrassed, and if one woman fails, all women feel the anguish. There could also be a touch of envy. The full range of human emotions comes into play when women judge each other. For whatever reasons, and some are better than others, women want more than gender to decide their vote.

Victoria Woodhull, the first woman to run for president, lost the support of women because her views on sex and marriage were too radical. She advocated free love and, because she despised sexual hypocrisy, published the details of preacher Henry Ward Beecher's affair with a parishioner's wife. The account hit the newsstands a week before the election in 1872 and cost her votes among men (women would not be able to vote for another half century). Though clearly accomplished—Woodhull opened the first female-run Wall Street brokerage firm, and in 1871 became the first woman to address Congress—her outspoken opinions on the sexual liberation of women unnerved the middle-class ladies in the suffrage movement.

Lawyer and feminist Belva Lockwood was nominated for president in 1884 by the National Equal Rights party. Lockwood had gained prominence in the suffrage movement, and when she was denied the opportunity as a lawyer to speak before the U.S. Supreme Court, she lobbied Congress for a bill that would permit women to practice in federal courts. She became the first woman to argue before the Supreme Court. Lockwood ran on a platform that called for uniform marriage and divorce laws, property rights for women, and equal pay for equal work in government jobs. She received over four thousand votes, not enough to make a dent in the electoral process but enough to win a place in history.

Eighty years passed before another woman sought the presidency. Margaret Chase Smith, the first woman to serve in both the House and Senate, entered the Republican race in 1964, and dropped out after coming in fifth in New Hampshire, the first primary. Prim-looking with crisply coiffed iceblond hair, Smith was a formidable presence on Capitol Hill. She focused on defense issues and had a reputation for being one of the most hawkish members of Congress during the cold war. Former defense secretary Melvin Laird says President Nixon would have lost the vote on the Anti-Ballistic Missile Treaty if Smith had not switched at the last minute to support the ban on missile defenses that was put in place to slow the arms race with the Soviet Union. Smith reluctantly agreed to back the treaty, but nobody ever mistook her for a dove even when she handed out her recipe for blueberry muffins.

Jeannette Rankin, a Montana Republican who served in the House and voted against entering both World War I and World War II, branded the stereotype of women as pacifists into the nation's consciousness. Her sister suffragists tried to convince her to join the majority and support World War I because they feared that women would otherwise be marginalized. Rankin rejected their pleas. But she could not ignore the public's wrath when, on the day after the Japanese attack on Pearl Harbor, she was the lone vote in the House against entering the war. Rankin did not seek reelection after that.

Shirley Chisholm stunned friends and colleagues in 1972 when she announced she was running for president. "I suffered from two obstacles—I was a black person and I was a woman," Chisholm recalled in an interview from her Florida home. "I met far more discrimination as a woman in the field of politics. That was a revelation to me. Black men got together to talk about stopping me. But I was not any weeping Annie. I confronted them. They said I was an intellectual person, that I had the ability, but that this was no place for a woman. If a black person were to run, it should be a man."

Chisholm was on the ballot in twelve primaries, and although she never got more than 7 percent of the vote, she made effective use of the soapbox her candidacy provided. A dynamic speaker, she wanted more federal spending for education and other social programs coupled with cutbacks in the defense budget. When the other Democratic candidates tried to exclude her from debates, arguing she wasn't "a real candidate," Chisholm took her case to the Federal Elections Commission, where she prevailed. She won only 150 of the party's 1,600 delegates, but is remembered fondly among Democrats as a passionate voice for the causes she championed. She still chuckles about how she surprised her male rivals, especially the hawkish Senator Henry "Scoop" Jackson, the candidate of Democratic moderates. "Scoop Jackson, may he rest in peace," she says. "He was taken aback by my ability to articulate the issues."

Born in Brooklyn in 1924, Chisholm spent most of her growing-up years living with her grandmother in Barbados, West Indies. Her grandmother was a powerfully built woman, well over six feet tall, with a will to match, and Chisholm credits her with everything she became. "She always told me, 'Stand up and be counted'," Chisholm says. "I would come home from school and she would say, 'Stand up, girl. Keep your head up. Approach me like you know where you're going.' She instilled in me my personality."

Chisholm's family was against her running for president, and her husband went along only halfheartedly. "He didn't try to block me, but he didn't like it," she says. She wouldn't have done it except for the response she got when she was quoted in an interview saying, "I can't run on the basis of moral supoort. I need money." Within a month, people had sent her more than $10,000. "I didn't want anybody to call my bluff," she says, laughing. "So I decided to take the plunge. I knew I wouldn't be president, but somebody had to break the ice, somebody with the nerve and bravado to do it."

Weeks before Elizabeth Dole decided against running for president, Chisholm predicted it. "When you make a bid for such a high office, you have to have energy," she said. "You have to be very outspoken and assertive, and not be afraid to offend people. She doesn't have the temperament. She's too cautious."

After the experiment of putting a woman on the ticket in 1984, both political parties backed away from playing the gender card in presidential elections. In 1988, Warren Rustand, a friend and adviser to presidential candidate George Hebert Walker Bush, suggested that Bush pick Supreme Court Justice Sandra Day O'Connor as his running mate. A former state legislator and a onetime candidate for governor, O'Connor understood politics. She was the right age (in her fifties), and her personal background had been vetted during the Senate confirmation hearings. "She is the most commanding woman of our time," Rustand told Bush. Choosing her would "do something for women and for the party," he said. Bush opted instead for Indiana senator Dan Quayle, a generation younger than O'Connor and someone whose fraternity-boy good looks would, at least in theory, appeal to baby boomers, male and female.

Quayle's unsuitability for the job quickly became known and has been documented elsewhere, but Bush's rejection of O'Connor remains puzzling. Did she not meet the one test that any vice presidential prospect must meet—the sure knowledge that she had the ability to step in and become president overnight should the need arise?

The climate for a woman president has improved since Margaret Chase Smith ventured into the New Hampshire primary in 1964. That was the year the Hollywood movie *Kisses for My President* debuted starring Polly Bergen as the first woman president and Fred MacMurray as her hapless spouse. On the couple's first night in the White House, they survey the separate bedrooms assigned to them. Hers is executive-style; his is frilly. He suggests the president's first official act should be ordering chintz curtains for her quarters. MacMurray's First Spouse is a study in wounded male ego. Sex is interrupted by phone calls from the secretary of state and secretary of defense. He sighs, "Another evening in front of a crackling fire with a good book." Immersed in her job, the president is oblivious to her husband's needs and those of her two children, who, by mid-movie, are transformed from two innocents into spoiled brats exploiting their mother's office. Having a woman president has upended the natural order. One man complains that ever since his wife voted for her, she's been "a pain in the neck. I should ship her back to the old country where she will learn who's boss."

The movie is a comedy, of course, and it was filmed before the women's movement got under way. The notion of a male First Lady was not only preposterous but humiliating for any man. "I'm the first First Lady with a background in electronics, and they don't know what to do with me," MacMurray moans in a self-pitying soliloquy. "I let her run, and what do I get for my act of generosity—four years minimum of being an absolute nothing." The president is juggling a foreign crisis and a balky legislature while her husband is supposed to plan meal menus. He can't take it and finally lashes out, telling the president, "I was a proud husband and a good father before you turned me into the First Lady, or whatever I'm supposed to be." Soon he's tempted to have an affair, and the viewer is left with the distinct impression that any woman elected president could not keep her marriage intact or her children from running amuck.

Just when the audience wonders how this will be resolved, the president faints. After some nervous moments, her press secretary announces, "The president is pregnant." In the next scene, the president is behind the podium with the presidential seal. She tells the country that she must either give up her strenuous duties as president or risk losing her baby, and she is therefore resigning. Moviegoers in

1964 no doubt were relieved that the traditional social order had been restored. The movie ends with some lighthearted but smug comments about the superiority of man, uttered by MacMurray, a happy former First Spouse. "It took forty million women to get you in the White House," he tells the first woman president, "and one man to get you out."

A prediction: There will be a woman president of the United States. When? Soon. The evolution of pop culture in the media age brings that goal closer with each passing year. The President 2000 Barbie doll—which, at Marie Wilson's insistence, will be available in African-American and Hispanic models as well as the standard-issue blond—will encourage little girls to dream. Fantasy will nudge politics to catch up with real life. Movies that feature a woman president are in the works. Writers and producers who watched Glenn Close's convincing performance as the vice president in the movie *Air Force One*, defying the demands of terrorists and staying cool in the face of danger, want her next to portray the president. Getting a woman on the ticket as vice president is, after all, the most likely stepping-stone to the presidency. If life mimics art, it is because art shapes the way we look at life.

ONE

Getting Organized

On a warm September evening in 1983, four women sat down for dinner in the restaurant at Washington's Watergate Hotel. All veterans of the feminist movement, they had come to plot strategy for the upcoming Democratic National Convention, which was ten months away. The women requested a corner table. They weren't there to see or be seen, and they hadn't come for the food or the atmosphere, neither of which was particularly notable. They had chosen the restaurant because of its convenience. The Watergate is an imposing complex of shops and high-rises on the banks of the Potomac near the heart of the city. One of the women had a small consulting firm and was renting an office in the Watergate tower. It was the same suite that the Democratic National Committee occupied at the time of the break-in that led to President Nixon's resignation. Perhaps because of its infamous past, she'd gotten a break on the rent.

At every convention since 1976, women activists highlighted an issue to pick a fight about. One year it was abortion, another it was the Equal Rights Amendment. Press coverage would follow and the male politicians would cower. What was the unfinished business that would define the 1984 convention and capture press attention? There were mixed signals when it came to women and their political clout. The ERA had been defeated in June 1982 after a long and bitter struggle, leaving the women's movement awash in recriminations over who was to blame. Yet there was oddly little left to accomplish within the Democratic party structure. The biggest fights had been won: The platform strongly supported abortion rights, and party rules mandated an equal number of women in each state delegation.

The best tool women had to command attention was growing evidence of a gender gap. In 1982, Democratic governors had won elections in New York, Michigan, and Texas on the strength of the women's vote. The gender gap had been identified as a split between the sexes over issues, with women putting more emphasis than men on a candidate's stand on health care, child care, education, and abortion rights. Pollsters started separating the genders in charting voter attitudes, and when an eight-point gap appeared in the election of Ronald Reagan in 1980, political analysts called it "the women's voting bloc." A staff aide preparing a chart at the National Organization for Women (NOW) couldn't fit all those words, and jotted in "gender gap." The phrase caught on and would inform political strategy for at least the next two decades.

Nobody remembers which of the four women proposed it first, but one of them said, "Let's try a woman on the ticket." Not any woman in particular, they agreed, but the *idea* of a woman. Even if it didn't happen, getting people used to the idea would be a building block for the future. They talked excitedly about how they would "crack the ticket" for a woman. First, they felt it was time. Six decades had passed since women won the right to vote in 1920. The women's movement had shattered the status quo and opportunities were opening for women everywhere. Second, beating Ronald Reagan would take a dramatic increase in turnout among women, where Reagan was weakest. Cutting back social programs, pouring more money into the arms race, scaling back environmental protections, and advocating a constitutional amendment to ban abortions had cost Reagan significant support among women. Putting a woman on the Democratic ticket could dramatize the differences between the two parties and generate the enthusiasm that would boost turnout enough to make the difference.

By the time the waiter brought the dessert menu, the women had settled on what role each would play in getting out the word that 1984 was the year for a woman. Kathy Bonk's job was to get reporters to float the idea in the media. Bonk had come to Washington in the early seventies, right out of college, and brought a winning enthusiasm to whatever she tackled. As part of a communications class project at the University of Pittsburgh, she had challenged the licenses of Pittsburgh's three television stations and gotten them to hire more women. Bonk had a number of friends in the media, and had no trouble persuading Jane O'Reilly at *Time* and Judy Mann at the *Washington Post* to write about the possibility of a woman on the ticket. Journalism being a pack profession, their articles spawned other stories until Bonk had a scrapbook bulging with clips from all the major media about how the gender gap was changing politics. What began as something of a lark over dinner soon gained enough momentum to force Vice President Walter Mondale, the presumptive Democratic nominee, to declare publicly that he would consider a woman as his vice presidential running mate.

At the time, Bonk was the communications director for NOW, the nerve center of the women's movement. Eleanor Smeal, a past president of NOW, and Molly Yard, a grandmotherly figure who would later become president, were also at the dinner, along with Ann Lewis, then the political director for the Democratic National Committee. Lewis had been active in Democratic party politics for a long time, and it was her task to talk up the idea of a woman with the party establishment. Smeal's job was to rally women. She had done her Ph.D. thesis in the early 1970s on women's attitudes toward women candidates. She and another student had recruited fifty volunteers through NOW to help them interview a thousand women. Based on that research, Smeal challenged the prevailing dogma of the political science profession that women didn't vote for other women, or on the basis of women's issues, and were in fact their own worst enemy when they entered the voting booth. Smeal found that women favored women candidates, but by a small margin, only 10 percent in her research. She knew that a woman on the ticket would not automatically bring out the women's vote, and that if the ticket lost badly, the whole venture could backfire.

Desperate to beat Reagan, they figured playing the women's card was worth the risk. Smeal took out a full-page ad in the *New York Times* in June 1984 headlined "We Want a Woman!" Paid for with funds from the Women's Trust Political Action Committee she had formed, the ad invited readers to join "The Gender Gap Action Campaign" by clipping a coupon and enclosing a contribution. Smeal estimates that the ad raised a quarter of a million dollars. Its placement in the *Times* had the intended effect of rallying East Coast opinion leaders and generating momentum that would prove unstoppable. What *Times* readers did not know is that the impulse for the ad originated with publishing heir Arthur O. Sulzburger, Jr., who had begun his ascent through the newsroom and was doing a stint in the Washington Bureau, where he had to show that he could sell advertising space. He called Bonk, who was a friend. "Do you know anyone who wants to buy an ad in the *New York Times*?" he wondered, eager to make a sale. Bonk conveyed the message to Smeal, who welcomed the opportunity. Sulzburger later sent Bonk a commemorative plaque of the ad, which she believes was the first he ever sold.

A woman on the ticket had become the mantra for women activists. "It was in the ether," says Joanne Howes, then the executive director of the nonpartisan Women's Vote Project and a member of "Team A," seven Washington-wise women most instrumental in propelling Geraldine Ferraro onto the ticket. Howes had always been fascinated by politics, and remembers sitting on the couch as a ten year old with her uncle listening to the 1956 roll call for president. She'd worked for liberal Democrats like Ted Kennedy and Barbara Mikulski, and lobbied for Planned Parenthood. She found the election of Ronald Reagan in 1980 devastating to her political ideals, but was heartened by the attention it had drawn to the gender gap. She hoped a woman in the race could regain the White House for the Democrats. Looking back on what she now regards as naïveté, she says, "Assumptions got made. I'm not sure they were as valid as we wanted them, that women would make that big a difference. But we predicted that women would come out of the woodwork."

There was little to disrupt the nominee-in-waiting aura that defined the former vice president. He and Jimmy Carter had lost in a landslide to Reagan, but many Democrats had convinced themselves that the aging actor was vulnerable, especially if the gender gap persisted. In 1982, a full two years before the next presidential election, Mondale's numbers cruncher, Tom Donilon, had declared in a meeting, "You guys better start thinking about women on this ticket."

Donilon didn't mention any names, but Mondale thought about it, talked about it, and worried a lot about the implications of Donilon's words. Were there qualified women? Which woman would he select if that's where the politics of winning took him? An earnest Minnesotan, Mondale took his role of presumptive nominee seriously. He viewed his time out of office as something of an interregnum, an opportunity for him as the president-in-waiting to study various aspects of governing. John Reilly, an old friend and political confidant, chuckles as he remembers Mondale striding confidently into his office in the summer of 1982 and proudly announcing, "I finally, finally understand the Federal Reserve."

"But who can you tell?" Reilly prodded him, adding a gentle jab. "You've been the vice president. You're supposed to understand the Federal Reserve."

On Capitol Hill, no female member of Congress would initially agree to have her name floated as a potential vice presidential candidate for fear of upsetting the Mondale camp. Nobody wanted to risk a sideshow that might distract from the party's goal of defeating Rea-

gan. A coalition of women leaders met regularly in a tiny room behind the statues in Statuary Hall that had been set aside for use by the
women members. New York representative Bella Abzug, a tart-
tongued pioneer in the women's movement, convened the sessions
and was often the only elected official present. They were all the
usual suspects, women attuned to politics, from NOW and other interest groups, plus a contingent of congressional aides who worked
mostly for liberal Democrats. Some of the female members of Congress dropped by occasionally, but at best their reaction was tepid.
The women quickly divided into two camps. One favored "the crusader position," which meant advocating for a woman on the ticket
but not backing any particular woman. The other camp didn't see the
point of pushing an abstraction, and supported "the candidate position" of recruiting and promoting a specific woman. Joan McLean,
who worked on the House Banking Committee, sided with those who
believed that once they sold the idea of a woman, they needed to be
ready with the name of somebody who could fill the bill.

They methodically ran down the list of prospective candidates, and
then imagined how each woman might fare in the initial news reports.
Dianne Feinstein? "Married three times, Jewish, mayor of San Francisco" was the consensus media shorthand. "Although it wasn't a problem for us, it's a lot for the public to get through each of these
circumstances," says McLean. "You have to deal with the religion—is
the country ready to have someone who's Jewish? You have to deal
with family values—one divorce, one died, one she's married to now.
To people sitting out there in mid-America, married three times seems
pretty exotic." Barbara Mikulski? "Four feet eleven, single, Catholic."
They loved the Baltimore congresswoman, but felt she was too un-
orthodox for mass consumption. Pat Schroeder? The independent-
minded Denver Democrat had far and away the best credentials as a
member of the House Armed Services Committee, but her reputation
was that of a gadfly. A few years earlier, on a trip to China, she had
donned an Easter bunny suit to entertain children at the American
embassy, and the way the story was reported, her exuberance came
across as juvenile behavior. "Flaky," the women feared the media
would label her. Gerry Ferraro? "Married, mother of three, part of the
leadership, elected three times." The women quickly zeroed in on
Ferraro, a member of Congress from Queens, New York, serving her
fourth term and regarded as a rising star in the House leadership.

Geraldine Anne Ferraro was the right age, forty-eight, with the
right résumé for the times. She was a liberal but not a limousine

liberal, the kind the Republicans would mock. Her immigrant Italian father died of a heart attack when she was nine, and she had attended a Catholic college on a scholarship. After graduation, she taught school in Queens and studied law at night. She married the same year that she got her law degree, 1960, putting her career mostly on hold to raise three children, and dabbling in Democratic politics on the side. As her children grew older, she found more time for political activities, and in 1974, she was appointed as assistant district attorney. Assigned to a Special Victims Bureau that dealt with cases of rape, domestic violence, and child abuse, Ferraro says her views became more liberal as a result of what she saw. She left the agency in 1978 in part because, as a married woman, she was paid less than her male counterparts. It was common practice then for employers to exploit the widely held assumption that since men were the primary breadwinners, married women were not as deserving on the salary scale. When that same year the congressman representing her Queens district announced he was retiring, Ferraro saw a chance to make a bigger impact on the issues she cared about. Her years of networking and her Italian heritage made her an obvious successor. She won with 53 percent of the vote.

Women were not that welcome on Capitol Hill in the late seventies, but Democratic House Speaker Thomas "Tip" O'Neill took an instant liking to the scrappy Ferraro. He made sure she got on some important committees like Budget, where real decisions were made, and Public Works and Transportation, which funded projects that were the lifeblood of urban communities like the district she represented. She was effective and hardworking. Her ethnicity as a working-class Catholic appealed to O'Neill, a Boston Irishman, and he backed her in her first leadership election as secretary of the Democratic caucus in 1980, and again in 1982. Secretary didn't sound like much, but it made Ferraro eligible to serve on the House Steering and Policy Committee, and she was widely regarded as a woman who'd made it as one of the boys. Yet she didn't forget the issues having to do with women and children that had made her political in the first place. Her crusty male colleagues and her feminist friends agreed on one thing. This slip of a woman with the trademark swirl in her hair had a bright future.

Democrats were looking for a way to beat Reagan, and the women's movement needed reenergizing. It was a marriage racing toward consummation. The women who called themselves Team A presented their case to Ferraro in November 1983 over take-out Chinese food in an efficiency apartment on Capitol Hill. They had concluded that the best way to advance the concept of a woman on the ticket was to rally around a plausible candidate. They argued that Mondale, a gray and cautious personality, needed something new to get people to take a second look at him. They told her that she would be good for the ticket, that it was time for women to command the national stage, and that she was the one who could pave the way. A fortune cookie specially ordered for the evening proclaimed, "You will win big in '84." Ferraro was pleased from the standpoint of her ego. But on leaving the dinner, she confided to an aide, "Those women are pretty crazy."

Ferraro wasn't eager to be the feminists' stalking horse, but she didn't say no either. She had accepted the dinner invitation, knowing in general what they had in mind. And by the end of the evening, she was at least willing to entertain strategic advice on what she should do to prepare herself. She thought she should press for a major role at the upcoming convention, perhaps chair the event. That would give her visibility, but probably too late to affect her chances to be named vice president. The women had a better idea. They wanted to see her named chairman of the Democratic Platform Committee, which writes the party's agenda for the election. It was a more substantive showcase, and a good way to boost her name recognition. Platform Committee hearings are held around the country, and would guarantee her a series of regional forums in the months leading up to the convention. The women brought their collective clout to bear. As players in the Democratic party with ties to organized labor, prochoice activists, and various liberal interest groups, their voices were heard. Ferraro became the first woman ever to chair the Democratic Platform Committee. Her skill in bringing together warring factions within the party and crafting fragile coalitions got her noticed.

As a composite, Ferraro was the best woman available on the Democratic side. She had the enthusiastic backing of the influential and colorful Democratic Speaker, Tip O'Neill. She had leadership potential, as evidenced by her colleagues electing her to a spot in the House leadership, and she came from an important electoral state. She was a mother and a wife, and at the time of her selection, that was all still positive. "And she was attractive but not glamorous—all the stuff you wished didn't matter," says Joan McLean, and the Team A member whose Capitol Hill apartment provided the setting for the first tentative step in Ferraro's historic odyssey. "She was attractive but not a raging beauty, so people could get by her looks and listen to her words."

McLean teaches a course now on women and leadership at Ohio Wesleyan University, and agrees that it would have been better if the first woman had been a senator instead of a mere House member. But that option simply did not exist. It would be another two years before Maryland's Barbara Mikulski would become the first Democratic woman senator elected in her own right. When the Mondale camp scrutinized Ferraro's legislative record, they were surprised to discover how little there was. "We didn't realize how parochial a congresswoman from Queens is," a Mondale aide confessed. "When we vetted her on the substance side, there was almost nothing there, literally." Once the decision was made to go with a woman, the paucity of Ferraro's legislative achievements mattered less than her compelling personal story and novel persona as a woman in what had been a man's role.

Mondale had hoped for an easy ride to the nomination, with ample time to consider vice presidential choices. But Senator Gary Hart of Colorado refused to drop out of the race, and the strength of his "new ideas" challenge forced Mondale to consider his arch-rival as his running mate. Mondale had developed a strong dislike for Hart, an aloof intellectual, and had no intention of naming him. So, in June 1984, having finally secured enough delegates to assure the nomination, Mondale created an elaborate smokescreen for picking a vice president, summoning a parade of possible contenders to his North Oaks, Minnesota, home, where he would interview them and divert attention from any claims Hart might make on the ticket. The media ridiculed the process, but there was no stopping Mondale. Among those making the trek were Los Angeles mayor Tom Bradley, an African American ("Age hurt him," says a Mondale aide), and San Antonio mayor Henry Cisneros, a Hispanic ("A bright, bright star," says the aide), who didn't make the cut because he was thought too young. Texas senator Lloyd Bentsen was the only white male in the group.

A pall of political correctness hovered over the process, which strengthened the determination of those pushing Mondale to name a woman. On the weekend of July 4, with the convention two weeks away, Mondale met with a delegation of twenty-three women in the conference room of a motel near his home. The group was led by Carol Bellamy, a member of the New York City Council, and included both elected officials and leaders of women's groups. Mondale and his aides braced for ultimatums and threats. They were pleasantly surprised when the women for the most part set aside their feminist rhetoric and calmly argued that it made political sense to put a woman on the ticket.

Ann Richards, then the Texas state treasurer, went so far as to bluntly announce that a woman was her second choice. "Really, I'm for Lloyd Bentsen," she said in her honeyed Texas drawl. "But if you can't have Lloyd, I'd take a woman." Resigned to what they called "Annie's Texas chauvinism," the women let the moment pass. "She always did her Texas politics first," says Carol Tucker Foreman, who coordinated women's events for the Mondale campaign. That approach served Richards well. Six years later, in 1990, she became the first woman elected governor of Texas.

John Reilly was the note-taker. He remembers writing down Betty Friedan's words: "Fritz, you've been talking about this all your political career—equal opportunity. You're one of the few who has a chance to do something about it." Friedan's breakthrough book *The Feminine Mystique*, published in 1963, had launched the women's movement with its vivid analysis of the discontent experienced by legions of housewives bored with their lives and not understanding why. A founding mother of NOW, she spoke as the dean of the assembled women. "What she said really hit him," says Reilly. Yet Mondale gave no hint during the meeting that he had been moved by Friedan's remark. He remained studiously noncommittal. Aides agreed later that the meeting was remarkably civil considering the participants and the passion they brought to the issue. "Nobody was obnoxious," says Reilly, apparently a high compliment in his mind when referring to women activists.

Mondale spent his evenings sitting in the den of his North Oaks home with Reilly and another aide, Jim Johnson, going over the pluses and minuses of potential running mates. "Then we would all go to bed and get up in the morning, and Mondale would go over everybody again," says Reilly. "There was no elimination, like in basketball." The process was tedious, but through it, Mondale had grown comfortable with the notion of putting a woman on the ticket. Friedan's words appealed to his loftier sense of self, and Johnson, the primary political architect of the campaign, argued that Mondale needed a series of dramatic initiatives to beat the popular Reagan. Choosing a woman would be one; proposing to raise taxes another. Both went against the grain of the times.

Two women had vaulted to the top of Mondale's list: Ferraro, the plucky congresswoman from Queens, and Dianne Feinstein, the San

Francisco mayor whose tough-on-crime reputation could help lighten Mondale's liberal baggage. As Mondale agonized about one versus the other, women leaders and the media voiced skepticism that, in the end, a conventional politician surrounded by male advisers would dare to choose a woman. "I can remember [Connecticut representative] Barbara Kennelly and several others saying there wasn't a shot this group of smart-ass white boys would do anything of that nature," says Reilly. "I was interviewed by members of the media who said, 'You guys don't have guts enough to name a woman.'"

Ferraro had gotten favorable reviews around the country for chairing the Platform Committee, just as her backers had hoped. Tip O'Neill said publicly that Gerry was his candidate, and he let Mondale know it. Mondale didn't know Ferraro, and he considered Feinstein a friend. Feinstein's husband, Richard Blum, had been a Mondale supporter and financial backer since 1974, even before he married Dianne. Feinstein was the early front-runner. Lawyers spent weeks poring over Feinstein's financial records and interviewing her husband. "We were in about as deep as you could get with him," recalls an aide. "There wasn't anything we didn't know about Blum—and he absolutely cooperated."

Yet Mondale couldn't decide on one or the other woman. Like a high school senior assembling college choices, he realized that he needed a backup in case his bolder choices fell through. Washington attorney Michael Berman got an urgent call from North Oaks ordering him to Boston to vet Michael Dukakis. The Massachusetts governor had agreed to be Mondale's fallback candidate, "The Safety." He would accept the nomination if offered.

Berman was in Boston when he got a call from North Oaks. "When can you get to New York to vet Geraldine Ferraro?" John Reilly wanted to know. Berman reacted with an expletive. He only had one set of financial forms, which he had left with Dukakis, and one marked-up copy of a broader questionnaire that he had thrown into his briefcase. "Tomorrow morning," he replied. "But what about Dukakis?"

Berman took the first shuttle to New York the next morning and had a car meet him at LaGuardia Airport. He had called two lawyers in Washington to see if they could join him because he knew Ferraro's husband, John Zaccaro, was a real estate developer, and that meant money, property, and business transactions to examine. One lawyer was able to meet him in New York. When Berman arrived at Ferraro's home in Forest Hills, Queens, there was an ABC crew waiting outside. The crew didn't ask Berman who he was and he didn't volunteer his identity.

When Berman first called to arrange time with Ferraro, she asked if his impromptu visit meant she had to reschedule her hair appointment. She was flying to California for preconvention committee business later in the day, and had planned to get a haircut on her way to the airport. Berman told her it might be useful to change her schedule, that his visit was relatively important. A combination of disbelief and sarcasm was evident in his voice. He couldn't believe her reaction. For her part, Ferraro couldn't understand what all the fuss was about. As the first woman to chair the convention's Platform Committee, she found nothing extraordinary in her desire to look good for the media attention that flows to a pioneer. It was the first of many such gender-based clashes between Ferraro and the Mondale camp.

Berman asked Ferraro and her husband a series of pointed questions during that initial meeting at their home. He told them about the kind of disclosure they would have to make, including releasing their tax returns to the media. They didn't fall over each other saying yes, but according to Berman, they didn't raise any objections either. Zaccaro called his accountant and told him to tell Berman anything he wanted to know. Another lawyer Berman had contacted agreed to meet him at the address that Zaccaro provided for the accountant. It was a Manhattan office building, and the two men felt reassured by the copious display of corporate nameplates.

Their confidence was short-lived. The contact name they had was for a one-room accounting firm with two persons on the payroll renting space from the corporate types. With the scanty information collected from the one person who was available, the two lawyers retreated to the New York office of Arthur Young, a prominent accounting firm, where they worked through, and talked through, the numbers. Sometime that evening they concluded that, on the surface, there was nothing disqualifying. They did no outside checking, with the exception of one call to one person in law enforcement in New York. Berman didn't know Mulberry Street from Park Avenue when it came to evaluating Zaccaro's real estate investments.

Ferraro was not vetted as exhaustively as Feinstein and other potential candidates. The Mondale camp had simply run out of time. But they had the tax returns that would later cause such problems when Ferraro, at her husband's insistence, refused to make them public. Zaccaro claimed he had promised Berman that he would release a financial statement, not the returns themselves. "There was absolutely

nothing wrong with the tax returns," insists Reilly, who remains mystified by Zaccaro's adamant stand. "He was in the real estate business,
which is a built-in tax dodge to begin with. But there wasn't a fear that
he hadn't paid taxes, or paid too little, or took deductions people
might be critical of. It was a tempest in a teapot as far as the campaign
was concerned."

More worrisome in the background check was the discovery of a
pending Bar Association complaint against Zaccaro for borrowing
money from the estate of an eighty-four-year-old woman whose affairs the court had appointed him to look after when she was no
longer capable. (Though he had repaid the debt with interest, the
court acted on August 30, the eve of the fall campaign, to remove
Zaccaro for unethical behavior as the woman's conservator.) The
question before Mondale's aides was whether this issue should
threaten Ferraro's nomination. How much should her husband's ac-
tions enter the debate? Should they have any bearing? They were
mindful of a possible double standard. "Do we investigate the wife of
a nominee?" asks Reilly. As it turned out, the aides were naive in
thinking they could separate Zaccaro from Ferraro.

The conventional wisdom is that Mondale passed over Feinstein
because of her husband's tangled finances. Not so, says Reilly, who
insists Blum "passed inspection." The real reason Feinstein wasn't
chosen was fear that the combination of having the Democratic convention in San Francisco ("That gay town," says an aide), and having
the former mayor of San Francisco on the ticket, would tar Mondale
as a social radical and give the Republicans an opening. Mondale felt
that Ferraro, being from Queens, the working-class community epit-
omized by Archie Bunker in the long-running television sitcom "All
in the Family," would better convey traditional Democratic values to
the country in the general election.

The primary season had ended with a big win for Hart in California, which kept him in the spotlight though well short of the delegates needed to win the nomination. Toward the end of June, Reilly
met secretly with Hart in Washington at the home of producer
George Stevens, a longtime Democratic donor. "It was part of the
regular order," says Reilly. "You go to the guy who's challenging you
the most, see if you can't pick up his support." The vice presidency
was on the table, and Hart wasn't being coy. "He wanted a deal," says
Reilly. "He wanted to be in charge of a number of things." According
to Reilly, Vice President Hart wanted to oversee the space program,

and he wanted to ensure for himself a role in governing by being the administration's point man on Capitol Hill.

Neither request was unprecedented. Lyndon Johnson had control of the space program when John F. Kennedy was president, and most vice presidents take an active role in congressional politics. The Constitution recognizes the vice president as president of the Senate with the power to cast the deciding vote in case of a tie. But Hart's demands were more sweeping, Reilly says. And Mondale, a former senator himself, was not prepared to relinquish control of Capitol Hill. "The risk-benefit ratio wasn't good," says Reilly. "There was great risk and small benefit."

With Hart never really in the running, and Feinstein fading, a consensus began to form around Ferraro. A key moment occurred when Representative Barbara Mikulski, recognized as a leader of women Democrats in the House, announced on "Nightline" that she was putting on a Ferraro button. Then she flew to Miami for the NOW convention, where there was a push to make a woman on the ticket a reality. Carol Tucker Foreman and another aide, acting on Mondale's behalf, had been assured by the NOW leadership that the organization would endorse Mondale. NOW had never endorsed before nor has it since, so this was a coup for Mondale, who needed to rally women in order to have a chance at victory in November.

Mondale appeared at the convention amid chants of "Win with a woman." The image was more Daniel in the lion's den than principled politician about to make history. NOW kept its word and endorsed Mondale. But the group upped the ante with an additional vote to demand that Mondale name a woman as his running mate. Foreman was on a plane heading home by the time NOW voted. She had to face Mondale's anger. "He chewed my ass, starting with my toes and going all the way up—and he should have. He said, 'I think I'm doing something courageous here. NOW made it look like I'm just caving in to pressure.'" A CBS News poll taken in June 1984 showed that for every woman excited by the prospect of a woman on the ticket, there was a man turned off by the idea.

Ferraro finally got the call to North Oaks, where she would meet with Mondale. Joan McLean and other Team A members briefed Ferraro before the crucial visit. They didn't want her to be caught flat-footed like Senator Ted Kennedy had been when asked in a 1980 television interview why he wanted to be president. Kennedy's halting answer severely undermined his prospects. The women attempted to prep Ferraro by asking "Why do you want to be vice president? What role would you play in the campaign? What role do you see your family playing?" Ferraro was not somebody who enjoyed this kind of preparation. She felt she knew herself and could answer forthrightly whatever was thrown at her, and she didn't want to be given some line. This feisty self-confidence, while admirable, would not serve her well as a vice presidential candidate, the most subservient position in American politics.

A week before the Democratic convention opened in San Francisco, the *New York Times* said in a page-one Sunday story that the Mondale campaign had all but decided against Ferraro, that she didn't do well in her interview. Her "apparent slippage," the article contended, was attributed in part to the Mondale camp's distaste for her maneuvering to secure the nomination. In her campaign memoir, Ferraro says she was so angered by the piece that she told Mondale to remove her name as a possible running mate. Mondale apologized, said he had nothing to do with the negative comments, and that she was still under serious consideration. He promised the leaks would stop, though that would prove impossible. Every campaign inevitably features conflicts among aides vying to advance themselves, or their point of view, and the Mondale campaign was more leakprone than most. Ferraro's interview had apparently not been decisive either way. Mondale's questions about how to address crime took her by surprise, though they shouldn't have, yet she handled them ably enough. And she more than held her own on the budget deficit and U.S. intervention in Central America, which would be hot topics in the fall campaign. Mondale resented the pressure placed on him to name Ferraro, but he didn't fault her personally. That was how interest-group politics worked in the Democratic party.

What made the situation more bizarre than it needed to be was the endless maneuvering between Mondale's people and Gary Hart, who either chose to believe or was led to believe, for the purpose of preserving political peace, that he still had a shot at being nominated. Dotty Lynch, Hart's pollster, acting on the *Times* story, reached Ferraro in her hotel room to offer consolation and suggest she give a speech to gain media exposure since she was no longer in the running. Lynch was an old friend, so Ferraro felt comfortable confiding in her. "I can't tell anybody this," she said, "but John Reilly is on his way to talk to me. It's not over. What are they telling Gary?"

"They're telling Gary he's in," Lynch replied.

In the meantime, Barbara Mikulski had rushed to Mondale the results of a survey of convention delegates conducted by the National Women's Political Caucus. The poll showed overwhelming support for a woman on the ticket, with Ferraro's name topping the list of hopefuls.

Reilly didn't leave Minnesota until six o'clock that evening. By the time he arrived at the Hyatt Embarcadero Hotel, it was quite late. Ferraro knew she was not the only person under consideration. Feinstein was still in the running. But this was serious. Reilly had been sent to ask what political professionals call "the Eagleton question." Named after former vice presidential nominee Tom Eagleton, the inquiry—"Is there anything else we should know about?"—is supposed to dislodge skeletons that might embarrass a running mate. Eagleton neglected to mention that he had been hospitalized for depression, a revelation that, when it became public, forced his removal from the Democratic ticket in 1972.

Prying into a politician's personal affairs made Reilly uncomfortable. "It's the worst thing you'll ever do in your life," he says. So he tried to keep the conversation on a high plane. He didn't ask about her husband, or the Bar Association complaint. He figured they knew what they needed to know about that. Instead, he talked about her previous elections, and what her opponents had said about her. He explained that the spotlight in a presidential campaign is much more intense. Her attitude was "I ran in Queens," as though that was the ultimate test. She was very feisty. She reacted as though she didn't believe Reilly when he warned how tough a national campaign would be in exposing her personal life.

Reilly told her Mondale would call one way or the other the next afternoon. "Sit by your phone," he said. Then he jumped in a cab and flew back to Minnesota.

The next morning, Ferraro called her husband in New York. Despite her bravado, Reilly's words had stung. "They'll dig into our lives just the way they did in 1978, but worse," she told him. Still, there was no turning back. When the call came, Ferraro knew that if she was named to the ticket, win or lose, she would be part of history.

"Will you be my running mate?" Mondale asked. The nature of a ticket as a political marriage is underscored when a woman is in the secondary slot, and much of the press speculation had centered on gender. When Mondale failed to greet Feinstein with a kiss at her interview, it was taken as a sign of her seriousness as a contender. Mondale's welcoming kiss of Ferraro when she was interviewed was therefore interpreted as a bad sign for her prospects. In *Ferraro: My Story*, she wrote that she remembered thinking, "What a pain this gender thing was going to be." Fritz and Joan Mondale kissed her when, as the chosen one, she arrived by private plane in North Oaks on the night of July 11.

The chambers of the Minnesota legislature were packed on July 12 with well-wishers, mostly state workers, when Mondale stood before them with his running mate. "This is an exciting choice," he said. "Let me say that again. This is an exciting choice." Minnesotans were proud of their native son and the momentous step he had taken. "God, I still get a little choked up when I think about it—the look on their faces, the sheer pleasure," says Reilly. "The picture was unbelievable, unbelievable." Joan McLean was in a spa in northern California when she got word of the impending announcement. She boarded the next plane to Minnesota. It was all anybody could talk about. The flight attendants were euphoric. If ever there was a moment of sisterly solidarity, this was it. Women in general were thrilled with the idea of a woman on the ticket.

Everything was quite celebratory when Mike Berman arrived in San Francisco to take care of party business. He had been asked by Jim Johnson to fire the Democratic party chairman, Charles Manatt, and replace him with Bert Lance, a Georgian who had been Jimmy Carter's budget director until he was forced to resign amid allegations of financial wheeling and dealing that predated his coming to Washington. Mondale knew Ferraro would not be a home run in the South, and Lance's appointment was designed to placate the good ol' boys by giving them the party leadership. But Democrats sympathetic to Manatt led a protest to rally support for him at the convention, and Mondale backed down.

The ease with which Democrats defeated Mondale's choice for party chair bothered Berman, but he had another, far more troubling matter to contend with. Awaiting him in San Francisco was a lengthy fax, three or four pages long, from *Washington Post* investigative reporter Charles Babcock. It was filled with questions about John Zaccaro's business dealings. Most of the alleged impropriety was news to Berman. He remembers thinking that if he had two or three weeks to investigate, he would have discovered this stuff too. Babcock had done the careful research Berman had not had time for. The reporter had visited various properties in New York owned by Zaccaro and uncovered a web of ownership and transactions that raised questions and suggested ties to organized crime. Ferraro's finances were technically not under assault. But Berman had been around long enough to know it was a distinction without a difference. He pushed the fax aside. Everybody was so busy with the hoopla around selecting the first woman, he couldn't have gotten anybody's attention if he tried.

The respite was brief, as it turned out. The week after the convention, stories began appearing from Babcock and others about various aspects of the Ferraro-Zaccaro family finances. They centered on possibly illegal loans Ferraro had taken from family members to finance her congressional campaign in 1978, her lack of disclosure about her husband's finances on congressional financial forms, and Zaccaro's renting of property to some shady characters. The revelations were the result of the hard digging that is done about anybody new to the national scene, and compounded by Ferraro's attitude that her privacy was being invaded. Her repeated use of a spousal exemption, allowed under the rules of Congress to keep from revealing her husband's finances, only whetted the media's appetite for the chase.

On the surface, Berman had not found anything disqualifying about Zaccaro. Admittedly, it was a rush job. But the actual combined income of Ferraro and Zaccaro was rather modest by his lights: $90,000 income in 1984 and a home in Forest Hills worth over $300,000 that they had purchased for $59,000. What they owned had appreciated. The alleged crime connection, which was much whispered, turned out to be tenuous. Zaccaro was heavily involved in real estate, and he was in the process of trying to shed some rental operations that could be construed as providing services to organized crime, though the businesses themselves were on the up and up. "There was not much there," insists a Mondale aide.

Ferraro had turned over the family's tax returns, and Mondale's aides had concluded there was nothing wrong. They remain mystified to this day as to why Zaccaro and Ferraro waged such a fierce fight to keep their financial information from going out to the media and public. Release of tax returns was becoming a routine practice for political candidates. Resisting seemed more trouble than it was worth. Ferraro said it was her husband's decision. "You people who are married to Italian men, you know what it's like," she said in a lame attempt to make light of the matter. The remark hit with deadly precision at the unease that voters have about a woman who might be president someday. If she couldn't stand up to her husband, how could she stand up to America's adversaries?

Ferraro's gender defined her candidacy in the best possible way, and the worst possible way. Campaign buttons popped up to proclaim, "Tits and Fritz." President Reagan's campaign manager, Ed Rollins, predicted (wink, wink) that "Geraldine Ferraro will be the biggest political bust in history."

Advisers spent hours discussing the body language permissible between Mondale and Ferraro. Any kind of embrace or touching was ruled out for fear it would convey the impression of a couple instead of a professional partnership. Ferraro's clothing became an issue. She favored skirts and dresses, but the Dress-for-Success look mandated suits. She wore a suit in her debate with Vice President George Bush, but defied the experts by continuing to campaign in colorfully patterned dresses.

Because Ferraro was new to national politics, one of the conditions the Mondale camp insisted on was using their people as her advisers. Elbowing aside Ferraro's aides naturally created resentment. Ferraro was permitted to have a few of her own people, most prominently Anne Wexler, a longtime Democratic activist who had been a senior aide in the Carter White House. Wexler sought out Reilly for advice on her role. "Gerry wants me to be her Reilly," she said. "What do you do?"

With a combination of Irish wiseacre instinct and wise-man gravitas, Reilly told her, "I sit around and pretend to know what's happening, and I never get operative," meaning he didn't make decisions.

Reilly thought he was being funny—and realistic. He believes the press requires a Reilly to interpret the candidate. By his self-description, he was the old gray-haired guy who's a contemporary of the candidate, who sees the candidate last at night and first thing in the morning. Everybody thinks he's making all the decisions when in fact the job is primarily handholding.

Wexler thought he was being flip, and dismissive of her genuine desire to do a good job. Reilly dates the lack of trust between the Mondale camp and the Ferraro camp to that conversation.

Back in Minnesota to map out the fall campaign schedule, the tensions escalated. Ferraro measured everything asked of her against her expectation of the demands that would be made on a male in her position. Her constant refrain was "I want to be treated the same as a white-haired senior senator." That was her way of invoking Lloyd Bentsen, whose wealth, connections, and patrician presence inspired deference in those who dealt with him. If Bentsen were on the ticket, Ferraro believed, he would be nobody's errand boy.

Ferraro rebelled at a scheduling meeting on August 1. She was told they would be going over a rough draft of the campaign schedule. But when they convened, she was presented with a fait accompli. Jim Johnson unveiled two charts with hers and Mondale's travel schedules inked in red and green for the next three months. Her first solo campaign swing was the following week. Mondale would not begin campaigning until later in the month. Ferraro flatly refused to go out that early. She felt she wouldn't have adequate time to prepare, and she didn't want to make a mistake. But what she said stung Mondale and his aides. As Reilly remembers it, Ferraro insisted she had to return to Washington to wrap up her work in the Congress, and that she then intended to go to Fire Island for a few days on a family vacation.

Mondale sat silent through Ferraro's outburst, his face reddening with anger. He didn't know what he had gotten himself into. "We were all pretty shocked at the time," says Reilly. "It was an unwritten rule that a vice president does what's asked."

Ferraro viewed everything through the prism of gender, which transformed the everyday humilities of being a vice presidential contender into a titanic struggle. In fact, Lloyd Bentsen would have said it was fine to provide him with a staff experienced in running a national campaign, as he did four years later when the Democratic nominee, Michael Dukakis, chose Bentsen as his running mate.

"What we didn't understand is that any vice president gets people the president wants," says Joanne Howes, a core member of Team A. "A vice president is not a free agent. You're locked to the hip of this person who just gave you this honor. We saw it differently, that if Mondale had any chance to win, it would be through Gerry, and if only they would pay attention to us, it would be different."

Ferraro had wanted her mentor, Tip O'Neill, with her on stage when the convention confirmed her nomination as vice president, but he refused, telling her, "I am the old politics, Gerry, and you're the new. I can only hurt you." The Republicans had tried to turn the portly, white-haired O'Neill into a symbol of what's wrong with Washington in the 1982 congressional elections, and he wanted to spare Ferraro any unnecessary grief.

The new politics glow of Ferraro's candidacy buoyed Mondale to the point where he was running even with Reagan (48 to 46 percent with 6 percent undecided) the week after the Democratic National Convention, according to a *Newsweek*-Gallup poll. The poll reflected a huge turnaround since Mondale had been behind by as much as nineteen points just one month earlier. Moreover, 64 percent of those polled said they considered Ferraro qualified to be vice president, up thirteen points from the week before.

The tears of joy elicited by Ferraro's groundbreaking candidacy had barely dried when questions about her family finances overwhelmed the Mondale campaign. New politics gave way to old politics, and Ferraro rapidly lost her luster as her campaign got mired in scandal. Ferraro was a novelty, and so was her husband. Reporters wanted to know everything about them. Responding was made more difficult by the campaign's internal squabbles. Ferraro's refusal to release her tax returns irked Mondale's aides. Reilly pleaded with her. "There are some things you have to do if you want to get elected," he said. She wouldn't budge. She said they were nobody's business, and that there was too much pointless scrutiny of private matters.

It became apparent that Ferraro was deferring to her husband on the returns. Not until he gave his permission did she relent. It was August 16, the night before the couple was scheduled for a marathon session with accountants hired by the campaign. By then, the Mondale campaign had lost valuable time. Reagan had reasserted himself in the polls, and was now leading Mondale by roughly twenty points, the same margin that existed before the Democratic convention and the outpouring of support for Ferraro.

The questions that arose about Ferraro's finances during the period after the convention dealt with potential criminal liability, so Mike Berman put together a team of lawyers and accountants who spent weeks doing all the digging they should have done beforehand. Then they confronted Ferraro and Zaccaro with what they had uncovered. Some of the information was troubling. And much of it was intensely personal, going to the heart of her relationship with her husband. Why, for example, did she take the spousal exemption on her congressional disclosure forms, claiming she was not involved with her husband's business, when she was listed as an officer and part owner?

Ferraro scanned the faces around the table, finally settling uneasily on Francis O'Brien, a congenial Boston Irish pol, who had been drafted by the Mondale camp to be her new press secretary. She never wanted him in the first place, and now she demanded to know why he was in the room when these private financial matters were being discussed. O'Brien thought to himself, Who needs this? So he got up and left the room. "You need him more than he needs us," Berman admonished Ferraro, silenced for the moment. With that, Berman got up to go after O'Brien. He caught up with him in the lobby and persuaded him to return. It was a close call. Had O'Brien gotten to the front sidewalk, he would not have come back. Ferraro's chief objection to O'Brien was that she didn't know him, and didn't feel comfortable sharing family secrets with a stranger. This was no time to assert privacy rights, a Mondale aide told her. Whatever they learned, the press had to be included.

In these soul-baring sessions with aides and her husband, Ferraro learned that her husband had created a trust fund for their son but not for either of their daughters. "It was a tiny little thing, maybe a thousand dollars for the boy, and nothing for the girls," an aide remembers. For Ferraro, the pain of discovery was compounded by having a roomful of political aides looking on and studying her reaction. She glared at Zaccaro. "We'll discuss this later," she said.

From the July convention until Labor Day, all the focus was on Ferraro and her family finances. Mondale stayed in Minnesota. "He knew in his heart of hearts that we'd blown it," says an aide. "We had not taken the time. Even in those days, when the scrutiny was far less. He was upset about that. We'd spent two and a half weeks on Feinstein. We had lawyers out there four or five days. Dick Blum was very forthcoming. There was never a question Dick was asked that he didn't answer."

Ferraro felt equally glum. She said that if God had shown her a videotape of what the next months would be like, she would have said, "Thanks, God, but could you do me a favor and choose Dianne?" On the road campaigning during the worst of it, she called home three and four times a day worried about her husband, who was devastated by the August 30 court ruling that removed him as the conservator of the elder woman's estate. The stream of stories leading up to the decision had taken their toll, and Ferraro recounts in her book how she brought her children together to tell them that their father was depressed, and that they needed to bolster him.

The cardinal rule in picking a vice president is to choose somebody who does no harm. If Mondale's advisers had done their homework, they might not have chosen her. But having chosen her, they should have been prepared for the questions from the media, and they should have had answers. Instead, they allowed themselves to be ambushed. "I'm from the 'lance the boil right now' school," says one top aide. "We weren't prepared to lance the boil."

It took most of August before the accountants, lawyers, and political advisers reached a comfort level with Ferraro's finances. They were then ready for full disclosure. The strategy called for two stages. First, they put all the high-priced lawyers and accountants in a room in Washington and let the reporters grill them until there was nothing left to ask. Then two days later, on August 21, Ferraro held a news conference at Kennedy Airport in New York in which she deftly used her gender to deflect criticism of her family's financial practices. Asked about large loans she had received from her husband to fund her 1978 congressional race, she blamed the sexist policies of banks that denied her loans without her husband as a cosigner. "I can give you a speech about how hard it is for women to run for office," she said, explaining that she was unaware that loans from family members are illegal under campaign finance law. The campaign's audit revealed she had underpaid her taxes, and she told the media she had paid the IRS $53,459 in back taxes. It was a simple miscalculation, she said, made by a well-meaning family accountant, a man she described as "a sweetheart." After an hour and twenty minutes, reporters had no more questions.

Mondale's aides were exuberant. "It's a ten!" one yelled when Ferraro finished. The story that had dogged them for weeks had finally spent itself. Berman called Mondale and said, "It's over." Ferraro's virtuoso performance persuaded the editors at *Time* magazine to kill an article about how she had let down the women of the country. Instead, *Time* put her on the cover with the caption "Under pressure, Ferraro passes a vital test."

Her candidacy reborn, Ferraro told NBC's Connie Chung with characteristic bravado, "I knew what I was getting into. I climbed into a boxing ring and I was ready to put on the gloves with any of the guys."

Ferraro received high marks for both courage and candor. Even now, many years later, the kind of no-holds-barred news conference she held is called "Doing a Ferraro." But the magic of her candidacy fell victim to the controversy. Women were still new enough to the political scene that voters didn't think of them as typical politicians, and expected them to be free of scandal. In the end, Ferraro's alleged wrongdoing was more smoke than fire. A better-handled presentation of her financial affairs on her own part, and by the campaign, could have helped her avoid much of the controversy. Her reputation suffered, as did Mondale's, and the campaign lost momentum. Analysts still debate the value of Ferraro's candidacy and whether she helped or hurt the cause of a woman vice president. "Anybody who says it was a negative thing doesn't know what they're talking about," Ferraro says. "If God were on the ticket with Fritz Mondale, even she would not have made a difference."

Granted, if defeating Ronald Reagan was the standard, Ferraro failed miserably. But her candidacy has to be judged in other ways. If it didn't change votes, did it change attitudes in a positive way? She believes it did. "The Secret Service told me they had not seen crowds like that since John F. Kennedy. People cried, they were so moved. But when they went to pull the lever, it wasn't me against anybody, it was Mondale against Reagan."

What Ferraro's candidacy accomplished so dramatically was to show the country what is possible. The picture of what politics could look like changed. It said to women that they could be included, and the lesson that a generation of women drew, in the words of Ann Lewis, was "Tell us what it takes. Next time we'll be ready." Emily's List was created two years later with the goal of electing women to the Senate, and more women, inspired by Ferraro, ran for office, not only nationally but also in state legislatures. A lot of women got excited about politics because of that night at the convention when Ferraro stood before a sea of delegates, more than half of them women and many of them crying, to accept the nomination of her party. She wore a pastel pink suit, as if to say, get used to it, this is a new power color.

What she didn't know then was how hard it would be to carry the weight of history along with all the baggage of any candidate at that competitive level of politics. There is a hazing quality to what anyone new to the national scene goes through. Just ask Dan Quayle. Compared to the way he froze like a deer in the headlights when questions first arose about his National Guard experience and his college transcript, Ferraro performed well in her trial by fire. "I proved I could handle the campaign—the hours and the stress. I wasn't going to burst into tears. I knew I was able to get through it, but I worried about my family," she says, looking back. "But you get up and get out and do your job. The people who are voting are not worrying if you're upset about something at home. My obligation was to them, and I showed I could do it."

One secret, though, never came out. The third day after Ferraro's nomination, a parent at the college Ferraro's son was attending told somebody in the campaign that young John Zaccaro, Jr., was involved in drug dealing at school. That person took the information to Berman, who decided not to tell anybody, not even Ferraro. "I just held my breath," he says. "I thought about it for two and a half seconds. Everything was so fragile. If I walked in and said your son is into drugs, I could imagine the reaction." It was minor peddling. Eventually, he was caught. The attention paid to her caused more attention to be paid to him, which caused the police to eventually do something about it. This was penny ante.

"I could not do it to Mondale either," Berman continued. "I've been in this business since 1964. Sometimes you just get lucky. I turned to the person who brought me the news and said, 'You've done what you're supposed to do. If it comes up, I'll take the rap.' "

Berman acted out of his candidate's self-interest. Neither Mondale nor Ferraro could have handled the prospect of another damning personal revelation. Besides, Berman had visited Ferraro and Zaccaro in their home in Forest Hills, Queens. He'd had his differences with them, but he believed they were good parents. They had a lovely home, a real home, where you could sit on the couch and not feel you were violating some code of conduct. Berman was sure he had done the right thing.

Mondale's people worked very hard to keep Ferraro's Team A pals off the campaign. They apparently felt that if people familiar to her were kept to a minimum, they could keep better control. "Why would we want to damage the ticket?" Joan McLean protested. They had a different take on how the campaign should unfold. For starters, Ferraro's women advisers wanted to know why "the white boys" weren't capitalizing more on Ferraro's star presence. Joint appearances with Mondale were initially kept to a minimum because the staff, not Mondale himself, legitimately feared that she was more dynamic and would quickly overshadow him. Mondale's men were also unsettled by reports that the Democratic party was being "feminized," and had lost its appeal among men. Showcasing Ferraro too much, they feared, could accelerate the trend. Mondale's men eventually came around to appreciate Ferraro's built-in star status as a historical novelty and scheduled more joint appearances.

Gender remained a point of contention. Ferraro knew she was selected because she was a woman, and was on constant alert for slights stemming from her sex. For example, it took six weeks for the Mondale staff to change the pronoun from "he" to "she" on internal memos outlining the fund-raising schedule for the vice presidential candidate. Some of the material had been in the works before her nomination, so the expectation of a "he" was understandable. But a six-week lag time seemed to Ferraro an intentional slight.

Her job was to rally women to the ticket, and she undertook the task with zeal. At the Democratic convention in San Francisco, she brought the delegates, half of them women, to their feet, telling them, "By choosing a woman to run for our nation's second-highest office, you send a powerful signal to all Americans. There are no doors that we cannot unlock." She pounded away at the theme throughout the campaign, declaring, "I'm happy there is no longer a sign [at the White House], 'White males only need apply.' It's *our* turn, folks." In a play on John F. Kennedy's famous line, she quipped in her acceptance speech, "The issue is not what America can do for women but what women can do for America."

As a pro-choice Catholic woman, Ferraro faced unrelenting attacks for her views on abortion. Protesters dogged her at public events, and Archbishop John O'Connor of New York openly campaigned against her. *Washington Post* writer Mary McGrory reflected the dismay within the Mondale campaign when she said of Ferraro in a September 25, 1984, column, "Here she is, a lifelong Roman Catholic, a product of Catholic schools and goes to Mass every Sunday. Yet the hierarchy of her church is acting like an arm of the Reagan reelection committee."

Republican representative Lynn Martin was campaigning among steelworkers in a bar in Dixon, Illinois, when she got the call from Vice President Bush asking her to play Ferraro in a series of practice debates. Normally, being called by the White House is something to brag about. But Martin didn't dare tell the steelworkers. Reagan's economic policies were not popular in the Rust Belt, and she was trying to survive her own reelection. She suggested other Republican women Bush might call. There was a pause, and Bush said, "Lynn, I'm vice president of the United States. That doesn't give me any power. But I get to pick who I want to do this. Now, if you don't want to do it, say no, but I didn't call you to ask who you thought I should pick."

Bush's typical self-effacing manner combined with his candor won over Martin. A pro-choice moderate active in the congressional women's caucus, she made a good Ferraro clone. She knew and liked Ferraro, and they were allies on many women's issues.[1] She even had blond hair. Martin plunged into the task with her customary energy. While she cheered the presence of a woman on a major party presidential ticket, this was a political competition and she was on the opposing team. Her competitive juices flowed maybe even more than if this was just another guy in a blue suit. She watched videotapes of everything Ferraro had done, paying particular attention to her debating style. New Yorkers talk much more quickly than midwesterners, and she wanted to get the tempo right.

---

[1] In January 2000, Ferraro and Martin announced a business partnership, G & L Strategies, to advise corporations on how to develop women leaders, and make the workplace more female-friendly.

The Bush family pride was at stake. Reagan's people had tried to avoid a vice presidential debate, fearing Ferraro would win simply by sharing a stage with the sitting vice president. The pallid crowds Bush attracted were constantly compared to the robust audiences turning out for Ferraro, prompting Barbara Bush to allude to Ferraro as "that four-million-dollar—I can't say it, but it rhymes with rich." Ferraro's family fortune had been put at $3.8 million, more than the Bush estate, though it was Bush who wore the label of privilege, not the immigrant's daughter from Queens.

Martin's job was to help Bush beat Ferraro, and the best advice she got came from Barbara Bush. "You go get him," she said of her husband. "He's too full of himself."

"Are you sure?" Martin replied incredulously. Because the more she thought about it, how could a victory over the vice president, even if it was just for practice, be a win for her? She was forty-four years old and a rising star in the party. Why tick off the GOP's heir apparent?

"Go at him," Mrs. Bush repeated, leaving no doubt that she meant what she said.

They had three practice debates, and Martin ripped Bush apart on issue after issue. She had modeled herself after the tough and combative Ferraro who appeared on the network news night after night. It wasn't until their third session that Bush got comfortable returning her volleys, and got his sound bites down to fighting trim. "We just tried to get him to give short answers on the parts where he was awkward," she explains. "Giving a longer answer and trying to explain how you're really a great guy is not a great plan. Just go at it, get it over, and go on."

The October debate in Philadelphia between Bush and Ferraro changed few minds, though the instant polls found more people thought Bush had won. Buoyed by the early returns, Bush boasted to a group of longshoremen in Elizabeth, New Jersey, the next day, "We tried to kick a little ass last night." The remark seemed gratuitously out of character for the patrician Bush, and left a more indelible impression than anything that had happened in the debate.

The legacy of 1984 was to energize women. Seeing one of their own in the national arena made women proud, and nervous. Wherever Ferraro went, fathers and mothers raised their young daughters on their shoulders to catch a glimpse of history in the making. Something happened to the body politic. It just didn't translate into votes. More women voted for Reagan than for Mondale, though in lesser numbers than men. The gender gap existed, but it wasn't enough to elect a president, at least not yet.

Mondale won only his home state of Minnesota, losing forty-nine states to Reagan in the biggest blowout in modern electoral history. Reagan got 55 percent of the women's vote, compared to 64 percent of the men's vote, proving the persistence of the gender gap even in the face of overwhelming defeat. Ferraro proved to be a good fund-raiser and a good trouper, traveling more than Mondale, and more than Reagan and Bush combined.

Ferraro still had to cope with the aftershocks of the campaign. Her son, John Zaccaro, Jr., was arrested in February 1986 on the campus of Middlebury College in Vermont, where he was a senior, and charged with possession of cocaine. He was sentenced to four months under house arrest and freed after serving three months of the sentence. The young Zaccaro finished his degree at Hunter College in New York, got a law degree at Catholic University, and has had no legal trouble since. In October 1987, Ferraro's husband was acquitted of charges that he had tried to extort a million-dollar bribe from a cable television company, an accusation dating to 1981. The evidence was so weak that Zaccaro's lawyers did not even present a defense case. Ferraro said her husband never would have been charged had she not been a candidate for vice president.

Whether Ferraro's candidacy had advanced or set back the cause of a woman on the ticket is a question still being debated. Women answered themselves by increasing their presence as voters and candidates, validating women at every level of politics, as if to say one losing election is no big deal. Still, so powerful was the Ferraro hangover that it would not be until 2000 that the two major political parties would again contemplate a woman on the ticket as a vice presidential contender.

If Ferraro was the wrong woman, finding the right woman became for a while the goal. After the election, early in 1985, Joan McLean was dispatched by the bipartisan Women's Campaign Fund to sound out Nancy Landon Kassebaum about a possible presidential run. Kassebaum was a well-connected Republican who had just been elected to her second term as senator from Kansas. She represented the heartland and she stood up on a variety of women's issues. Her father, Alf Landon, had run for president in 1936. It would be a wonderful tale to have the daughter of the failed presidential candidate complete the legacy. But when McLean met with Kassebaum in her Washington office to propose she run for president, Kassebaum was dumbfounded. "I have a ranch in Kansas. Why would I want to do that?" she asked. McLean remembers thinking that her response was exactly why they wanted her to run. She knew what was truly important to her, and she had no interest in vying for a place on her party's ticket.

McLean next trained her sights on Sally Ride, the first woman astronaut. Ride had been a Ferraro supporter, and McLean had met her a couple of times and been impressed. McLean often used Ride as an example of the kind of woman who could someday be president, and had dreamed up a time line for her trajectory. If Ride were groomed for high office, the way men are, she would make the perfect presidential candidate in 2000. Well-respected and with high name recognition, all she needed was electoral experience. California's Alan Cranston was expected to retire from the Senate soon; if Ride ran for his seat and won, she would be on her way. McLean calculated that Ride's contacts in the vote-rich states of California, Texas, and Florida because of the space program would help enormously in a presidential run. McLean also figured Ride might have a sentimental edge in the New Hampshire primary, which helps decide each party's nominee. Ride had distinguished herself by asking tough questions as a member of the commission investigating the 1986 *Challenger* disaster, in which a crew of astronauts had died along with New Hampshire schoolteacher Christa McAuliffe when their flight capsule exploded seconds after liftoff. McLean anticipated that Ride's involvement in investigating the tragedy might translate into an advantage in McAuliffe's home state.

Ride, who left NASA in 1987 for a science fellowship at Stanford University, was a natural when it came to foreign policy and defense experience. As McLean viewed it, anyone who sits on top of a rocket and gets blasted into space should automatically have credibility on national security issues. It worked for John Glenn.

One complication: When an intermediary approached Sally Ride and probed her about her future ambition, Ride slammed the door shut on electoral politics. Serving on the commission looking into the *Challenger* explosion had turned her off politics. She didn't like the compromises you have to make and the spin that people put on information as compared to dealing with straight scientific data.

Women activists came to realize that conjuring up an ideal woman for a presidential ticket was a lot simpler than finding a real-life woman who could be nominated. The dream died with Ferraro. The hard work lay ahead.

TWO

Women Raising Money for Women: The Creation of Emily's List

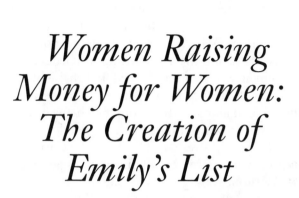

Ellen Malcolm is a tall and imposing woman with broad shoulders, a sturdy build, and a ready smile. She grew up in Montclair, New Jersey, the daughter of a Republican committeewoman and the granddaughter of a woman so staunchly Republican she insisted throughout her life that Herbert Hoover solved the Depression while Franklin Roosevelt, a Democrat, stole the credit. Malcolm was programmed to follow the same political path. But like many who came of age during the Vietnam War, her life's direction changed. At Hollins College, a women's school in Roanoke, Virginia, Malcolm got involved in the antiwar movement and Gene McCarthy's presidential campaign. She changed her registration from Republican to Democrat. After graduation in 1969, she worked at Common Cause in the early 1970s and as press secretary for the National Women's Political Caucus, a bipartisan organization dedicated to the advancement of women in politics. In 1980, she joined the White House staff as press secretary for Esther Peterson, President Carter's special assistant for consumer affairs.

Co-workers and even close friends did not know at the time that Malcolm was a wealthy woman. Her father had died of colon cancer at age twenty-eight when she was only eight months old. His grandfather was one of the founders of IBM, and the family had generously ensured young Ellen's financial well-being. She was accustomed to keeping her wealth hidden. She wanted to be accepted for herself, not the funds she could provide. "I was a shy girl," she says.

In what appeared at the time a happy coincidence, checks for $5,000 from an anonymous donor arrived periodically at the offices of the Caucus and other groups dedicated to the advancement of women. The checks were signed by a trust officer at a bank in Boston to preserve the donor's privacy. Five thousand dollars was a lot of money in those days, and the women couldn't believe their good fortune. "I thought it was a mistake," says Judith Lichtman, then with the Women's Legal Defense Fund, a recipient of the anonymous gifts.

Malcolm rejoiced along with the others whenever a new check arrived. But she was growing restless with the hand-to-mouth existence of the nonprofit world. After a brief stint in the Carter White House, Malcolm enrolled at Georgetown University to get a master's degree in business. Without telling anyone, she also created a foundation, naming it after the street where she lived. The Wyndham Fund became the vehicle for Malcolm to contribute money anonymously to her favorite projects.

Meanwhile, the checks kept coming to the women's groups, drawn now on the Wyndham Fund. Malcolm would sit stone-faced in meetings while others speculated about the identity of the mysterious donor who underwrote the Wyndham Fund. "Somebody would say, 'It's some Rockefeller that so-and-so is dating,' " Malcolm recalled. "And all I could think of was, 'Oh, my God, just breathe. Nobody will ever know it's me if I don't do anything. I'm sure I'm not blushing.' "

Over time, Malcolm decided it was silly to keep pretending. She should assume the power of what she was doing. By then, the Wyndham Fund had moved into a funky building at Twentieth and P Streets in downtown Washington, and Malcolm, now with her MBA, arranged to "rent" an office in the Fund's suite. Amazingly, none of her friends drew the obvious conclusion. The building housed a number of nonprofit groups, including the Women's Legal Defense Fund. One day, Malcolm strolled across the hall to Lichtman's office. "I have something to tell you," she said in a serious tone. The two women sat on the couch, and Malcolm blurted out her secret. "It's me. It's my money you've been getting."

The news stunned Lichtman. "Just think, I *like* you!" she exclaimed, the past flashing before her as she wondered whether she would have gotten those checks if she and Malcolm had not gotten along. Malcolm calls it "coming out of the philanthropic closet." It freed her to think bigger than she had dared before.

In 1982, Malcolm had worked hard to get a woman, Harriett Woods, elected to the Senate. Woods had come up through the ranks of local politics in Missouri, where, like many other women, she was motivated by social justice and community causes. After eight years on the city council and six years in the Missouri State Senate, she was ready to move up. Popular with voters, knowledgeable, and patrician in her bearing, Woods was a strong candidate. But she couldn't get "the money boys" to take her seriously. One of the party's biggest contributors told her that people would see her as "nothing but a housewife from the suburbs." He said she would not be able to raise the money needed to run for the Senate.

The Democratic establishment backed a local bank lobbyist who had the connections to bankroll his race. But Woods defeated him in the primary with her strong reformist agenda and came close to unseating incumbent Republican John Danforth in the general election. Danforth's aloofness from the voters and support for "Reaganomics" at a time of double-digit unemployment made him vulnerable. Woods lost by only 27,000 votes, about one percent of the votes cast, a margin narrow enough that more money could have made the difference.

Women were angry that the Democratic party had not fully supported Woods. Even after she became the nominee, party leaders had so little confidence in her that she received only token financial help. A woman running for the Senate was such an oddity in 1982 that the mostly male leadership could get away with their cavalier attitude. Frustrated by the male establishment's refusal to recognize the power of Woods' candidacy, Malcolm decided it was time for women to act on their own.

The year 1984 was not a good year for women to assert their political independence. True, several Democratic women ran for the Senate that year, but none had a real chance to win. They were either running in heavily Republican states or were so underfunded that they could not compete. Still, Malcolm sent out a chain letter describing the women who were running. Assuming women wanted to elect more women to Congress, the letter asked them to contribute to the candidates of their choice, then pass the letter along to a friend. Malcolm had no way to track the results, but enough women sent positive notes and checks to make her believe the effort had potential.

As expected, not a single woman won a Senate seat in 1984, and Geraldine Ferraro's historic candidacy for vice president ended in a humiliating defeat. Sizing up her first effort at women funding other women, Malcolm concluded that too little money had been spread too thin to do anybody any good. What good was it to divert precious dollars to candidates she knew would, at best, get no more than 40 percent of the vote? From here on, she decided, money would go only to those candidates who had a chance to win.

As Harriett Woods geared up for a second Senate try in 1986, Malcolm decided to put the full force of her fledgling organization behind her. Malcolm vowed that a shortage of money would not handicap Woods this time. "Early money is like yeast—it makes the 'dough' rise," Malcolm liked to say. That's how Emily's List got its name, along with a logo modeled after Fleischmann yeast packs. Fleischmann's prime audience was full-time homemakers who baked from scratch. Most of Malcolm's crowd had never opened a yeast packet. Yet Malcolm was sure all women would get the message.

Only a small percentage of women would be eager and able to contribute to candidates, Malcolm knew, so she challenged those women to give more generously than they might have otherwise. She proposed that women participating in Emily's List pay a $100 annual membership fee and give $100 or more to at least two candidates per year, a minimum annual commitment of $300. "Are you crazy?" Lichtman asked. That was a lot of money to ask of women. Most had never before given to political candidates. But Malcolm insisted that women had to dig deep if they hoped to make a difference in politics. Two dozen women assembled in Malcolm's basement, Rolodexes in hand, to send letters to their friends seeking contributions to pro-choice Democratic female candidates.

Following the lead of Tupperware saleswomen, Malcolm traveled the country holding "Rolodex parties" in people's living rooms. She had never raised money in her life, and was terrified of public speaking. But her idea had power, and women responded to it. They paid their $100 membership fee just to hear Malcolm's pitch, and they wrote checks for hundreds and sometimes thousands of dollars. And they didn't always wait for permission from their husbands.

Malcolm had created a new product for a market segment. She had done so against the advice of her marketing professor at Georgetown. He had strongly discouraged his star pupil from working in the non-profit world. "You'll hate it," he told her. "It will drive you crazy. They're incompetent." As Emily's List took hold, Malcolm thought of inviting her old professor to assign a student to write a paper on her venture so the professor could revise his thinking.

In 1986, its first year of operation, Emily's List attracted six hundred donors, raised over $350,000, and claimed some of the credit for the first Democratic woman elected to the Senate in her own right, although not the one who everyone thought would break the gender barrier. Women activists expected Woods to win on her second try in Missouri. She had positioned herself perfectly during the intervening years, running as a pro-choice reform candidate and winning a statewide race in 1984 to be lieutenant governor. Then a second woman announced she was running for the Senate. Barbara Mikulski was a social worker and former city council member from Baltimore who had been elected to the House in 1976.

The four-foot-eleven Mikulski seemed an unlikely prospect for a seat in the Senate. She was an old-style politician with her roots in the neighborhood, and her constituents in city council and later Congress felt comfortable with her; she was one of them. And she could get things done. When no one else was able to persuade authorities to keep open the neighborhood Polish-American Catholic church, Mikulski went over the heads of the archdiocese and got the Maryland Historical Society to declare the church, the oldest of its kind in Maryland, a historic site. When a freeway threatened the neighborhood, she organized local citizens into the South-east Baltimore Citizens Organization, and together they stopped the freeway. But those were local matters. Washington's elite could not picture her as a member of "the world's most exclusive club," as the Senate is known.

Twelve years earlier, Mikulski had tried to leap directly from the Baltimore City Council to the Senate. Hoping to capitalize on the anti-Republican sentiment following President Nixon's resignation in 1974 in the wake of the Watergate scandal, Mikulski had challenged Republican senator Charles "Mac" Mathias. She lost by 150,000 votes against the popular Mathias. Two years later she was elected to the House, defeating Baltimore lawyer Samuel A. Culotta, a Republican member of the state House of Delegates. The outspoken Mikulski quickly earned the nickname "The Mouth." She championed the causes of women, labor, and minorities, treating the legislative arena as an extension of her social work. She was sometimes abrasive, confirming what an instructor told her when she was earning her master's degree in social work, "Ms. Mikulski, you don't have a therapeutic personality."

Mikulski's decision to risk her safe House seat for a second try at the Senate was deeply personal. She was going to be fifty years old, and she was ready for a new life. Public policy and public advocacy had been her passion going back to when she was a community organizer and a social worker dealing with child abuse. She longed for a bigger stage where she could have more impact. The idea sounded foolhardy even to her biggest backers. Carol Tucker Foreman, a friend and ally, remembers thinking, "Does she really want to do this? She's a lowly congresswoman from innercity Baltimore." Foreman had watched other female House members try to move up to the Senate and wind up losing their foothold in politics. New York's Bella Abzug's narrow loss in the Democratic primary in 1976 to Daniel Patrick Moynihan was especially painful. Abzug ran for other elective offices, but never regained the platform she had had in the House. Besides, Mikulski didn't look like a senator. Her short stature and bulldog demeanor would never have gotten her past central casting for the role she wanted to play. Democratic activist Ann Lewis, Mikulski's first chief of staff in the House, said, "I know. Jesse Helms looks like a senator. I want to change the image of what a senator looks like."

Rarely does a Senate seat come open, and when it does, politicians line up to run for it. Mathias' retirement created a stampede to replace him. In the primary election, Mikulski ran against a sitting governor, Harry Hughes, and a popular congressman, Michael Barnes, who represented Maryland's affluent Montgomery County in Congress. Hughes' standing with Maryland voters had slipped, making Barnes the real competition. As a leading opponent of the Reagan administration's adventurism in Central America, Barnes had made requent appearances on "Nightline" and other TV shows, enhancing his name recognition. But Maryland's Democratic voters were concentrated in urban areas, with almost 60 percent of the vote in Baltimore, Mikulski's home turf. Barnes' strongest backers were good-government people residing in the bedroom communities of Montgomery County. Many of them registered as independents and could not vote in the primary.

Mikulski had to prove she could compete dollar-for-dollar with the boys. Running for the House, she hadn't had to rely on expensive media consultants. She could count on fund-raising gimmicks like "Bagels for Barb" and "Bicycle Riders for Barb" to make do. Now, running statewide, she had to raise ten times as much money, and that's where Emily's List played a key role. Emily's List financed a statewide poll that showed Mikulski was a formidable challenger. By making the poll public she established her credibility as a Senate candidate. That helped her raise enough money to compete with Barnes, which was what Emily's List wanted to accomplish with its early contribution.

Barnes' strategy was to portray Mikulski as an unpleasant, sharp-elbowed person and himself as a genial, pleasant guy. Mikulski turned the caricature to her advantage with the slogan. "When it comes to Maryland, I'm a fighter." The slogan was so effective that people polled after the election would repeat it word for word, as though they had discovered she's a fighter without prompting from a television ad. Mikulski's advisers neutralized her image problem with film footage showing an exchange with the butcher at a local supermarket.

"You're looking good—you lost some weight," the butcher says.

Beaming, Mikulski replies, "I'm counting my calories, and counting my votes."

Mikulski faced whispers that she was a lesbian, a charge used against many female candidates. Mikulski's opponent in the general election, Republican Linda Chavez, a former Reagan appointee, emphasized her marital credentials and said that Mikulski was out of the mainstream. She portrayed Mikulski as "a San Francisco–style Democrat," a thinly veiled suggestion of homosexuality. But the smear tactics didn't work. Mikulski had already been elected to Congress five times. A third-party candidate, a woman running on the LaRouche ticket, regularly said Mikulski was a lesbian. Voters thought her opponent was the weirdo, not Mikulski. "There are a lot of women like Barbara in Baltimore, in ethnic Catholic families—the unmarried sister," says a former aide, explaining why the charge failed to move votes. "Some go into the convent, others stay home and take care of their parents. The unmarried schoolteacher, the unmarried social worker, these are common occurrences in working-class ethnic homes. It was new to me," says the aide, "but it exists."

Mikulski, the daughter of a Polish-American grocer, was not daunted by the challenge of becoming the first Democratic woman elected to the Senate on her own. She had done so many things where she was the first that she didn't think much about it. "Some guy didn't have to die for me to get my job," she quipped. But she occasionally reminded her supporters that they were part of a historic endeavor. Only eighteen women had served before her in two hundred years. And of that eighteen, the Senate historian told Mikulski, only three had been elected in their own right: Maine Republican Margaret Chase Smith, Kansas Republican Nancy Landon Kassebaum, and Florida Republican Paula Hawkins.

In the primary, Mikulski won the Senate nomination with 53 percent of the vote over Barnes (29 percent) and Hughes (13 percent). She went on in November to defeat Chavez, 61 to 39 percent. She was reelected easily to a second term in 1992 and a third term in 1998.

Mikulski's breakthrough candidacy was a first for female Democratic candidates for the Senate and a first for Emily's List. Now she had to prove herself. In the House, Mikulski had gravitated to what she called "affinity groups," like-minded colleagues, typically Democrats to the left of center, who together championed the issues they cared about. The Senate was different. It was a club that frequently worked across party lines, melding policy with personal relationships. Mikulski knew that most of the senators regarded her as a loose-lipped liberal, and that she had to answer the question "Is she serious?" She laid out a strategic plan. She knew that simply having a strategy would be noticed and admired. As a pacesetter, she would set the tone for successors not yet born. She would pave the way for other women by setting a good example. "She wanted playmates," says Foreman.

Getting on the right committees would signal her seriousness. She set her sights on Appropriations, a traditional center of power because it controls the purse strings. She didn't want to be a back-bencher, the term for junior members relegated to B-list assignments. She paid personal visits to every key senator. Other freshmen lobbying for Appropriations had to fly in and cram all their courtesy calls into one afternoon. Living in nearby Maryland, Mikulski could drive to Capitol Hill in an hour and did so frequently to accommodate the schedules of senior senators. She called it "playing the Maryland card." Her lobbying paid off. She edged out several other contenders for a seat on Appropriations. Two years later, she was made chairman of the Appropriations subcommittee dealing with the space program and veterans affairs. NASA contracts are important to Maryland, and making sure she is taking care of veterans is important to Mikulski. Her opposition to the Vietnam War had made her vulnerable with veterans, a powerful constituency. When she recognized a weakness in herself she set out to correct it.

Mikulski reveals the anxiety she experienced in the mystery novel *Capitol Offense* that she co-authored in 1996 with the writer Mary-louise Oates. The book's central character, freshman senator Eleanor "Norie" Gorzack, pays a courtesy call on the Senate majority leader, a man's man who wears cowboy boots and twirls a rope that he fashions into a noose at her feet during their conversation.

Gorzack wants to avoid being tagged a "bleeding heart" liberal. With that in mind, she asks for the Labor and Veterans Affairs committees, which deal with union types and veterans. The majority leader says that both committees are magnets for fund-raising, and that all senators, not just a female senator, want issues "close to men's souls." He drags out the word *souls* until it stretches between them like a syllable to hang herself with. If she were on one of these committees, he concludes slyly, which subcommittee would she like?

Gorzack is stumped by the question, thereby violating a rule that Mikulski lives by: Know how it works so you can work it. The fictional Gorzack, representing Pennsylvania, gets assigned to Government Operations and Agriculture, the equivalent of Siberia for a senator from a mostly urban, northeastern state.

Mikulski dug into her new job and earned the respect of her colleagues. She shunned the limelight and focused on being the senator from Maryland, not just Baltimore, which meant traveling the state. She smoothed the rough edges of her reputation for mouthiness. A decade had passed since she won her congressional seat. She had matured. She had authored bills that became law. With the benefit of age and accomplishment, she could afford to tone down her demeanor. She wasn't a fluke, and she desperately wanted to fit into the clubby world of the Senate. "I wasn't here as fins on an automobile," she says. "I really wanted to be a senator."

Mikulski relied on a half-dozen senior Democrats who counseled her. She called them the "Galahads," after chivalrous Sir Galahad, a knight of King Arthur's legendary roundtable. Senators Paul Sarbanes of Maryland and Ted Kennedy of Massachusetts were especially helpful. They helped get her on the Appropriations Committee, a good perch from which to raise money for the next campaign, and they tutored her on the rules of the Senate. Mikulski soaked up the advice and found acceptance in the old boys club. Six years later, in 1992, she won reelection with 73 percent of the vote, and is widely viewed as having one of the safest seats in the Senate.

Mikulski's success helped offset Malcolm's disappointment with Harriett Woods, who had held such promise for Emily's List. Woods was back home in Missouri, again nursing defeat. She had lost a second bid for the Senate and her political career was over. This time lack of money was not the main cause of her defeat. She had raised $3.7 million, more than any other woman running in the country. It was less than the $4.4 million raised by her Republican opponent, former Missouri governor Christopher "Kit" Bond, but more than enough to be competitive. The seeds of her defeat were planted by a

series of TV ads that Washington media consultant Bob Squier created to erode Bond's popularity.

Squier called his trio of ads the "Crying Farmer." After seeing
them, Woods says she told him, "Bob, you may win an award for this,
but I could lose an election."

"Don't worry," he told her. "This is a silver bullet. I won't use it till
the fall, or when we really need it. This is a killer. We'll put him away
with this one."

Squier's silver bullet was a serial ad that literally said, "To be continued" at the end of each of the first two installments. It assumed that
voters would watch all three parts. Squier's researchers had found a
farmer facing foreclosure by an insurance company where Bond served
on the board. Woods had gone to the farm to talk with the farmer on
camera. During their conversation, the farmer broke down and cried
about losing his farm. The result was an emotionally powerful scene
that Squier felt sure would undermine Bond's good-guy image.

In early July, Squier, unnerved by Bond's climb in the polls, convinced Woods to unleash the "Crying Farmer" ads. She resisted. Her
gut told her no, but she thought, "Why do I pay these high-priced
consultants if I don't follow their advice?" Squier made the case that if
Woods didn't do something immediately to cut Bond's lead, she
would not be able to catch him by election day.

The first of the three TV spots created a public furor all right, but
not the one Woods had been promised. Instead of blaming Bond,
viewers criticized Woods for intruding on the farmer's private hell.
The farmer added to Woods' image as an opportunist by telling a
local newspaper he didn't know the conversation would be used in a
political ad. Bond turned the sorry episode into a commercial attacking Woods. The controversy pointed up the potential peril for a
woman unleashing attack ads because going negative shatters the
sugar-and-spice-and-everything-nice public stereotype of female
politicians.

When Woods fired Squier and her pollster, Harrison Hickman,
she believes they used their Washington connections to make her
look like the loser. The political community and the media skewered
Woods for running an inept campaign, a perception she feels the
ousted consultants happily perpetuated. "I felt that was very disloyal
and unprofessional because we were still in the middle of the race and
they were saying, 'Boy, we're glad we got out of there'," says Woods.
"I often wondered whether they would have done that with a male
candidate. But when I fire someone, it's 'You know how women are.' "

Woods' claim to higher office was based on a career in public service, but the "Crying Farmer" ad made such a bad impression that it blurred her accomplishments. She had reformed nursing homes. She cared about the homeless. She had pushed through tax reform. She wasn't going to just sit there and take it. She fought back with negative ads, and positive ads, but she could never penetrate Bond's image as an affable and competent chief executive. He was no longer governor, but his easy familiarity with the voters made him seem like an incumbent.

Following the election, Woods accepted an appointment to the Kennedy School at Harvard, the public-policy school that has become a haven for losing politicians of both parties. Woods was disappointed in the race she had run, and Emily's List, which had banked on her success, was equally upset by the outcome. When Woods proposed soon after the election that she maintain her donor base through direct mail in case she wanted to run again, Malcolm accused her of trying to steal her mailing list. The battle escalated and got nasty before Woods finally dropped the idea and any thoughts of running again.

Woods also suffered from bad timing. She ran for the Senate both times in non-presidential years, when turnout among core Democratic voters, chiefly blacks and labor, typically is much lower. The year she won as lieutenant governor coincided with a presidential election. Woods might have had a better shot in 1992, when Bill Clinton became the first Democrat to win the White House in sixteen years. But by that time her passion for politics was gone.

When a call came exploring her interest in heading the National Women's Political Caucus (NWPC), Woods was not interested. She couldn't imagine why anyone would want to head a women's organization. She felt women's groups had been marginalized, and that running one would be frustrating. She had at times been trapped into doing tasks for the NWPC, but avoided taking a larger role. Then Jody Newman, who had volunteered in Woods' first statewide race for the U.S. Senate, called to say she'd given up on saving the beaches in Florida and had taken a job with the NWPC. Would Woods take on the presidency? Knowing that she and Newman were a good team, she agreed.

Woods couldn't get herself elected to the Senate, but spent the next several years promoting other women for office, including Republican Christine Todd Whitman, who in 1993 became the first female governor of New Jersey. In 1992, Woods helped raise money for

Carol Moseley-Braun, an African American who was given no chance of toppling an incumbent senator in a Democratic primary in Illinois. "I said, 'Hey, I remember,'" says Woods, recalling the dismissive attitude that greeted her first bid for the Senate. "I went to Chicago and helped put on a fund-raiser and talked to Carol about ways for her to raise money." Emily's List, she points out, contributed money only after Moseley-Braun looked like a winner.

Malcolm makes no apologies for the tight screen Emily's List imposes on candidates to gain her group's backing. Arnie Arnesen, a New Hampshire Democrat who ran for governor and then Congress, did not get support from Emily's List in part because she proposed increasing taxes. Emily's List concluded she could not win in tax-averse New Hampshire. "A week before the primary, they got word that I was kicking ass and winning, two to one, and they hadn't given me a dime," says Arnesen. "So they sent me a $5,000 check so they could claim ownership." Arnesen won the Democratic primary in 1994 but lost the general election to Republican Steve Merrill, who opposed new taxes. Emily's List offered more enthusiastic support for Arnesen two years later in her bid for a congressional seat. She still lost.

Democratic representative Loretta Sanchez from California's Orange County got minimal help from Emily's List in 1996. Sanchez challenged GOP incumbent Robert Dornan, a rabid right-winger known as "B-1 Bob" for his zealous support of a bomber even the air force didn't want. Emily's List didn't include Sanchez in its mailing, so she didn't get "bundled" contributions, the money collected from women around the country and funneled through Emily's List. Sanchez won by a handful of votes out of tens of thousands cast, making her a heroine to Democrats and many Republicans for ousting Dornan, long a thorn in the side of progressive or even moderate politicians.

The many women who credit their victories to the group's support outnumber the races where Emily's List guessed wrong. Accepting credit for launching Mikulski's senate career, Emily's List anticipated backing another woman for the Senate in the 1988 election. "How many women are running?" Malcolm asked. They started with Alabama and they were down to Vermont before they came up with a strong candidate, Governor Madeleine Kunin, who in the end did not run. In the opinion of Emily's List analysts, there was not one viable female candidate for the Senate in 1988.

Could Emily's List get its donors to care about women running for the House of Representatives when many voters cannot even name their congressman? With all 435 House seats contested every two years, the opportunities seemed to be plentiful. But the reelection rate for incumbents in the 1980s was 95 percent. Unless a retirement created an open seat, any challenger had a tough time. The cold war had frozen the political landscape in men's favor. Voters trusted men more when it came to national security and defense issues. Malcolm calculated that it took fifteen open seats to get one new woman elected.

Progress had stalled. In 1972, there were fourteen Democratic women in the House. In 1988, after fifteen years of the women's movement, there were twelve. Emily's List sent out a mailing recommending nine women running for the House in the 1988 election. Only two won, New York's Nita Lowey and Oregon's Jolene Unsoeld. On the encouraging side, twelve hundred women sent checks, twice the number that had backed Mikulski and Woods for the Senate two years earlier. Many were not first time donors. Malcolm realized she had tapped into a network of women who were committed to backing the cause over the long term.

The year 1990 seemed like a promising one for women running for office. The collapse of the Berlin Wall and the end of superpower tensions shifted the public's interest to quality-of-life issues like health care and education, which female candidates emphasized. But that changed with Iraq's invasion of neighboring Kuwait in August and the subsequent military buildup for the Gulf War. Dianne Feinstein, the dynamic former mayor of San Francisco, lost her race for governor in California to former senator Pete Wilson, an unexciting but safe Republican, and Claudine Schneider, a moderate Republican congresswoman, failed to unseat the aging Senator Claiborne Pell in Rhode Island. Both had been favored to win before the nation became preoccupied with war. Not a single incumbent was defeated that year.

Among those disappointed in 1990 was moderate, pro-choice Republican Lynn Martin of Illinois, who lost a bid for the Senate. It was her first election loss since eighth grade. Martin had been elected to the House in 1980. She succeeded John Anderson, a liberal Republican, who left Congress to run for president as an independent against Ronald Reagan and Jimmy Carter. It was a big year for Republicans, who captured control of the Senate and elected a record four women, including Martin, to the House. The women were such a novelty that they were invited to appear on Phil Donahue's daytime television talk show, which was the "Oprah" of its day. Martin, a single mother at the time, said the TV appearance was the only thing that impressed her two young daughters.

Martin's irreverent style and quick wit made her a favorite with the media, but it wasn't enough to sustain a serious race against her opponent, the bow-tied all-around nice guy Senator Paul Simon. She didn't make a dent in Simon's support, and, by her own admission, ran a terrible campaign. She thought her political career was over until she recalled advice from Lee Atwater, the Republican strategist most responsible for the harshly negative campaign that had propelled George Bush into the White House two years earlier. "Remember, if you win, you're everybody's top dog. And if you lose, you're not dead."

Martin was in Florida with her husband after the election when a friend called telling her she had better return to Washington immediately if she wanted a job in the Bush administration. "If you want to do anything, you've got to tell him what you want," the friend advised. Having played Geraldine Ferraro in practice sessions before the Bush-Ferraro vice presidential in debate in 1984, Martin felt she was close to Bush. "Oh, he'll know," she said. Looking back on the episode, Martin says, "I think this is gender specific. Women always believe men will know. Men don't know. You give men a list. Don't fight it. We spend our lives saying, 'I don't want you to need a list.' And this guy said, 'You tell him what you want.' Good advice." Martin flew back to Washington and called Bush, who soon after named her secretary of labor.

Emily's List rallied its donors behind two women running for governor in 1990—Dianne Feinstein in California and Ann Richards in Texas. Of the two, Feinstein was the favorite. If a woman could win anywhere, surely it would be California, the frontier of progressive politics. Richards wasn't supposed to win. Texas was, after all, a state noted for its macho politics, not a good venue for a woman.

The silver-haired Richards had been elected state treasurer in Texas, a good stepping-stone for a woman in politics. "If people think you can manage money and make money, then you must be smart," she says. "It's a very male kind of thing." Her saucy rhetoric and her unashamed admission of past alcoholism conveyed toughness that both men and women found reassuring.

But style and positioning can carry a candidate only so far. Richards needed money, and for that, she could count on Emily's List. "I would never have been governor of Texas without it," she says. "It was being able to buy that television time up front that made the difference. You cannot communicate a message if you don't have the money. In a state the size of Texas, money is the number one thing. I don't care what anybody tells you."

Richards was also blessed with an unabashedly retro opponent in Republican Clayton Williams, whose attitude toward women became a central issue in the campaign. "He was going to 'hoof me' and 'head me' and drag me in the dirt or something like that, referring to what they do to cows when they brand them," says Richards. Williams exceeded the boundaries of taste with the comment that fog is like rape—"if it's inevitable, just relax and enjoy it."

Even then, Williams might have survived. What defeated him was his refusal to shake Richards' hand at a public gathering. His bad manners registered with men and women. The incident occurred in Dallas, a conservative city where old-fashioned courtsey is valued. Richards extended her hand. Williams looked her in the eye and said, "I refuse to shake your hand." The media recorded the moment. The reaction was immediate. "You don't do that," says Richards. "You don't even do that with another man. But doing it to a woman is much worse."

Williams' boorish behavior cost him the election. Texas-born CBS News anchor Dan Rather said the race was "so nasty it would gag a buzzard." At one point, Richards trailed Williams by 15 percent in the polls, but when the ballots were counted, Richards won, 51 to 49 percent. Her narrow margin made the victory bittersweet and foreshadowed the difficulty she would have as a woman and a Democrat maintaining her hold on the office in an increasingly Republican state.

However fragile the victory, it was another plum for Emily's List. The excitement around electing a woman governor had almost tripled the number of women contributing, from 1,200 in 1988 to 3,500 in 1990. Malcolm was right about the women of America; they wanted their fair share of political power, and they were willing to put their money behind their dreams.

Progress was slow, but it was real. Reflecting on the changes in an interview in her office in Washington, Richards said, "I've reached the age where I can accept that our progress has been remarkable if I will just stop and look at it. My grandmother could not vote for a period of her life. Idiots, imbeciles, the insane, and women could not vote in Texas. Here, one generation later, I was the governor. So I know we're going to have a woman president. And it's not going to be just a popularity contest. This woman is going to be good, she's going to be smart, she's going to be prepared, and she's going to win. I hope I live to see it. But if I don't, I really want quality that first one out."

By the 1990s, Emily's List was the single most important endorsement for a Democratic woman candidate. "If you're a male candidate running against a woman who gets the Emily's List endorsement, you go have a couple of whiskey sours or shots," says Saul Shorr, a Philadelphia-based Democratic consultant. To gain backing from Emily's List, a woman candidate must be pro-choice and have a reasonable chance of winning. With a lengthening list of women seeking support, Malcolm prevailed upon her friend Judy Lichtman to develop a candidates' questionnaire to determine precisely where they stood on a range of issues. Some candidates, for example, called themselves pro-choice yet they supported numerous restrictions on abortion rights.

Lichtman and her staff at the Women's Legal Defense Fund worked diligently and produced a thirty-seven-page questionnaire "with every issue you could think of nuanced and with sub-parts," she says. "Ellen looked at the questionnaire and waited respectfully for a moment. My political naïveté was stunning. She said, 'Judy, we're not in the business of *excluding* people. We'd like to find candidates we can support. There isn't a human being in America who could pass your litmus test.' It was a powerful lesson to me."

In the early days of Emily's List, it was just Malcolm and Lichtman. Their offices were across the hall from each other. They shared a copying machine and a fax. "We evolved," Lichtman says. "When we started, we thought we were about as sophisticated as you get as women in the Democratic party. But we evolved to be even more sophisticated. When I think of the millions we've raised and the women we've helped get elected, I think, dammit, we really did something."

By 1998, Malcolm's network of women had grown to nearly fifty thousand members in all fifty states. That year they contributed $7.5 million and helped elect seven new pro-choice Democratic women to the House, the largest increase of Democratic women in a nonpresidential election year. Emily's List had established itself as a player in American politics.

With influence comes controversy, and in 2002, Emily's List took heat from Democrats for taking sides in key primaries. Needing six seats to regain control of the House, Democrats didn't want to dilute their effort with internal fights. In two high-profile races in the Midwest, the women candidates backed by Emily's List lost to Democratic men favored by the party. Emily's list fared even worse in the general election. Caught in the downdraft of 9/11, the group posted a victory in only one of ten competitive congressional races it targeted.

THREE

Women Running and Winning: The Post-Ferraro Babies

The charges were explosive. University of Oklahoma law professor Anita Hill claimed that Clarence Thomas, President Bush's nominee for the Supreme Court, had sexually harassed her when she had worked for him a decade earlier in Washington. Emma Jordan, a law professor at Georgetown Law School, heard the report on National Public Radio. If Hill proved credible, she could doom Thomas' nomination, an outcome devoutly wished by liberals opposed to Thomas' conservative views. Hill surely would be summoned for questioning before the Senate Judiciary Committee, which was sharply divided on Thomas' merits.

The phone rang in Jordan's northwest Washington home. "Do you know Anita Hill?" asked Judith Resnick, a law professor on the West Coast.

"I've met her. I'm not a close friend," Jordan replied.

"Some of us were wondering if she has legal representation," Resnick said.

Jordan was president-elect of the Association of American Law Schools, the premiere organization of law schools and law professors. She was the first African American to hold the post. She had met Hill in the early 1980s when both women made presentations at an association meeting. They were the only black women there. Hill was on a panel where she talked about teaching commercial law. Jordan thought she did a wonderful job.

Jordan tried calling Hill but got a busy signal. After several attempts, she gave up. Early the next morning, Jordan tried again. This time Hill's answering machine clicked on. Jordan had forgotten the time difference; it was only 6 A.M. in Norman, Oklahoma, where Hill lived. Jordan started to leave a message: "Anita, this is Emma Jordan calling to see if you might need . . ." Hill came on the line. "Hello, Emma," she said in a languid voice that Jordan would later refer to as "her Anita way."

"Do you have legal counsel?" Jordan inquired. "It looks like you're going to be asked to testify. You could be subpoenaed. This is a high-stakes matter. You need to know you have a support structure. I can provide law students to be gofers to help your lawyer."

"Well, in fact, I don't have a lawyer," Hill replied.

Jordan couldn't believe it. A scant four days before her grilling, Hill had no lawyer. Jordan took a deep breath and volunteered to pull together a team.

She thought immediately of Charles Ogletree, a prominent black criminal defense attorney who taught at Harvard Law School. "Tree" had been president of the Stanford student body when Jordan was there on a teaching internship in the early 1970s. While other students worried about career advancement, Ogletree wore a bandanna on his head and raised money for starving children in the war-ravaged West African territory of Biafra. He wasn't afraid of controversy. Hill, it turned out, had spoken to Ogletree but had not formalized any arrangement.

Hill didn't seem to grasp the enormity of the task ahead, but Jordan and Resnick did. They quickly drew up what they called "a dream-team list." They agreed the team should be interracial, and include men and women, so the races and the sexes would not be pitted against each other. In Jordan's mind, this diversity was essential. Otherwise, she feared Hill would be seen as a dupe of the white feminist movement, and her charges dismissed as special pleading by a feminist with a black face.

Liberal groups had mounted a ferocious attack against Thomas, a conservative appellate court judge whose opposition to affirmative action made him a favorite of the Republican right. Thomas' relative youth (forty-three) and obscurity made him an unlikely heir to the retiring Thurgood Marshall, who had argued *Brown v. Board of Education of Topeka*, the landmark school desegregation case, before the Supreme Court. Marshall had been a federal judge before President Johnson named him to the high court, the first black so honored. Apart from skin color, Thomas seemed to have little in common with Marshall.

Thomas' prospects for confirmation by the Senate had been damaged by a lackluster rating from the American Bar Association and opposition from civil rights groups, led by the venerable National Association for the Advancement of Colored People (NAACP). But Thomas' African-American heritage and his personal story, a moving tale of triumph over poverty, touched people and made Democratic members of the Senate wary of the reaction back home if they voted against him.

Into this maelstrom walked Anita Hill, a quiet, deliberate, and dignified presence with a tawdry tale to tell. Her story had to stand on its own, apart from politics and independent of the views that Thomas represented. She would face hostile questioning from Republicans on the Judiciary Committee. In a flurry of phone calls, Jordan, Resnick, and Ogletree assembled in a day a distinguished team of lawyers, all working for no money and paying their own expenses. John Frank, seventy-three, a constitutional law attorney and an expert on Supreme Court nominations, flew in from Phoenix to head the team. Frank was a hero among civil libertarians for arguing the 1966 Miranda case before the Supreme Court that requires police to read suspects their rights before questioning them.

Ogletree did not know Hill, and he wanted to test her truthfulness. Joining the other lawyers closeted with Hill in Washington to preview Hill's testimony, Ogletree confronted her with what he claimed was evidence that contradicted her testimony in the form of records that showed she had been terminated from a job because of a relationship with a man. "I have it right here," he said, practically shouting to lend credibility to his ruse. Ogletree watched to see whether Hill revealed any fear that there was something in her background that could be shaken loose by such a browbeating. She didn't flinch. Ogletree subsequently arranged a polygraph test for Hill, which she passed.

Hill and her advisers had only a few days to prepare. After being lobbied by women Democratic lawmakers on Monday, Senate Majority Leader George Mitchell had agreed to hear Hill's testimony that Friday. Usually, congressional hearings are carefully choreographed, with everything negotiated in advance so there are no surprises on either side. "It's not just a matter of showing up and talking," says Jordan. "Every step is planned like a ballet." The rush to complete the hearings and send Thomas' nomination to the full senate left so little time for preparation that Jordan and the others felt they had embarked on a kamikaze mission.

Late Thursday night, only hours before Hill's scheduled testimony, the Judiciary Committee announced that Thomas would answer

Hill's accusations *before* Hill testified. Hill had been assured that she would be the leadoff witness. But Senator Joseph Biden (D., Del.), the committee chairman, granted a request from the Bush White House to let Thomas go first. "They double-crossed us," said Jordan. "This is a Democratically controlled Congress?"

The last-minute switch in the lineup had one unexpected benefit. Analyzing why the White House had insisted on Thomas going first, Georgetown law professor Susan Deller Ross concluded that the White House wanted to exploit the television imagery of a learned and noble black man on trial. That led to thinking about the image Hill would project to a national TV audience. Jordan realized that having two white lawyers seated with Hill while she assailed the truthfulness of a black man before an all-white committee would look like a Caucasian conspiracy to get Thomas. Having a black woman represent Hill also would be counterproductive because men, black men especially, would look on it as an anti-male tirade by the "sisters."

By elimination, the obvious choice to head Hill's team was Ogletree. His history of social activism on behalf of blacks everywhere would insulate him from the tensions within the African-American community over a sister's challenge to a brother's making it in the white world. Ogletree would have to be persuaded to take charge. On the morning of the hearing, Jordan and Ross banged on the door to Ogletree's room at the downtown Marriott Hotel. He greeted them half-dressed with the phone to his ear. When he hung up, Jordan stated her case.

"Tree, you've got to be the lead on this," she said.

"Oh, no," he replied warily. "I didn't sign up for that. What about you, Emma?"

"I'm a woman. We need gender balance. Otherwise, she'll be vulnerable to attacks that she's being manipulated by feminists," Jordan said.

"I don't have tenure," Ogletree protested. Jordan understood immediately. When she was on the faculty of the University of California, she had signed a friend-of-the-court brief opposing a hearing for the Bakke case, a white student's challenge of affirmative action in medical school applications. The educational establishment wanted the suit to go ahead, hoping the court would establish clear guidelines. The chair of the university's board of regents had summoned Jordan to his office where he asked her, bluntly, whether she had tenure. She said no. "It was an intimidating question," Jordan recalled. Ogletree wasn't a kid anymore, and he didn't want to risk his career on what could be a fool's errand.

Jordan pressed for an answer and Ogletree stalled, saying, "I have to check with some of my boys." They were already almost a half hour late for a breakfast meeting with the legal team where the strategy and tactics for the day would be finalized. Jordan demanded an answer before the meeting. Ogletree finally relented, "Okay, I'll do it."

Ogletree insisted that Jordan break the news. He did not want to look like he was leading a coup against Frank, a legal legend, who had handpicked another highly regarded attorney, Warner Gardner, to be his deputy. Jordan told the team that millions of people would watch Hill's televised presentation. What they saw was as important as what they heard. Then she blurted out, "We've decided we need a prominent black man. Tree has to be the lead counsel. I can't do it. It's not a matter of ego. It's a matter of practical necessity." Addressing Frank and Gardner, she said, "You are the most distinguished people on the team. We need you. But for the public face and the symbolism, we need a black man." No one objected.

Despite the lawyers' best efforts, Hill's testimony was weakened considerably by Thomas' preemptive claim that he was "the victim of a hightech lynching." He portrayed her as the sexual aggressor, and said she was delusional and a liar. When the hearings ended early Monday morning, October 14, 1991, polls showed more Americans believed Thomas than Hill. Hill's credibility gap was even wider among blacks. The next day the Senate voted, 52 to 48, to confirm Thomas for a lifetime appointment to the Supreme Court.

It was not until months later that the hearings produced an unexpected political aftershock. The first hint that Hill's treatment by the Judiciary Committee and the Senate—patronizing, rude, and ultimately dismissive—would alter the chemistry of campaigning in 1992 in the Illinois Democratic primary. Carol Moseley-Braun, virtually unknown outside of Cook County, where she held the lowly post of recorder of deeds, upset Alan Dixon, an affable two-term senator. She would go on to become the first black woman ever elected to the Senate. Her secret weapon was Dixon's vote to confirm Thomas, which she used to rally white and black women alike.

The same phenomenon took place in other parts of the country as well. Despite polls that showed Thomas "won" and Hill "lost" in the hearings, women of both races—and some men—were offended by the Senate's insensitive grilling of Hill. In California, Senate candidates Dianne Feinstein and Barbara Boxer capitalized on the anti-male climate to generate enthusiasm among women voters. "The sense of rage I felt as I watched what they did to Anita Hill has not subsided with the passage of time. I am sure you feel the same," Feinstein wrote in a fund-raising letter. Boxer plastered pictures everywhere of her and other Democratic women members of the House marching on the Senate to demand that Hill be heard. The scene was reminiscent of the early suffragettes storming the Capitol.

From beginning to end, the male-dominated Senate failed to grasp how women across the country would be affected by Hill's charges of verbal sexual harrassment. After first ignoring her allegations, then failing in the eyes of many women to take them seriously despite agreeing to reopen the Thomas hearings, the senators infuriated women. Although the principal figures on both sides were African Americans, it was clear to women that a black man was assumed to be more credible than a black woman—even a black female law professor.

In a column under the headline "Why Women Are So Angry at the Senate," the *Washington Post's* Judy Mann wrote, "No matter what come out of these hearings, there is one overriding lesson for women. And that is that they cannot depend on men to protect their interests. Women have to run for the House and they have to run for the Senate and they have to win. If there had been a couple of women on that committee, this debacle would not have happened."

Pundits declared 1992 the Year of the Woman—and this time the designation seemed to fit. Besides the backlash to the Thomas hearings, female candidates had more opportunities because redistricting based on the 1990 census redrew the lines of many old districts and created some new ones. That year, four Democratic women won election to the Senate, and twenty-one Democratic women captured House seats. A jubilant Patricia Schroeder, who had been in a distinct minority since winning in a Denver district twenty years earlier, declared, "The cavalry has arrived."

Fulfilling its own prophecy, the media lavished attention on women running for office. Politics usually was a turnoff for most Americans, but people responded enthusiastically to this new crop of candidates. Untold numbers of women participated actively for the first time as campaign volunteers and paid staff.

The choices women candidates offered the electorate resulted in several upsets. Lynn Woolsey, a former welfare mother in California, would triumph over a lavishly funded campaign waged by the son of Louisiana senator Bennett Johnston, whose connections normally would have been insurmountable. Blanche Lambert, barely thirty years old and a Washington lobbyist, would knock off a sitting incumbent in her home state of Arkansas to capture a House seat. And Marjorie Margolies Mezvinsky, a former television reporter in Philadelphia, a Democrat initially dismissed as a hopeless underdog in a heavily Republican district, would charm the media and emerge a winner in her House race.

One discordant note, however, reminded the sisterhood that politics requires painful choices. A New York Senate race pitted two prominent Democratic women against each other. Geraldine Ferraro was the sentimental favorite. Attempting her first comeback since the bruising presidential race eight years earlier, she led the polls and, until two weeks before the September 15 primary, seemed assured of victory. Then Elizabeth Holtzman, New York City comptroller and a former member of Congress, unleashed a hard-hitting attack on Ferraro's ethics. She accused Ferraro of failing to keep a commitment she had made during the 1984 presidential race to have her husband, real estate developer John Zaccaro, evict a child pornographer from a rental property that he controlled. The charge revived memories from the 1984 race when Ferraro's family finances dragged down the Democratic ticket. Ferraro reacted angrily and defensively, accusing Holtzman of using ethnic stereotyping to unfairly link her to organized crime.

Like Ferraro, Holtzman had been one of the women pioneers in politics. Taking office in 1973 at age thirty-one—to this day the youngest woman ever elected to Congress—Holtzman and Representative Barbara Jordan of Texas became nationally known as members of the House Judiciary Committee during the Watergate hearings that led to the resignation of President Nixon. Those hearings, which captivated much of the nation, were a prelude to the power of television that would alter politics twenty years later in the wake of the Thomas hearings. "I don't know that I saw the significance of TV from a gender point of view," said Holtzman, who didn't own a television at the time.

Two points about Holtzman's House career are worth exploring further. First, she was elected in 1972, a postcensus redistricting year that was a forerunner of the Year of the Woman in '92. There were sixteen women members of the House at the time, three of them from New York, and Holtzman felt certain that many more women would follow. "I thought the floodgates would open," she said. "I thought this was only the beginning." After a steady increase in their numbers, women have reached a plateau in the House of fifty-six members, still less than 13 percent. The second point is that women members of the

House bonded in a bipartisan way far more readily than their male counterparts. Holtzman and Margaret Heckler, a feisty Republican from Massachusetts, teamed in 1977 to form the Congressional Women's Caucus. Republican women worried that their more aggressively feminist Democratic colleagues would embarrass them. Democratic women fretted that they would be typecast as members of a female ghetto if they championed women's issues. So the women in the caucus agreed to take only those positions they could agree upon unanimously. Even at that, they frequently found common ground.

From the start, the Congressional Women's Caucus demonstrated how having women at the table alters the legislative agenda. In 1977, caucus members met with cabinet secretaries and other officials of the newly formed Carter administration on issues ranging from health care and child abuse to housing and employment. Even before President-elect Ronald Reagan took office in January 1981, he held a working lunch with the caucus. At that lunch, he voiced his commitment to naming a woman to the Supreme Court. In 1983, Reagan named Heckler, a caucus co-founder, as secretary of health and human services. Heckler's successor as Republican co-chair, Senator Olympia Snowe of Maine, drew media attention when she led a group of Republican women to the White House to meet with Reagan. The women cautioned Reagan that the widening gender gap posed substantial risks for Republican candidates.

George Bush's promise upon assuming the presidency in 1989 of a "kinder, gentler" approach to governing did not extend to the most important issues on the caucus' agenda: family and medical leave and a change in the National Institutes of Health's (NIH) policy that routinely excluded women from many studies, such as one that studied the effects of aspirin on heart disease on 22,000 male physicians. That changed when the 1992 elections almost doubled the number of women in the House and tripled the number of women in the Senate. The enlarged and energized women's caucus found a friend in the new president, Bill Clinton. The Family and Medical Leave Act was the first legislation passed by Congress and signed into law by Clinton. Under Clinton, the National Institutes of Health codified a policy requiring the inclusion of women and minorities in research and authorizing additional money for research on breast and ovarian cancer, contraception and infertility, and osteoporosis.

One small, but symbolic example of how women brought a new way of thinking to the legislative branch was the practice of naming

hurricanes. Traditionally, hurricanes had always been named alpha-
betically after women. At a meeting with Juanita Kreps, the commerce secretary in President Carter's administration, the women's
caucus raised the issue: Why should women be linked symbolically
with the deaths and destruction caused by killer storms? Kreps hadn't
thought of it before, but she quickly agreed to change the policy.
From then on, hurricane names alternated between the sexes.

The caucus' biggest disappointment was the defeat of the proposed
Equal Rights Amendment (ERA). The amendment was first introduced in 1923, three years after women gained the right to vote. It
languished for forty-nine years before the caucus pushed it through
the House and Senate. The language of the proposed amendment was
straightforward: "Equality of rights under the law shall not be denied
or abridged by the United States or by any state on account of sex.
The Congress shall have the power to enforce, by appropriate legislation, the provisions of this article." Thirty states ratified the amendment in the first year, but repeated attempts over the next nine years
fell short of the thirty-eight states needed for ratification. The
amendment died in 1982 at the hands of the conservative religious
and political organizations that lobbied against it. The fight over the
ERA exposed a fissure between conservatives and moderates in the
Republican party.

In 1980, Holtzman gave up her safe House seat to run for the Senate. She defeated popular consumer affairs advocate Bess Meyerson, a
former Miss America, in the Democratic primary, but she lost the
general election to Republican Al D'Amato. Sidelined from Congress, Holtzman ran the next year for district attorney in the work-
ingman's borough of Brooklyn.

The race for D.A. taught Holtzman a lesson about gender and politics. She had come close to winning a Senate seat, and this race was a
lot lower on the ladder of politics. Still, she almost lost to a male opponent she considered "a total nobody" because, as a woman, she
didn't fit the image of what a district attorney is supposed to look like.
Her opponent exploited Holtzman's image problem by running radio
spots that she says described her as "a very nice woman. I'd like her
for my daughter, but not D.A." Holtzman said the image of a D.A.
many voters had in mind was that of the character on TV's "Perry
Mason." She recalls one man telling her how much his wife admired
her. "What about you?" she asked. "I never vote for women," he said.

By 1992, Holtzman, who had moved up the political ladder to city
comptroller, was ready for another run for the Senate, even if that

meant taking on Ferraro. The media treated the contest like a cat-fight. In one debate, Holtzman whirled around to face Ferraro and forcefully argue her point until the moderator pleaded, "Ladies, ladies . . ." Holtzman could not understand why reporters portrayed her as the heavy. She and Meyerson had campaigned hard against each other in 1980 and "nobody said boo," Holtzman said.

As polls showed her support fading fast in the final days of the campaign, Ferraro played on the perception that she was the victim of vicious and unfair attacks. In a last-minute television appeal she looked into the camera and said, "My opponents have tried to turn me into an evil figure from the shadows. . . . I know of no other way to respond than to look you in the eye and swear to you that I have never been involved with organized crime."

When the votes were counted, neither woman had the nomination. Ferraro came in second, a percentage point behind Robert Abrams, New York's district attorney, a lackluster candidate who was defeated by D'Amato in the general election. Holtzman ran a poor fourth. (No woman had ever won on her own in New York statewide until 2000, when First Lady Hillary Rodham Clinton defied expectations to decisively beat Republican Rep. Rick Lazio for the Senate seat of retiring Democratic Sen. Daniel Patrick Moynihan. Ferraro had tried a second comeback in 1998, this time losing the Democratic Senate nomination to Rep. Charles Schumer, who went on to defeat D'Amato.)

Emily's List got caught between Ferraro and Holtzman. Both women fit the profile of the kind of candidates the fund-raising organization wanted to support. Both had backers on the board of Emily's List. Ellen Malcolm, the founder and executive director of Emily's List, tried for a while to stay neutral in the race. But after conducting a poll that showed Ferraro would be a stronger candidate against D'Amato, Emily's List put its money behind Ferraro.

"Emily's List made up its mind before I even got in the race," said Holtzman, still smarting from the snub in an interview six years later. "I asked for an opportunity to appear before their board. They called me the day before. I was scheduled to be in Buffalo, and there was no way I could get back." Holtzman said she had a poll that showed she was the stronger candidate, but that Emily's List refused to consider contradictory research. Holtzman said Malcolm was a friend and major supporter of Ferraro.

To Emily's List and other activist women, Holtzman was a spoiler with no real chance of winning the nomination or of beating D'Amato. When Holtzman not only stayed in the race but also challenged Ferraro forcefully, critics said her candidacy would undermine the public's belief that women politicians were higher-minded and fairer. Holtzman said she hadn't campaigned any differently than a man would have, and was "surprised by the notion that somehow as a woman I didn't have the right to raise issues I thought were relevant."

As the first female district attorney in Brooklyn, Holtzman had prosecuted organized crime figures and child pornographers. The crime figure about whom she charged Ferraro and her husband with being lax in evicting ultimately did leave the property, and was subsequently murdered by the mob figure John Gotti. Asked what conclusions she drew from that, Holtzman replies, "I don't draw any conclusions from that. I'm not fighting that civil war all over again. I clearly learned another lesson—that when the criticism may be just, some people do not want to hear it."

Was Holtzman the victim of a double standard that says girls have to play nicer than boys? Not necessarily. More likely she just crossed an invisible line of civility that governs the conduct of any candidate, man or woman, who runs against a woman, especially an icon like Ferraro had become because of her historic candidacy for vice president. Ferraro conceded recently that she probably would not have won the nomination in 1992 even with Holtzman out of the race, because Holtzman's Jewish support would have shifted to Abrams. That makes the price Holtzman paid especially severe. She sought reelection as city comptroller and lost, a defeat she attributes to the backlash from the Senate race.

In the excitement over the Year of the Woman, Holtzman and Ferraro were just a footnote. A new wave of women arrived in Washington. The media portrayed them as outsiders who would shake up the system. That was at least half wrong. The newcomers brought with them plenty of experience as officeholders. They were savvy pols who had risen through the political ranks like their male counterparts.

The large number of female candidates inspired young women to work in politics. Amy Walter was one of them. Graduating Colby College as a political science major in the spring of 1992, Walter couldn't wait to go to work for the Women's Campaign Fund, where she had interned as a student. "I caught the fever of it," Walter says. Marjorie Margolies Mezvinsky was Walter's favorite. Walter campaigned for her, then went to work in her Capitol Hill office.

Walter paid a backhanded compliment to the new class of female politicians, calling them "good ol' boys in skirts." She cited the example of Karen Thurman in Florida. While a member of the Florida state legislature, Thurman saw to it that the lines in the congressional district she had her eye on were redrawn to give her maximum benefit, a traditional gambit for politicians hoping to move up in a post-census year. Thurman's skill at playing inside politics paved the way for her election to Congress.

Senator Barbara Mikulski smiles as she recalls "the day of the flashing lights," when the four new women senators posed for pictures with her. At last, Mikulski had female company: Dianne Feinstein and Barbara Boxer from California, Carol Moseley-Braun from Illinois, and Patty Murray, the "mom in tennis shoes," from Washington State.

"Are you having tea?" a reporter asked Mikulski.

"No, I'm conducting a power workshop," Mikulski fired back.

"What's that?" the reporter wanted to know.

"Keep an eye on us and you'll see," said Mikulski.

Later that day in her spacious, blue-and-yellow-toned office, Mikulski distributed homemade how-to manuals to share with the new women senators the advice she had received as a freshman six years earlier. "Getting Started in the Senate" stressed the importance of a clear set of organizing principles. "Campaign themes, such as 'a proven leader' or 'a voice for change,' are not organizing principles," Mikulski cautioned. "They will not help you decide which staff positions to fill first or how to respond to constituent mail." She urged the women to define their overall goals and objectives, and to set priorities.

Their first homework assignment, she said, was to land a spot on the right committees. She offered four rules: (1) find a mentor; (2) know where the openings are; (3) know your strengths and weaknesses; and (4) lobby hard for what you want. She passed out a sheet listing the most prestigious committees, along with a rundown of vacancies. The distribution of committee assignments resembles the seating at a Georgetown dinner party, with A-list and B-list guests. Mikulski identified four "Super A" committees: Finance, Appropriations, Foreign Relations, and Armed Services; eight "A" committees, and a host of lesser "B" committees. To get an "A"committee, she said, a new senator has to be as competitive as she was to get elected in the first place. A senator can serve on as many "B" committees as she wishes.

The excitement over electing a record number of women was absent in the committee rooms of Capitol Hill. Veteran lawmakers grumbled that the influx of women made the House look like a shopping mall. The Democrats in charge of the House, old bulls like Dan

Rostenkowski of Illinois and John Dingell of Michigan, ran their committees with an iron hand, and with strict adherence to the traditions of seniority. Freshmen barely qualified for a good-morning greeting. "The boys didn't see these women as an asset," says Walter. "They didn't look out for them. All the momentum from the 1992 election just stopped in the House and Senate—and the White House—where they did nothing to encourage the reformers."

The newly elected women soon confronted partisan reality in Washington, where Republicans and some Democrats blocked the sweeping changes President Clinton's election had seemed to promise. Clinton's faltering first year culminated in a desperate attempt to corral enough Democratic votes to pass the federal budget. The Democrats held the majority in both the House and the Senate, but many balked at supporting a budget that raised taxes, even if only of the wealthiest taxpayers.

The freshman women strongly supported Clinton, and the White House counted on that support. Several of the women had won by narrow margins in districts where they could not afford to offend moderate Republicans and independents. Representative Marjorie Margolies Mezvinsky, for one, represented an upscale, Republican-leaning district of Pennsylvania. She could support the White House on liberal social legislation affecting abortion rights or gay rights without fear of voter repercussion. But her well-heeled constituents adamantly opposed raising taxes on themselves, and expected Mezvinsky to vote accordingly. She would have to be allowed to vote in her best political interests if the Democrats wanted to keep her seat in the '94 election.

But on the first budget fight between the White House and Congress, Clinton found himself desperate to win. Losing that vote, he would tell Mezvinsky and the others he lobbied personally, would undermine his power and credibility so much that it could effectively end his presidency before it started. Vice President Gore and health and human services secretary Donna Shalala also pleaded with Mezvinsky to vote with the president. She stood her ground and, on the day of the vote, the calls stopped. Thinking that her vote was not crucial after all, Mezvinsky announced that she would vote against the Clinton budget. Her sound bite played on the television news in Philadelphia. That advance announcement, she would say later, hurt her as much as the actual vote.

That evening, with only minutes left before the vote, Clinton called Mezvinsky.

"My presidency is riding on this vote," he told her. "What will it take?"

"More spending cuts," Mezvinsky replied.

Clinton promised to support legislation that was pending to reduce spending. He also agreed to Mezvinsky's request for a White House conference outside of Washington on problems facing social security, Medicare, and other entitlements that comprised the biggest portion of the budget. Compared to the goodies that her colleagues were extracting from Clinton in exchange for their votes—from roads and bridges to judgeships for political pals—Mezvinsky's demands were easily accommodated.

"One more thing," Mezvinsky told the president. "I will only be your last vote."

Mezvinsky could have rebuffed the president. Many other Democrats did. She could have put her own reelection ahead of Clinton's perception, real or imagined, that his presidency was on the line. But she didn't. Instead, she promised to wait until the very end and see how the vote went. If he needed her, she would support him. Mezvinsky knew she was gambling, but the odds were with her. Only twice in history had a single vote made the difference in the House. One was for the impeachment of Andrew Johnson in 1868; the second, the Selective Service Act of 1917, establishing the military draft. This was her president, and he would be a lame duck for the rest of his term if he failed this first test of leadership, she decided. It was as simple as that.

It would take 218 votes either way to settle this. Amy Walter sat with Mezvinsky on the House floor watching the vote tally reach 214, 215, 216. . . .Then it stalled. As the time for her to vote drew nearer, Mezvinsky rose. She listened as other Democrats standing near her agitated over whether to change their votes from "no" to "yes." Besides Mezvinsky only two other Democrats—Pat Williams of Montana and Ray Thornton of Arkansas—had not yet voted. "We have to do this," Williams said, casting the 217th yes vote. Thornton, who was from Clinton's state and claimed to be the president's friend, demurred. "I promised I'd never vote for a tax increase," he said. He voted no. It was 217 to 217 with only Mezvinsky left to vote. All eyes turned to her. She took out her coded voting card and slipped it into the slot. The electronic tote board above the press gallery flashed her vote: Yes.

The Republicans, perhaps never expecting to win but pleased at coming so close, expressed their delight with applause and cheers—and with catcalls for Mezvinsky.

"Bye-bye, Marjorie," they chanted, mockingly informing her that this would be her first and last term in the House. Once the voters in her district heard that she had cast the deciding vote after promising to vote against Clinton's budget, winning the seat away from her would be a cinch for almost any Republican who wanted it.

Amid the clamor, Mezvinsky strode calmly up the aisle to a small reception room with red walls. She sat on a sofa and let the enormity of her vote sink in. Several colleagues, mostly women, alternately congratulated and consoled her. "Your vote made my vote count," said a grateful Karen Shepherd, who also had gone against the wishes of a majority in her district by voting for the tax increase.

Shepherd, a freshman like Mezvinsky, defied all her advisers, including her husband, to support Clinton's budget. She had announced her decision well in advance of the vote. If the budget had failed to pass, then her courageous vote would have been meaningless. "What's the worst thing that can happen to me?" she remembers thinking. "I can lose. I never expected to be here in the first place, and I would feel terrible if I cast a vote I didn't feel good about. It was partly naïveté, and partly we weren't career politicians. I never thought I had to come and stay thirty years."

Mezvinsky called her husband, Ed, a former congressman, to tell him what she'd done.

"You did *what*?" he bellowed.

"I had to," Mezvinsky replied stoically.

The more senior women among the Democrats complained that the White House had leaned on Mezvinsky, a vulnerable freshman, while giving male Democrats in safe districts a free pass. Mississippi's Sonny Montgomery, for one, easily won reelection every two years and had no fear of a backlash from his voters. And then there was Thornton, Clinton's home-state congressman. Former White House aide George Stephanopoulos monitored the roll call as the votes were cast. When he told Clinton that Thornton had voted "no," the president was incredulous. "I made him president of Arkansas State," Clinton said. "I can't believe he's doing this to me."

The women concluded that the good ol' boys didn't care about protecting the new women members. When White House lobbyist Susan Brophy appeared on the House floor, Representatives Rosa DeLauro of Connecticut and Nita Lowey of New York assailed her for sacrificing the politically vulnerable women when there were other options. At the White House, the Clintons celebrated, and Hillary Clinton let her husband know who had saved his administration from humiliation. "You know what my wife just said, George?" the president asked Stephanopoulos, chuckling. "'Every woman in the Congress voted for you. They've got more balls than the men.' "

Mezvinsky's constituents viewed her vote as a betrayal, made worse because it was done at Clinton's bidding. The president was anathema in her district. Campaigning for reelection in 1994, Mezvinsky aroused such anger among some voters that she needed a police escort at community meetings. "I understood that I would have a lot of explaining to do," she said. "What I didn't understand is that I wouldn't be able to explain it." At one particularly contentious town meeting, she jabbed her finger in angry frustration at a questioner, insisting, "That's exactly wrong." A camera crew working for her opponent captured the moment and created a thirty-second ad that didn't use any sound, only the picture of a wide-eyed, crazed-looking Mezvinsky pointing. At the end, a voice said somberly, "She lied to us."

With her political career at stake after only one term, Mezvinsky scrambled to raise enough money for TV and radio ads to answer her critics. Among those whose help she sought was Thornton, whose own lack of courage had put her in a predicament on the key vote. She felt he owed her. A few days later, Thornton told Mezvinsky he had found a donor willing to give her $5,000. But because of her vote to raise taxes, the money would have to be funneled through somebody else, he said.

"You're the only person who can't say that to me," she told Thornton. "I don't want his money."

Thornton, too, paid a price for his cowardice. Many of the women House members and some men, too, shunned him. "He was a pariah," Mezvinsky said. "Members would come up to me and say, 'I'm not speaking to Ray Thornton anymore because he put you in that position.' " Thornton quietly ended his congressional career after three terms to run for a seat on the Arkansas Supreme Court.

In the 1994 election, the Republicans won control of the House for the first time in forty years, and captured the Senate as well. Eight of the twenty-one Democratic women elected during the Year of the Woman lost their seats. Among the casualties were Shepherd and Mezvinsky.

Losing hurt. After winning in 1992, Mezvinsky wrote a letter to her youngest son, Andrew, saying that she hoped in the year 2000 no one would be talking about the Year of the Woman because enough women would be in office to have real clout. Now, with her own loss looming, she wrote a second letter to Andrew. She said that she looked forward to attending more of his games. She read the letter as her concession statement, struggling not to cry, no small feat for a woman who says she cries at bank openings. She stayed dry-eyed, but twelve-year-old Andrew was inconsolable. Screening the tape months later, she realized how wildly upset her children were. A German television crew captured the scene of Mezvinsky consoling her brood of eleven children, some her husband's from a previous marriage, some hers, and some theirs. "Guys, it's going to be OK," she said. "It's just an election, OK?"

Did Mezvinsky's vote show that she had more guts than the male Democrats who turned their backs on the president? Her constituents didn't think so, particularly the women. Their support had made the difference for Mezvinsky in her first election; the second time, they voted for her opponent or simply stayed away on election day. "They said she kowtowed to some guy, that she was too weak," Walter said, attributing the reaction to the women's "self-hate."

On October 20, 1995, eleven months after the '94 election, Mezvinsky was working out on a treadmill when a *Wall Street Journal* reporter called to ask what she thought of Clinton's confession at a Dallas fund-raiser that he had raised taxes too much. Her response made the front page of the *Wall Street Journal*. "Marjorie Margolies Mezvinsky, who cast the deciding vote for the 1993 increase and then wasn't reelected, sighed, 'Oh,my.' "

Mezvinsky would make an attempt at a political comeback that ended badly. In 1998, she ran for lieutenant governor, not because she had a realistic chance of winning, but to nurture a statewide network for a run for the Senate in 2000 against Republican Rick Santorum. In the Senate Democratic primary, she found herself competing against four men and another woman, state senator Allyson Schwartz. It became clear that the two women would draw votes from each other, probably preventing either from winning.

On the night of January 3, treasurers from the campaigns of the two women met and agreed on a proposal to allow an independent arbitrator, after reviewing financial information and polling data, to decide which of the two should continue in the race. The other would drop out voluntarily. Mezvinsky agreed to the plan, but Schwartz rejected it, prompting her finance chairman, Peter Buttenweiser, who had been one of the negotiators, to resign. Two weeks later, Mezvinsky, who led Schwartz in the polls but trailed in fund-raising, issued a statement saying she was withdrawing from the race.

Mezvinsky said the rejection of the binding arbitration proposal "became a catalyst for a reassessment of my candidacy." She explained that her commitment to the race had been weakened by the failing health of her eighty-seven-year-old mother, whom she had spent six weeks caring for in the hospital. Mezvinsky did not refer to the legal and financial troubles facing her and her husband, also a former member of Congress. A few days after Margolies Mezvinsky dropped out of the race, Ed Mezvinsky filed for bankruptcy. Soon afterward, Margolies Mezvinsky also filed for bankruptcy. Her attorney, Eric L. Frank, said, "After evaluating all of the information which has come to her attention in the past few weeks, she concluded that, unfortunately, the immense amount of debt created by Ed's business dealings left her no alternative."

Although Margolies Mezvinsky had said dropping out of the race for the Senate nomination would not rule out a future run, the family's financial collapse appeared to shut the door on that option.

Anti-Clinton and anti-Democratic sentiment drove voters in the '94 election. Women, the last ones in, were the first ones out. Among the many disappointments was Ann Richards' loss to George W. Bush, son of former president Bush. Richards was a popular governor, with high approval ratings, but Bush beat her by a wide margin. Her loss stunned women activists. "Don't romanticize Ann," cautions a Texas political analyst. "She's good role model, and a good woman, but she couldn't get anything done, and her razor-sharp wit, if that's what it is, backfired when she referred mockingly to George W. as 'Shrub.' " Bush responded with a television ad saying he would treat his opponent "with respect" and that issues, not personal attacks, should guide the campaign.

Richards lost largely because Texas is good ol' boy heaven and she did not fit the profile. "Half the time, she was one of them, cussin' and carryin' on, and half the time she was whinin' and cryin' that the men didn't know how to deal with her, and part of it was her own fault," says the analyst.

Richards agrees that fitting into a political world created by men with rules made for men is difficult for women. She did what most women do once they get elected. She spent her time trying to establish credibility in areas in which she was presumed weak, and downplayed the issues that got her elected in the first place, like education, health care, and child care. Bush accused Richards of being soft on crime, and attacked her for signing a law requiring that minor drug offenders, for example those caught with less than a gram of cocaine, receive probation instead of jail time. "Hard prison time, not automatic probation, will send a message that criminals cannot snub their nose at Texas's criminal-justice system," he said. Richards had embarked, as governor, on a major, $2 billion prison building program to handle the rising prison population. Automatic probation for nonviolent, small-time offenders was done primarily to free up penitentiary space for violent felony convictions. "Everybody assumes George Bush is going to be tough on criminals. I have to prove that I'm going to be tough," Richards said. "You see the difference? And being tough doesn't ring any bell with women voters. It doesn't make them say, 'Oh boy, I'm going to charge the barricades and put that woman in office.' I can tell you there was not near as much enthusiasm for me as a female candidate from the female community when I ran for reelection as there was when I ran for election the first time."

The second time around, Richards was no longer a phenomenon. Reporters ignored gender, and so did Richards, at her expense she believes. "We very foolishly, I think, did not play to the women's issues," she said. "Like I told you, women are convinced that once they get in office they have to appear to be in charge, strong, tough, able to get in there toe-to-toe with the men. If they don't do that, they're going to get beat. But if they do that, they're very likely going to get beat." A strong women's vote is key to any Democrat's chances, adds Richards. "White men don't vote for Democrats. I don't care how hard we try, stand on our head, do somersaults, they simply don't."

Male bonding trumped partisan politics in Texas. Richards never worked well with her lieutenant governor or the speaker of the Texas state house, although they were Democrats. Within an hour after Bush was elected, he called both men and invited them to work with him for the good of the state. He even showed up at fund-raisers for them in the next election. He didn't contribute to their campaigns, of course, but he lent his presence. His party was furious, but he insisted. Bush worked so well with Bob Bullock, the Democratic lieutenant governor, that the veteran politician endorsed him for reelection in 1998 over his Democratic rival. When Bullock died in 1999 at age sixty-nine, Bush eulogized him as "the largest Texan of our time." The close relationship they forged across party lines is largely responsible for Bush's reputation as a man who values consensus and can rise above partisanship.

Richards' sharp tongue and partisan edge have their place, and she is a political celebrity, in demand at Democratic events around the country. After losing the governorship, she took a job as a lobbyist with a mainline law firm in Washington. Part of her job is to maintain her ties with influential politicians, and to spot newcomers who may prove helpful in the future. Democratic women candidates across the country call on her for help raising money. Explaining her motivation for getting into politics, Richards said, "I had passion and I had drive. Part of it was my being a woman. I very much wanted to have little girls say, 'If she can do that, I can do that too.' "

USA Today called 1994 the "year of the angry white man." Emily's List surveyed the Democratic women who had voted in 1992 and two years later stayed home. "They were the wives of the angry white men, and they just bailed out," says Malcolm. "They felt the Democratic Congress hadn't done anything. They think politicians get elected and come to Washington to play with the lobbyists and further their own careers, that Congress could do something to improve their lives and chooses not to. There is tremendous cynicism and anger. They're working two jobs. They can't get home to be with their kids, and they're scared about that. They're right on the edge of complete crisis. One respondent in a focus group said, 'If the car broke down, I don't have the money to fix it, and it's the only way I can get to work.' "

Republicans turned out their vote, and many Democrats didn't. "I hate paranoid lefties who say the Right is electing all these people. But they're right," Malcolm concluded. "They pulled the whole Republican party to the right, and they pulled the whole country to the right. We want to bring women back not because women have a unified view, or are all liberals, but because women have more of a sense of community, how to solve problems together, how to work together. If we can figure out how to bring women consistently to the polls, then we have a counterforce to the right."

Malcolm's thesis that even conservative women serve as a moderating force in the political arena was borne out in the 104th Congress, the first led by Speaker Newt Gingrich. Republican women in the House, including some who oppose abortion rights, went to their male leaders and asked them to stop scheduling votes on the abortion issue. The votes had the goal of curbing abortion rights and satisfying social conservatives. Most failed to garner enough support for passage, but they conveyed the impression of a party preoccupied with the issue of abortion. "Enough is enough," said Representative Tillie Fowler of Florida. She and other Republican women wanted a limit set on the number of abortion votes. "We didn't think it was positive for the party to have these battles," she said. The leaders turned a deaf ear. There were more than a hundred votes on abortion in the 104th Congress. "We weren't real successful," Fowler concedes.

When the 1994 election results were in, women had held their own with forty-seven seats in the House, but the politics of the women holding those seats had shifted to the right as Republican women replaced Democrats. The new breed of conservative women made it harder for men to automatically dismiss women as bleeding hearts, a welcome counterbalance to the stereotype of women politicians.

The biggest setback that year for women's prospects for the presidency was Richards' failure to win reelection. Her loss underscored the difficulty women have winning and holding on to executive positions, an obvious stepping-stone to the White House. Women have made great gains in politics over the last twenty years. Polls show that as many as three-fourths of Americans would not hesitate to vote for a "qualified" woman for president. But election after election demonstrates that voters trust women in legislative offices, where they are one of many, but not as executives of states, much less the country.

Holtzman, one of the women who helped pave the way, said a woman running for president "runs against Washington, Lincoln, and Jefferson. People are willing to see women in legislative positions because that's talking, and women can do that. But running the show? They worry about that. There are so few women role models. It's tough, but I'm sure it will ultimately happen. It will just take longer than we think."

FOUR

Competing to Win Elective Office: The Obstacles Women Face

Pat Schroeder's tearful retreat from the 1988 presidential race marked a setback for women in their quest for the office. Schroeder is defensive about it to this day, pointing out that male politicians who cry in public win praise for their sensitivity. For years, her chief of staff maintained a "crying folder" where he would tuck away every reported instance of a male power figure shedding tears. The file bulged with clippings that captured the lachrymose moments of such manly men as General Norman Schwarzkopf, U.S. troop commander in the Persian Gulf, former Russian president Mikhail Gorbachev, Marine Lieutenant Colonel Oliver North, and Chilean dictator Augusto Pinochet.

The rules are different for women. "The number one negative for women is emotional instability," says Republican pollster Linda Di-Vall. "What we don't need is another Pat Schroeder, in and out, in and out, and then crying about it."

Schroeder's 1988 candidacy—or rather almost-candidacy, since she never actually entered the race—was an afterthought. She had been co-chair of Gary Hart's presidential campaign, and decided to explore running herself only after he dropped out. Under the circumstances of Hart's departure from the race, Schroeder felt betrayed by her fellow liberal from Colorado. Early in May 1987, Schroeder had filled in for Hart at a campaign event in California after he claimed he had pressing business elsewhere. After checking into her hotel, Schroeder learned of Hart's other engagement. The Democratic front-runner was in Bimini, where he was photographed aboard the yacht *Monkey Business* with a much younger woman who was not his wife on his lap. The ensuing media storm forced Hart from the race. Hart's reckless behavior dashed the hopes of many people who had placed their confidence in him. Hart was unapologetic. He believed he was the victim of intrusive media tactics, and he never called Schroeder to explain. Less than a month later, in June 1988, when Schroeder announced her exploratory campaign, Hart pointedly endorsed New York governor Mario Cuomo, who wasn't even running.

In Congress, Schroeder enjoyed a reputation for independence. She won reelection with margins large enough that her seat was considered safe, yet she refused to take spears for her party, routinely voting against measures to boost congressional pay, which infuriated the Democratic leadership. Her independence was a plus with voters, but made her untrustworthy to her Democratic colleagues. Not a single prominent Democrat endorsed her for president. Representative Lynn Martin felt sorry for her colleague across the aisle. "She can be a little cutesy sometimes," said Martin, perhaps referring to Schroeder's penchant for drawing smiley faces in her signature. "But why shouldn't she have the right to be as ambitious as those other dopes?"

The media dubbed the crowded Democratic field "Snow White and the Seven Dwarfs." Political heavyweights like Cuomo and New Jersey senator Bill Bradley, a former basketball superstar, stayed out of the race. Schroeder's campaign was pitched to women partly out of necessity. That's where the enthusiasm burned for her candidacy.

And enthusiasm was the wellspring for campaign money. In Minnesota, two elected female officials, the lieutenant governor and secretary of state, hosted a reception for Schroeder. They invited two hundred people, and eight hundred showed up. Schroeder had roots in the state, having graduated magna cum laude and Phi Beta Kappa from the University of Minnesota in 1961. She was among friends, so she made a direct appeal for money, asking everyone to write a check on the spot to her campaign. Kathy Bonk traveled with Schroeder during this period, and she remembers walking away from that event with almost $50,000 in a bag. Schroeder and Bonk returned to the hotel, dumped the bag out on a bed, and counted their take. They could put away their American Express cards, at least for a while. They were in the money.

But Schroeder was no more prepared to run for president than the country was to have her. Her exploratory campaign lasted three months. In August, she ran third in a *Time* magazine poll, which was respectable but not good enough to convince potential contributors that she could win the nomination, Women's groups withheld their financial support, fearing another Geraldine Ferraro-like debacle. Schroeder herself had wanted to be Walter Mondale's running mate in '84. Her husband, Jim, a well-connected attorney, wrote an impassioned letter to Mondale touting his wife's attributes. She was deeply disappointed when women activists and her Democratic women colleagues in Congress backed Ferraro instead.

Issues mattered to Schroeder. When she, at last, decided against running, her finance co-chair, Gary David Goldberg, creator of the TV sitcom "Family Ties," offered a consolation prize. He put up the money for what Schroeder called her "Great American Family Tour." She and noted pediatrician Barry Brazelton visited key primary states and held public forums so that when the presidential candidates came through, they would be asked about family issues. Schroeder regarded it as a triumph when Vice President Bush conceded in the summer of 1988 that it was acceptable for both parents to work, and that there was a real need for day care. Some social conservatives portrayed families as aberrant if both parents chose to work when they had young children.

Once was enough for Schroeder. When she retired from Congress in 1996 at age fifty-six, she dismissed any suggestion that she run again. "I beat my head on cement long enough," she said. "Why do it again?" Schroeder is eager to have the next generation of women take up the causes she championed, such as women's reproductive rights. "If I get one more Margaret Sanger award [honoring the founder of Planned Parenthood], I'll be Margaret Sanger," she said.

Conventional wisdom has it that the first woman president will be a Republican. In the post-Reagan era of centrist politics, the thinking goes, it would be too big a step for the country to elect a woman *and* a liberal. Most Democratic women are liberal, but the common perception is that *all* of them are. In 1993 and early 1994, Lynn Martin, a progressive, pro-choice Republican, made one trip to Iowa and three to New Hampshire to test the receptivity to her possible presidential candidacy. After four terms in the House and a losing race for the Senate, Martin had been President Bush's labor secretary. The Republican party chairman in New Hampshire urged Martin to enter the early contests. He said that he needed a woman "to offset some of the crazies." The prospective GOP field tilted right and included Bob Dornan, the caustic congressman from California who moonlighted as Rush Limbaugh's substitute host, and Morrie Taylor, a tire salesman from the Midwest who had never held public office.

It took Martin less than a month to decide the venture was not for her. At best, she figured she would be positioning herself for vice president. She couldn't make herself believe that she had a chance for the nomination. "You have to kid yourself," she said. "When somebody says, 'What do you mean you're going to swim the Hudson? You haven't learned to swim,' it's harder for women to say, 'I can do it.' "

Running for president is the ultimate ego trip. By nature or by acculturation, women have been less likely to presume that out of 281 million Americans they are the best one for the job. In the wake of Ferraro's loss, Schroeder and Martin were the only women for more than two decades in the major parties who even thought about running for president. Limited aspirations were a product of the times for women who came of age in the thirties, forties, and fifties. They were just getting accustomed to running for lower offices; the presidency seemed out of reach to a generation of women raised to defer to men.

Martin learned early that boys operate out of self-interest. She lost an election for eighth-grade president by one vote—her own. She had cast her ballot for her soon-to-be ex-boyfriend. He voted for himself. She went on to become active in student government in high school and was a student senator in college. It did not occur to her that she would run for anything else, ever. Martin graduated in three years from the University of Illinois in 1960, got married the following year, and had her first baby nine months and two weeks later. She was part of the first generation of women who attended college in great numbers, although many enrolled mainly to find a husband. Martin and her husband settled in Rockford, Illinois, where she was the first visibly pregnant teacher in the Rockford school system. She taught up to the day she gave birth.

By the 1960s, the birth-control pill had liberated women from the fear of unwanted pregnancy. But professional opportunities had not yet materialized. Bored housewives with Phi Beta Kappa degrees found a much-needed outlet in politics. Martin's ambition flourished in the company of her women friends, all married with children, all Junior Leaguers, all thirsting for a challenge outside the home. Four of them gathered regularly on the side porch of one of their houses, drank iced tea, and talked about how to reform local politics.

In the early 1970s, female candidates were rare even for local offices. With the support of her gal pals, Martin ran for the county board and was as surprised as anyone when she won. In 1976, after one term at the county level, she ran for the Illinois State Senate. Her campaign symbol was a birdhouse drawn in purple ink with the slogan "Put a Martin in the House." She served her daughter's friends hot dogs as reward for working the neighborhood, door-to-door. "They were seventh-graders; you know, cute little girls with pigtails, pony-tails," Martin says, shaking her head and smiling at the memory. "Shameless," she says softly.

Martin's seat was known as the woman's seat. Two women, both Democrats, had preceded her. When Martin ran for Congress in 1980, however, she could not convince any woman to replace her. By then, Martin was a single parent with two daughters. She probably would not have run for Congress if she had stayed married, yet she doesn't blame politics for the breakup of her marriage to her college sweetheart. If it hadn't been politics, it would have been some other calling, Martin says, as she and other women of her generation experienced "the rush of the outside world." With one daughter under ten and the other a teenager, she was reluctant at first to enter the crowded primary to succeed liberal Republican John Anderson, who had launched a third-party presidential bid to protest Ronald Reagan's candidacy. But congressional seats rarely open up, and she felt she couldn't walk away from the opportunity.

Reagan won in a landslide, carrying forty-four states and helping to elect a Republican Senate, the first in a quarter century. Republican candidates across the country benefited from the surge of votes for the former Hollywood actor. Martin was one of four Republican women elected to Congress that year, a record up to that time for either party in a single election. And none of the women was the widow of a deceased congressman. Each had carved out her own career instead of inheriting it, which in earlier decades had been a common route to Congress for women.

Reagan's election was a triumph for conservative politics, but Martin kept her moderate bearings. She often broke with the Reagan White House on domestic policy and reproductive rights. A reformer at heart and a feminist, she held a press conference to expose unequal pay practices in the House, where women staff members received lower salaries than men in similar jobs. She went public when the male Democratic leadership in Congress did nothing to correct the pay structure after she twice pointed out the imbalance. She realized the men were humoring her and that they would make changes only if she mobilized public opinion through the media.

In 1988, Martin gave up her safe seat in the House to challenge Senator Paul Simon, a folksy intellectual whose bow tie was his signature. Even if she had done everything right, Simon probably was unbeatable. But Martin killed any chance of winning by running a cautious, overly polite race. To beat a popular incumbent, she had to be willing to expose his vulnerabilities with a barrage of negative campaign ads on the issues separating them. She wasn't willing to do that. It was the first race she had lost since the eighth grade.

Martin was one of several promising women who lost bids for the Senate that year. The reasons for each candidate's defeat can be enumerated—and maybe they all deserved to lose—but collectively women have had a tougher time than men becoming senators and governors, the traditional pipelines to the presidency.

For women, the key to winning is demonstrating toughness while not surrendering their inborn empathy. Republican pollster Frank Luntz once quipped that the ideal female candidate for president is a combination of Jack the Ripper and Mother Teresa. Any candidate, male or female, combining a steely, unblinking toughness with a missionary's compassion would be formidable. Nobody conveyed strength better than British prime minister Margaret Thatcher, who "had those artifacts of the male body that are usually described as courage," Martin said. "You can disagree with the manner in which she did it. You can argue with the Falklands enterprise. But the point is if you had to say who is the toughest person out there, the answer would be Margaret Thatcher."

Thatcher exploited that image. Campaigning for reelection in 1983, she was criticized for waging war with Argentina over the Falklands, an island primarily inhabited by sheep. She was accused of using excessive military force to prove she was any man's equal. Unemployment had more than doubled since she took office, and the cutbacks she ordered in social spending prompted chilling visions of the return of a Dickensian England. Facing reelection, she was the most unpopular prime minister in the history of polling. Thatcher lightened her hair (a must for aging women, she confides in her memoir), and hired Christopher Lawson, a former corporate marketing director, to work the same magic for her that he had for Mars candy bars. "The man from Mars," as Lawson was called, was an expert in creating the right mood for the message. He had martial music piped into the pressroom when Thatcher unveiled her Conservative manifesto for the campaign. The patriotic music and Thatcher's characterization of her platform as "robust" set the tone for an upbeat campaign of renewal while the opposition Labour party preached gloom and doom.

Thatcher never deviated from her message, expressed in the slogan "Britain's on the right track, don't turn back." Like her friend and idol Ronald Reagan, she delivered prepared speeches from a Tele-PrompTer, sarcastically dubbed "the sincerity machine" by the British press. Repetition was her friend, spontaneity her enemy. She gave so few interviews that the reporters assigned to her campaign composed a ditty to the tune of "A Bicycle Built for Two" that began, "Maggie, Maggie, give us an interview. . . ."

After Thatcher's comeback from the depths of unpopularity to re-election, a British newspaper called her "an astonishing bird." It was meant as a compliment.

As prime minister, Thatcher was not particularly helpful to women. She didn't surround herself with female advisers. She didn't promote women. And she was Reagan's soul mate in her zeal for slicing spending on social welfare. Yet none of that detracted from the important role she played in smashing the negative stereotype of women as weak, overly emotional, and indecisive. She was known as the Iron Lady.

Thatcher's example can be an inspiration or a curse for the women in her wake. Kim Campbell found that out when she rose to the leadership of the Conservative party of Canada and, for a brief time in 1993, was Canada's first female prime minister, only to suffer a humiliating defeat in her bid to retain that office. Jeff Marshall, twenty-three, one of the Conservative party delegates who voted for Campbell to succeed the retired prime minister, Brian Mulroney, told a reporter, "She is our Mrs. Thatcher, and that's what attracts us to her." Campbell was not a Thatcher clone and had no desire to become one, but was unable to escape the shadow of expectations that she would be Canada's "Iron Lady."

Born Avril Phaedra Douglas Campbell in March 1947, she began calling herself Kim when she was twelve. She describes her childhood as unhappy. Her mother, Phyllis, left home for several years to work on boats in the Mediterranean and West Indies, and their father, George, a prosecutor, raised Campbell and her older sister. She was valedictorian of her high school class and, as a teenager in Vancouver, British Columbia, set her sights on becoming the first female UN secretary general. She worked as a high school teacher to pay her way through law school and studied the Russian political system at the London School of Economics. At age twenty-five, she married a man twenty years her senior, the first of two marriages that ended in divorce.

Campbell's first husband was a member of the Vancouver school board. When he gave up his seat to run for city council, she ran in his place; despite her husband's insistence that his was the better-known political name, she ran and won under her maiden name. Campbell advanced quickly from local government to the provincial legislature in 1986, and to the House of Commons in 1988. By then, she was married to a Harvard-educated American lawyer. When Mulroney named Campbell as Canada's first female justice minister and attorney general in 1990, it was a boon to her career but a blow to her marriage. "It was really hard for him." she says of her husband. The two separated soon afterward. In January 1993, Mulroney rewarded Campbell with another first for a woman, making her Canada's defense minister. "I was just flabbergasted," Campbell said with typical candor. "When he told me, I probably said, 'Holy cow, Prime Minister, leapin' Lizards, Daddy Warbucks.'" Her career dreams were coming true even as her personal life was disintegrating. Responding to a newspaper analysis that described her as "crushingly ambitious," Campbell said, "I find that extraordinary because, in the course of my life in Ottawa, my marriage has ended, I'm very far from home and I find life here sometimes unspeakably lonely and very difficult."

When Mulroney announced his retirement from office, effective in June 1993, Campbell instantly became the party establishment's choice as his successor. She was the dynamic, fresh-faced, popular leader the party needed if it hoped to overcome the Tories' low standing with the voters after ten years of Mulroney. The outgoing prime minister's popularity rating was 11 percent, which one wag noted was less than the 12 percent of Canadians who believed Elvis Presley was still alive. Campbell wanted to resign as defense minister to prepare for the leadership contest and her turn as prime minister, but Mulroney said that would be disloyal, so she stayed. Instead of assembling a campaign team and laying out a strategy for the national election, she found herself mired in controversy over the brutal torture and killing of a teenager by Canadian soldiers in Somalia. At Mulroney's urging—to show the vibrancy of the Conservative party, he said—Jean Charest, the thirty-four-year-old minister of environment, challenged Campbell for the party's leadership position. Campbell wound up winning on the second ballot, but the intraparty contest sapped her energy and cost her precious time that could have been put to better use preparing for the prime minister's race.

On June 13, 1993, Ellen Faircloth, Canada's first female cabinet minister, appointed in 1957, nominated Campbell for the Conservative party leadership, setting the stage for her to become Canada's first female prime minister twelve days later. She resigned the leadership on December 13 after a national election in which the Tories won only 2 seats in the House of Commons, a precipitous slide from the 153 seats they had controlled under Mulroney. Campbell did not even retain her own seat in Parliament. *Newsweek* summed up the election: "Campbell . . . ran a spectacularly inept campaign, rarely opening her mouth, it seemed, except to change feet."

Over dinner five years later, Campbell offered a more nuanced version of her demise. Yes, she deserved a big share of the blame, she said. She was, after all, the candidate. But she said she was saddled with Mulroney's old campaign team, who ran things the way Mulroney liked them, even if it did not suit her style at all. The mostly male Mulroney team never understood her needs, Campbell said, from the extra time a woman needed to get ready in the morning (all Mulroney had to do was shave and shower), to wanting time to review and rehearse speeches before delivering them (Mulroney liked to get the text ten minutes in advance), to liking the thermostat dialed up (Mulroney favored air-conditioning even in cold weather). Campbell had promised Canadians "a different kind of politics," but the good ol' boys managing her campaign practiced the old politics. She fought them at first, she said, but finally gave up.

The worst moment of the campaign came on October 14, 1993, when her campaign ran a TV ad showing an unflattering photograph of Campbell's main opponent and the eventual winner, Jean Chretien of the Liberal party, with eyes closed, a dazed look, and his mouth distorted, the result of a birth defect. Campbell had not seen the ad in advance, but had signed off on the concept of an attack ad against Chretien. When she finally did see it, she ordered it taken off the air. Too late. Canadians howled their disapproval. Some of Campbell's campaign workers threatened to quit. Chretien, who had joked about his facial deformity, saying at least he wasn't one of those politicians who spoke out of both sides of their mouth, added to Campbell's embarrassment with his humble reaction to the ad: "God made me the way I am."

Canada, like the United States, had not had a female candidate for the nation's top elected position before Campbell. She was a novelty and the press gave her extra scrutiny. After the election, news analysts found she had received more coverage on television and in newspapers than any of her rivals. But Lydia Miljan, director of the National Media Archives, noted that most of the discussion of her as a leader was negative.

Analysts differed over whether Campbell was treated more roughly because she was a woman, but there was no disputing the singular attention paid to her looks, clothes, and hairstyle. Consultants gratuitously advised her in print to wear pastels in Quebec and bright colors in Ontario, to darken the roots of her extra-blond hair, and to abandon her favorite pearl earrings. She mostly ignored the advice. "Give me a navy blue suit with some kind of scarf or blouse and I'm happy as a clam," she said. "I feel comfortable. I feel secure." There were references in the press to Campbell's "sparkling blue eyes," but no mention of the eyes of any of her male opponents. As justice minister in 1992, Campbell had posed for a photograph with bare shoulders, holding her lawyer's robes in front of her. It became known as The Photograph and was brought up in every profile of Campbell in the 1993 campaign.

Reporters admitted during and after the campaign that they were ready to pounce on any Campbell mistake of word or deed. Tom Van Dusen, a Campbell aide, later wrote, "The intensity of the attack on her, the relentless pursuit by a press pack that refused to give her a favorable nod, left me reeling throughout the seven-week campaign." Campbell said the media not only commented on what she said but how she said it: "I don't have a traditionally female way of speaking. I don't end my sentences with a question mark. I'm quite assertive. If I didn't speak the way I do, I wouldn't have been seen as a leader. But my way of speaking may have grated on people who were not used to hearing it from a woman. It was the right way for a leader to speak, but it wasn't the right way for a woman to speak. It goes against type."

Campbell told her side of the story in *Time and Chance*, her autobiography, published in 1996. Many critics savaged the book, saying she blamed everyone but herself for her downfall, but the public liked it enough to make it briefly a best-seller in Canada despite its hefty price tag of $34.95.

Campbell's appeal to female voters neutralized the Tories' gender gap, but not all women were pleased with her brief stint as prime minister. When, as attorney general, she declared herself a feminist, Campbell said, "there was an audible intake of breath from sea to shining sea." Yet she governed not as a radical but as an Edmund Burke moderate, approaching politics as the art of the possible. She offended some on both sides by striving for consensus on controversial issues like abortion, sexual abuse, and gun control. Susan Swan, a Toronto novelist, complained that Campbell put her economic conservatism ahead of her feminist instincts. "It is a bitter pill for all of us who expected to see women's issues dealt with," Swan told *Maclean's* magazine. "I had this naive view that the first woman leader was going to be more virtuous and more caring, the fantasy of the perfect mother. In the real world it doesn't play out like that." Sheila Copps, a member of Parliament and deputy leader of the Liberal party of Canada, said that, woman or not, Campbell was still a Tory following Tory policies.

Despite her crushing defeat, Campbell sees much good coming from her breakthrough to prime minister. She met many young women during and after the campaign who told her she had inspired them to think they could be prime minister someday. "They felt it was a huge milestone for the country," Campbell said. "Whether a woman could become prime minister was no longer an abstract question." Some political analysts took the opposite view, saying that Campbell's disastrous campaign had set back the cause of women in politics, noting that Geraldine Ferraro, who was also part of a landslide loss, is still the only woman ever put on a national ticket in the United States. But Copps said Campbell's quick rise and fall was not the beginning and end for women aspiring to political heights in Canada. "We are two elections away from throwing the whole issue of gender aside for good," she predicted. "Once the number of women in politics approaches that of men, it stops being an issue. The fall of Kim Campbell will not be the fall of womanhood."

Campbell says she will not run for political office again, but she has not completely abandoned the notion of a position at the United Nations, perhaps as Canada's official representative. In August 1996, Chretien generously awarded Campbell the plum assignment as Canada's consul-general in Los Angeles. She shared the consul's official residence with Hershey Felder, a composer and concert pianist. For the first time, she said, she had found a man who doesn't require mothering, although he is twenty years her junior, "We're a couple," she said, "We each carry our share of the burden. It's really been quite wonderful."

Perhaps with the Thatcher model in mind, a growing number of U.S. voters—90 percent according to a poll taken in the spring of 1998 by Democratic pollster Celinda Lake—say they would vote for a woman as president. When the Gallup Organization first asked people in 1936 whether they would "vote for a woman for president if she qualified in every other respect," only 31 percent said yes; 65 percent said they would not. Over time, attitudes evolved and women were accepted in politics even as they took their place in law, medicine, and the military. The ranks of city councils, school boards, county commissions, state legislatures, and the like are well populated with women. But higher up the pyramid of electoral politics, women still are a scant presence.

Where do presidents come from? Most recent presidents—Carter, Reagan, Clinton, and George W. Bush—have been governors. John F. Kennedy was a senator, Dwight Eisenhower a military hero. George Bush the elder was Reagan's vice president for eight years and before that served as a member of the House from Texas, and held major appointive posts, including director of the Central Intelligence Agency and U.S. envoy to China. Except for Bush senior, a longstanding member of the Washington elite, the others campaigned as outsiders. But they were not strangers to the political process.

The requirements are no different for women. Getting more women into the pipeline for the presidency means winning more Senate seats and governorships. At the dawn of the twenty-first century, there are only thirteen women among the one hundred senators and only six female governors in the fifty states. These stepping-stone offices are the political equivalent of baseball's farm system. Electing women senators and governors may be the best way to nurture ambition and hurry history.

Are there any shortcuts? Maybe. With the country at peace and enjoying full prosperity and the public wary of professional politicians, the truly exceptional woman, or man, might be able to bypass the long initiation process if she presents alternative credentials that are convincing. The challenge is greater during wartime when voters seek comfort from experienced officials and are less likely to take a risk. Elizabeth Dole on the Republican side held two cabinet positions under two different presidents—transportation under Reagan and labor under Bush—and for eight years was president of the Red Cross, which has the budget and workforce of a major corporation. She had never run for office, but neither had retired general Colin Powell when Republicans tried to draft him to run for president in 1996.

On the Democratic side, Hillary Rodham Clinton's candidacy for the Senate from New York sparked speculation that her ultimate goal is the presidency. This Clinton had never before run for office, and couldn't even claim a string of appointive posts. Voter interest in Clinton's candidacy seemed to spring from a desire to reward the First Lady for her dignity and grace in handling the revelation of her husband's dalliance with a young White House intern, Monica Lewinsky.

It is admittedly a stretch, but if there is a plausible analogy, it is with Eisenhower. Just as Eisenhower was drafted for the presidency after proving himself on the battlefield, Hillary's steadfastness through a year of humiliation proved her mettle in the age of "Oprah."

Men traditionally use their military service to erase doubts about how they might handle the responsibilities of commander in chief. But lacking a war, most of the country's future leaders will not have had military experience. Women have to look for other ways to show toughness. Democratic pollster Geoff Garin found, for example, that a female candidate who has survived breast cancer gets equivalent respect from voters as a man who has suffered a war injury.

The Senate is a proving ground for future presidents. A standing joke says that when senators—at least male senators—look in the mirror, they hear "Hail to the Chief" playing in the background. Three years before the 2000 presidential election, a dozen senators were mentioned as possible contenders. They weren't all heavyweights, or even nationally known. The only woman senator speculated about for higher office, and then only for vice president, was Senator Dianne Feinstein of California. "If Dianne were a male with California's mother lode of electoral votes, she'd be an automatic candidate," says Senator Susan Collins of Maine. Collins, a Republican, also noted the double standard in assessing the presidential prospects of California senator Barbara Boxer. "Boxer is too strident," Collins said, "but [Minnesota senator Paul] Wellstone isn't? That's gender. Two outspoken liberals, but the man gets praised for sticking up for his principles while the woman is marginalized."

Reacting to the partisan rancor that infected the 1996 election, Senator Barbara Mikulski proposed that the women of the Senate meet periodically. There were nine of them at the time, a record, and Mikulski thought if they got to know each other better, they might find common ground on issues. Since then, every four to six weeks, the women have gathered at one of their homes, or at the Monocle, a favorite Capitol Hill restaurant. When it's Mikulski's turn, she typically serves Maryland crab cakes. Collins relies on lobster stew from Maine and apple crisp, another Maine specialty, which in her first turn as hostess she stayed up until midnight the night before to prepare. The dinners sometimes yield substantive victories, such as the women's bipartisan decision to support standards for mammography testing. Together they drafted a "Dear Colleague" letter that began, "We the women of the Senate invite you the men of the Senate. . . ." When the women agree, they send a powerful message because they span the ideological spectrum from Texas Republican senator Kay Bailey Hutchison, a conservative, to Maryland Democrat Mikulski, a liberal.

They also enjoy a lot of laughs, sometimes at their male colleagues' expense. "At one dinner we were talking about all the men running for president—a lot of them senators—and here we were, nine women senators, and not a single one of us thinks of herself as president," said Collins. "That's got to be gender-related. I remember Lynn Martin speaking at a Women's Campaign Fund event saying a man who sells Toyotas thinks he's an expert in international trade while a woman thinks she needs a Ph.D. in economics before she can comment. We went down the list of the men who were running, and they weren't more experienced or more capable. They have a confidence, or is it an arrogance? I don't know what it is. We got up to about a dozen senators, both sides of the aisle. We laughed about it, but the essential truth of it struck all of us."

For Collins, running for public office was not a big leap. Born in 1952, she grew up in the tiny town of Caribou, Maine, where first her father and then her mother served as mayor. Both parents were politically active. Her mother headed the school board. Her father, grandfather, and great-grandfather all served in the state legislature. "Community service and politics were part of what you did. You were expected to give back to society," she says.

Collins had a role model during her growing-up years. Margaret Chase Smith was a senator from Maine. Smith had filled her husband's seat when he died in 1948 and was the only woman in the Senate for a quarter century, until she retired in 1972. The indomitable Smith was one of the few lawmakers who spoke out against the Communist witch-hunt conducted by Senator Joseph McCarthy. When Collins was in high school, she spent a week in Washington and got to meet Smith, who gave her a copy of her declaration of conscience against McCarthy. "It honestly was an inspiring moment," says Collins. "Twenty-five years later, I ran for her seat. I go to schools all the time and tell the students, especially young girls, that if I could go from the halls of Caribou High School to the U.S. Senate, so can they."

Collins started as an intern for Representative William Cohen, who later was elected to the Senate and then tapped by President Clinton as secretary of defense. Becoming a paid member of the staff, she continued to work for Cohen from 1974 to 1984. She returned to Maine, where she ran for governor in 1992. Although she was vastly outspent and lost the three-way race against two self-financed candidates—one a Democrat, the other an independent—Collins emerged with statewide name recognition and a reputation for being a good loser. She didn't blame anybody for her loss. Four years later, she was well-positioned to win Cohen's seat when he left the Senate for the Pentagon.

Collins is a hard worker who comes across more like the staff person she was than a high-wattage senator. She has an independent streak in her voting, and her down-to-earth style is popular in Maine, even among Democrats. But any freshman facing reelection for the first time is vulnerable, and Collins won in 1996 with only 49 percent of the vote. In 2002, she faced former state Senate Majority Leader Chellie Pingrie, who is something of a folk hero in the state as the principal author of Maine Rx, legislation that lowered the cost of prescription drugs. With each senate seat crucial in the closely divided Senate, the Maine race was a test case of whether President Bush's war popularity would rub off on other Republicans, or whether Democrats could successfully challenge the Bush administration on domestic issues. Collins won handily. A moderate, Collins says she often feels like a "pariah" among her conservative male GOP colleagues. When the emotionally explosive issue of banning late-term abortions arose in the Senate, Collins looked across the aisle to Democratic women for help in deciding how to vote. "I'm Catholic. I had my bishop call me. My parish priest raised it," Collins said. To deal with the pressures, she turned to Mikulski, the Senate's senior woman, and to Mary Landrieu, a freshman senator from Louisiana, both Catholics. They would, she knew, understand the dilemma she faced personally and politically. They, too, struggled with the issue. In the end, Collins voted against the so-called late-term abortion ban, contributing to its narrow defeat. So did Mikulski. "My family, like hers, thought my vote was appalling," says Collins. Landrieu supported the ban, as she had pledged to do during her campaign.

Landrieu is the first female senator with young children, perhaps a forerunner of things to come as more young women in all professions combine work and family. She describes herself as a typical firstborn child: stubborn, strong, and opinionated. But she coats her personality with a soothing, soft-spoken southern veneer. Just forty when she was elected in 1996, she is a hot political commodity. "A white woman from the South and a Democrat—wow!" says a Democratic party candidate recruiter. Landrieu comes from a colorful political family.

Her father, Moon Landrieu, is the former mayor of New Orleans and was housing secretary during the Carter administration. A traditionalist, the elder Landrieu once said women's role in politics is to stuff and stamp campaign envelopes, or, as he put it, "Women do the lickin' and stickin'."

Landrieu is the oldest of nine children and not the one her father imagined carrying on the family name in politics. Growing up, Landrieu, too, did not envision a political career. Her mother had stayed home and cared for the family while her father pursued a career as a lawyer and politician, and she could imagine herself marrying a politician and having nine children. When, at age twenty-three, she told her father that she wanted to run for the state legislature he smiled but said nothing. Weeks later, he noticed her campaign signs springing up in the neighborhood.

"I guess you're running for the legislature. Your signs are all over the district," he said.

"Well, what did you think?" she replied, a little miffed that he hadn't taken her seriously. From then on, he offered advice and encouragement.

Landrieu did marry a politician, a lawyer named Frank Snelling who had been elected at the local level. But the children did not automatically follow. "I never thought I'd have trouble having my own, and I did," says Landrieu, who turned to adoption to complete her family. "Frank was adopted out of an orphanage from Ireland when he was five years old. So, when I married him, it was kind of like God telling me that I would have adopted children because I knew Frank wouldn't object. You don't know when you get married, maybe your husband doesn't like that idea. So it was quite a natural thing for me." They adopted two children, a boy and a girl.

With a degree in sociology, Landrieu set out to be a social worker. She once considered becoming a nun, and in college was active in the Campus Crusade for Christ, an interdenominational Christian organization. She hoped to get a staff position as a lay minister when she graduated. When she didn't, it was a big disappointment. She returned home unsure of her career path. Her father suggested that she work as a volunteer in the campaign of a family friend who was running for judge. He was the underdog, and when he won Landrieu and the other young volunteers who made it happen felt proud of what they had accomplished.

Soon afterward, local labor leaders approached Landrieu about running for the legislature. She thought about it overnight and said yes. For six months, for four hours every day, she walked the district knocking on doors until people literally told her, "Mary, please don't come back here. We're voting for you." Having the name Landrieu was magic enough, but it was her youthful innocence that captivated people, especially the legion of older women left behind by families fleeing to the suburbs. "I'd knock on the door and these old ladies would say, 'Oh, sweetheart, come in. It's so nice to have young people interested in politics.'" In her debut on the ballot in November 1979, she ran ahead of three other candidates in the field and defeated a three-term incumbent.

Being in the spotlight as a candidate sometimes unnerved Landrieu. Although good at giving speeches in school, she suffered bouts of anxiety and self-doubt when speaking to a prestigious audience. Before one scheduled debate, Landrieu was so nervous that she got no farther than the parking lot. She had a friend tell the host that she was sick. On another occasion—a speech in the New Orleans garden district before "the kind of la-de-da crowd" that could make or break her candidacy—Landrieu came back to her campaign headquarters and collapsed in despair. "I was hysterical," she said. "I threw myself down and beat my fists on the floor." Her stunned campaign staff tried to console her, but she kept blubbering, "I know you all think I can do this, but I can't. I just can't do it. I cannot make these speeches. I can do the canvassing. I can write the letters. I know the issues, but I just can't do this."

Landrieu had overcome most of her novice's fears by the time Ann Richards met her. Richards had been elected state treasurer of Texas and was called upon from time to time to make speeches in neighboring Louisiana. Richards liked the younger woman from the start and would come to think of her "almost like a daughter." Richards immediately saw Landrieu's potential in politics and Landrieu was eager to have Richards as a mentor.

Richards urged Landrieu to run for treasurer as a step toward eventually becoming governor. Landrieu took the advice and won in 1987. After almost eight years of seasoning, Landrieu joined the race for governor in 1995. She had her heart set on being governor. So did several others, apparently. Landrieu got squeezed out in a primary crowded with candidates who siphoned off the good-government vote and divided her African-American support. She ran third in a field of nineteen, missing the runoff by a percentage point. The experience almost drove her from politics. "I thought this is just too tough a business for me, and the sacrifice is so great. I didn't take it personally, but I was thinking, is this worth it? I had a three-year-old child. I have a husband who needs me. And then you think all the money it cost, and the time."

Landrieu was taking a hiatus from politics when John Breaux came calling. As the soon-to-be senior senator from Louisiana and a known charmer, Breaux's job was to find a candidate who could keep the seat vacated by the retiring Bennett Johnston safely in the Democratic column.

"You need to get your running shoes back on," he told Landrieu.

"Oh, no, you better find somebody else," she protested.

The last thing Landrieu wanted was another statewide race. She had closed her headquarters and begun to pay off her campaign's $50,000 debt. Her brothers and sisters were as devastated as she was by the loss and skeptical of the merits of entering another race so soon. Her father, surprisingly, held a contrary view. This was no time for her to lay back and nurse her wounds, he told her. "If you don't want to still serve the state, then go ahead and quit," he said. "But if you want to run again, you cannot sit out for four years. You've got too much invested."

Louisiana's voters seemed to welcome a Landrieu candidacy. Her poll numbers actually went up after her losing race for governor, an anomaly that increased the pressure on her to run for the Senate. Norma Jane Sabiston, Breaux's chief of staff and a close friend of Landrieu's since they were seventeen, offered to leave her job and run the campaign. Landrieu's husband, longing for a less hectic existence, would have been happier if she chose not to run. But he relented. "Let's do it," he said.

Landrieu seemed headed for a relatively easy victory when opposition came from an unexpected and unwelcome source. Less than a week before the November '96 election, retired New Orleans archbishop Philip Hannan told Louisiana Catholics that it would be a sin to vote for Landrieu because she supports abortion rights. Landrieu's poll numbers dropped twenty-five points in one heavily Catholic rural area of the state. Her once-comfortable lead all but disappeared. "Had the race been two days longer, we wouldn't have gotten in," says Landrieu. The archbishop's words devastated Landrieu's parents, staunch Catholics who regarded the prelate as one of their closest friends. Nowhere else did the Catholic Church intrude so directly in a political campaign. "Since I'm not the only Catholic with my views, why would I be the only one out of the whole country that the church singles out?" Landrieu wondered.

The race was the closest in the country. Of 1.7 million votes cast, Landrieu won by only 5,788 votes over Republican Woody Jenkins, a state representative aligned with the Christian Right. Jenkins refused to concede, and instead insisted on an investigation of alleged voter fraud in the black parishes of New Orleans. When state officials refused to overturn the election based on scanty and unconfirmed allegations, Jenkins got the Republican-controlled U.S. Senate to intervene. After a ten-month investigation that left Landrieu $600,000 in debt, she was finally able to claim her seat.

The first woman Democrat from a Deep South state, Landrieu's political future looked bright. Political analysts generally agreed that the year 2000 was too soon to put her on the ticket as vice president, that she's too young and, as a freshman senator, too green. "She's got, what, six presidential cycles ahead of her," says Rich Masters, her communications director and senior policy adviser. The day after Landrieu was elected, she was invited to appear on CNN's "Crossfire" and NBC's "Meet the Press." Masters turned down both. "We didn't want her to be a white-hot star," he said, explaining the danger of putting Landrieu into the national spotlight too quickly. After sixteen years of focusing solely on state issues, it would take time for her to master national issues, and mistakes are better made away from the media glare, he said. Masters compared the process to the pacing of a thoroughbred, which calls for saving strength for the stretch run. "For the first two years at a minimum, we decided we were going to take a passive role, raise our hand, and wait to be called on," he said.

Landrieu welcomed the go-slow approach. She arrived in Washington happy but tired, the kind of bone-tiredness familiar to women juggling work and family. She didn't want to moonlight as a talking head on television. "I ran for three years in the most grueling, tough state," she said. "My children need me. My husband needs me. I'm going to take my time and learn the Senate. I'm very respectful of this institution. I think it's a place where you should come and really be quiet for the first couple of years until you really learn the place. There's so much history here and there is a rhythm to the place. The senior members do most of the talking on committees. That's fine with me. I listen. I have plenty of time."

Bleak statistics drive Landrieu's legislative agenda. Louisiana has the highest percentage of children in poverty and the highest percentage of people working at minimum wage. She launched an early childhood development initiative called "Steps to Success," which matches volunteer mentors with parents to create a better home environment for children. And she pressed for a greater share of offshore oil drilling revenues for her state. Her voting record is determinedly centrist. Among the votes that distance her from the liberals of the Democratic party was her opposition in the spring of 1998 to toughened alcohol standards in a highway transportation bill. Mothers Against Drunk Driving (MADD) supported the measure and it had received sympathetic coverage in the media. Reporters scrutinized Landrieu's financial reports under the assumption that she had received large contributions from the beer lobby to vote the way she did. But she hadn't. "I'll bet she gets some [contributions] for her reelection," an aide said, chuckling.

Landrieu faced reelection in 2002, and she prepared herself for a strong challenge. "I know people are sittin' out there thinking, 'There's no way she can win again. It was a fluke. She only won by five thousand votes.' So I have to be ready for it. Also, being a woman, you just feel like you can never really rest. I learned early I can't rely on the political establishment. They won't come to my rescue or to my defense. I run every race like the only people I can count on are myself, my husband, my mother, my father, and my brothers and sisters. One thing that's been beneficial for me, and I think for many women, is that men generally underestimate women. In a race, it's to your advantage to be underestimated by your opponent, whether you're a marathon runner or a political runner. And I've come into every race with everybody saying there's no way she can win. So I overprepare. It's good to be overprepared and ready and underestimated by your opponent. It gives you an advantage."

Republican dreams of unseating Landrieu turned nightmarish when their leading candidate, Louisiana Rep. John Cooksey, attracted national attention with a boorish remark about Muslims who wear turbans. Cooksey endorsed racial profiling in the wake of the 9/11 attacks, and said that law enforcement authorities should question anyone wearing "a diaper on his head and a fan belt wrapped around the diaper." The White House rebuked Cooksey for the remark, and Republican leaders quickly regrouped, settling on a strategy to take advantage of a quirk in Louisiana law. If Landrieu failed to get 50 percent of the vote on Election Day, she would be forced into a run-off. The GOP encouraged a multi-candidate field to oppose Landrieu, knowing that would increase the odds of her falling short. Republican Suzanne Terrell, the state's election commissioner, was the second top vote getter (with 27 percent to Landrieu's 46 percent). The GOP's gamble paid off. Terrell was a much more appealing candidate than Cooksey, and Republicans were optimistic that

Bush's high popularity in the state would rally voters to Terrell. Landrieu's play-it-safe, centrist policies made it hard for her to energize the state's African American voters, who she needed to turn out in order to win. "One Republican Party is enough," said Cleo Fields, a black state representative. "Two is almost unconstitutional." Landrieu's pro-choice politics were also seen as a handicap in dominantly Catholic Louisiana. Terrell supports a constitutional amendment to ban abortion, and opponents of abortion rights are typically more apt to vote on that issue alone. The runoff was scheduled for Saturday, December 7, competing with Christmas shopping and football. President Bush planned to barnstorm the state on Terrell's behalf, and Republicans poured so much money into the race that Louisiana Sen. John Breaux called it "the second Louisiana purchase."

In a debate, Landrieu portrayed Terrell as a "rookie" who could not accomplish much for the state; Terrell countered that Landrieu's "clout" was overrated. Republicans circulated flyers showing Landrieu embracing Nancy Pelosi, the newly elected Democratic House leader and a card-carrying liberal. The post 9/11 political climate promised to test all of Landrieu's skills as a centrist Democrat in an increasingly conservative part of the country. In the end, Landrieu won, 52% to 48%, and by winning, she kept alive her prospects for returning to Louisiana to run for governor after a second term in the Senate.

After Landrieu's election in 1996, she and her husband settled into Washington as if expecting to stay for a long time. They bought property on historic East Capitol Street, just four blocks from the Capitol, and spent months overseeing the construction of a custom-made Victorian row house. Landrieu says their home will double as an informal embassy for the state of Louisiana, complete with the state flag displayed prominently outside. They share responsibility for their two children, with each parent committed to being at home two nights during the week. Landrieu is extra-organized. "I just think you've got to be," she says. "Every Monday night we have a date night. And Saturday night is our time to go out with our friends." The couple has a full-time nanny.

As a working mother, Landrieu is a role model for young women who think that politics and rearing children don't mix. She worried when she first ran for office that finding a suitable spouse might be harder if she pursued a political career. "But then I thought: Am I going to give up what I love because I'm single and I might not get married? I decided no, I want to show young women that they don't have to wait until they're fifty to get into politics. They don't have to wait and have all their kids and then get in. They can make choices just like men."

Landrieu didn't fully appreciate the value of female role models until the day she took her then six-year-old son, Connor, to court with her to finalize the adoption of an infant daughter, Mary Shannon. Two women judges presided that day. Connor stood wide-eyed as he watched the judges come off the bench resplendent in their black robes. One of the judges offered to take the little boy on a tour of her chambers. When she asked if he had any questions, he looked up at her and said, "Yes. I didn't know girls could be judges. Can girls be judges?"

Traditionally, women enter politics later in life, when their children are older. But with so many mothers with young children in the workforce, voters are not as judgmental as they once were. A generation ago, in 1967, two-thirds of men in their first year of college thought women should stay home and raise the children. In 1996, less than a third voiced that opinion. The late Sonny Bono's mother said publicly that her two grandchildren "would essentially become orphans open to abuse by strangers" if Mary Bono won the congressional seat left vacant by Sonny's death. If anything, the elder Bono's remarks created a backlash. Mary Bono won a special election in April 1998 with 64 percent of the vote, routing Democrat Ralph Waite, an actor who had played the father on "The Waltons."

Bono has company on Capitol Hill talking child-care arrangements with other women. More than a dozen women members of the House have school age or younger children in contrast to an earlier era when mothers with young children rarely sought elective office. In 1974, California representative Yvonne Braithwaite created a stir when she became the first member of Congress to give birth. Twenty years later, when the Republicans gained control of the Congress for the first time in forty years, Speaker Newt Gingrich accommodated two nursing mothers in the Republican ranks, Utah's Enid Greene and New York's Susan Molinari, by setting aside a small room off the House chamber for breast-feeding.

Progressive attitudes sometimes have to yield to practical realities. Blanche Lambert Lincoln was a second-term member of Congress from Arkansas in 1996 when she became pregnant with twins. Realizing that hers was a high-risk pregnancy and not wanting to campaign in the heat of summer, Lincoln announced she would not run for a third term. Yet when the twins were not yet two years old, Lincoln returned to the campaign trail, this time in pursuit of a Senate seat.

"She was walking a very fine line," says Celinda Lake, who did Lincoln's polling.

The lure of an open seat jolted Lincoln off the mommy track. When Arkansas senator Dale Bumpers announced he would not run again, she saw an opportunity that might not come again for another generation. Yet, by running, she risked looking like a hypocrite after declaring upon leaving the House that staying home with young children is important to teach them values. With the increase in households where both parents work, voters have become more tolerant, but some still think less of women who seem to put their political ambition ahead of family duties. Lincoln had compounded the problem with her self-righteousness. She would have to find a way to neutralize the issue.

Lake put the twins in an ad with Lincoln's husband to show voters someone was taking care of them. To make sure there would be no surprises, Lake tested tough ads against Lincoln with focus groups. One ad resurrected Lincoln's syrupy statements on motherhood and declared, "Sorry, Blanche, but we don't think kids have all their values at two and a half." Older women and younger men reacted negatively to Lincoln's decision to run for office while her children were so young.

The campaign braced for the expected attacks. They never came. The closest another candidate came to exploiting Lincoln's turnabout occurred in the Democratic primary when Scott Ferguson, a radiologist, said that of all his titles, "Dad" meant the most. Asked if he was sending a message to Lincoln and other working mothers, Ferguson insisted he was not. He added that he wouldn't dare because his wife is a dentist, and they, too, juggle child care.

Lincoln's Republican opponent, Fay Boozman, an ophthalmologist and state senator, forfeited his right to raise any gender-related issue after stumbling into the abortion debate with the bizarre assertion that rape victims are unlikely to become pregnant. The ensuing uproar forced Boozman, a religious conservative who opposes abortion rights, to apologize. He did not back away from the statement, however, which he said was "based on personal experience and not scientific fact." Lincoln won the election comfortably with 55 percent of the vote.

Lincoln began her political career answering phones for Arkansas representative Bill Alexander after graduating from college in 1981. A decade later, at age thirty-one, Lincoln defeated Alexander in her first race for public office. When she told her boss that she planned to challenge him, he found the idea laughable. "Why not run for the Senate?" he responded with more than a hint of sarcasm. Alexander turned out to be an easy mark after he was named as one of the biggest abusers of privileges extended by the private House bank. An audit revealed that Alexander had 487 check overdrafts but paid no penalty. Voters were outraged that members of Congress enjoyed this perk while they had to pay a fine for every bounced check.

If breaking into politics is hard for women, moving up the political ladder is even harder. When Lincoln, a proven vote-getter as a House member, said she wanted to run for the Senate, local Democratic officials tried to dissuade her. They already had a candidate in mind, a man, and they reflexively dismissed her chances. As women strive for higher office, they face unrealistically high expectations. Bella Abzug, a leading feminist and a member of Congress from New York in the early seventies, once said that the real goal of the women's movement is not to advance the superstars but to make sure every mediocre woman gets the same chance to fail as her male counterpart.

Only a few women have dared to contemplate the biggest leap in politics—to the White House. Political analysts, most of them men, put a ceiling on women's aspirations at the level of president's help-mate, the vice presidency. These analysts speculate about the good prospects for a woman on one or both major-party tickets, but impose stringent standards when it comes to identifying a particular woman.

When Charles Cook, a highly regarded political handicapper, mentioned California representative Nancy Pelosi as a prospective running mate for the Democratic nominee, Marc Sandalow, a columnist with the *San Francisco Chronicle*, mocked the idea. "Vice President Pelosi? Have the political cognoscenti lost their minds?" he wrote.

A few days later, in her office in the Rayburn Building, Pelosi waved a copy of the article to punctuate her thoughts about qualified women being dismissed by the so-called experts. She wasn't just defending herself. Sure, she was flattered that Cook had thought of her as a potential vice president, but the *Chronicle* columnist had written off practically every other woman running for public office before he got to her. And then he poked fun at her too.

"Compared to the other women being talked about, Nancy Pelosi is a titan," Cook gushed. "It is true that Pelosi is among the most respected lawmakers in Washington," Sandalow conceded. Inevitably there's a "but" . . . Pelosi knows what's coming.

"Too liberal," she says.

In the centrist Democratic party created by Bill Clinton and Al Gore, Pelosi's liberal voting record is in tune with her San Francisco district, but too far left for the likely Democratic nominee, and so her name is struck from most lists of vice presidential prospects. Her circumstances would not be noteworthy if she were an exception, but she is just one of many women in politics cavalierly eliminated from contention for the second spot on the ticket, because . . . well, because.

One by one, the most promising prospects for 2000 were removed from consideration: Arizona governor Jane Hull, ready for retirement; New Jersey's Christine Todd Whitman, anathema to the GOP's right wing; New Hampshire's Jeanne Shaheen, comes from a no-count state, electorally speaking. So much for the women governors. As for the senators: Maryland's Mikulski and Washington State's Patty Murray, not "presidential"; Louisiana's Landrieu and Arkansas' Lincoln, too young and inexperienced; California's Feinstein, too independent, and Boxer, too strident (a disparaging adjective with a strictly feminine connotation); Texas' Hutchison, not with fellow Texan George W. Bush at the top of the ticket; Maine's Snowe and Collins, too pro-choice for today's GOP and from too small a state.

That leaves? Well, that leaves Elizabeth Dole, whose padded shoulders for a brief time carried the aspirations of many women as the greatest democracy the world has ever known embarks on a new century.

FIVE

The 2000 Election: No Women Wanted

An aide to Elizabeth Dole telephoned a reporter in *Newsweek's* Washington Bureau. "I have a tip for you," he said. "In this week's Conventional Wisdom chart, how about giving an up arrow to Elizabeth Dole, and a down arrow to her husband." The aide was doing classic damage control. Earlier in the week, a story on the front page of the *New York Times* had Bob Dole, former senator and presidential candidate, ruminating in an interview about his wife's exploratory presidential campaign. He said she was having trouble raising money, and he wasn't sure she would decide to run because of the financial hurdle. Dole also confided that he was thinking of contributing money to a rival candidate, John McCain, a colleague from the Senate who, like himself, is a war hero.

The *Times* story infuriated Elizabeth Dole, whose fledgling campaign was struggling to gain a toehold in the competitive world of presidential politics. "The boys are still standing in the clubhouse door, her own damn husband included, and saying, 'She's not one of us,'" griped one adviser. Dole's remarks prompted a great deal of pop psychology over his motives. The women working for Elizabeth were convinced that Bob Dole's patronizing assessment of his wife's chances had more to do with the locker-room atmosphere so prevalent in politics than any personal angst he might feel over her candidacy.

A friend fumed that if Elizabeth had publicly contemplated giving money to one of her husband's opponents when he ran for president, "His campaign would have been feeding her poisoned chocolates." But money for McCain wasn't the worst of it. Writing a personal check to the Arizona senator could be rationalized. He was, after all, a good friend to both Doles, and a thousand dollars, the maximum allowed under federal law, would be mostly a symbolic gesture.

Far more damaging to his wife's campaign was Dole's suggestion that Elizabeth might not see the race through. A comment like that might scare off potential contributors. Donors don't bankroll a candidate who's not committed to the run.

Bob Dole didn't mean to sabotage his life partner's political dream, but that was the practical effect of his remarks. Contributors to political campaigns assume that someone savvy about politics wouldn't say what Dole said unless it was true. Why underwrite a campaign that lacks staying power?

In the first quarter of 1999, Elizabeth Dole had raised only $700,000, a pittance next to the $13 million amassed by Texas governor George W. Bush, the Republican front-runner, and not enough to remain viable in the high-stakes game she wanted to play. A major reason she had been taken seriously as a presidential contender was her talent at fund-raising. She was one of very few women who had a national network to tap for the millions needed for a presidential run. In eight years as president of the Red Cross, she had raised $3.4 billion. Her inability to transfer this fund-raising prowess to her candidacy was crippling, and potentially decisive in the crowded Republican field. Bob Dole had spoken the truth in revealing her money woes, but as journalist Michael Kinsley once observed, only in Washington is speaking the truth treated as a gaffe.

Elizabeth heeded advice to handle her husband's unwelcome remarks with humor. "He's been banished to the family woodshed," she told reporters, smiling brightly. Her lighthearted demeanor, however forced, enabled others to join in the frivolity. Majority Leader Dick Armey guffawed that Dole "would be singing 'Strangers in the Night' for some time," and wouldn't need the Viagra he touted as a paid spokesman for the Pfizer Pharmaceutical Company. Pollster Linda DiVall insisted to reporters that the campaign remained on track and that Dole would formally announce by late summer or early fall. In the meantime, DiVall said dryly, "My guess is there will be a lot of frozen casseroles in the deep freezer for him."

The perception that she was merely dabbling in presidential politics to position herself for the vice presidency had plagued Dole from the start. Now was no time to give ground to the skeptics. Sick with laryngitis, she stuck doggedly to her schedule, traveling to New Hampshire and shaking hands with voters despite a fever of 103 degrees. If she disappeared from public view, claiming illness, rumors about a deteriorating campaign could become a self-fulfilling prophecy. It was only May of 1999. The New Hampshire primary was nine months away. "She's determined. She doesn't want anybody to think she's not going to do this," said a top aide. "If she goes down, it will be because George Bush beat us fair and square."

Once a week, Dole's campaign manager, Tom Daffron, a trim and mild-mannered man, dropped by Bob Dole's downtown Washington office to bring him up to date on his wife's campaign. It was a delicate mission, not unlike briefing an ex-president about a sensitive foreign policy matter. The advice is valued, but there's only one president or, in this case, one candidate. Bob Dole has a good intuitive sense of politics, and he understood the minefields that Elizabeth's candidacy presented. "I don't want to look like a guy who couldn't get to the White House through the front door and is riding in on her," he told Daffron early on. "I don't want to trade on her. It ought to be her campaign."

During Bob Dole's disastrous campaign in 1996, many commentators said the wrong Dole was on the ticket. Bob agreed in his wry way, and after the election, he had caps made up with lettering that said "Elizabeth 2000." He said he only ordered six "because I don't want to be stuck with a big inventory." For a man in his mid-seventies, he seemed remarkably comfortable with his wife's turn on the stage. He joked about being the first First Lady named Bob. Elizabeth, for her part, seemed relieved at her husband's willingness to adapt to the new configuration in their political status. At the same time, everybody around the Doles was aware of the delicate balance in their relationship, both personal and political. Bob Dole is not accustomed to sitting on the sidelines. The good news, says a campaign aide, is that Elizabeth has a high-profile surrogate. The bad news, he adds, is that Elizabeth has a high-profile surrogate. Bob Dole's crusade on behalf of erectile dysfunction was a source of both embarrassment and mirth in the Dole camp. Like most Americans, Elizabeth's advisers credited Dole for forthrightly discussing a subject that afflicts many men. Still, it annoyed them how oblivious he was to the burden his activism placed on his wife. "I hope they're both getting filthy rich off that so it's worth it," said a friend, referring to Dole's televised ads extolling Viagra, the miracle pill developed to treat impotence. Elizabeth typically wore a frozen smile when reporters, trying hard to conceal their smirks, questioned her about her husband's role as an ED spokesman.

Bob Dole knew his wife had gotten off to a late start and needed more money. The fat cats who bankrolled his presidential runs did not come through for her. Eager to get out of the woodshed after the *Times* interview, a chastened Dole agreed to hit the road to raise money for his wife. The campaign laid on a half-dozen fund-raisers he would do solo in the spring and summer of 1999 in places where he remains a draw—on Wall Street, in his native Kansas, and less obviously, Las Vegas. He soon discovered that hustling dollars for Elizabeth was hard because she doesn't have a powerful position like he had when he was running for the Republican nomination. "When you're chairman of the Senate Finance Committee, they slide the checks under your door," says a Dole aide. It was the reason why McCain, substantially behind Elizabeth in the early polls, outperformed her in raising money. "This is not brain surgery," says the Dole aide. "McCain will either be the nominee, or he'll be chairman of the Commerce Committee. The word is out, if you want to do business in front of the Commerce Committee, you better contribute. She'll either be the nominee, or she'll be back at the Red Cross, or wherever she goes."

Dole compounded the problem by waiting too long to signal her intentions. By the time she stepped down from the Red Cross on January 18, 1999, to consider a presidential run, most of the party's big donors and best activists were already taken. Governor Bush had agents in the field wooing donors a full year before Dole's name even surfaced on the radar screen. "There is no real good explanation for why she didn't start sooner, or make two thousand calls to her closest friends and say, 'This is what I'm thinking of doing, keep your powder dry,'" says a campaign aide. "You can't make up for lost time in this business."

Running for president involves lots of tests along the way, some real and some self-inflicted. By the summer of 1999, Elizabeth Dole had gained credibility on issues. She took a tough stance on prosecuting the war in Kosovo and, alone among the Republican candidates, supported stricter gun laws, holding up a childproofed aspirin bottle as a prop to emphasize the need for safety locks on guns. Polls showed that 53 percent of Republicans favor gun control, and aides gleefully proclaimed the issue "gangbusters" for Dole. Keeping kids safe from violence in school and on the streets emerged as a top issue for voters. After the Columbine High School shootings in April, support among Republican women for gun control reached 78 percent, according to Democratic pollster Celinda Lake.

On the divisive issue of abortion rights, Dole attempted to steer a middle ground by saying she would not actively pursue a human-life constitutional amendment, as mandated by the 1996 Republican platform, but that she remained personally opposed to abortion. Her stance displeased activists on both sides, but fortified her image as a centrist, making her more electable if she could survive the divisive primary process.

The next test that loomed was money. She needed to attract more financial support to dispel the cloud of doubt over her campaign. The media and the other candidates would measure her staying power in the race by the dollars she raised. Every three months, candidates must report the contributions they receive to the Federal Elections Commission. At the end of the first quarter of 1999, Elizabeth was so concerned by her poor showing that, in a desperate last attempt to catch up, she wanted to make an additional hundred phone calls herself to solicit money. Daffron thought that this must be a female characteristic, to suppose that somehow the whole campaign can be rescued if you just work harder. Another woman he once advised, Susan Collins of Maine, reacted much the same way, blaming herself for the campaign's shortcomings, and thinking if she shook more hands, that would make the difference. "I used to tell her: Money and media—nothing else matters. If it isn't covered, it didn't happen. You can shake five hundred hands a day. A congressional district has five hundred thousand people. It will take you a thousand days, almost three years, longer than your term."

The synergy for a Senate seat, let alone the presidency, was bigger than any phone list, even with another hundred calls tacked on.

Politics is a young person's business, but Daffron's gray hairs and long résumé, on behalf of mostly moderate Republicans, give him a perspective that some of the younger and more fiery partisans lack. "There are such horrendous ups and downs in a campaign," he confided. "You have to find a balance, or you'll get emotionally short-circuited." The previous Sunday, while he was at brunch, Dole had called him on his cell phone with nine questions. He didn't know Dole before he signed on to manage her campaign, and he assumed that Bob Dole's campaign associates had recommended him. When he met with Dole, she had done her own due process, calling three of the politicians he had the longest history with: Senator Fred Thompson of Tennessee, Senator Collins of Maine, and Defense Secretary William Cohen. "She wanted to know was that sixteen and a half or seventeen years with Cohen?" Daffron jokes. "I told her that was in the ballpark."

Dole is a perfectionist, hard on herself and hard on others. One Republican media consultant says, "I'd rather have my eyeballs ripped out than go to work for her." In the world of politics, tales of Dole's icy stares and backstage tirades regularly circulate throughout Washington, but Daffron insists she is "unfailingly gracious" in private, unlike other politicians he has dealt with. "One guy I worked for punched the walls," he says.

The lacquered exterior and scripted style that eased Elizabeth's climb to the top imprisoned her as a presidential candidate. She was like a character in the movie *Pleasantville*, a spoof on the 1950s obsession with manicured lawns and neat lives. No words left her lips that weren't calculated. There was no sense of daring, spontaneity, and imagination, qualities voters seek in an inspirational leader. "If she had lurking within her the soul of Jeane Kirkpatrick, she'd be a great candidate," mused David Keene of the American Conservative Union Former ambassador to the UN Kirkpatrick, a former Democrat turned hawkish Republican, never worried about who she might offend with her views. Dole was too polite. Her demeanor seemed more like that of the hostess of a garden party than a candidate scrapping for position.

In the early spring of 1999, NATO air raids against targets in the Serbian province of Kosovo presented Dole with an opportunity to showcase her humanitarian skills against a backdrop of a foreign policy crisis. The bombing resulted in a massive exodus of ethnic Albanian refugees fleeing from atrocities inflicted by the Serbs, and from NATO's bombs. Dole yearned to visit the makeshift camps set up by relief groups working with the North Atlantic Treaty Organization (NATO). But she worried that such a visit would be seen as a publicity stunt. "You are the former head of the largest humanitarian organization in the world," aides assured her. "You have credibility in the same way that John McCain has credibility." McCain, a former prisoner of war in Vietnam, had postponed his presidential announcement in deference to the war. He was getting lots of face time on television to press his view that only a full-scale ground invasion of Kosovo could successfully end the conflict. The media declared him the winner of the "Kosovo primary," though he lagged far behind Dole (and Bush) in the polls.

Several weeks into the crisis, Dole managed to coax an invitation from a refugee organization to inspect a camp in Macedonia. The visit produced a riveting image of Dole in her khaki pants being interviewed by satellite while holding a child's hand. The reason she was so good, observed an aide, is that she forgot for a minute she was Elizabeth Dole, and she got involved in the lives of the people in the camp.

No one assailed her for seeking publicity. After she returned from Kosovo, Daffron marveled that every woman he talked to volunteered the opinion that Dole's hair was much better, sleeker, and more flattering. She had toned down her steely coiffure, and people whose opinion she valued liked her new look. "It's not good and it's not bad—it's a fact," he shrugs. "Appearance does matter with female candidates."

That sealed it for Elizabeth. The helmet vanished. Her hair was more relaxed, even if she wasn't.

The image of Elizabeth Dole as "tighter than a nuclear submarine," in one aide's words, had taken hold in the media and in the popular culture. Daffron argued valiantly that no candidate ever got in trouble for being overprepared. "Ad-libs get you milk and smoking," he said, recalling Bob Dole's tortured insistence during the 1996 campaign that tobacco is safer than drinking milk.

Cartoonist Garry Trudeau lampooned Elizabeth Dole in his "Doonesbury" strip as a Stepford-like personality who spouts sound bites on command, never varying so much as a semicolon. Her fictional handlers despair that even her ad-libs seem rehearsed. Scanning one of the first strips in the series, Daffron shakes his head with bemusement. "I never can figure out whether these things are good or bad," he says, "At least somebody's paying attention." Dole's communications director, Ari Fleischer, wondered why men are called "disciplined" and "on message" while women are "scripted." He chided reporters about a double standard in the way they covered Dole.

Pollster Linda DiVall told the *Wall Street Journal* that she warned Dole early on that the media and campaign rivals would question her temperament and, by extension, her suitability for office. Voters think women candidates have greater honesty, integrity, and trust than their male counterparts. But Dole would have to cope with "outrageously sexist" talk that she is too tightly wound to be president, DiVall concluded.

Journalists noted that Dole required aides to count the number of steps to a podium, and that silver gaffer's tape marked the spot where she was to stop to take a "spontaneous" question after announcing her resignation as president of the Red Cross. Women journalists were among Dole's severest critics: *New York Times* columnist Maureen Dowd, who won a Pulitzer for her commentary about the Lewinsky scandal and President Clinton's inadequacies as a leader, contemplated in a March 31, 1999, column how "even more scary" it would be to have Elizabeth Dole in the Oval Office running the war. "It's hard to imagine the woman who likes to coordinate the color of her shoes with the color of the rug on the stage where she gives a speech, dealing with any crisis that involved a lot of *variables*, a lot of unpredictable turns that she could not *control.*"

Asked how Dole handled the drumbeat of criticism, a confidante says, "A lot of that she writes off as sexist crap."

Reporters don't warm to Dole the way they did to her husband with his wry asides. She's too programmed. Every anecdote, every story, every self-revelation has been said before, and judged safe to repeat. It's all there, indexed and cross-referenced. She is a walking Lexis-Nexis search. She doesn't engage in the kind of off-the-record banter that gives reporters the illusion they are glimpsing the person behind the sound bite. The choreography was acceptable when she was the candidate's spouse, and winning points for a supporting role that far outshone her husband's public persona. "Wow, gold medal performance, why isn't she on the ticket?" NBC anchor Tom Brokaw enthused when Dole ventured into the audience, during the 1996 Republican National Convention, with a stirring tribute to her husband, the party's standard bearer. The groundswell for Elizabeth as a candidate was so powerful that the Dole campaign tested Elizabeth in focus groups as his vice presidential running mate. The voters didn't buy the idea.

Once she was the candidate, Dole found the media a much harsher filter. On a February 1999 trip to New Hampshire, a National Public Radio reporter noted that the press was kept so far away, they couldn't see her facial expressions. Aides thought she might get a fairer shake from reporters if they knew her better. She had never done anything to personally ingratiate herself with individual reporters, but she made a stab at it in the early spring of 1999. An aide dubbed it "Operation Cold Call." Dole phoned a handful of reporters out of the blue to invite their questions. Most were so startled that they got little that was newsworthy from the conversation, other than the fact that it occurred. The outreach effort rapidly lost momentum when Dole did not slip comfortably into the role of telemarketer for herself.

By summer 1999, Dole had lost much of her early luster. She was a distant number two in national polls to Bush, whose "compassionate conservatism" and Clintonesque charm captivated the media. McCain had drawn even with her in New Hampshire. The rest of the Republican field languished far back in single digits. Yet Dole still had enviable resources: almost universal name recognition and an approval rating in the seventies. She consistently drew big crowds, with women the majority of the well-wishers. Linda DiVall was heartened when David Yepsen, political editor for the *Des Moines Register*, told her, "I don't know who these women are." That meant they weren't the party activists who turn out every four years. To win, Dole needed to expand the pool of voters to suburban women and independents who had rejected the Republican party in recent years because of its preoccupation with hard-right conservative social issues. The excitement around Dole's candidacy was real, but nobody could say for sure that it would turn into votes.

In June 1999, Dole appeared on Rosie O'Donnell's show, a popular daytime talk show geared to stay-at-home women. She brought her mother's recipe for pecan cookies. Then the two women talked about their shared interest in gun control. Fox News commentators Fred Barnes and Mort Kondracke (the "Beltway Boys") snickered at Dole's performance, as if to say that girl talk has no place in the man's game of politics.

Dole did better in the second quarter of 1999, mustering $2.8 million in contributions, just ahead of McCain, who raised $2.5 million. Bush was many millions ahead, but Dole was still fighting for a sliver of the electorate. Two key tests loomed: an August straw poll in Iowa, followed by the third-quarter fund-raising report, which would show whether Dole could sustain even a modest campaign. The initial soundings in Iowa were disheartening. Dole was losing eight to one. Aides prepared three scenarios. A poor showing was dubbed "life support," and would have forced her departure from the race. A middling performance was called "waiting for a mishap," meaning she could continue with minimum resources and be available in the event Bush stumbled. The best outcome was "overdrive," which Dole achieved with a surprise third-place showing. Bush and publisher Steve Forbes captured the first and second spots, but they had spent substantially more money than Dole.

Dole pulled out her surprise finish by targeting women voters. She benefited from the turnout of her Tri Delta sorority sisters, but she also courted other sororities, women-owned businesses, and high school girls excited about the prospect of a female president. Those who turned eighteen by November 2000 could participate in the straw poll. Two-thirds of her votes came from women, many of whom had never before participated in politics.

Dole was ambivalent about a race where she touted herself as a symbol. She had always played in a male world, and reached out to women as her prime constituency only as a last resort. "We're still interested in getting men's votes, but you go to the areas of highest probability," said Daffron, likening the effort to former president Jimmy Carter capitalizing on the excitement among southerners over his candidacy. "That's her base," said another aide. "To not target women would be like having Jesse Jackson stay out of black churches."

The gamble paid off, and Dole had a brief second wind as a candidate. Around the same time, she modernized her appearance, wearing simpler blouses and suits, and discarding what one observer called her "First Lady look—from the Nixon administration." She looked as if she was ready to fulfill the early promise of her candidacy. But she needed a stronger calling card than "I'm your sorority sister." She delivered what aides billed as a major speech on education in which she stressed discipline and unnerved First Amendment protectors with her advocacy of school-locker searches. Aides promised a series of policy speeches, but they never materialized. A *Washington Post* story on August 17, 1999, described Dole's stump speech as "a verbal version of skipping stones across a New Hampshire pond." She didn't stick with any subject long enough to make an impact, and the impression took hold that on issues, she was lighter than air. This was an extraordinary turnabout for Dole, a person who had always done her homework, and prided herself on being prepared. Charles Cook, a respected political analyst, recalled that at one of Dole's speeches, he and several female reporters stood in the back of the room making faces at each other to share their dismay at her lack of substance.

Dole compounded the problem with her attitude toward the press, parceling out her time in tiny increments and having an aide abruptly end press conferences at the first sign of a troublesome question. "A female candidate who avoids questions might as well be saying, 'Hit me for not being substantive,'" said Cook.

Bush wasn't any more accessible than Dole, but he won praise for being disciplined, and having a controlled message. One reporter whom he respected offered Daffron some advice. He said all reporters are not the same, and Dole should pick out a few she respects and deal with them more candidly. Everybody makes mistakes, he added. The message was clear. Fear of making mistakes is a greater impediment in a political campaign than the mishaps themselves. But a sixty-three-year-old woman does not change overnight.

Elizabeth Dole is a woman who has never failed at anything. She comes from a performance-oriented environment where she was always expected to do her best. Her childhood and young adulthood were a steady march of achievement, from president of the bird club in third grade to Phi Beta Kappa, student-body president, and May Queen at Duke University. She learned early how to steer the tricky terrain between beauty and brains by excelling in both, and then packaging the combustible combination in a sticky sweet exterior of southern charm.

The summer after she graduated from Duke in 1959, she was in eight weddings, always as a bridesmaid, never—"by choice," she emphasizes—as a bride. "I don't know why I listened to the beat of a different drummer," she says. "But I'd never lived in another part of the country. I felt like I wanted to broaden my horizons. I really wanted to go to graduate school. I wanted to work. I wanted to do this, do that. And why? I don't know. I can hear my mother now saying, 'I hope you'll live next door.' And when I told my parents I'd like to go to law school, my mother's words were, 'Don't you want to be a wife, a mother, and a hostess for your husband?'"

Dole's mother had given up a promising career in music to marry and move to tiny Salisbury, North Carolina, and she expected no less from her daughter. Academic degrees were fine, but at some point they should be set aside to embrace a more conventional life of marriage and children. Elizabeth Hanford earned a master's degree in education from Harvard, and then went on to attend Harvard Law School, where she was one of only 24 women in a class of 550. Elizabeth was a Democrat then, and like so many young people of her generation, she looked upon government service as an honorable calling. It was a special time. The country had been inspired by the leadership of President Kennedy, and devastated by his assassination. Vietnam had not yet taken its awful toll.

Beginning from a junior position at the Department of Health, Education and Welfare, Elizabeth Hanford built a career focused on consumer advocacy. When Democratic president Lyndon Johnson, beset by poor health and a war gone sour, declined to run for a second term, and the Democrats lost the White House to Republican Richard Nixon, Elizabeth could have been a casualty herself. But she so impressed her new bosses that she was made deputy director of the White House Office of Consumer Affairs under the legendary Virginia Knauer, a Republican consumer activist who served three Presidents. One of Dole's accomplishments was helping persuade supermarkets to date products for freshness. She was later named to the Federal Trade Commission, where, as the only woman on a panel of five, she pressed for enforcement of the Equal Credit Opportunity

Act. Divorced or widowed women were often denied credit because their assets had been in their husband's name.

A prodigious appetite for work left little time for socializing. Elizabeth was thirty-nine years old in 1975 when, after a three-year courtship, she married Bob Dole, a divorced senator from Kansas. When Dole was named Gerald Ford's running mate a year later, Elizabeth took a leave from the FTC. In 1980, she resigned the post when Dole announced his bid for the presidency. When he dropped out, she turned her energy toward electing Ronald Reagan. He rewarded her with a job on his White House staff, and later named her secretary of transportation. She focused on safety issues and is credited with pushing through both air bags and the third brake light that is now mandatory on all new cars. Her zeal was remarkable. She once stood in the parking lot with a bright red "Stop" sign while checking to see that employees wore their seat belts.

It was during this period that she was dubbed "Sugar Lips" for her apparent ability to talk members of Congress into doing what she wanted. Former Representative Tillie Fowler of Florida, a close friend since they served together on Knauer's staff, says, "An adoring smile and a southern accent make it easier to do what you need to do. Even though she believes in many of the same things that feminists do, she's a softer person."

Dole is an attentive godmother to the younger of Fowler's two daughters, and if she has regrets over not having had children of her own, she has not shared them publicly. Her attitude in interviews is that she recognized that because she was older when she married, if motherhood happened, it would be fine, but she wasn't going to indulge in any of the Herculean efforts to reproduce so popular among women today.

Many profiles of Dole feel compelled to point out that she is "childless," an adjective that, when applied to a woman, sounds pejorative. A long Sunday piece on April 11, 1999, by the *Washington Post's* Ceci Connolly ended with this paragraph: "And after a detailed recitation of a résumé that includes two Cabinet posts, a seat on the Federal Trade Commission and the Red Cross, the childless Dole made this observation: I think the most important career a woman can have is that of a mother raising fine young future citizens.' " Fairly or unfairly, the remark invited the observation made by the reporter. Still, a Dole adviser took umbrage. "Would they say that about a male candidate? I don't think so," she said. Conservative commentator Patrick Buchanan also happens to be childless, though that is rarely mentioned when he offers his paeans to the traditional family unit. "Do they ask him: Did he try to have children?" the aide asks, ending with an exasperated, "Puh-leeze!" Some months later, when another profile points out that Dole married late and had no children, campaign spokesman Ari Fleischer observed that Ohio congressman John Kasich, another Republican exploring a possible presidential run, also married late and had no children, yet those facts didn't seem especially pertinent to his candidacy. (Kasich subsequently dropped out of the race, and learned soon after that his wife was expecting twins.)

To have or have not is tricky when it comes to female politicians and children. Women candidates with young children risk the charge that they are abandoning their family to indulge their own selfish needs. Adolescent children need less hands-on attention but are riskier bets when it comes to politically correct behavior. Divorced women have their own baggage, and single women face the inevitable whispers that they are lesbians. The wry belief among those who track women and politics is that a widow makes the best candidate: She's proved she can get a man, but he's not around to create problems. The fewer encumbrances the better.

Maybe because Dole has not had to juggle the raising of children with her career, she has had more opportunity to indulge her perfectionist tendencies. The media seem most uneasy with this aspect of her personality. "Sure, it's sexist," says a television talk-show producer. "We don't talk about how long Trent Lott spends on his hair." The Republican Senate leader has a striking black pompadour with every hair in place. A former cheerleader in college, the Mississippi-born Lott is a renowned perfectionist. His wife told the *Washington Post* that he keeps his socks so neat and color-coded that he can reach in the drawer at four in the morning and without turning on a light immediately find the pair he wants.

In a talk with Dole near the end of her tenure at the Red Cross, she relaxed once the tape recorder clicked off, signaling the end of the interview. Asked why more women aren't running for high office, she said, "A lot of women think power is almost a dirty word. I'd like to get them to see it depends on what you use power for. You can use it to do good things. You can't get anything done if you don't have a place at the table." Because the interview had technically concluded, we agreed to run these rather harmless quotes by Dole's press secretary to get permission to quote her. Days later, a fax arrived from

Dole's office with a version that scrubbed every bit of spontaneity from her words, and that any self-respecting journalist would find unusable. Read for yourself:

> At the grassroots level many women learn valuable skills of leadership and develop a sense of mission, dedication, and commitment to good government. It's interesting to note that some of the women who've risen through the ranks with this dedication to good government have viewed the achievement of power with mixed emotions and sometimes even with distaste. Some believe that concepts such as power and ambition are inconsistent with the mission guiding their steps and their conscience. Over the years, though, women have more and more come to realize power is a positive force if it is used for positive purposes. They've come to realize that they cannot have an impact on the issues they care about unless they have a place at the policy table, direct public attention to their cause, and get out and raise the necessary money.

Dole calls herself a "recovering perfectionist," meaning she is trying to wean herself from her need to do everything at 100 percent. By her own admission, she's homing in at 98 percent, not exactly loosey-goosey. She was devastated, for example, when she spoke at a New York luncheon in April 1999 organized by the *Ladies' Home Journal* and was coolly received by the audience of mostly young professionals. "I had this opportunity and I'm a dismal failure," she said afterward, her dejection deepened by the knowledge that several prominent New York columnists were there for a first look at her campaign style. Her mood brightened when CNN's "Inside Politics" praised her speech, declaring she had come "out of the closet" as a feminist. An aide assured her the audience was not typical. "These were Upper East Side Democrats wearing black," he said. A survey of Dole versus the Democratic front-runner, Al Gore, had Dole winning in three quadrants of the country while getting tromped in the East by twelve points. "She provokes a visceral negative reaction in the East," said an aide. "It's a Goody Two-Shoes, Miss Perfect image that they get sore about."

The skepticism tended to be generational as well as geographical. Younger people saw Dole as belonging to a different decade, and they either couldn't or didn't want to relate to her struggle to make it as a professional. She aligned herself with the women's movement of the early 1970s, declaring, "Although I predate the revolution, I was deeply involved in living it." Her mother wanted her to marry and live nearby, but she chose to attend law school, where patronizing professors didn't think women belonged. Her stories of what it was like back then elicited little response or warmth from the twenty- and thirty-somethings who compete equally with men in law school and almost everywhere else, and who don't want to acknowledge a debt to an earlier generation. "She cut the path, but younger women look out and see a freeway," said a Dole aide.

Republican women under fifty and independents, voters whose support she needed, did not warm to her immediately. "St. John's Steel" is how one professional woman in her early forties described Dole, who favors the famed designer's knit suits. A neighbor of the Doles' in the Watergate complex in downtown Washington recalls seeing a rack of St. John's knits in assorted colors from banana to pistachio wheeled to the Doles' apartment to clothe Elizabeth for the 1996 campaign. Tight-fitting and tailored, they convey an image that is rich, Republican, and matronly to a boisterous political world that is populist, independent, and skewed to younger and more diverse demographics.

Worrisome signs of bio-fatigue showed up in the Dole camp's polling data, and not only among young people. Dole risked looking outdated when she recounted her thirty-year battle for equality. Voters wanted to know what she would do for them in the future. Just as Bob Dole relied too much on World War II to define him as a candidate, Elizabeth Dole couldn't expect women to flock to her on the basis of gender solidarity. Yet her campaign was primarily defined by gender, because at this stage in the nation's history, a woman running for president is notable. If Dole had made it to New Hampshire, she would have been the first woman to appear on the ballot in the presidential primaries for one of the two major parties since 1972, when Shirley Chisholm, an African-American congresswoman from Brooklyn, New York, ran for the Democratic nomination. Her vote never exceeded 7 percent in the twelve primaries she entered but her powerful voice and spirit echo through history far more than the legions of white men who have come and gone as candidates. She said of her two handicaps, being female put more obstacles in her path than being black.

In the twenty-eight years since Chisholm ran for president, women have become more commonplace in all fields. Yet gender is the most obvious characteristic that set Dole apart in the Republican field, and she tried to use it to her advantage, just as McCain promoted his singular status as a war hero against rivals who avoided active military service. When does she stop being a woman candidate for president and become just a candidate? Daffron mused at one point. "When did JFK stop being a Catholic? When he became president, people forgot about it. We're hoping for a certain consideration from women. A lot of women have not been in the process. Look at the finance committee of a candidate. There's no women, or one token woman. The professions of law, business, and medicine are more balanced than politics. She wants to bring more women into the Republican party."

Dole's aides were under no illusion. George W. Bush, increasingly known only as "W," was so far ahead that it would take more than a minor gaffe or two to dislodge him from his presumptive status as the Republican nominee. If at the time of the convention in July, polls show that Elizabeth Dole as a running mate could move five or six points in a national race, and it's a close race, she could end up on the ticket. "But if George W. is way ahead and doesn't need her, I can tell you there aren't any factions in Austin clamoring for her," says a senior aide. Practical politics would in the end triumph.

The fading historical significance of Dole's candidacy was underscored to Daffron when Hillary Rodham Clinton announced she would form an exploratory committee for a Senate run in New York. Political strategists struggled to assess what a Hillary candidacy would mean for New York, for the presidential race, and for the overly analyzed Clinton marriage. "Someone even suggested to me that there'd be less interest in a woman running for president now that Hillary's running for the Senate in New York," said Daffron. "That's ridiculous. There are nine women in the Senate. It's not necessarily novel except she's a First Lady." Hillary Clinton had upstaged her lame duck husband much the way Elizabeth Dole had seized the initiative in her husband's losing campaign in 1996. Now they would compete against each other for a place in the history books.

On a long flight back to Washington, D.C., from Seattle, Elizabeth Dole concluded that she couldn't stay in a fight she had no chance of winning. Fund-raising was not going well, and the persistent buzz that she wouldn't stay the course had prompted a huge drying up of campaign funds. Dole wasn't the kind of candidate who could live off the land, bunk with supporters, pick her spots, and wage a guerrilla operation. At a press conference stacked with supporters in a downtown Washington hotel on October 20, 1999, Elizabeth Dole withdrew her candidacy before she had ever formally declared it. She focused on the financial disadvantage that she had, suggesting it was prohibitive. She had attended over 70 fund-raising events, and another 108 fund-raisers were planned. The campaign had taken to auctioning off the floral centerpieces at these events for five dollars each in a desperate effort to generate cash. Yet however hard they worked, the results were underwhelming. Governor Bush and publisher Steve Forbes enjoyed an eighty-to-one cash advantage.

The media coverage pointed out that Dole appeared "chipper" and kept a smile on her face, while her husband seemed sobered by the occasion. Elizabeth turned to Bob for comment at one point, referring to him as "my precious husband." The endearment was like chalk on a blackboard to Dole's detractors, and underscored the cultural bias she had to overcome as a southern lady.

At a forum moderated by Kathleen Hall Jamieson, dean of the Annenberg School for Communication at the University of Pennsylvania, to discuss gender on the campaign trail, the media's preoccupation with Dole's clothing and style was discussed. Gwen Ifill, host of "Washington Week in Review" and a former *New York Times* reporter, defended reporters who routinely included what Dole was wearing in their stories. "We've never had a president before who wore a yellow suit," said Ifill. "It's legitimate to mention what is different about a candidate." But Ifill was stumped when Jamieson wondered why a *New York Times* piece on the occasion of Dole's withdrawal from the race mentioned that Dole's pollster, Linda DiVall, is unmarried and childless. "I am trying to think of another male pollster about whom that would be written," Jamieson said. "And what relevance does it have to her ability to poll? What was the underlying message of that—if there was one?" Without defending the commentary, Ifill guessed at what the reporter might have been trying to convey. "She wasn't in touch herself, so how could she know what Elizabeth Dole was lacking." What's unspoken is that if you're unmarried and childless and a woman, there is something wrong with you, said Jamieson.

Money wasn't Dole's only problem, or even her most significant difficulty. By reason of personality and temperament, she did not take advantage of the extraordinary resources that she had going into the race: name recognition, widespread respect, gold-plated credentials, and the historic novelty of being a woman going after the country's top job. "She so blew it," said Republican pollster Frank Luntz. "In politics you get one big wave—one tsunami, and there are no aftershocks. And she didn't ride hers. What she should have done is quit the Red Cross and forty-eight hours later announce a nationwide whistle-stop tour—and gone after the one constituency that is more frustrated than men in the Republican party: women. If she had 40 percent of the vote of women and no percent of men, she would have been there with 20 percent of the vote, and that would have guaranteed her second place on the ticket, at worst. What she did was too little, too late."

Dole made some progress in changing the landscape for women because her candidacy was taken seriously, and nobody asked her why she wasn't home baking cookies. She drew big crowds, and mothers brought their daughters to see her and get inspired. "It's almost as if you see some women sit up a little straighter because you are trying to empower them to understand that they can do it, they can really make a difference," she said at her press conference. On the practical side, she had some success in motivating new women voters, and getting them to give money. "Win, lose, or draw, she leaves with a network of women donors that other candidates are going to want," says Ari Fleischer, Dole's former communications chief who joined Bush's campaign and became White House press secretary. Yet Dole's premature exit left political activists with an empty feeling. How do you change attitudes if you never reach the starting line? Jamieson said she wished Dole had stayed in the race long enough to participate in the debates, "where she would have looked like she belonged."

Dole had never run, much less won, a competitive race before, and it showed. Her inability to capitalize on the few openings that came her way underscores the difference between politics and public service. The legendary Democratic Speaker of the House Sam Rayburn once counseled President Lyndon Johnson about becoming too enamored with the "best and the brightest" advisers of the Kennedy administration, saying, "I'd feel a whole lot better about them if just one of them had run for sheriff once."

Dole is the type that when she starts something, she finishes it. Withdrawing from the race was hard, but given the financial disparity between her and the front-runner, she had made a practical decision. She relied on herself all through her life to get ahead, but that isn't enough when you run for president. The Republican establishment had spurned her in favor of another moderate, Bush, and it hurt when she looked around for her friends and they weren't there. Dole understood the formalities of losing, and being gracious. She had been through it with her husband. And she knew if she hadn't tried this, she would always have wondered what could have been. "I'm a long way from the twilight," she said with a smile that seemed fiercely genuine.

When North Carolina Senator Jesse Helms announced his retirement in mid-2001, Dole didn't hesitate to throw her hat in the ring. Polls showed her well ahead of any Democratic rival, and Republicans cleared the field so she faced only token opposition in the primary. This time, money wouldn't be a problem. And, aides hoped, neither would her husband. "As long as I stay away, everything's OK," Bob Dole said in his familiar, wisecracking way. But there were early signs that some of the problems that plagued Dole in her presidential campaign remained. Conservative columnist Robert Novak in a February 2002 column reported home-state criticism about her obsession with details and how her Washington-run campaign was keeping her shielded from the press, and the people. Though she had adjusted her views and was more pro-gun and anti-abortion than she had been as a national candidate, she was no Jesse Helms, and was having difficulty energizing the conservative vote she would need to win.

Some North Carolina Republicans griped that she wasn't the hometown girl any more, having lived in an apartment at the Watergate in Washington for almost three decades, since her marriage to Bob Dole. Democrats couldn't with a straight face accuse her of being a carpetbagger, not since Hillary moved to New York to run for the Senate, having had no history in the state other than liking Manhattan. Most Democratic Party officials privately thought Dole couldn't be beat by her Democratic challenger, former Clinton chief of staff Erskine Bowles. A colorless technocrat with the demeanor of an accountant, Bowles had deep roots in North Carolina and was raising a lot of money. But his Clinton connection was an albatross.

Dole was the name brand, and if she didn't make a major mistake, victory would be hers. In an early stumble, she got caught in the back draft of the scandal over Enron, a major energy company that had gone bankrupt, leaving employees and shareholders with worthless stock while top executives managed to cash out with millions. The company's founder, Kenneth Lay, was George W. Bush's biggest financial backer, and the company had lavished campaign money on two-thirds of the Senate and half the House of Representatives, receiving in return what appeared to be little government oversight of its activities. Dole made it easy for Democrats to implicate her in the scandal when, after the terrorist attacks on September 11, she said she would suspend all campaign activities and then went ahead with a fund-raising lunch hosted by Lay at a hotel in Houston, where Enron was headquartered. Democrats jumped on the issue with a negative ad linking her to Enron, giving her the dubious distinction of being the first prominent politician targeted by a political ad in the Enron mess.

It is risky to run negative ads against a woman, and the Democrats' goal was more to rattle Dole than to do serious political damage.

How she handled attacks on her ethics was the test here. Could she roll with the punches? And did she have the stomach and the staying power for the race? The answer was yes. Dole won convincingly.

Talking about a woman on the ticket is one thing; picking a particular woman is another. Faults can be found with each of the prospects whose names have been put forth. The problem may not necessarily be that this woman or that woman does not measure up, but that the standard for any woman is too high. To get in the right frame of mind for this, consider the names of some recent choices for the second spot on various presidential tickets: Spiro T. Agnew, Richard Nixon's vice president, who was, in a word, corrupt; Dan Quayle, whose mention here requires no explanation; and, of course Ross Perot's first running mate, Vice Admiral James Stockdale, a Medal of Honor winner whose one appearance in a nationally televised debate will be remembered for his clumsy self-introduction, "Who am I? Why am I here?" No doubt, readers can think of other examples of less-than-perfect choices for the job.

That's the point. Nobody's perfect. And the women we spoke to for this book repeatedly told us that they—the women who make up more than half the electorate and vote in greater percentages than men—deserve the same opportunity to be less than perfect that has been afforded men since this country's beginning.

With that in mind, who besides Elizabeth Dole should have been on the short list in 2000?

The senator from Texas is wearing a purple suit. The high ceilings of her office in the stately old Russell Office Building make her seem more petite than she appears to be on television as she emerges from behind an expansive executive desk to greet an interviewer. The office is done in rich royal blue and sunny yellow, primary colors that are both bold and feminine. An array of candies and tiny cakes adorns the coffee table.

Nothing unusual so far. But then this: Kay Bailey Hutchison wants to run for president and she's not embarrassed to say so. Not right away, mind you, but down the road, when Hutchison will have been in the Senate for more than a decade and be ready to move up. An influential voice on the Armed Services Committee and a force for moderation on social issues like abortion, Hutchison thinks she has the right mix of positions and experience to be a credible presidential candidate. The fact that she's a woman, well, gender be damned! "If Benazir Bhutto can be elected prime minister [of Pakistan], I really think we are big enough to handle it. Good heavens, a Muslim country!" she says.

As surprising as Hutchison's ambition is her willingness to acknowledge it publicly. A woman who openly expresses presidential ambition invites, in order, astonishment, disbelief, and belittlement. "I'm saying a prayer for the Republic," says a Texas journalist who has followed Hutchison's career. Yet this analyst, like most, believes that the first woman president will come out of the Republican party. "The Democrats still have a Ferraro hangover," she says. "Democratic women look too wussy, too liberal."

With her honeyed hair teased into a Texas-sized frame around her fine features, Hutchison could be the model for the Senator Barbie doll. Her prettiness and what the Texas journalist called her "sweetsypoo demeanor" put off some people, but these ultrafeminine qualities have served her well in a state where good ol' boys hold sway. She was the first Republican woman elected to the state legislature and the first woman of either party to represent Texas in the U.S. Senate.

Texas governor Ann Richards saw Hutchison coming. Richards called President-elect Bill Clinton in Little Rock after the November 1992 election to warn him that if he appointed Texas Democrat Lloyd Bentsen as treasury secretary, the Democrats would lose Bentsen's Senate seat. "I can't hold it," she told Clinton. "You've got to know that I can't promise you that I'm going to give you a Democrat."

Hutchison was state treasurer at the time, having succeeded Richards in that post in 1990 when Richards became governor. "She knew before I made the decision to run that I was going to be the candidate to beat," says Hutchison. "She's just a wise old bird."

Hutchison is sometimes described as the Republican Richards. The comparison holds only in the sense that each woman used the treasurer's job as a springboard to higher office. Stylistically, the two are very different. Richards is a master of barbed humor. As governor, she wanted to be one of the boys. Hutchison is standoffish and demure. Yet she had greater success dealing with the male legislators than her Democratic counterpart. "She puts a velvet glove on, and they eat out of her hand," marvels the Texas journalist.

Feminist leader Gloria Steinem calls Hutchison a "female impersonator," a commentary on Hutchison's lukewarm support for reproductive rights. Yet Hutchison has come a long way from her hometown of LaMarque, Texas, where feminist notions were as exotic as Manhattan bagels. "If I had told my wonderful father, 'Daddy, I'd like to be a United States senator someday,' I know he would have patted me on the head and said, 'Kay, there are a lot of wonderful things you can do with your life, but that's probably not one of them.'" In fact, Hutchison's girlhood aspirations did not approach such heights. She told an interviewer that she went to law school "because I didn't find someone to marry while I was in college." She did marry while attending law school, but the brief union ended in divorce.

Hutchison entered politics through a side door. She graduated from law school in 1967, a time when few law firms hired women. After knocking on doors for a couple of months with no success, she was uncharacteristically dispirited. On a whim, she stopped by a Houston television station to inquire about a job as a reporter. "I've never had a lawyer apply and I'm sort of intrigued," the news director said. A couple of weeks later, he offered her a job covering the Texas legislature.

Hutchison had majored in government at the University of Texas, but the legislative antics she witnessed bore little resemblance to her civics lessons. For the most part, the elected representatives she covered did not impress her. Like many reporters on legislative beats before and since, she thought she could do at least as good a job, probably better.

That notion was only a pipe dream until she met Anne Armstrong, the newly elected co-chair of the Republican National Committee. Hutchison interviewed her for the local news and discovered the elegant, designer-dressed Armstrong could also turn a phrase. This time, Hutchison was impressed. So was Armstrong, who the next day recruited Hutchison to come to Washington as her press secretary.

Suddenly steeped in Republican politics, Hutchison saw the potential for a newcomer like herself. Six months later, she was back in Texas running for the legislature. It was 1972, a good year for Republicans with Richard Nixon's landslide win over Democrat George McGovern. Hutchison won. The four other women in the legislature were Democrats, including Sarah Weddington, who would gain fame as the attorney who successfully argued the groundbreaking *Roe v. Wade* abortion-rights case before the Supreme Court.

Hutchison found common cause with the Democratic women in a legislature controlled by Democrats, authoring a bill that made it harder to introduce a rape victim's sexual history as evidence in a trial. After two terms in the legislature, Hutchison was tapped by President Gerald Ford to be vice chair of the National Transportation Safety Board (NTSB). She moved to Washington. Her old boss, Anne Armstrong, would be one of four finalists as Ford's vice president in the 1976 election. The affable Ford, who had pardoned Richard Nixon in

1974 after becoming president, was thirty-three points behind his Democratic challenger, Jimmy Carter, in the first poll taken after the Democratic convention, and he needed to do something dramatic to change the dynamic. Putting Armstrong, a quick-minded Texas rancher, on the ticket could give Ford, a drab midwesterner, just the boost he needed. Ford was ultimately dissuaded by polling data which showed that resistance to a woman among core Republican voters would offset any benefits gained from selecting Armstrong. Ford settled on Kansas senator Bob Dole, but later wrote in his memoirs, "In retrospect, if given the opportunity to make that decision again, I might well have said, 'Damn the torpedoes,' and gambled on Anne."

Once Ford lost the election, Hutchison returned to Texas, where she married her current husband, Ray Hutchison, a Dallas bond lawyer, and started a new life as a businesswoman. The failing candy company that she bought and revived earned a mention years later in *The Book of Political Lists*, published by *George* magazine, among members of Congress who had had unusual occupations before they were elected. The former owner of McCraw Candies is listed with Ohio Democrat John Glenn, astronaut, and Colorado Republican Ben Nighthorse Campbell, horse trainer and jewelry designer.

Kay Bailey's marriage was a merger of political forces. She had met Ray Hutchison when they served together in the legislature. Charming, ambitious, and outgoing, he seemed slated for big things. But when his bid for governor was unsuccessful, he dropped out of elective politics. He recognized that his political career was over while his wife's was just beginning, and he relished the role of her adviser and manager. "Her husband is her brains," says the Texas journalist. "They have a close partnership and both get what they want out of it." In 1982, an anonymous flyer suggested that Kay Bailey was responsible for wrecking her husband's first marriage. The flyer was circulated as she attempted to reenter politics by running in a Republican primary for a congressional seat. She lost the race.

Another opportunity would not come for nearly a decade. In 1990, Hutchison jumped into the contest for state treasurer to succeed Democrat Ann Richards, who was running for governor. At the time, voters had never elected a Republican for any statewide job below governor, except railroad commissioner. The GOP had no statewide officeholders, and the Republican candidate for governor, Clayton Williams, was widely seen as a buffoon. Without his coattails, Republicans were given little chance of winning. Hutchison's victory was so unexpected that Alan Greenspan, the Federal Reserve Board chairman and a friend, called her the next morning to say he was sorry she had lost. "I won," she said. "You really won?" he sputtered.

Two years later, Hutchison proved the victory had been no fluke. She got 67 percent of the vote—a record for Republicans at the time—to win the special election over Bob Krueger, the Democratic congressman appointed by Richards to fill the seat vacated by Bentsen. Her victory confirmed Richards' warning to Clinton.

Hutchison's political honeymoon was short. District Attorney Ronnie Earle, a Democrat, produced evidence that, as state treasurer, Hutchison had used state employees to perform personal and political chores. A Texas grand jury indicted the new senator on five counts of records tampering and misuse of public office. Hutchison spurned a proposed plea bargain—her Senate seat for her freedom—and maintained, instead, that she would be vindicated by a fair trial. A judge eventually dismissed the charges against her. "They thought the lady would crack," Hutchison said triumphantly.

Although Hutchison portrayed herself as the victim of a Democratic vendetta, her primary accusers were Republicans who worked for her, including Sharon Ammann, the daughter of former GOP governor John Connally, who alleged that Hutchison beat her with a notebook when she failed to produce a phone number quickly enough. Hutchison voluntarily took a lie detector test to refute the charge.

After her dismissal, Hutchison dared the prosecutor to make public the evidence he had gathered against her, evidence she had fought to keep out of court because it was obtained illegally without a search warrant. The high-risk maneuver worked to her benefit. Although the materials showed political activity went on during business hours, and that Hutchison knew about it, her willingness to come clean dwarfed the indiscretions. When Hutchison faced the voters in November 1994, this time for a full six-year term, she won with 61 percent of the vote.

Hutchison did not want her name floated as a possible vice presidential contender in 1996. One reason was that she feared the national media might reopen the investigation. But she leapt at the chance to give a major speech at the 1996 Republican convention in San Diego. The Republican nominee, Bob Dole, eager to present the GOP as diverse and inclusive, approved making the convention's opening night "ladies night." Hutchison joined the keynoter, Representative Susan Molinari of New York, and Governor Christine Todd Whitman, from New Jersey, for prime-time appearances.

Hutchison's convention speech was the kind that politicians call "red meat." The Christian Coalition had tried to block Hutchison from joining the Texas delegation because of her wishy-washy position on abortion, so she may have felt she had something to prove to the party's right-wing foot soldiers. After a video showed President Clinton engaging in a mock debate with himself, Hutchison went after the president in a blistering tirade. An abbreviated sample: "America, it's time to wake up to President Clinton and his high-taxing, free-spending, promise-breaking . . . drug-coddling, power-grabbing, business-busting . . . FBI-abusing . . . overregulating . . . class-baiting . . . values-crushing, truth-dodging, Medicare-forsaking . . . job-destroying friends."

The hard-core Republicans in the convention hall hooted and hollered their approval. But the speech bombed with a group of mainstream voters wired by a pollster working for one of the TV networks to get instant reaction. Newspaper editorials in the next few days would scold Hutchison for being mean-spirited. "We must admit to being more than a little disappointed in Senator Hutchison's transformation into a Republican attack dog," said the *Lufkin* (Texas) *Daily News*. "One of the things we have always admired about Senator Hutchison is her ability to work on both sides of the aisle, to keep above the politics. . . ."

Hearing the reaction, Hutchison was furious that she'd been set up. The party had sent out a woman to do the dirty work while the men hid behind her skirt. And the party hadn't even tried to "spin" the speech as a success. "I want you to go out and tell every reporter that you see what a great speech it was," she ordered one startled consultant. Angry that she had gotten bad advice, she collared a mid-level party operative and demanded to know why a speech tailored for partisans had been broadcast to a wider audience in the first place.

Nobody made Hutchison deliver the speech. Indeed, she was eager for the prime-time exposure. What triggered her fury was the tin ear her party had shown in crafting the speech for her, and then assuming, because she was a woman, she could smile her way through the harsh rhetoric. She had misread the moment, and all she could think to do was blame the experts.

That Hutchison is hard on the people around her is true, yet it's hardly disqualifying and certainly better than being regarded as a pushover. The boys who dominate the political culture in Washington mock her perfectionism. A Republican consultant jokes that when he was invited to her home for dinner, "I had to put on rubber gloves and agree not to get within five feet of the walls." Hutchison gets it from women too. A Republican colleague in the House says if Hutchison ran for higher office, she would be "vulnerable to the charge of overemotionalism."

But if Hutchison is deterred by such criticism, she doesn't show it. She confers regularly with Republican party elders and consultants for tips on broadening her portfolio and positioning herself for a nationwide run. After the 9/11 attacks, she took a prominent role in advocating tighter airport security, including pushing for a federalized security screening force, something which many Republicans abhorred. She has taken a lead on military issues from combat readiness to sexual harassment, and serves on the Defense Subcommittee of the Appropriations Committee. On issues of particular interest to women, she has championed homemaker IRAs and joined with Democratic women senators to increase breast cancer funding and improve mammography standards. She also sponsored antistalking legislation that makes it a federal crime to harass people across state lines. Hutchison has experienced stalking firsthand. A man broke into her campaign office in 1971, stabbing a poster of her with an ice pick. He has pursued her periodically for more than twenty-five years. "Women bring issues forward that men don't disagree with, but they just never put them out front," she says.

As the senior Republican woman in the Senate, Hutchison also serves as an informal den mother for her less-seasoned colleagues. One thorny issue she had to confront: what to do about the straying hands of the senior senator from South Carolina, Strom Thurmond, a well-known ladies' man whose advancing years may have slowed but have not deterred his amorous advances. A woman new to the Senate complained to Hutchison that when she passed Thurmond's desk on her way to vote, he invariably groped her. Hutchison convinced her colleague not to lodge a formal protest largely out of deference to Thurmond's age (ninety-nine on December 5, 2001). Hutchison devised a circuitous route to the well of the Senate that allows her female colleagues to avoid Thurmond.

Hutchison's national ambition is best illustrated by her campaign war chest. As of January 2002, Hutchison had $4.7 million in campaign cash on hand. After winning reelection with 65 percent of the vote in 2000, she said she planned to "start looking at the lay of the land [for a presidential run]. I think I have every capability to run on my own."

"She talked to me," says Lynn Martin. "I said, 'By God, if you want it, you've got to go do it.'"

Hutchison was a good prospect for the vice presidential spot on the GOP ticket in 2000, but not as George W. Bush's running mate. The Constitution prohibits candidates from the same state running together. But Bush's candidacy raised another prospect for Hutchison—a bid to replace him as governor. Hutchison was already being talked about as a prospect for governor whether or not Bush won the presidency. Hutchison did nothing to dampen speculation when she said that she'd rather be governor than senator. "If you said to me, you can, in an open field with no other issues, run for governor or run for senator, I'd rather be governor," she told the *Dallas Morning News.* "But it's not an open field and it's not a decision that would be made in a vacuum."

In March 2001, with Bush in the White House and a newly designated Republican in the statehouse in Texas, Hutchison announced that she would stay put, and not run for governor. She didn't say so publicly at the time, but her life had taken a dramatic turn with the decision to become a parent. In August 2001, Hutchison, fifty-eight, and her sixty-eight-year-old husband, Ray, announced they were adopting a seven-month-old daughter. The congratulatory notices were still coming in when the couple revealed they were also adopting an infant boy. Hutchison's spokeswoman said the Hutchison home was beginning to look like "Romper Room." Hutchison's detour into motherhood may alter her priorities, at least for now. But she remains a prime prospect for a Republican ticket.

On the Democratic side, California Sen. Dianne Feinstein is a Quadrennial favorite.

The morning after the 1994 election, Republican senator John Chafee of Rhode Island had a list of congratulatory calls he wanted to make. Feinstein was at the top of the list. "He couldn't wait to call her," says Josie Martin, then Chafee's press secretary. "I told him it was too early in California, so he waited until noon."

A courtly but tough-minded New Englander, Chafee was dean of the dwindling band of moderate Republicans in the Senate. Chafee got to know Feinstein during the Clinton health care debate, and he really liked and respected her. When he strayed from GOP orthodoxy, he found Feinstein a willing ally in fashioning a centrist approach to issues. He was eager to congratulate her for her narrow victory over conservative Republican Michael Huffington, who had spent $30 million of his own money in a sharply negative campaign to defeat her.

Feinstein picked up the phone herself, which both startled and pleased Chafee. "I had to go through five people to get to [Senator] Jim Jeffords in Vermont," he told her. "And there are barely five people in the state of Vermont." Feinstein was delighted to hear from Chafee, and told him he was the only Republican to call and congratulate her. "Can you imagine that?" Chafee exclaimed in a disbelieving tone as he hung up the phone. "Well, Senator, we did run a Republican against her," his press secretary gently reminded him.

Feinstein tops everybody's list as the woman with the best combination of experience and temperament to secure a spot on the Democratic presidential ticket. A former mayor of San Francisco, now a senator from California, she has impressed people for a long time with her sense of command and her cool media presence. Yet in 1983, when *Ladies' Home Journal* touted her as a hot prospect for the 1984 Democratic ticket, Feinstein found the notion preposterous. "I'm on my third marriage," she exclaimed. "This job is hell on my private life. My husband, Dick Blum, is a most patient man. President? Me? I'm not ambitious for higher office. I've got to survive as mayor."

Does she still agree with that sentiment fifteen years later? "Yes, absolutely," she says. "You know, people have always attributed some sort of ambition to me that I really don't possess. I have finished every job I've started—always."

In early 1998, California Democrats wanted Feinstein to run for governor. She said no. She wasn't ready to leave the Senate after only five and a half years. But her reasons were more complicated. She had run for governor, unsuccessfully, in 1990, and though she clearly coveted the job, she wasn't prepared to go through what it takes to get there. Polls showed she was the Democrats' most formidable candidate. Yet not even President Clinton in a highly publicized phone call could convince her to enter the race. She realized that if hearing from any one person would push her over the brink, it would be the president. When she remained ambivalent after her conversation with Clinton, she knew she really didn't want to run. She had barely survived Huffington's challenge four years earlier, and the idea of facing another self-financed millionaire, this time former Northwest Airlines chairman Al Checchi, a Democrat, made her stomach churn. She announced her decision in a telephone news conference, citing the "very debilitating campaign environment."

The fact that she and Checchi were in the same party offered no guarantee of civility. A Democratic primary could be vicious, as she discovered in 1990. Democrat Gray Davis, who was behind in the polls, tried to jump-start his campaign with a negative ad that portrayed Feinstein behind bars as a Leona Helmsley look-alike, equating convicted tax cheat Helmsley's crimes with campaign-reporting allegations against Feinstein. Democratic loyalists were aghast. "For more than a year he couldn't walk into a room without getting booed," says Feinstein. "He never understood why that ad was so venal. I know because he came and talked to me about it after the race was over." Feinstein, who is Jewish, felt the ad played on "a very subtle anti-Semitism" in linking her with the haughty hotel owner who had been jailed for tax evasion.[1] "I've never met the woman," Feinstein adds. Davis later apologized for the ad, calling it "a big mistake."

Feinstein won the primary fight, but Davis' negative attacks took their toll, and she lost the general election to Republican Pete Wilson. Feinstein wilted under the barrage of personal innuendo, prompting political analysts to whisper that she lacked fire in the belly for higher office. "I had it cut out," Feinstein says. Her wry joke refers to the hysterectomy she underwent just weeks before the race commenced. "I was very anemic," she recalls. "I had had massive bleeding for a long time. I was so debilitated that it took me a period of time to come back." Feinstein's wish for privacy combined with the political taboo of admitting frailty made her lackluster performance more mysterious than it needed to be. Eight years later, Feinstein endorsed Davis in his positive, issue-oriented California governor's campaign and he won handily, succeeding Wilson, and returned power in the state to the Democrats. The lesson in politics, as in life, is to forgive even if you can't forget.

Feinstein leans forward when she wants to emphasize a point, as if proximity to the person she's persuading increases the importance of her words. Though she is in her mid-sixties, her face is unlined and girlishly alive with intelligence and determination. She sits for our interview in a sparely decorated and businesslike conference room be-

---

[1] The voiceover for the ad said, "Leona Helmsley and Dianne Feinstein. Hotel queen Helmsley misreported $1 million to the IRS; Feinstein misreported $8 million to the Fair Political Practices Committee. Helmsley blames her servants for the felony. Feinstein blames her staff for the lawsuit. Helmsley is in jail. Feinstein wants to be a senator? Truth for a change. Gray Davis: Democrat for U.S. Senate." CNN, November 3, 1998.

tween her private office and a busy outside reception area. She is clad in a bright kelly-green suit and a navy blouse. An award on the wall honors her for fiscal prudence as mayor of San Francisco, a city not normally noted for prudence of any sort.

Feinstein was a "new Democrat" before the label was created. She backed measures that were tough on crime while advocating gun control. In the Senate, she gained a reputation for hard work and a willingness to cross party lines to reach consensus. Few people thought she would succeed as a freshman senator in 1994 when she pushed through a ban on military-type semiautomatic assault weapons despite the full-court lobbying efforts of the National Rifle Association. As the Senate debated the proposal, Idaho senator Larry Craig, a major NRA backer, disputed one of Feinstein's assertions, adding gratuitously, "The gentle lady from California needs to become a little more familiar with firearms. . . ." Feinstein responded, her voice tight with passion and fury, that she was "quite familiar" with firearms, having become mayor in the wake of her predecessor's death by an assassin's bullet.

Feinstein's career is a case study in overcoming obstacles. Her mother, a Russian émigré, suffered from tuberculosis and, as a child, was confined to a sanitarium. She had no formal schooling. She was a beautiful woman and worked as a model for a major department store until she married Feinstein's father, a surgeon. Beneath the exquisite surface, however, the parts of her brain that control memory, judgment, and reason were deteriorating, the result of an insidious fever linked with her earlier illness. Bizarre behavior was the result. It wasn't until years later that a CT scan revealed an organic basis for the way she acted.

Her mother's unpredictable nature made Feinstein fearful of the disruption that could burst forth without warning. She often sat in the car doing her homework rather than chance going in the house, not knowing what might happen. "The deterioration started when she was still a relatively young woman, and it had a profound impact on all of us," says Feinstein. "From the outside, it appeared that I had a very easy childhood. From the inside, it wasn't easy at all."

Dianne attended San Francisco's Convent of the Sacred Heart, where the benefits of a rigorous academic curriculum outweighed any qualms her family might have had about the school's religious orientation. Author Patricia Bosworth remembers her friend Dianne Goldman as "a slender, immaculate brunette" who captured the ribbon for "good conduct" given out at assembly. Putting up a good front was important to Dianne. When she closed the door at home to go out into the world, she left the turmoil behind as best she could. At Stanford University, where she did her undergraduate work, she ran for student body vice president. "She was always political," says classmate Carla Hills, a Republican party activist who was secretary of housing and urban development during President Ford's administration.

A brief early marriage resulted in Feinstein's only child, a girl, Katherine, who is an attorney in San Francisco. Her second husband, nineteen years her senior, died in 1978 after a three-year battle with cancer. "He was the sun, the moon, and the stars," she says wistfully. Her current husband, Richard Blum, is an investment banker whose overseas holdings periodically get cited as possible conflicts for Feinstein. The fact that she had run statewide three times and faced extraordinary scrutiny from both Democratic and Republican opponents made it unlikely that skeletons would tumble from her closet if she were on the presidential ticket in 2000.

Just as male politicians have had to learn to work with increasing numbers of women colleagues and to meet the expectations of female constituents, successful female politicians must have a way with men. Feinstein commands men's respect, both as colleagues in a mostly male environment and as voters. "I've had to get along in a male world," she says. "I am of an age where when I first applied for a job, it was women need not apply. So the way I've chosen to go is to show that I can be effective." To illustrate, she reaches back to 1967, when a subcommittee of a crime commission on which she sat held a meeting at the Pacific Union Club, which didn't admit women. She protested and was told not to worry about it since not much would happen anyway. She's long since forgotten what the subcommittee decided upon at the meeting from which she was barred, but she loudly opposed whatever it was. She took up so much time making her case that the men didn't dare exclude her again. "I sent a message that it was a mistake to do it that way," she says, smiling at the memory.

Some women have interpreted rejection by the voters in a single election as a death sentence pronounced upon their political careers. Not Feinstein. She ran for mayor twice unsuccessfully before achieving the office. Yet even she was ready to give up after her second loss, in 1975, when she came in third after being heavily favored to win. "I became convinced I had something really lacking in me, that I was not electable," she said. In 1978, she announced to the press that she would not run again for mayor. Later that same day, a crazed former city supervisor and ex-cop walked into City Hall and fatally shot

Mayor George Moscone and city supervisor Harvey Milk, San Francisco's first openly gay elected official. Feinstein was the first to find Milk's body. "I put a finger on his wrist and it went through a bullet hole," she says, grimacing.

As president of the Board of Supervisors, Feinstein was next in line to ascend to mayor. Her announcement only hours earlier that she would not seek the job was relegated to a historical footnote. She served out her fallen predecessor's term and went on to win two four-year terms. The image of a shaken but steadfast Feinstein summoning the strength to deal with the assassinations vaulted her into the nation's consciousness. She steadied the city through the trauma and riots that followed when the killer, Dan White, received only a minimal sentence. The experience forged in Feinstein a commitment to gun control that is a consistent thread in her public policy. Feinstein herself has been the target of violence. She had the windows of her beach house shot out, and a bomb was discovered in a window box at her home in San Francisco outside the bedroom where her daughter was sleeping. Once, when she was walking precincts, a man pointed a pistol at her head and pulled the trigger. Fortunately, it was a cigarette lighter. The *Los Angeles Times* reported that for a time in the 1970s, Feinstein carried a .38-caliber pistol in her purse.

Another lesson Feinstein learned from personal experience is, as she put it, "Hell hath no fury like a man beaten by a woman." Feinstein won reelection to the Senate in 1994 by 165,562 votes out of more than 8.5 million votes cast. Her opponent, oil heir Michael Huffington, claimed that fraudulent votes cost him the election, and he refused to concede. After months of investigating, the Senate Rules Committee finally dismissed the case when Huffington could not substantiate his allegations. Fighting the challenge was expensive and distracting for Feinstein.

Just how angry it made her was evident a few years later when she leapt to the defense of Louisiana senator Mary Landrieu, another Democratic woman senator whose male opponent couldn't accept the fact that he had lost the race. Feinstein vowed she would filibuster in order to block efforts by the Republican-controlled Rules Committee to subpoena witnesses and expand the scope of the investigation into Landrieu's narrow victory. "You have no idea how hard it is for a woman to be elected to the U.S. Senate," Feinstein said, staring at the all-male panel. Republican senator Rick Santorum of Pennsylvania shook his head and rolled his eyes at Feinstein's outburst. Democrats claim that Santorum then turned to a colleague and said, "What a bitch." Democrats circulated a videotape to prove their point, but Santorum's words are not clear. A spokesman insists he muttered, "Can you believe it?"

Even in this age of raised consciousness about sex stereotypes, the language used to describe women subtly differentiates them from their male counterparts. A January 1998 story in the *Wall Street Journal* portrayed Feinstein as "imperious" and "temperamental," adjectives rarely applied to male politicians. Feinstein has a reputation for being "difficult," another pointedly female adjective. "Sure, she's difficult, but a lot of guys are difficult too," says a former Senate aide, a woman. "And she's not insisting everybody on the staff sleep with her. There's difficult, and then there's that."

Legislating was new for Feinstein, and she was surprised to discover that she liked it and was good at it. Previously, she had gravitated toward the management and administrative side of government. "It's clearer, more decisive," she says. "You can do things as opposed to discussing, convincing, and cajoling. Getting things through in the Senate is a long process. Having said all that, when I got here, I found out I can be effective."

One reason Democrats shy away from Feinstein as a running mate is her independence and fear that she couldn't play the dutiful supplicant's role required of the vice president. A friend who knows her well says it would only be a matter of time before Dianne felt compelled to hold a press conference explaining how her views are different from the president's position on some matter of national importance. Besides, any Democrat who needs her to carry California will by definition be so weak he can't win the presidency.

"People have talked to me about running for president, to be honest with you, and I sort of laughed at it," she says laughing even as she says this. "I mean, one of these days it's going to happen, whether it's me or someone else. I'm not sure the time is right."

Her reservations, she admits, are based on "vibrations," or intuition, which she concedes "sounds dumb" when stacked against all the objective data about women's capabilities. But the double standard is alive and well, she reminds: "The woman who does it is going to have to be tested and steadfast, her credentials assured. The question is still pressed, you know, as to whether you really know your stuff. A woman still isn't taken at face value. You have to prove yourself."

Nobody expected Christine Todd Whitman, a political neophyte from Somerset Hills, New Jersey's wealthy horse country, to hold her own against Bill Bradley, the cerebral basketball superstar turned

U.S. senator. She hadn't voted in local school board elections because her children attended private school, and she had led a life of extreme privilege. Her aides fretted about her "rich bitch" image, and were constantly after her to warm up her frosty demeanor. As the date neared for their first debate, pundits predicted that Bradley, a former Rhodes scholar, would expose Whitman for the dilettante she was, especially when the questioning turned to foreign policy. "Poor Christie's out of her league," they said. Whitman secretly reveled in the role of underdog. "Nobody thought I was going to know squat," she said, "so I had the advantage."

Neither Bradley nor anyone else knew much about Whitman then. Had they inquired they might have been surprised to discover that she had majored in international government in college, had lived overseas, and had crammed for the debate. "Not only did I not get buried, I scored some points," Whitman recalls with pleasure. "In those days, expectations for women were lower, and if you strung a couple of sentences together intelligently, they thought, 'Oooh, she's not so dumb.' It's a little tougher now to get away with that."

When Whitman nearly beat Bradley, a prince of his party, a president-in-waiting, it was a life-changing experience for both of them. Bradley, determined never again to lose touch, resigned his Senate seat six years later to plunge into presidential politics. Whitman's trajectory pointed up.

Politics was the family business in the Todd household. Christie's father, Webster Todd, was the GOP state chairman in New Jersey in the 1960s and 1970s. Christie was only twelve when she attended her first Republican convention in 1956, and presented the nominee, General Dwight Eisenhower, with a leather golf tee holder she had sewn herself. Young Christie was such a devoted Republican that she donated the proceeds from her lemonade stand to the party. Yet her parents expected that her brothers would be the ones to seek office, not their youngest daughter. Her oldest brother, John, was involved in local politics until his death in 1988. Dan Todd, next in line, envisioned a life as an elected member of Congress, but his career path was disrupted when, after one term in the state assembly, he took a job in Washington with the Nixon administration. After the Watergate scandal, he realized his association with Nixon had made him unelectable. He chose to move to Montana.

When Whitman first ran in 1982 for the Somerset County Board of Freeholders, New Jersey's equivalent of a board of supervisors, it took her father some time to get over the fact that his daughter and not his son was the candidate. "He was supportive, but you could see that he expected it to have been Danny, not me," she says. Eleanor Todd, however, cheered her daughter's entry into politics. Eleanor was known as "The Hurricane" for her fearsome energy. Her friends said if she had been born a generation later, she would have sought elective office.

Near the end of her life, Eleanor was her daughter's biggest booster, arguing against admitting defeat in the 1990 race against Bradley until the last vote was counted. "Boy, she didn't want me to concede," says Whitman. "She was ready to raise Cain. She nearly took off my campaign manager's head. I said, 'Mother, it's time now.' We were, I forget, how many votes behind, but I knew Essex County [a Democratic stronghold] hadn't come in yet, and I said, 'We ain't making up the difference now.'"

Buoyed by her strong showing against Bradley, Whitman ran for governor in 1993. She ran a clumsy campaign, one that was plagued with gaffes and lacked focus until the final weeks, when she belatedly called for a 30 percent cut in the state income tax. She had earlier resisted Republican calls for tax cuts, calling them "cynical." The tax-cutting fever took hold, and she managed to wring out a victory against James Florio, the Democratic incumbent who had angered voters by raising taxes after promising that he wouldn't. In victory, Whitman got a hint of the toll that politics takes on mothers in office. The night the returns came in, her daughter, Kate, then sixteen, raised a glass to toast her mother. "I want to . . ." she began, then burst into tears. She could not get through it. Later, she told her mother that she had wanted to wish her good luck, "but if you won, I was afraid I was going to lose you."

Whitman immediately served notice that she would govern differently from her male predecessors. She named the first woman attorney general and the first female African-American secretary of state. On the outside for the first time, men grumbled about the statehouse being an "estrogen palace."

Whitman's first term generally was judged a success. She gained prominence because of her proposal to slash state income taxes. Most economists and editorial writers ridiculed the idea as unworkable, but she delivered the tax cut ahead of schedule. Republicans around the country looked to her as a model. She also was in the forefront of the privatization movement, turning over various government functions to the private sector. But Whitman made enemies too. Some Republicans thought she was timid in cutting back government for fear of angering the welfare bureaucracy. Some Democrats accused her of masquerading as someone sympathetic to the concerns of minorities and the poor, only to side in the end with the rush to squeeze government programs endorsed by the newly elected conservative Republican majority in Congress.

House Speaker Newt Gingrich understood that Whitman was an asset to the Republican cause despite, or perhaps because, she was liberal on social issues. He chose her to deliver the GOP's response to President Clinton's State of the Union address in January 1995, an honor that symbolized the party's commitment to return power to the states. Gingrich also named Whitman chairman of the Amtrak reform council, a valuable appointment for her since New Jersey commuters rely on the heavily subsidized rail line. Periodically, the federal government threatens to withdraw or at least substantially decrease its funding for Amtrak. Whitman would be in a position to look after her constituent's interests.

In 1997, New Jersey's first female governor became the first woman ever to win reelection in a major state. By most measures, she would have been an ideal candidate for vice president in 2000. But putting her on the ticket would have inflamed the conservative wing of the Republican party, and prompted widespread protests at the GOP's July convention in Philadelphia. Whitman's stand in favor of abortion rights makes her anathema to the GOP's social conservatives.

The 1997 campaign exposed the fissures between Whitman and her party. Steve Forbes, the billionaire publisher and perpetual presidential candidate who had been a friend since childhood, came home to New Jersey and lobbied the Republican-led legislature to overturn Whitman's veto of a ban on partial-birth abortions. Forbes' ambush surprised Whitman. "He had been pro-choice," she says. "I guess he's got his reasons, and I presume he believes now in what he says. We really haven't ever talked about it. Maybe it's an evolution. To me it looks like a change, but I'm sure it's an evolution on his part."

Whitman tries to give her old friend the benefit of the doubt, but she can't conceal her disdain for Forbes' flip-flop. "One of his primary reasons for getting involved [in running for president] would be to overturn *Roe v. Wade*—not that the president has the ability to do that," she says with a derisive laugh. Actually, whoever won the presidency in 2000 could tip the fragile Supreme Court majority that upholds *Roe v. Wade*, the 1973 ruling that legalized abortion. If court watchers are right in predicting as many as three retirements among the aging justices over the next four years, a president committed to overturning the ruling could shape the court to guarantee that outcome.

Whitman believes that her pro-choice position springs from conservative values about limiting the role of government and keeping it out of private decisions. She had asked that any ban on partial-birth abortion include exceptions for the life and long-term physical health of the mother. "I don't want a legislator standing over my surgeon in the operating room telling him how to proceed," she says. "I'm pro-choice, not pro-abortion. That's a fine line that a lot of people don't distinguish, but it's real." The New Jersey legislature overturned her veto, dealing Whitman a political reprimand. Social conservatives defected from her candidacy and almost cost Whitman her reelection.

When it comes to standing up for abortion rights, Whitman has few peers among Republicans. She has stared down her party's leadership and held firm even on favoring federal money to help poor women pay for abortions. It's hard to find liberal Democrats willing to take that stand anymore. Yet she faults herself for not confronting her critics directly on the partial-birth abortion issue. She thinks she could have done a better job defending the way she rewrote the law to provide legal protection for a viable fetus except when the mother's life is in danger or her physical health is at risk. "I wanted to talk about it, and I was advised by the gurus in the campaign, 'Don't talk about it. You've got to just get over it and go on.' I thought that was a mistake. I should have been more aggressive in telling people what it was that I'd done."

Whitman is thought to be so divisive a figure in her own party that any Republican presidential nominee who dared to name her his running mate would prompt a walkout by social conservatives at the convention. Geoff Garin, a Democratic pollster, says a ticket including her would be so progressive, it might even get his vote. "If they have a presidential candidate brave enough to go to the convention with Whitman, that would make me think twice," Garin said, adding, "He'd be a daring fellow. No such person exists in the Republican party. That would be excessively provocative, stupidly provocative. It just can't happen."

Rather than wait for some Prince Charming to put the magic slipper on her foot, Whitman may be carving out her own path to the presidency. For a time, she toyed with running for the Senate in 2000 to replace retiring Democrat Frank Lautenberg. She would have been a formidable candidate and, if she had won, been promoted as a possible presidential candidate in 2004 or 2008. Some political visionaries had already been speculating on a presidential contest that pitted Whitman against Hillary Rodham Clinton, assuming the First Lady's bid for a Senate seat proved successful. Then on September 7, 1999, Whitman stunned the political world by calling a press conference to announce she would not be a candidate. Republican leaders greeted the news somberly as if there had been a tragedy in the family. But Whitman was almost giddy with delight at her decision. "It's a huge relief," she said. "It will be fun to think about policy issues without having to factor in the possible political consequences. It allows you to do what you think is right and take on some of the sacred cows."

Whitman felt tugged one way on issues as governor, and another as a potential Senate candidate. "The psychologists call it cognitive dissonance," says a campaign donor. "It was wearing on her." She hated the way everything she did was scrutinized for its political intent, and she felt hamstrung by the cynicism. There were practical considerations as well. She said she couldn't do her job as governor and raise the money she would need to compete, which she put at $100,000 a week. Her opponent, Democrat Jon Corzine, the former chairman of Goldman, Sachs & Co., a blue-chip investment firm, said he was prepared to spend from his own fortune of an estimated $300 million whatever it took to win (winning the seat in 2000 cost Corzine $63 million).

Whitman also concluded she could not overcome resistance from social conservatives and their determination to bring her down. A third-party candidacy loomed on the Right, which would drain away votes from Whitman, whose margin of victory in New Jersey in 1997 was an anemic single percent. In the early spring of 1999, when she was still actively considering a Senate run, she had her friend and ally, Wall Street investor Lew Eisenberg, contact Ralph Reed, the former head of the Christian Coalition, to seek his advice about mending fences with social conservatives. The two men, along with Whitman's chief of staff, met in a hotel on Capitol Hill in Washington. Eisenberg offered Reed a contract for his consulting services, but Reed politely declined. The Christian activist turned consultant explained that signing on with Whitman would make them both look like hypocrites.

Reed is regarded as the most realistic and accommodating of the Christian Right leaders, and his refusal to even consider a consulting contract with Whitman was a wake-up call. After all, Reed seemed to have no compunction about advising Texas governor George W. Bush, who had been a client for months. Whitman felt squeezed by her party's social conservatives, and their resolve to see her defeated even if it meant electing a Democrat. Winning them over would mean compromises she was not willing to make personally or politically. By pulling out of the race, Whitman avoided a bruising battle, and was gambling she could still get to Washington in a cabinet job if the Republicans won the White House.

Her bet paid off when the newly elected Bush named her head of the Environmental Protection Agency, one of the few Cabinet-level appointments where her pro-choice views would not come into play. The job turned out to be a mixed blessing for Whitman. While it gave her a national platform, she quickly learned the limits of her authority. Just weeks after assuming the job, Whitman was forced by the White House to backtrack on a commitment she had made, and that Bush had made during the campaign, to limit carbon-dioxide emissions, the leading contributor to global warming. Greg Wetstone of the National Resources Defense Counsel called it "one of the most immediate and embarrassing eviscerations of a new cabinet secretary." Many of her admirers thought she should have resigned in protest. A week later, with environmentalists already angry, Whitman announced that the Bush administration was postponing a Clinton regulation limiting arsenic in the water supply. The political furor was predictable, cutting into Bush's support across the board and especially among suburban women. Whitman seemed unprepared for the negative reaction, explaining that additional study was needed. She eventually re-instated the Clinton standard, but the damage done to her reputation as a progressive leader makes her future in national politics uncertain.

More stories followed about how Whitman was being ignored, and how her recommendations were overruled in an administration bent on deregulation and determined to do everything different from its predecessor, Bill Clinton. She had taken so many hits that Secretary of State Colin Powell took to calling her the administration's "wind dummy," a military term for a device dropped from a plane to test air currents. "You push the dummy out the door and see what happens to it," Whitman explains. At the 2002 spring dinner of the Gridiron Club, where journalists and politicians take turns spoofing one another, Whitman delivered several sharp barbs about the way she'd been treated. "I used to be somebody," she began plaintively, noting that she was one of only a handful of pro-choice Republicans on the vice-presidential short list for two successive elections. "Ironically, none of us made it past the first trimester," she said as many in the audience winced. With President Bush looking on, she plunged ahead, declaring that she knew the location of the hideaway where the Secret Service had been secreting Vice President Chaney since the 9/11 terrorist attacks. "It's where no one would think to look for him—the

EPA," she said triumphantly, "or what the president calls the Department of Sticks and Berries."

Advocating for the environment in an administration headed by two oilmen, Bush and Chaney, is a stiff challenge. Republicans in general, as the party of big business and corporate America, have not been sensitive to environmental concerns. "People have to realize, when you give a Republican the choice between more poison and less regulation, we need some time to think about it," Whitman said. As EPA administrator, Whitman is not a member of the Cabinet but is allowed to attend meetings. "I don't even mind the folding chair in the corner," she quipped. Still, the jokes revealed the depth of the disappointment Whitman has experienced. "Arsenic, whether I'm poisoned or not, will be in the first paragraph of my obituary," she said, adding in a jab at her privileged upbringing that the incident was "way overblown. Nobody drinks tap water any more, do they?"

Whitman's once promising future has fallen victim to the politics of the moment, yet she is the prototype for the kind of woman who could become the nation's first female president. She has star quality that is both stylistic and substantive. She offers proven executive experience, a record on issues of national concern, and a confident media image. Her aristocratic bearing and aquiline nose give her the look of royalty, yet she's not afraid to get down and dirty when it comes to politics. "I grew up as a tomboy and I grew up with two older brothers, so the rough-and-tumble part has never bothered me," she says.

Her steely calm can come across as chilly and uncaring. She has had to work to overcome the "rich bitch" image that accompanied her entry into statewide politics. Her advisers remind her to smile more when she faces a camera, and to sprinkle her statements with personal anecdotes. "When I catch myself on the news, I say, 'Remember to smile, would you? And look a little more relaxed.' People like to paint me as being above it all. Do I care? Of course I care," she says. "But there's no way to convince somebody who's just lost their job that I give a damn if I'm the one who put them out of work. And you can't sit back and say, 'Well, there's a greater good,' because that's not the answer either. The answer is that there's a balance that's got to be struck, and unfortunately, some people are getting hit by that."

Whitman has not been a big vote-getter in New Jersey. She won both races for governor with only 49 percent of the vote, and an extremely low turnout (8 percent) among black voters in 1993 is credited with turning the race in her favor because blacks historically vote for Democrats.

Because Whitman wielded executive power in a big state for longer than any other woman in American history, we asked whether she thinks she treats power as a man would. Former New Jersey representative Millicent Fenwick, an iconoclast who inspired the "Doonesbury" character Lacy Davenport, maintained that once women were in power for a period of time, they'd be just like the guys. Perhaps to prove her point, she enjoyed a good cigar. As much as Whitman admires the late Fenwick, she disagrees. Women, says Whitman, are "not that comfortable with power."

"Women tend to come to government because of something they want to accomplish," she said. "It's not so much another something to add to the résumé, or a power trip. They want to get something done, something they believe in deeply. A lot of women start out with local issues—a school-guard crossing or something like that. They decide they have to be involved. Then we do our homework because we have to. We do it more than a lot of the guys because, again, nothing's going to be handed to us."

Whitman thinks women govern differently because their life experiences are different. "If you give a woman a choice between capital construction for a bridge or for a halfway house for troubled teenagers, we'll go for the halfway house first," she said. "That's not because we don't understand the importance of infrastructure repair, but because we tend to focus on the human side first. Then we'll get to the other." Citing women's affinity for consensus building, Whitman said, "Anybody who's been a mother knows there is no all-right or all-wrong way. And because we haven't been in power, we're not threatened by bringing new people to the table. A power structure that has tended to be white male has something to lose. We really don't have anything to lose."

Listening to Whitman champion women, it is surprising to learn that she, like her male Republican counterparts, suffered from a gender gap in elections. Despite the fact that she is one of them, women have not flocked to Whitman, and her Democratic opponents get the benefit of the gender gap, though less so against Whitman than they might against another candidate who is not as progressive. She substantially closed the gap in her second gubernatorial run, but she knows she can't take women for granted. She and other women running for office get a second look from female voters eager to support one of their own. But focus groups that probe the thinking of women voters have found that most will not vote for a woman "just because she's a woman." Issues matter, and Democrats have the edge over

Republicans on domestic issues that matter most to women, like education, health care, and reproductive rights. But that edge was almost non-existent in the 2002 congressional elections when security concerns dominated the political landscape, and women—like men—placed more trust in Republicans to keep them safe.

Whitman predicts that we will see a woman at the top of the ticket within the next twelve years. She sees the future in the faces of the high school and college women in the audience for her speeches. Her own daughter, Kate, says she will never run for public office—"never in her whole life," her mother reports. "But who knows?" she quickly adds. "She majored in international government. People accuse Generation X, her generation, of being disengaged, but I see a lot of social awareness. Inevitably they're going to come to politics because if you really want to change the system, that's where it happens."

SIX

Senator Clinton

Hillary Clinton was motivated to run for the Senate in part by Elizabeth Dole's running for president. Seeing Dole get all the attention as the first possible woman president got under the First Lady's skin in ways that were primordial. Dole had played it so safe for so long, why should she get the credit for stepping out boldly while Hillary sat quietly by? Clinton had been on the frontlines, stretching the limits of what was permissible as the wife of a president, then retreating and standing by her husband as he became embroiled in an embarrassing sex scandal. As the first First Lady with professional credentials, she had tried to broaden the traditional role of helpmate by taking on a policy job in her husband's first term. But her failure to achieve her goal of universal health care tarnished her aura of superiority, and she was badly shaken by the experience. Polls showed the country liked her best when she stayed away from policy and stuck by her man, even when they deplored his behavior.

Her friends thought that eight years in a White House as besieged by scandal as the Clinton administration would have been enough for Hillary. But being at the center of government only whetted her appetite for more. This is a woman with a strong sense of history. She had gotten a taste of what was possible, and she was tantalized by the prospect of taking the sympathy the public felt for her and turning it into something concrete, namely a U.S. Senate seat.

Months of anticipation led up to the July day in 1999 when Clinton announced an exploratory committee to look into her running for the seat of retiring New York Senator Daniel Patrick Moynihan. She was at the outer edge of the precipice of what was acceptable for women in politics, and many analysts remained disbelieving that she would go through with a campaign, much less win.

Moynihan stepped away from the microphone, seeming to forget momentarily why he was there. With a smile fixed on her face, Hillary Rodham Clinton didn't move a muscle, or betray any emotion. Maybe it was the rustling of the camera crews, or the air of expectancy that clung to the event like early morning dew, for Moynihan immediately sensed his error. "My God, I almost forgot," he said, scurrying back to address the media throng assembled at his farm in upstate New York. "I'm here to say that I hope she will go all the way. I mean to go all the way with her. I think she's going to win." There was a sprinkling of laughter among well-wishers familiar with Moynihan's egocentric ways. The First Lady had won him over, but not completely. "If Moynihan were a university, endorsements would be the equivalent of an honorary degree," observed a former aide. "He doesn't think much of them."

Receiving Moynihan's blessing, however tepid, was a victory for Hillary Clinton. Stepping to the microphone and beaming broadly, she thanked the man she hoped to succeed in the U.S. Senate, hailing him as "probably the wisest New Yorker we can know at this time." There is nothing she won't say to flatter Moynihan, a gifted intellectual accustomed to having others behave around him like supplicants. Having announced her exploratory committee a month earlier on "Good Morning America," here she was on a sunny summer day at Pindars Corner, the heart of Moyniland, a coup in itself and the result of months of courting both the senator and his influential wife, Liz Moynihan. If Hillary had undertaken this kind of full-court press of Moynihan back in 1993 and 1994, who knows, maybe she could have altered the fate of her health care bill. Instead, the mercurial Moynihan, frustrated by the imperious and self-righteous First Lady, would amuse visitors to his Senate office by holding aloft her 1,342-page plan and letting it drop to the floor with a thud to signal his disdain. As chairman of the Senate Finance Committee, Moynihan was a critical player for Hillary to have on her side. Alienating him as she and others in the White House did helped doom what many believe was a rare opportunity for health care reform.

Engineering major social change as First Lady proved to be an unworkable combination. Now Hillary would discover whether campaigning for a U.S. Senate seat as First Lady would prove just as lethal an experiment. "Why the Senate and why New York and why me?" she said, posing the questions on everybody's mind. She cited her deep interest in education and health care, the fact that she has been a "tireless advocate" for those and other issues, and she hoped she could convince New Yorkers that "what I'm for is as important if not more important than where I'm from."

Getting the quirky Moynihan on her side was essential in her first bid for elective office. He had won reelection three times with his highbrow mix of principles and parochial interests. One of the most successful politicians in the state, and indeed the country, he managed always to seem above politics, a master at combining the politically expedient with the intellectually workable. With Moynihan telling voters that Hillary will best carry on his centrist policies, and that she will act in the highest tradition of a philosopher senator, it becomes much tougher for Republicans to paint her as a radical liberal whose pro-government views would damage the interests of New Yorkers.

Hillary Clinton had learned a lot about being a politician in her years as First Lady, and her handling of Moynihan is Exhibit A. "The animosity that existed before is completely gone," marvels a former Moynihan aide. Yet he warns that Mrs. Clinton needs to keep up the courtship. "She can't cross it off her to-do list at all. The Moynihans are high maintenance. And for her to conclude that she's done enough, and not do more work, is a big mistake. To know them is to know that," the aide says. Moynihan sees Hillary enhancing his stature if he can help get her elected. And he doesn't talk just to hear himself talk (although sometimes it feels that way); he cares about issues, and he cares about ideas.

Instead of just trying to charm Moynihan, Hillary is listening to those ideas. After one of their meetings in the early spring of 1999, Moynihan sent the First Lady a note. She was overseas at the time, and when she returned, she called him at ten o'clock at night to apologize for not having responded. The next day, Moynihan noticed that some of his thoughts on the ethnic conflict in Kosovo, as expressed in his note, were incorporated into a speech President Clinton gave.

There were almost as many legacies at stake in Hillary's Senate run (four including Moynihan) as there are boroughs in New York City (five). Win or lose, she stole some thunder from her husband, which could well have been at least a subliminal motivation for her to enter the race. If historians judge the success of the Clinton presidency by its staying power, then Hillary's victory is every bit as critical to her husband's legacy as Vice President Al Gore's. Many analysts think the First Lady's political ambition made it harder for Gore to break away and be his own man when the stage remains crowded with Clintons, his and hers. Finally, there is Hillary herself. Leaving the White House after eight hard years, in which her image with the public rocketed from pathbreaker to power-seeker to poor victim, why would she risk further battering in a race where the outcome is uncertain?

That's what Liz Moynihan wanted to know when Hillary first broached with her the idea of running. "Are you crazy?" she asked. "Why do you want to do this?" Mrs. Moynihan pointed out that a junior senator doesn't have the power or the platform of a former First Lady, and that the race would be tough. She managed her husband's three Senate campaigns, and knows that New York is a minefield of ethnic politics that can explode the hopes of a novice like Hillary. She cautioned the First Lady against getting talked into running by Democrats desperate for a celebrity candidate to raise the funds to compete for the seat. Prominent among those privately advising Hillary was Harold Ickes, a liberal and longtime activist in New York politics whose father served in Franklin Roosevelt's cabinet. The senior Ickes once urged Eleanor Roosevelt to run for the U.S. Senate from New York. Mrs. Roosevelt turned down the idea, writing in May of 1945, "I feel very strongly that running for office is not the way in which I can be most useful." She believed that public office was too constraining, and she wanted to preserve her ability to speak out "free of any obligation."

Half a century later, Hillary Clinton sees public office as a liberating experience and a way to gain legitimacy. As a little girl, Hillary looked up to Margaret Chase Smith, one of the few people in the Republican party who dared to defy Joe McCarthy. "I admired her kind of flinty Yankee integrity," she says. But when the young Hillary was deciding her own career, her role models were Marion Wright Edelman of the Children's Defense Fund and Jane Addams, the pioneer social worker, women who labored in the trenches on behalf of children's issues and women's issues. Elective office wasn't part of Hillary's life plan. "I always just saw myself as an activist, a citizen activist," she said. Yet those who know her have long viewed her as a potential candidate for office.

"I always thought she would run," says William Galston, a former White House domestic policy adviser. "She desperately wants her own voice. This notion that the Senate is a comedown, I don't buy. She's a person who speaks out about public policy. That's who she is. From a state like New York, with its political tradition, it couldn't be a better forum."

Mrs. Clinton had toyed before with running for public office. Pollster Dick Morris says that in 1990, the Clintons commissioned him to do two polls to test the receptivity in Arkansas to Hillary succeeding her husband as governor. The first sounding confirmed her popularity with voters but determined she had not created enough of an independent image to be a credible candidate. Unhappy with the results, Hillary sent Morris back into the field with more nuanced questions, but the results remained the same.

For a woman with the intellectual promise that Hillary exhibited, growing up at the height of the women's liberation movement, it must have rankled her that her power and influence were so derivative. The yearning to get out on the high diving board on her own, and take the plunge, must have been overpowering. Clearly she wanted emotional and political independence from Bill Clinton, or she would not put so much at risk. Only minutes after the Senate acquitted Clinton on charges of perjury and obstruction of justice in the Lewinsky affair on Friday, February 12, 1999, Hillary sat down to lunch at the White House with Ickes to begin war-gaming her political future. "After that whole thing was over, she felt as if she had crawled out from under a rock—and it was her turn," says a friend. "She had to think about what she was going to do with the rest of her life."

Ickes laid out the promise and the perils of a potential Senate campaign. He was characteristically blunt. She had never run for office. New York might be the toughest state in the union for a politician with its overlay of ethnicity that, as a Midwesterner, she had no experience with. New Yorkers had never elected a woman statewide, though several talented women had tried, including Geraldine Ferraro, twice. Raising the necessary funds would be a formidable task. During the last eight months of his candidacy, Charles Schumer, who won the New York Senate race in 1998, spent 75 percent of his time fund-raising.

On the positive side, Ickes said that in a presidential year, Democratic registration exceeds Republican registration in the state by two million. Next to Arkansas, Bill Clinton ran up his highest victory margin in New York. The economy had thrived under President Clinton's policies, and she could tie her likely opponent, New York mayor Rudy Giuliani, to the unpopular Republican majority in the House. (In late April, Giuliani was diagnosed with prostate cancer, putting his candidacy in doubt. Then, longstanding strains in his marriage burst into public view. Burdened by health and marital problems, Giuliani withdrew from the race. Ickes could not have foreseen this development. Even so, it would not have changed his diagnosis of what lay ahead.) The race would be close, he told her. Polls showing her ten points ahead were fantasy. She and Giuliani would both be tough, articulate candidates, and if neither makes any fatal mistakes, the winner might not be known until election night.

The conversation stretched over four hours. On one occasion, the president came in to try out the statement he would later read on the North Lawn of the White House responding to the Senate's decision to acquit him of charges of perjury and obstruction of justice. "It was out of a Fellini movie," recalls Ickes.

Deciding to run is fundamentally a personal decision, but friends warned Hillary that if she became a candidate, she would have to change her attitude toward the press. Eight years of scandal and scrutiny had left her wary, and she had sought refuge in the protective bubble that aides willingly provided. She would have to choose between the shred of privacy that she had left and her desire to become a political figure in her own right. For better or worse, she was a celebrity now. She could write her own ticket. She could become the head of a foundation, write books, give lectures, and sit on corporate boards. She looked at a lot of options, and reached some conclusions. "I don't want to work for anybody," she told a friend. "I want to be my own boss. I'm not interested in making that much money."

For a woman portrayed as so worried about building a financial nest egg that she cut corners as a lawyer to ensure her family's future, she was tossing away perhaps $20 million in private-sector income and lecture fees should she win election to the U.S. Senate. The annual salary of a senator ($150,000) is a fraction of what Mrs. Clinton could earn. If we know anything about Hillary Rodham, a Yale Law School graduate who could have earned big bucks on Wall Street, she's in public life for the psychic income, not the money.

Now it's her turn to run for office, and his turn to pay the bills.

Clinton will do penance the rest of his life for the humiliation he heaped upon his wife and daughter during the yearlong Lewinsky saga. When the scandal first broke, Hillary's friends were mortified for her, and furious at him. One former aide said, "I wanted to write her a letter to say I'd come over and we'd take all his ties [some of them gifts from Lewinsky], and cut them up and fling them off the Truman Balcony, and send them sailing across the South Lawn. My husband talked me out of it." Another aide, who had publicly defended the president's version of the story, contemplated quitting after Clinton confessed he had lied about the nature of his relationship with the former intern. In the end, the aide decided to stay.

Why? "I didn't want to leave Hillary alone with those SOBs." Which SOBs? The lawyers who helped craft Clinton's hair-splitting answers? The White House aides who wanted Hillary to deliver an all-is-forgiven speech when she was still barely on speaking terms with her husband? "Both," the aide replied.

When the most serious scandal of the Clinton presidency hit in January 1998, the initial reaction from the president and his aides was a curious paralysis. Stunned by the charges that Clinton had had an affair with a young intern, the normally efficient Clinton attack machine went suddenly silent. It took Hillary's personal intervention and strategic common sense to pull together the stricken aides and organize the response that could well be credited with saving the Clinton presidency.

For a time in the winter of 1998, the American public got a glimpse of what it might be like to have a competent woman at the helm. Hillary did not know the extent of her husband's lie, and one wonders whether that would have made a difference. Coming to his rescue was not a new role for her. She has done it repeatedly over the years, most memorably during the 1992 campaign when she appeared on "60 Minutes" to defend her husband in the midst of charges that he had had a twelve-year affair. She was "not some little woman standing by my man like Tammy Wynette," she said spiritedly. She had forgiven him, so should the voters.

Hillary Clinton has the same ability her husband has to suspend reality and put on a game face. Why she apparently turns a blind eye to his philandering is a matter for conjecture. Critics and friends alike believe that the answer lies in her dedication to the political goals that she and her husband share. If his presidency collapsed and he had resigned, she would no longer have been First Lady. She would have lost her access to the levers of power. The agenda she painstakingly pursued for herself would have come to an abrupt end, from working behind the scenes to draft progressive adoption policies to playing roving ambassador to women around the world. Hillary is the most-traveled First Lady in history, having taken more than fifty foreign trips, half of them on her own, and often accompanied by her daughter, Chelsea.

Given what she had at stake, it is not surprising that she would defend her husband. If the Clintons had left the White House in disgrace, history would remember Hillary as the First Lady who knew her husband had affairs with other women, and who didn't do anything about it. Public opinion would likely turn on her, especially among women. She would no longer be seen as a strong and loyal wife, but as a victim of her own denial.

By handling herself and the office of First Lady with dignity and grace, she converted the sympathy people instinctively felt for her into a groundswell of support for her as a public figure. "You get gravitas by going through a crisis and holding your head up. Every woman can relate to it," says Andrea Camp, a former aide to Representative Patricia Schroeder (D., Colo.).

Through the Starr report and its humiliating details, a media feeding frenzy and fascination with Monica Lewinsky, Hillary soldiered on, never revealing a hint of what she must have been feeling inside. "Nobody, save perhaps her husband, shrugs off public humiliation as elegantly as Mrs. Clinton," declared the British weekly *The Economist*, crediting Hillary's nineteen-state campaign tour for the unexpected gains that Democrats made in the November 1998 congressional elections. One adviser who visited with the First Lady at the White House on a regular basis during the height of the scandal reported, "It's as though Monica does not exist. I have never heard the word *Monica* uttered in that building." Friends referred to Lewinsky as "the woman whose name we do not speak." Yet on the February afternoon the Senate acquitted Clinton, it was Hillary who carried over a box of valentine chocolates to the West Wing to thank the aides who had stood by him. "In private, she rips his head off," says a former aide, confirming numerous stories about Hillary's volcanic anger over minor issues as well as her husband's recklessness in jeopardizing so much of what they had worked for. "But she's able to remove herself and treat their personal problems as political problems," says the aide. "If anything happened to her, he'd be one sick puppy. He depends on her for everything. She's his closest political adviser."

Hillary had campaigned hard in 1998 for Democrats, and when in the midst of the impeachment drama her party made significant gains, confounding historical precedent, she rightly got credit, especially in New York, where she had campaigned tirelessly for Schumer in his upset win over Republican Alphonse D'Amato. On the Thursday night after the Tuesday election, unbeknownst to Hillary, Moynihan told the legendary New York newsman Gabe Pressman in a taped interview that he would not run again. The interview would not air until Sunday, but Hillary's phone immediately started ringing with New York Democratic elected officials and activists calling to propose she run for the seat.

"I thought it was an off-the-wall idea, and told them so," said the First Lady, recounting the story in our interview. She assumed that somebody would quickly step forward and shut the door on any notion of her running. But that didn't happen. "And so everybody kept pushing me and pushing me, and then one day, I think it was in February, I went to church, I came home, and the phone rang, and a friend of mine said, 'Did you see Bob Torricelli on "Meet the Press?" ' "

Torricelli, the New Jersey senator who headed the Democratic Senatorial Campaign Committee, was responsible for candidate recruitment. He predicted that Hillary would run for the Senate from New York. When Mrs. Clinton found out, she called Torricelli.

"What are you talking about?" she asked him.

"You're going to do it," he said.

"I'm not going to do it," she replied.

Retelling the story months later, she said, "I'm having an argument about my life with Bob Torricelli! But the idea just kept coming back, and people kept coming to see me. And so then I began to put my toe in the water, and I began to call people in New York. I called county chairs, and local elected officials, and other activists. But I still just wasn't convinced or committed." In the late spring of 1999, New York representative Nita Lowey, who had expressed interest in running, told Hillary she really wanted to make a decision. If she had any prayer of winning, she needed to start raising money and traveling around the state. Hillary said, "Look, if you want to do this, go ahead. I can't make a decision yet because I am not clear at all that this is the thing to do." Lowey found Hillary's ambivalence unsettling but decided against risking her safe Westchester seat in an expensive year-long marathon against Giuliani and the Republican establishment.

"And so then I took the next step with this listening tour," Hillary says. "But every step along the way, I had to stop and say, 'Am I doing this because Bob Torricelli said I was going to do it? Am I doing it because [New York representative] Charlie Rangel keeps calling me and saying that I'm going to do it, or wants me to do it, or whatever?'"

The seat being vacated by Moynihan had a proud history, one that appealed to Hillary, whose idealism and sense of public service was honed as a child of the sixties. Robert F. Kennedy had won the seat in 1964 in the aftermath of President John Kennedy's assassination, and used it as a platform to launch his bid for the presidency before he was cut down by a gunman's bullet on the night he won the California primary in June 1968. To walk in the footsteps of Kennedy and Moynihan would be a high honor for Hillary, just as a single handshake with

President Kennedy became a life-changing experience a generation earlier for the young Bill Clinton.

Early polls added to the allure with numbers that showed her beating Giuliani. Determined to make a decision of the head as much as the heart, Hillary diligently did her homework. She filled endless pages of yellow pads with the pros and cons of entering the race, and she consulted local leaders across the state to gauge the receptivity to her candidacy. "She's not down to receivers of tax, but she's going into pretty deep soil doing her spadework," said Tony Bullock, Moynihan's chief of staff in the spring of 1999. "So when and if she announces, and the local reporter goes to the mayor and other town officials for reaction, they will say nice things because they were all touched by her."

Some administration officials worried about the conflicts of interest that a Hillary campaign posed for an administration already seen as ethically challenged. White House lawyers advised creating an exploratory committee, but delaying an official announcement as long as possible. They found themselves in rare agreement with the political side of the White House, which saw no need for a formal declaration of candidacy until February 2000.

On Sunday afternoon, February 6, 2000, Hillary Rodham Clinton walked onto the stage at the State University of New York in Purchase with her husband, daughter, and mother. She had never been more prepared. She had practiced her speech over and over until she got comfortable using the word "I," which as First Lady she had consciously avoided for so long that it had become instinctual. "I realized for me to stand up and say, 'I believe,' not 'We believe' or 'He believes' or 'America believes,' which I've been able to do in the past, it's very different," she confessed. This was so much Hillary's day that commentators afterward noted that she didn't even introduce her husband, the president. Blue posters proclaimed simply "Hillary."

She had a few good lines that were repeated in the morning papers. "I'm new to the neighborhood, but I'm not new to your concerns" confronted the carpetbagger issue head-on. "I'm a little older, a little blonder" evoked knowing laughter and had just the right self-deprecating touch. But the speech was too long for a kick-off rally, and too densely packed with positions on issues. It was the kind of speech that only a policy wonk could love. A fifteen-minute video prepared by Hillary's old friends, the Hollywood team of Harry Thomason and Linda Bloodworth-Thomason, tackled the more problematic, personal side of the elusive First Lady. In the film,

Hillary's mother, Dorothy Rodham, tells how Hillary as a child held her own with the boys on the block. Various friends and colleagues offer testimonials to Hillary's steadfastness on children and family issues. Bill Clinton's appearance is limited to a cameo while Hillary brags on camera about how she can "make a mean tossed salad and a great omelet." Focus groups later revealed that women found the boast about her culinary skills "fake," to which Hillary protests, "That was a joke!" She couldn't believe people thought she was serious when she meant to signal that she's a dunce in the kitchen.

Women voters, expected to be Hillary's natural allies, were the most resistant to her campaign. A February poll in the *New York Times* showed Giuliani leading among white women. Yet Hillary's advisers sounded unconcerned. If there was one group she had a chance to win over, it was women. "Women know they're with her on the issues, and they know they should like her," says a White House aide. "So the more exposure they get to her, the theory is that they will move to her. And if she can turn women, they will turn in droves." Still, feedback from focus groups commissioned specifically to probe the attitudes of women toward Hillary's candidacy was "sobering," says a campaign adviser. Women suspected she was running to advance her own ambitions and not to serve the voters of New York, and they wondered who the real Hillary is. They remembered the early Hillary Clinton, the woman who wore headbands, who was outspoken and independent, and they hadn't seen that Hillary yet in her campaign they thought she was playing it too safe. They wondered whether she was a creation of her husband, and they questioned whether she would have gotten this far on her own.

Hillary listened intently as we ran down the list of concerns about her. She looked resplendent in a peach-colored suit and radiated the kind of feisty confidence that women once routinely expected from her. "I'm the most unknown known person you can imagine," she said. "Nobody knows what I did for thirty years in both the public and the private sector, and people don't know much about what I did in the White House. . . . I step out and people say, well, what has she done? Who is she? So, what I find is that that's what the beauty of a campaign is. You introduce yourself to people and you can't assume anybody knows anything about what you've ever done or what you care about."

She likes to compare her situation to the one Vice President Gore confronted when he ventured out on his own as a presidential candidate. "He was very well known and nearly totally unknown," she says.

"Nobody outside of Tennessee knew he'd been a senator. Their image was that he was the guy behind the president. So, why should you vote for the guy standing behind the president? He had to reintroduce himself to the American people, and I think it was a big surprise to him. It was a big surprise to me when I watched the campaign unfold. I have found exactly the same thing."

She was right that her standing with women improved as they learned more about her. A Gore adviser agreed that she and the vice president had the same challenge of President Clinton overshadowing them, and each had to build an independent identity. The adviser thought Hillary had the tougher challenger "With Hillary, there is resistance to reintroducing her. The cynicism is much higher, and it's harder for her to say, 'This is who I am.' People know things about her they don't know about their next-door neighbor. They know her marital problems. You can't create a new bio for her.

"I think she should run what I call a Popeye campaign: 'I am what I am. I will go to the Senate and shake things up.' Who cares that she can make an omelet. I don't believe it, and if I don't believe it, the people of New York sure won't."

Softening her image will work up to an extent, he argues, but she should play to her strengths. "She is the only woman running that nobody will call weak or vacillating or indecisive—the usual attacks you get against women candidates. So for better or worse, she's pretty strong."

What the political establishment in Washington found most puzzling about Hillary's candidacy is why she wanted to run for the Senate, knowing that if she won, she would have her days decided by Majority Leader Trent Lott and the Republicans who tried to oust her husband from office. "What a comedown, taking orders from Trent Lott and having to sit so far to the back of the room. Even if she were named to the Senate Finance Committee, she wouldn't be on the dais," said Lawrence O'Donnell. A former Moynihan aide who had migrated into the world of television political commentary, O'Donnell couldn't fathom how the First Lady could handle the life of a junior senator, which is not unlike being a plebe at a military academy, the chain of command is so rigid. "She's not accustomed to waiting until who knows all speaks before she gets a turn. She knows all that from her dealings with the Senate on health care," he said. Over and over he asked himself, why would she want to do it? Why would she want a demotion? It finally hit him. "She wants to be president," he concluded. "It's the Bobby Kennedy model."

Hillary's women friends also struggled to understand her motivation. "Nobody's written what will happen to her after she's a senator," said one. "Trent Lott and the Republicans will try to block everything Hillary tries to do. Sure, she'll have a platform for speeches and the like, but she'll have a tough time establishing herself legislatively. And it's not just the Republicans who'll resist her. The Democratic women won't want to share the spotlight. Barbara Mikulski especially, who is accustomed to being top dog. She's not going to defer to Hillary as the leader of the pack. The Senate's customs and rituals require freshmen to be seen and not heard. They won't even want Hillary to be seen."

To quiet the qualms of those around her, Hillary called a staff meeting to declare her intentions and to explain herself. Her White House staff was almost all women, and Hillary was emphatic. She was going to run for the Senate because that was the way to get things done. One of the women remarked later that she was really struck by what a believer Hillary is in government. At a time when confidence in government and voter participation had reached historic lows, Hillary can still get misty-eyed about public service. "She's in awe of Ted Kennedy," says an aide. "She thinks he wields a lot of power."

The Ted Kennedy model is how Hillary envisions a career in the Senate. Kennedy is widely respected by Democrats and Republicans for his legislative prowess. His staff is consistently rated one of the best on Capitol Hill, and there isn't a piece of social legislation over three decades that Kennedy has not sponsored or played a major role in shaping. Yet Kennedy in his early years had no bills or legislative record that he could claim because jealous elders in both parties put obstacles in the path of the young man they viewed as a spoiled son of privilege. Kennedy was only thirty years old when he was elected to the Senate, so he had time to make his mark and to overcome doubts about his abilities as a lawmaker because of the lapses in his personal behavior.

Warnings about the hard life of a junior senator don't impress the First Lady. She retains the naïveté of the Watergate generation that politics can be fixed, and that public service is a high calling if the right people get involved. The notion that being a senator is a comedown makes no sense to her. "A comedown for her is an ex–First Lady with nothing else on her résumé," says an aide.

Campaigning for Democrats in the 1998 elections was Hillary's coming-out party after months of the Monica mess and its strain on public discourse. The change was subtle, but word went out from

Hillaryland, the name given to the First Lady's White House universe, that Hillary was no longer under wraps. She had been doing substantive work behind the scenes, and now she was ready to take credit for that work. She didn't trust journalists, and turned to Carl Sferrazza Anthony, a historian who specializes in writing about First Ladies. In an article titled "Hillary's Powers," which appeared in the November 1999 issue of *George* magazine, Anthony wrote at length about the First Lady's hidden hand in pushing social reforms. Her efforts at overhauling the nation's adoption laws were deemed so popular that the president's aides wanted to steal the issue for his reelection platform in 1996. Hillary resisted out of worry that exposing her involvement would revive concerns voiced during the health care debate that she was usurping power as an unelected official and was secretly staging a takeover of the presidency.

Many months before Hillary or her putative rival, Mayor Giuliani, would officially announce, the race between them was shaping up to be the biggest mobilization and countermobilization of any political race ever. The White House braced for criticism that she was abusing government privileges by traveling on government planes and bringing White House aides with her on what appeared to be purely political trips. The criticism came, and to the surprise of her aides was not very harsh.

The more stinging criticism, certainly for a woman, centered on Hillary's ambition, and whether she was using the Senate seat as a stepping-stone to the presidency. The specter of Hillary picking up where Bill left off did not endear her to voters ready to close the book on the Clinton soap opera. Tim Russert on NBC's "Meet the Press" advanced the theory that if Vice President Gore loses in 2000, then the Democratic challenger in 2004 picks Hillary as his running mate. If Gore wins, she mounts her own campaign in 2008. Conservative columnist George Will, in a column that ran on July 5, 1999, two days before Hillary announced her exploratory committee, asserted that the First Lady wants Gore to lose "so she can fulfill her manifest destiny in 2004." A fund-raising appeal sent to Republicans by the chairman of the Alabama State GOP envisioned a Hillary presidential campaign in four years. "Scary, isn't it," the letter warned.

The attacks on Hillary reflected the frustration of the Clintons' political enemies that the yearlong Monica scandal ended with the president persevering and his wife running for office. The *Weekly Standard*, a conservative opinion publication, suggested with acid tongue that she skip the Senate and go straight to the presidency.

That way, if she and her husband split up, she gets to keep the house. James Pinkerton, a speechwriter in the Bush administration, commented on the Fox News Network that with Hillary's "cool, condescending tone," she would make a good East German border crossing guard. Reminded that Giuliani, a former G-man and a prosecutor, is not exactly warm and cuddly, Pinkerton jokingly conceded off camera that Giuliani would make "a good Mussolini."

As the battle lines formed, Deborah Tannen, a professor of linguistics at Georgetown University who specializes in gender studies, said that Hillary better get used to it. "A woman in the public eye is going to provoke a hatred and anger from men" that is visceral. "I've never heard women rail against men the way men do against women," says Tannen. She was once on a radio show when a man called in and declared, "There can only be one boss, and in my house, it's me." The show's host, a woman, responded by saying marriages should be on an equal footing. The next caller, a man, accused her of being like all women, and wanting to take over. "Excuse me while I scream," the host responded, and she did just that. For Tannen, it was an enlightening experience. "There is no equal," she concluded, in male-female power relationships. "She had said equal, and he had heard dominance."

The buzz that Hillary really wanted to be president, and was interested in the Senate only for selfish careerist reasons, became so pervasive that her advisers went to the First Lady and told her she had to say something to defuse it. "Her reaction was to laugh," says an aide. "We had to say, 'This is real. This is what people are accusing you of.'" On the second day of a campaign "listening tour" of upstate New York, on July 8, 1999, Hillary Clinton pledged to serve a full six-year term if elected to the Senate.

One of the reasons the speculation took hold is that it's not hard to imagine Hillary as a presidential candidate, or as president. Hillary Rodham Clinton is the closest we've come to having a woman president. "Buy one, get one free," Bill Clinton enthused as the couple campaigned together in 1992. Though forced to temper his rhetoric as the campaign progressed, Clinton still turned to Hillary for advice on every major decision. And when she said she wanted to lead the effort to reform the nation's health care system, Hillary's boosters pointed out that with her credentials, she would be on the short list for almost any cabinet post if it weren't for nepotism rules. Clinton unhesitatingly turned over policy-making authority to his wife—and he didn't take a poll to see what voters might think of the idea. If there was a co-president, the chattering classes declared when the

Clintons took office in January 1993, it was Hillary, not Al Gore. Poor Al, the joke went, he's a heartbeat from the *vice* presidency.

Like her husband, Hillary has shown extraordinary resilience. Her travails in office are well known, and the conventional wisdom is that she engineered a comeback by refashioning her role in more traditional terms. She also had to face both publicly and privately the airing in the media, and in an impeachment proceeding, of the evidence of her husband's philandering. Clinton would never have survived politically without her visible support.

Hillary did not invent herself out of whole cloth. First Ladies have been powerful partners before. Eleanor Roosevelt is often cited as a pioneer, and serves as an enduring role model. Betty Ford phoned members of Congress to lobby for the Equal Rights Amendment. Rosalynn Carter sat in on cabinet meetings and represented her husband on a trip to Latin America the first year he was in office. Polls taken at the time showed wary voters demanding "Who elected her?" Nancy Reagan was perhaps the most powerful First Lady in recent times. She controlled her husband's schedule with the help of astrologers, forced the firing of a chief of staff and several national security advisers, and pressed her husband to set aside his "Evil Empire" rhetoric to meet with Soviet president Mikhail Gorbachev. "Everybody wonders when we will have the first female American president, but what will become evident here is that we've already had her," said Neil Meron, producer of an ABC mini-series about Nancy Reagan.

What Hillary Clinton did that was different was to take that power out of the closet, put a title on it, and take an office in the West Wing of the White House, traditionally a male domain. When that experiment failed, in part because of Hillary's penchant for secrecy and her refusal to hold herself as accountable as any other high-level policymaker, and in part because the country wasn't ready, Hillary made herself relevant in other ways.

"There is no ordained role for First Lady," says presidential historian Arthur Schlesinger, Jr. "Hillary Clinton is an expression of the culmination of the women's movement. Eleanor Roosevelt was a more familiar type, a social worker type. She didn't represent the threat to manhood that Hillary Clinton did, who wasn't a social worker or a teacher, but came into a man's world and said, 'Anything you can do I can do better.' "

She learned she could get things done behind the scenes like her predecessors, and she could adopt a more vigorous public role in areas that were acceptable, like foreign travel that focused on the advancement of women around the world. "When the history of Hillary is written, it will say that she was caught in a historical time warp," says Kathleen Hall Jamieson, dean of the Annenberg School for Communication at the University of Pennsylvania. "At a time when a majority of American women work outside the home in all professions, she thought she would be accepted. But Americans are still conflicted about the roles women play in public and private life."

Initial polls showed her leading Giuliani by ten points, but by October 1999 the polls had flipped, with Giuliani ahead by ten points. Republican pollster Frank Luntz found Giuliani leading Clinton by thirty points among men over sixty years of age, while Clinton led Giuliani among women by seventeen points in a June 1999 survey. "You can't find an older man voting for Hillary Clinton even if you searched for it," said Luntz. "You can't find a younger woman voting for Rudy Giuliani if your life depended on it." The historical odds did not favor Hillary's candidacy. New York had never elected a woman to statewide office except as the governor's running mate. Every other state, except West Virginia, has broken that barrier. Less than 20 percent of the state's congressional delegation was female, and New York was in the bottom half of states in the percentage of state legislative seats held by women. Combine the state's apparent inbred resistance to electing a woman with Hillary's polarizing personality, as evidenced in her high disapproval rating, and it is not surprising that rumors persisted throughout 1999 that she would in the end decline to make the race.

The fact that Governor Christine Todd Whitman pulled out of the Senate race in New Jersey and Elizabeth Dole withdrew from the presidential race before the primaries got under way made Hillary's supporters question whether she would stick it out. "That created a real ripple," the First Lady acknowledges. Both Whitman and Dole cited the difficulty of raising money as the major reason for their decisions. Contributors to Hillary's campaign sought reassurance that she would not change her mind at the last minute. "In one part of their heads American voters know it's tougher for women," says Hillary. "That doesn't make them more sympathetic. That makes them say, 'Go out there and prove yourself.'"

Hillary's advisers insisted she would remain in the race despite her reluctance to formalize her candidacy. They blamed the pervasive talk of her bailing out on Republicans eager to drive her from the contest because she is a formidable opponent. Tony Blankley, an urbane Brit who once served as Speaker Newt Gingrich's press secretary, dismissed the First Lady's formulation. "We want her in the race," he said, speaking for Republicans. "She's the tar baby." The First Lady's closest friends and advisers said the race was "in her bones" and that rumors of her quitting got her competitive juices flowing. A member of the Clinton cabinet pointed out that if Mrs. Clinton decided the race was unwinnable, or she didn't want to spend her final year as First Lady scrounging for dollars and beating back political attacks, she could always say she's needed back in Washington. She would anger the New York Democratic party, but the country would probably think she had come to her senses. Senator Dianne Feinstein of California, who backed away from her state's governor's race in 1998, put it this way. "Political life and running for office is a life capsule sped up. You see so many things. There are moments of creativity and moments of absolute dejection and despair. It takes people with unusual drive and staying power to go through it."

Hillary set out with pad and pencil on what she called a listening tour of New York. Meeting with groups of voters and diligently recording their concerns, she hoped to become a familiar figure around the state and neutralize charges she is a carpetbagger. A huge contingent of media followed her everywhere, gently mocking her schoolmarmish approach, and soon tiring of her careful answers to questions posed by New Yorkers. One caller to C-SPAN during this period questioned the validity of the First Lady's claim she was listening, "because every time I see her on television, she's always talking." Deborah Tannen saw Hillary's approach as classically female in the way she sat and took notes, together with the issues she raised, which were of particular interest to women—gun control, education, and health care.

On the July day in 1999 that Hillary kicked off her bid for the Senate at the Moynihan farm, President Clinton was on a poverty tour of America, trying to revive his waning powers and recapture his party's liberal base. He visited South Dakota's Pine Ridge Indian Reservation, one of the poorest communities in the country, where three out of four people are unemployed. Clinton attracted far less media coverage than his wife. White House aides confirm that the sidelines are excruciating for Clinton, who draws sustenance from the spotlight much the way living things depend on oxygen. But to have him accompany her accentuates how derivative her power has been, and she looks weak. New York was Clinton's second best state in 1992 (he got 58 percent of the vote), and his third best in 1996 (he won by 1.8 million votes). Yet he must reconcile himself to the backseat. "Our roles are almost completely reversed now, you know," he mused in a CBS interview in November 1999. "All the things that she did for me over more than twenty years—all the encouragement, reminders, helpful suggestions, all the things—we've just kind of reversed roles, and I'm enjoying—I'm trying to do a good job in my new role."

At Hillary's announcement, Clinton paced backstage while the video extolling his wife's life played. Offered a chair, the president declined, saying, "I'm nervous as hell." Tony Bullock, Moynihan's chief of staff, said later, "He reminded me of one of these skating coaches at the Olympics wondering whether she'll make that triple axel."

Their political ambition joins them, and now it's Hillary's turn. It's part vindication and part legacy. It's what they do. Yet this is a dramatic change in a marriage where his career has always come first. There are bound to be missteps, perhaps unconscious ones, as Bill Clinton adjusts. For a man who loves the campaign trail, and excels at schmoozing, he diminishes any politician by comparison when it comes to people skills. Just ask Al Gore. Hillary now is not only a wife, or a First Lady; she's a politician. Senator Feinstein suggests he campaign for his wife "with discretion." Probed for what that means, she says, "It's not my business, but I think he should do the fund-raisers, but let her campaign alone. Because all women basically campaign alone. That's a whole other topic, but you do." Asked if he is more of a liability than an asset, as some polls suggest, Clinton responds with his characteristic aplomb. He thinks the voters want his wife and his vice president to "sell themselves"—and he wouldn't expect anybody to vote for them "just because I say they should do it."

Hillary's delay in formalizing her candidacy rested on the shaky rationale that she could prolong the benefits of incumbency. In 1996, President Clinton had never officially announced his bid for reelection, and the above-the-battle pose had worked for him. Vice President Gore tried the same approach in the run-up to his 2000 presidential bid, but found that voters don't respond in the same way to a politician staying vice presidential. Faced with a serious primary challenge from former New Jersey senator Bill Bradley, Gore moved up his planned announcement from September to June, and gave up the pretense of maintaining his official duties in order to campaign full-time.

Hillary's distaste for the media argued for sticking with the safety of her role as First Lady. The media are the same people, generally speaking, who hadn't understood her for seven years, from the time she first burst onto the national scene wearing a headband that became the focus of endless commentary. The longer she could avoid becoming a common politician, the longer she could put off the merry-go-round of media availabilities, press conferences, and interviews required of a major political candidate.

The turning point arrived in November 1999, when Hillary traveled to the Middle East against the advice of her political aides, and discovered firsthand just how lethal it was to mix her ceremonial role with her hopes for political office. The First Lady carried with her on the trip extensive rewrites of a book she had contracted to do about White House entertaining. The ghostwritten volume would have to be totally redone now that she was a political candidate. "When you're running for the Senate, you don't want to look like Martha Stewart," said a publishing source.

And maybe you don't want to look like a First Lady either. On a stop in Ramallah, an Arab section of the West Bank, Mrs. Clinton sat impassively as Suha Arafat, the wife of Palestinian leader Yasser Arafat, accused Israel of deliberately poisoning Arab women and children, and causing an increase in cancer cases. Mrs. Arafat apparently meant the use of tear gas by Israeli security forces. It took the First Lady's traveling entourage a dozen hours to muster a response disavowing Mrs. Arafat's remarks, which meant that Mrs. Clinton violated an important campaign rule that missteps should be corrected in the same news cycle. Mrs. Clinton had not taken any campaign aides with her so as to emphasize the official nature of the trip. But they had to be consulted as her statement was drafted along with diplomats worried about the political fallout on the ongoing Middle East peace negotiations. The overall hesitancy in handling the situation sparked a wave of criticism of Mrs. Clinton's political acumen. Giuliani's supporters said that if he had been confronted with Mrs. Arafat's unwarranted accusations, he would have stormed out of the event, or challenged her on the spot. A picture of the First Lady Kissing Suha Arafat made the front pages in New York. *Newsweek's* "Conventional Wisdom" chart gave Hillary a down arrow, declaring "First Lady Kisses up to Mrs. Arafat—and kisses off a lot of New York voters."

To win, a Democratic candidate running statewide in New York needs to carry the Jewish vote by a substantial margin. Polls showed Clinton and Giuliani dividing Jewish voters equally. In a *New York Times* survey, Hillary's negative rating among New York voters had climbed to 38 percent, up from 22 percent in the spring. In the same time period, her favorable rating plummeted from a high of 52 percent to 37 percent. Democrats who once salivated at the prospect of having the First Lady as their candidate had gotten more disillusioned by the day. Former vice presidential contender Geraldine Ferraro, who had run for the Senate in New York the previous year and was now a Fox News Network political analyst, advised the First Lady to "give up her day job" and move to New York after the first of the year. Ferraro spoke from experience. Friends and supporters had urged her to give up her job as co-host of CNN's "Crossfire" in order to raise money and campaign. She resisted, a decision that compromised her ability to wage a competitive race, and proved decisive in her defeat.

The crescendo of bad news properly panicked the First Lady and her advisers. In a series of transcontinental conference calls, the campaign cooked up a response that would signal Hillary was running, and would shore up her image as a strong political candidate and not some hothouse flower who would wilt at the first sign of trouble. Barely forty-eight hours after returning from ten days abroad, the First Lady was back in New York, holding forth at an education-related event and braced for a horde of reporters with one thing on their minds: Is she really running? "This is the kind of event where the media is the message," explained a top adviser. By returning to New York so soon after her contentious visit to the Middle East, the First Lady's presence spoke volumes. "In a campaign in which the other side is going to say 'I'm tougher,' this is a test of strength, showing she will be there for people whatever is thrown at her," said the adviser.

Hillary's campaign strategy revolved more around Giuliani self-destructing than on her ability to sell herself. The famously autocratic mayor was known for his inability to work and play well with others, and from a personality standpoint was not suited for the clubby Senate. The *New Yorker* cover of July 19, 1999, captured the essence of the race from Hillary's standpoint. It pictured an innocent-looking Hillary jogging in Central Park while a sinister-looking Giuliani lurks behind a tree waiting to mug her. "That image will stick," predicted Bob Squier, the noted Democratic media consultant, who believed Hillary had drawn the perfect opponent in Giuliani. "He just bites at everything. He's like a hungry trout." As Squier predicted, Giuliani's temperament became an issue when New York police shot an unarmed black man who was hailing a cab, and the mayor, instead of consoling the family, said the dead man was "no altar boy." Patrick

Dorismond's death was the third high-profile wrongful killing in little more than a year, and denigrating the deceased raised questions about Giuliani's judgment.

Giuliani is a left-leaning Republican who favors abortion rights and gay rights, and who wouldn't otherwise energize the GOP's conservative base. His supporters argued that with Hillary in the race, every right-wing male in the country will see it as his patriotic duty to defeat the country's leading liberal feminist.

Then in May 2000, six months before the election, in an emotion-packed news conference, Giuliani pulled out of the race. His health, his marriage, his iron-man image had all come apart, and the Republicans would have to find another contender to take on the First Lady. Within twenty-four hours, Long Island congressman Rick Lazio stepped forward. He had wanted to run originally but under party pressure had deferred to Giuliani. A pro-choice moderate like Giuliani, Republicans cheered him as Giuliani without the baggage. He had a progressive legislative record especially on health care issues, yet next to the First Lady, who had never been elected to anything, he had an over-eager manner that made him seem lacking in stature.

Their first debate on September 13 proved decisive. Convinced he had to assert himself in the race or Clinton would win by default, Lazio crossed the stage to demand she sign a pledge to forego ads paid for with soft money. The issue, while meritorious, was irrelevant. What mattered to viewers was Lazio's aggressive stance, and the way he invaded Clinton's space. Women thought Lazio was a bully, and in the polls and focus groups conducted after the debate, women voters moved to Hillary in droves. She won the election by twelve points, an astounding margin given all the predictions of how close the race would be. "Sixty-two counties, sixteen months, three debates, two opponents, and six black pantsuits later—here we are!" she enthused on election night. While the results of the presidential election would not be known for several weeks, Hillary had defied history and would become the bearer of the Clinton legacy. Gore failed to carry his home state of Tennessee, conceding defeat to George W. Bush after a controversial 5-4 Supreme Court decision in December ended the vote recount in Florida, in effect handing victory to Bush.

Early inklings of Gore's difficulties were apparent even in New York, a Democratic stronghold in the spring of 1999. Hillary's friend and confidant, lawyer Harold Ickes, approached some folks in the Moynihan camp about the rumor that Senator Moynihan planned to endorse Bill Bradley for the presidency. The message Ickes got back through intermediaries was blunt, and reflected the Moynihans' thinking. "Which race are you worried about? Don't press us on all fronts." If Ickes wanted Moynihan's endorsement for Hillary, he should lay off trying to win an endorsement for Gore. Moynihan never liked Gore, who he thought too white-shoe, too buttoned-down, and too entitled as the privileged son of a former senator. "Moynihan likes interesting people," says a former aide. "He doesn't do well with legacies." Better to take out on Gore his long-held animosity against Clinton, a classless fellow in Moynihan's mind, than on the well-meaning if hapless Hillary. As expected, Moynihan endorsed Bradley on September 23, 1999.

Why would Ickes bother to intervene on Gore's behalf? Because Bradley could raise money, and there's not an infinite amount of money for political candidates. Ickes wanted to save it for Hillary. The less mess there was on the Democratic side the better. If Bradley caught on, a three-way race for money would make it harder for Hillary. She set a goal of raising $25 million, the ticket of admission for a competitive race in an expensive media state like New York. She ended up spending $41 million; Lazio spent $40 million. The demands of the money chase sapped her energy, and made her friends wonder all the more why she chose such a difficult path for herself. "I think she's a lunatic for running," said a White House colleague.

Hillary had the issues on her side. New Yorkers wanted progress on health care and education, and the voters seemed to have forgiven her for failing to achieve the reforms in health care that she worked for in her husband's administration. They blamed political and economic interests for blocking reform and not Hillary. In October 1999, the Republican-controlled House of Representatives passed a Patients Bill of Rights, including the right to sue an HMO for denying medical treatment. The Republican-led Senate did not take up the bill, and it died with the close of Congress and the Clinton presidency. The House tried again in 2001, passing a Patients Bill of Rights with a limited right to sue, which the Democratic-led Senate pledged to put on the agenda in 2002. Partisan politics prevented final action, but Congress' steps vindicated a lot of what Hillary was saying in 1993, that the health care industry is out of control and needs regulation. It showed that asking for health care reform isn't ridiculous, and made her seem less of a pro-government Marxist crazy, which is how Republicans liked to portray her on the issue.

A *New York Times*/CBS poll published on February 25, 2000, showed the race still in a dead heat, with 45 percent of New Yorkers supporting Giuliani, 44 percent backing Hillary, and 9 percent undecided. The good news for Hillary was that voters overwhelmingly saw her as running a positive, issues-oriented campaign while Giuliani was perceived as spending more time attacking her than saying what he would do in the Senate. The carpetbagger issue had lessened as a problem. As *Washington Post* columnist David Broder noted, more than a third of those serving in the Senate were not born in the states they represent. Giuliani did slightly better with Jewish voters, a potential problem for Hillary, who needs to carry that community, and the two candidates split women, who are having the most trouble navigating the personal terrain of a Hillary candidacy. "It's like a soap opera where the queen steps off the stage and starts talking to the audience," explained a campaign adviser. "There are a lot of memories, and people have a lot of trouble putting them to rest." The goal is to get beyond "the celebrity phase," said a White House aide. "Once we get to issues, we're golden."

The GOP's playbook against Hillary read like this: She's a walking advertisement for the Clinton scandals. She's a doctrinaire liberal. She's responsible for the failed Clinton health care bill. She's a carpetbagger. Those are not hard charges to counter, and scandal-fatigued voters will punish Republicans for dwelling on the past. Caricaturing Hillary as a liberal might work in Mississippi, but not in the state that gave rise to Rockefeller Republicans. Voters clamoring for government regulation of HMOs are likely to see Hillary in the Senate as a savior, not as a threat to free enterprise. Finally, the carpetbagger charge: Remember, running for the Senate wasn't initially her idea.

It is a powerful lure for a sixties activist like Hillary Rodham to succeed Senator Moynihan, the resident intellectual of the Senate, and to occupy the same seat Robert F. Kennedy held when he campaigned for president. Kennedy was a carpetbagger too, though he had lived in Bronxville, a suburb of Manhattan, as a child. During his 1968 campaign, he attempted to lead a busload of reporters to his childhood home, and was embarrassed when he couldn't find it. Voters didn't seem to mind what the *New York Times* politely referred to as the "late-breaking residency" of Kennedy and Republican James Buckley, another carpetbagger who held the seat for one term, from 1970 to 1976. "Empire State voters tend to regard anyone famous as an honorary New Yorker," the *Times* opined. Giuliani as a college student penned an editorial for the school newspaper praising Bobby Kennedy's candidacy and dismissing the carpetbagger charge as irrelevant. The way candidates learn is by running, but they've got to be careful. All those upstate hamlets and Long Island townships with Native American names—mispronounce one and you're dead.

Hillary has the intellect and the drive to make it on her own in the political arena. But does she have the political instincts? Republicans seethe over the cavalier way the First Lady, a lifelong Chicago Cubs fan, declared she was also a New York Yankees fan. Picking out a team in another league to root for is something everybody does, she says. No they don't, howl the red-blooded males who call conservative talk-show host Rush Limbaugh daily to rail against Hillary the she-devil. She will never win over those voters, but the doubts about her political skills go deeper than the Yankees cap she donned. When she suggested that the American embassy in Israel be moved to Jerusalem, a position at odds with her husband, who favors leaving the status of Jerusalem to the peace settlement talks, a former Moynihan aide observed dryly: "New York politics is a study in the art of subtlety. Hillary is the opposite of subtle."

When reporters asked when her husband would be moving into the home the Clintons bought in suburban New York, Hillary said she hadn't yet talked to him about whether it would be his primary residence. Jaws dropped across America. Was Hillary telling us something? Aides explained that she's a lawyer to the core and is concerned about the tax implications of the family's move to New York, which could be tempered by Clinton claiming residency in Arkansas. "Plus he's trying to raise a boatload of money for a library in Little Rock," said an adviser. Clinton ultimately shifted his residency to New York, and made a show of spending the first night in their new home with his wife. Still, Hillary's language was unfortunate. She tends to react to things strongly, when what's needed is a lighter touch.

She hates to make mistakes—and a Democratic strategist who worked in the White House predicted she would make five huge ones in this campaign, and so will her staff. "It's New York politics," he shrugs. "To be a good politician, you've got to take risks and anger people sometimes." Hillary got a taste of what lay ahead before she had even formally announced. She was slow to clean up the controversy over the release of imprisoned Puerto Rican nationalists, who were conditionally pardoned by President Clinton despite objections from the FBI. After seeming at first to support her husband's judgment that those released had been given sentences too harsh for the crimes they had committed as members of the ultra-nationalist FALN, the First Lady then said that the release offer should be retracted. By then it was too late, their release was in motion, and her comment was read as an effort to gain distance from the negative political fallout of the president's decision. The public discourse revolved around what Hillary knew and when she knew it, and whether Clinton took the controversial action in a misguided effort to help his wife with the Puerto Rican vote. It took Hillary several days to regain her footing, but she was able to put the episode behind her and regain favor with Puerto Rican leaders, who were mostly mad at her for not consulting them before she went public in the first place.

Hillary Clinton is a polarizing figure. People tend to love her or hate her. She knows that, and sometimes it paralyzes her. Her instinct then is to play it safe and not offend. But a campaign that is too safe has no momentum. It stalls in the fast-paced media environment. That's part of what happened to Elizabeth Dole, who dropped out of the Republican presidential race before even officially declaring her candidacy.

American politics is a slugfest. And any woman who doesn't feel that way, who doesn't want to dirty her skirts with the rough and tumble, is going to be terribly disillusioned. Hillary calls the campaign environment in New York "a constant hazing" that each day tests her resilience. "It's daunting, and it's off-putting, I'm sure, for men as well as for women," she says. "But once you get into the rhythm of it, you see what's really going on. They dump on you, and you get back up and keep going. It's like a little check mark. Then they dump on you again. You get up and keep going, and it's like anything, once you do it for a while, you get the sense of how it works, and you're either ready to do it or you're not."

Asked if in the dark of the night she thinks about losing, Hillary replied with an air of defiance that is, well, so Hillary. "I'll have an interesting, full life, no matter what happens in November," she declared the words tumbling out, as if to dare the listener to feel sorry for her, or question her choice. "I want to do this because I really would like to serve in the Senate, and I'd like to be on the front lines of solving problems that I see in New York, and that I know exist around the country. I wasn't planning to do this, and I was looking forward to living in New York, and writing and speaking, and maybe working at a foundation, or in some other capacity, doing the work that I've always done on behalf of children and families, and women's issues. And so in one way I would continue that work in the Senate, and if that didn't work out, I would continue that work anyway.

"So for me the losing does not hold any fear at all. I think you get out there every day, you do the best you can, you try to get better so that you convince more people to vote for you, and you try to have fun doing it.

"Now that I've got my footing, and I'm into the rhythm of it, I'm having a good time. I like it. I like meeting people. I like talking about issues. I like the give-and-take. It's more like what I did before the White House, being a lawyer. I just can't overstate how different it is if you believe that you're here in the White House to further a presidential agenda than if you're either on your own as a lawyer before, or as a candidate now. This has been a lot of fun," she says, sounding like a woman eager to chart her own life and reclaim her independence.

Michael Deaver, who worked in the Reagan White House, is most remembered for the artistry he brought to a photo opportunity, and the way he used pictures to send signals to the country. "If somebody says she's going to be like Hillary Clinton, which Hillary is it going to be?" Deaver asks. "What role would you copy? Activist? Wife? Defender?"

Now Hillary has added successful senate candidate to the list. By stretching the role of First Lady to the breaking point, she shakes up the stereotypes and invites the country to look at her as a whole human being, not a crusader for one or another aspect of womanhood. She's not the caricature her critics create, or that her admirers seek to emulate. But she's in the arena, and that's the necessary first step to getting anywhere in politics.

Clinton barely had time to savor her victory when she was once again in the midst of controversy, some of her own making, much of it attributable to her husband. An $8 million book deal raised ethics concerns and charges of cashing in; and $190,000 in gifts from friends and political acquaintances seemed designed to beat the $50 Senate gift limit. Hillary's well-honed sense of entitlement came through when she explained with a touch of self-pity that she and her husband were furnishing homes in New York and Washington. But the scandal that struck with volcanic force had to do with a flurry of pardons President Clinton issued during his last hours in office. Several were questionable on the merits. Some were intertwined with donations to Clinton and the Democratic Party. Perhaps most embarrassing for Hillary was the revelation that her brother, Hugh Rodham, had been paid $400,000 to intervene on behalf of two felons seeking pardons. The whole affair underscored the poisonous role of money in politics. And while nothing illegal was proved after a year long investigation by the U.S. Attorney of New York, the bad taste of pardons for sale lingered in the public mind.

Rebuilding her battered image was nothing new for Hillary, and she went about it methodically, keeping her head down and her profile low, the way a freshman senator should. She reached out to conservative Republican senators, who had been her husband's tormentors, joining several of them in a weekly prayer group. She did her homework, asked no special favors, and turned down far more television requests than she granted. The gaggle of reporters who hung on her every word soon tired of the innocuous statements she doled out publicly. They resigned themselves to the fact that Clinton was a serious legislator who would not play the sound bite game, and who wanted to get along with her colleagues, not engage them in combat. Early coverage about Hillary's hair, flatter now than when she had daily coifs done at the White House, gave way to how much she loved being a senator and sitting through those boring budget hearings. There was even speculation that her real goal in life was not to be the first woman president, but the first woman Democratic Majority Leader. Her political action committee, HILLPAC, gave away $292,000 in 2001, a tip off to her future ambition. Only California Rep. Nancy Pelosi's "PAC to the future" gave away more money ($500,000), and Pelosi was waging a winning race to become the first woman elected party leader.

In May 2001, the Democrats took back control of the Senate for the first time since 1994 when Vermont Republican Jim Jeffords left the GOP and became an independent. Economic projections forecast budget surpluses as far as the eye could see, and the two political parties geared up for a debate on how to spend the windfall. Republicans favored tax cuts; Democrats wanted more investment in social programs. By early September, a slowing economy had begun to eat into the projected surplus, threatening both parties' agendas. But the partisan fights would be set aside, or at least postponed, as the country rallied to respond to the devastating attacks on New York and Washington the morning of September 11. Minutes after the first plane crashed into the World Trade Center, Giuliani was at Ground Zero, exhibiting leadership that would transform his final months in office into a case study for how politicians should respond in a crisis. His effectiveness combined with an unexpected compassion opened up limitless possibilities for him in the private and public sector, with the presidency perhaps even in reach. It was a reminder of how quickly and dramatically political fortunes can change, a lesson Hillary Clinton had lived many times over.

SEVEN

Go West, Young Woman

Betsy Bayless graduated from college with a Phi Beta Kappa key, degrees in Latin American studies and Spanish, and an interest in international banking. "My problem," she says, "was that it was 1966, and I found that a woman could not enter the professional world, at least not very easily, and certainly not in Arizona." Bayless finally did get a job in international banking—as a file clerk—and soon figured out that if she stayed she would always be a file clerk. "Being an achiever, it never occurred to me that I wouldn't be able to continue achieving," she says. She went back to school for a master's degree in public administration at Arizona State University. An internship led to her taking a job with the state govenment at minimum wage. As better jobs opened up Bayless applied, and a supervisor would say, "Well, we don't know whether a woman can do that job or not, but we'll at least give you a chance."

Bayless turned every opportunity to her advantage eventually becoming Arizona's secretary of state, the second-ranking position in state government. She was elected in November 1998 as one of the "Fab Five" women who held the top five jobs in the Arizona government. Governor Jane D. Hull, Attorney General Janet Napolitano, Treasurer Carol Springer, and Superintendent of Public Instruction Lisa Graham Keegan round out the all-female statehouse team. Arizona is a conservative Republican state, and Napolitano is the lone Democrat among the five women. They were sworn in by another prominent Arizonan, Justice Sandra Day O'Connor, the first woman on the U.S. Supreme Court. O'Connor praised the "independent and wise voters" who put the state's government in the hands of women.

By the spring of 2002, the vicissitudes of politics had splintered the Fab Five. Prevented from running for reelection by term limits, Hull served out her final months as governor. Bayless and Springer announced they would run for the Republican nomination to succeed Hull. The two women faced a formidable foe in former Congressman Matt Salmon, a conservative Republican, who was considered the front-runner. On the Democratic side, Napolitano sought the nomination against former State Senator Alfredo Gutierrez. Keegan was the first to split from the all-women's team. She resigned as state superintendent of public instruction in May 2001 to become CEO of the Education Leaders Council, a Washington education think tank that she helped found. Hull appointed a male Republican to replace her.

History has not yet rendered judgment on the Fab Five's performance in office, but that didn't prevent the *Phoenix New Times*, an alternative newspaper, from editorializing that "fab has turned to flab over the past few years, as these five have proven that women can be just as mediocre as men when it comes to governing." Hull's most lasting accomplishment has been her own face-lift, the paper said. It chided Napolitano and Bayless for "spending most of their time in office eyeing Hull's spot," said Springer "failed to notice that Arizona's alternative fuel tax credit was about to bankrupt the state," and said Keegan "gave us unregulated charter schools and onerous standardized testing—then split early for a lucrative private-sector job." Summing up, the paper said, "Lesson learned. The best man for the job is not necessarily a woman. . . ."

In the first half of the nineteenth century, the advice of newspaper editor Horace Greeley was "Go west, young man." At the start of the twenty-first century, the recommendation applies equally to young women interested in careers in politics. Besides the unprecedented female takeover of Arizona's government, seven of the ten women serving as attorney general—a stepping-stone to the governor's office— were elected in western states. And if state legislatures are the farm system for national office, the first female president will hail from west of the Mississippi. As of 2002, the top five states with the highest percentage of women in their state legislatures were (1) Washington, 38.8 percent; (2) Arizona, 35.6 percent; (3) Nevada, 34.9 percent; Colorado, 34 percent; and (5) Oregon, 33.3 percent. The model for women in politics is California, with two female senators, seventeen women serving as U.S. representatives, two women in state executive offices and 28.3 percent women in the legislature.

By electing large numbers of women to office, western states are laying the foundation for future generations. Girls growing up in Arizona and Washington, for instance, regularly see role models on television. Once women become an accepted fact of political life in a state, their numbers increase.

Why is the West more receptive to women in politics than other regions of the country? Women who hold office in those states point to the pioneering ethos of the West, where from the beginning women worked side by side with men to carve out the new frontier. The West is newer and open to new ideas, they say. From her ninth-floor office with a panoramic view of Phoenix, Hull, a no-nonsense redhead, credited her rise to the state's top job to the ongoing pioneering spirit. "In a lot of the West, you've constantly got new people coming," she said. "We have 100,000 new people coming to Arizona every year. There's not that sense that you have in the older eastern cities that you have to be a Rockefeller, that you have to have been born into the inner circle to get anywhere."

Machine politics that for years dominated in states from Massachusetts to Illinois and through much of the south never took hold in the West. Springer, the Arizona treasurer, broke into politics in 1990 by defeating an eighteen-year incumbent from her own party for a seat in the state senate. The daughter of a bricklayer—"We're just very ordinary people, very blue collar"—Springer ran because she was "ticked off" by the incumbent's vote for higher taxes. Eight years later, she was her party's nominee for treasurer. Springer is a conservative but supports abortion rights, as do the other members of the Fab Five, all except Hull.

The voters' reaction to scandals involving male politicians also has played a role in women's success in Arizona. The state's first female governor, Democrat Rose Mofford, took over in 1988 following the impeachment and conviction of Governor Evan Mecham, a Republican. Hull moved into the job by constitutional succession in September 1997 upon the resignation of Governor Fife Symington after his conviction for financial fraud. Bruce Merrill, a pollster and political scientist at Arizona State University, said that in the wake of those scandals and another that led to the indictment of several legislators, Arizona voters perceived the female candidates as more honest, fairer, and more compassionate. Springer quoted a male voter who told her, "Well, the men have screwed it up. We might as well let the women have a chance at it."

As newcomers to politics, women are held to a higher ethical standard. "For the first few decades of women in power we will be cognizant of the fact that we're first," says Keegan, the education superintendent. "And that has a heavier responsibility. It's not a good idea to screw up here because you've got a bunch of people standing behind you who would like to follow in your footsteps." Pressed about the prospects of women falling prey to corruption, Bayless, the secretary of state, said, "I just think women are smarter than that. I think women at this point generally have more ego control, maybe because we're working with a smaller ego to begin with."

Not all women politicians fit the profile. One of the most prominent offenders in Arizona's biggest political scandal was a woman, former state senator Carolyn Walker. She was sentenced to four years in prison for her role in Azscam, a 1991 sting that netted eighteen legislators and lobbyists for taking bribes from casino gaming interests.

The seemingly overnight success of Arizona's Fab Five came after years of preparation and persistence. "I wish I could say there is something in the water or some tremendous ideological movement in Arizona that supports women," said Merrill, the ASU political scientist. You have to look at the five elections individually to find out why they came out the way they did. Two of the women ran unopposed. The other three "ran the best campaigns and were the best candidates regardless of their gender," Merrill said. Hull ran as the incumbent Republican in a heavily Republican state enjoying its healthiest economy in decades. Bayless held major government positions in both Democratic and Republican administrations, and she was the incumbent by appointment before the election. Napolitano's election was the only surprise. But she had earned a tough-on-crime reputation over four years as the U.S. attorney in Arizona. Still, she might not have won had a vicious GOP primary not weakened the Republican candidate.

Women served as lawmakers of the Arizona territory before statehood and before women's suffrage, but they have not had it easy. Mofford, who was the first female secretary of state before her elevation to governor, began a half-century career in government after graduating from high school in 1940. "At first I thought being a woman was going to be a handicap because of the salary difference," she recalled. "I held a job as secretary to the tax commission. The man who had it before me made $250 a month, which was a lot of money in those days. When I got it, they paid me about $150. I didn't complain. I just went ahead and did my job." When she reached the top of the political ladder as governor, Mofford appointed more women as judges than any previous governor.

Arizona's experiment in governance by women raises the question, does having women in power make a difference? Hull thinks it might.

"Women tend to want to put people around the table and talk. Men order things, like ordering dinner." Hull said she expected less infighting in the all-female administration. "In the past, there seemed to be the attitude, 'if I'm mad at you, I'm going to make sure that the whole world knows it,' " she said. "That's not my style. I don't think you are going to see outright headline wars from us. I think we tend to talk out our disagreements before we introduce them to the press."

Napolitano, the lone Democrat, said there are differences even among the Republican women, whose ideology ranges from mainstream moderate to far-right conservative. "We're very different politically, but it's not acrimonious," she said. "I think fundamentally we all view ourselves as having jobs to get done. We haven't devolved into the kind of chest-thumping posturing that characterized Arizona under Governor Symington." Bayless said the women are "more inclusive in decision-making" than their male predecessors, and Keegan added that the women share a family-friendly approach to governing. "Most of us lead with our families," she said. "That's where we live. It's the first issue in the morning and the last one at night. If you listen to the five of us, we are usually talking about the future in terms of children. I think until recently men didn't have the luxury of leading with children and families because it was seen as soft."

Arizona's attorney general has made improving care for foster children one of her priorities. She dubbed them "plastic-bag children" after the sacks they use to tote belongings from one foster home to the next. "You have to reach people who ordinarily wouldn't spend any time thinking about these kids by creating an image like 'plastic-bag children' that will stick in their minds," said Napolitano. But that doesn't mean women running government are, to invoke a stereotype, "soft." "This is a big death-penalty state, and I've supervised four executions in ten weeks," Napolitano said early in her term. "Some of my friends are very anti-death penalty. They are disappointed that I've said, 'Look, we're going to do this,' and we've done it."

Hull and several of the other women talked about their "consensus approach" to governing. But Springer pointed out a contradiction. Republicans control the state legislature, but Hull vetoed twelve bills in her two years as an appointed governor and continued to wield the veto pen frequently after she was elected. Her twenty-one vetoes in 1999 were the most by any governor in more than twenty years. "You don't build consensus on all the issues," said Springer, described by those who know her as "tough as any man." "Why would a Republican governor veto a Republican legislature's bill if consensus was the way you always worked?" she asked. "Sometimes it's who has the hammer. And she has the hammer."

Does ideology trump gender? Springer thinks it might. "Each of us is different philosophically even though four of us are from the same party," she said. "We don't always agree on issues. So I don't see how you could say that government will be run differently than if there were five men, if the five men were of the same persuasion politically as these five women." Springer said the five women were elected not because of their sex but because of their experience and stands on issues. "Gender was never an issue during the campaign," she said. "In my view, that's the bigger story. The voters didn't set out to elect women. Nobody really thought about it until after the election." Merrill's polling confirms this view. He did not detect a gender gap. Men and women voted equally for the Fab Five.

Once in office, however, the women pursued different priorities from the men who preceded them. Hull prides herself on being a fiscal conservative, but the former schoolteacher put tens of millions more dollars into education in her first two-year budget than had been projected by her predecessor. Arizona's Republican legislature would have opted to use the money for across-the-board tax cuts. As House Speaker Jeff Groscost put it, "Education is next to godliness, but in Arizona, cutting taxes is godliness." The new governor succeeded in passing an education-funding measure that many said took a woman to champion. "Education is where the action is," she said, simply.

Hull's frequent run-ins with Groscost, a fellow Republican, point up the friction created when women take the top jobs once held exclusively by men. For the most part, Groscost treats his standing with Hull and the other female leaders with self-deprecating humor. In speeches, he says he is "the most powerful man in elective office in the state." Then, after a pause, he adds, "Of course I'm the only man left in elective office in the state." In a less-guarded moment in the summer of 1999, Groscost accused Hull of being a liberal and compared her to Hillary Rodham Clinton, which is no joking matter in conservative Arizona.

Groscost, a paid consultant on the presidential campaign of Arizona senator John McCain, was miffed when Hull endorsed Texas governor George W. Bush. In an interview with the *New York Times*, Hull said McCain had an explosive temper and was temperamentally unsuited for the presidency. This led to stories and editorials questioning McCain's ability to cope with the pressures of the Oval Office. Soon after Hull's remarks were published, Groscost gave an interview to a *USA Today* reporter in which he recounted a conversation between Hull, Bayless, and senate president Brenda Burns on a car ride where he felt left out. According to Groscost, the women talked about which hair curlers produce nicer curls, two-inch curlers or quarter-inch curlers. "I finally understood what ladies have long talked about: having to endure men's talk about football and basketball games," Groscost said.

Hull turned the incident into a bad hair day for Groscost. Addressing an audience of two thousand Hispanic professional women, she brandished the *USA Today* front page, where the story appeared, and said, "I haven't seen those pink spongy curlers for thirty years. Believe me, we do not talk about our curlers. I will send a pointed message to the speaker . . . to remind him we don't talk about curlers. We talk about issues, and we talk about what's good for the state of Arizona."

Groscost also has had strained relations with two other politically powerful women, Arizona State Senate president Brenda Burns and house majority leader Lori Daniels, who is second in command behind Groscost. Both women are Republicans. Groscost bragged about his intention to line up votes for a male senator who hoped to unseat Burns, but it was Groscost himself who was unseated when he tried unsuccessfully for a seat in the Arizona Senate in 2000. "There's not a lot of love lost between us," Daniels said.

In an interview before his fall from power, Groscost said the women in the Arizona statehouse "span the spectrum from my most liberal members to my most conservative members. We have members who consider the John Birch Society to be something of a leftist organization, and we have among our ladies some on the far left who probably knew Mao Zedong personally." Describing Daniels, he said, "My majority leader is tough. That's why I love her. I don't have to play the bad cop all the time." In a separate interview with the *Arizona Capitol Times*, Daniels sounded nothing like Groscost's description. "To be perfectly honest," she said, "I kind of consider myself Mom. I kind of feel like whenever members have problems or need some help, I'm the one they're supposed to turn to."

With five women in charge, men have had to play unfamiliar roles. Keegan quotes Hull, saying, "When you see a line of men holding women's purses while the women talk, you can be sure you're in Arizona." Laughing, Keegan says, "I have seen the governor hand off her purse to a man on a number of occasions and it cracks me up."

Yet some things don't change. Keegan and her husband, John, are the parents of five children, three of them from his first marriage. On the day Keegan was interviewed, she had stayed home from work to care for the two younger children, who had colds, while her husband, who is the mayor of their town of Peoria, outside Phoenix, tended to business at city hall. "That's still the nice thing about being a man," Keegan said. "Women who whine about that just need to grow up. I wouldn't give up the ability to play hooky with the kids. . . . But it's absolutely true that my husband has more liberty in how he chooses to spend his time than I do."

By coincidence, the day after Keegan gave her observations on women's dual role, her point was demonstrated by another female politician-wife-mother. This time the setting was Olympia, Washington, another capital where women have seized a large share of political power. On the lawn of the capital building, Christine Gregoire, the state's highly rated attorney general, held a news conference to end speculation that she would challenge Republican senator Slade Gorton in the 2000 election. Washington already had one female senator, Patty Murray, a Democrat who campaigned as a "mom in tennis shoes." But Gregoire, who was described in a newspaper article that morning as "the strongest among possible Democratic challengers," said she had more pressing responsibilities at home.

"With a fourteen-year-old daughter still at home, and an elderly mother who needs her family more than ever, I have decided I will not run for the U.S. Senate," she told a clump of reporters and photographers. "The timing may be right politically, but it is wrong for my family. I have one daughter who is a college sophomore, so I know how quickly the years pass and our children leave home. I also want to be there for my mom—just as she was there for me for all those years. . . . I therefore have concluded that being the best mom I can be, the best daughter and wife I can be, and the best attorney general I can be are the most fulfilling roles for me at this time."

Would a man with a good chance of winning the Senate seat have pulled out for the sake of his family, or does family responsibility put more pressure on a woman? "I've tried mightily to say it doesn't," Gregoire said. "But the bottom line is I think female candidates think differently. In the end, I think almost every female candidate that I know always talks about family and how important family is. So it weighs very heavily on a female candidate's mind, possibly much more so than it might on a male candidate."

When she dropped out, Gregoire was at the peak of popularity. Her role in spearheading a multibillion-dollar settlement between tobacco companies and the states suing them had earned Washington a $495 million bonus in addition to the $4 billion due to the state. *Good Housekeeping* chose Gregoire for its highest award for women who "made a difference" in 1999 (ethics rules prevented her from accepting the $25,000 prize) and her standing with the state's voters hit an all-time high. Gregoire did not rule out a future run for governor or the Senate, but the opportune moment had passed her by.

With or without Gregoire in the Senate race, Washington is a female-friendly state in American politics. No sooner had Gregoire dropped out than state insurance commissioner Deborah Senn announced she would seek the Democratic Senate nomination. She set a goal of raising $1 million by the end of 1999 to prove her viability. At a news conference in Washington, D.C., Senn distributed a briefing book citing the high number of women in her state's legislature as proof of the strong support for female candidates. "The women statewide elected officials are perceived as having done really good jobs," she said, "and so I think people are very enthused about electing women."

Punctuating the point, former representative Maria Cantwell announced in January 2000 that she would challenge Senn for the nomination. In 1992, Cantwell became the first Democrat in forty years elected to the U.S. House from the state's First District. Two years later, her political career was cut short by the Republican landslide of 1994. Commenting on Cantwell's attempted comeback after five years out of politics, Democratic consultant Cathy Allen likened Cantwell to a bungee jumper who is afraid of heights. "It's something she's got to do," Allen told the *Seattle Times*. "She can't live with that last loss. This is her confronting and overcoming her greatest fears."

Typically, women take political losses personally. Many give up after a single defeat, as if the voters had delivered a verdict for life. Cantwell's defeat hurt, but she says, "I don't know how you can engage in learning experiences unless you get out there and try to hit the mark. And if you miss, you get back up and try again."

After her loss, Cantwell became an e-commerce executive with RealNetworks, an Internet start-up company specializing in video-streaming software. The company enjoyed phenomenal success, growing from ten employees when Cantwell joined to more than seven hundred when she took a leave of absence to run for the

Senate. In five years, her stock holdings grew to be worth more than $12 million.

"Every day at an Internet start-up it's like the two weeks before an election," Cantwell said. "In software, there's a term, 'periscope up,' because you're so underwater, immersed in your own world, you don't even know what's going on." She said the experience was "a great education for me about business, about decision-making, about how the future will impact people." After deliberating for several months, she decided to try again for elective office, in part "because I work with a bunch of twenty-and thirty-year-olds that are writing off the system. I'm motivated to engage them in a campaign that shows that government doesn't have to be an anchor that drags behind the technology economy. When people write off government, we get bad social policy."

In addition to her two years in Congress, Cantwell had six years' experience in the state legislature. But she was at a disadvantage against Senn, who had twice been elected insurance commissioner in statewide balloting with whopping majorities of 83 and 75 percent. Even as Senn, a hell-raising populist, raised campaign money and gathered endorsements, some Democrats publicly urged the moderate, pro-business Cantwell to get in the race, fearing that Senn's take-no-prisoners liberal politics would fail against Gorton.

Cantwell spent more than $11.5 million on her political comeback, including $10.3 million from her own high-tech fortune. She defeated Senn easily in the primary and went on to win the Senate seat narrowly after a drawn-out recount. But a dramatic plunge in the value of her RealNetworks stock left her more than $4 million in debt, including $3.8 million in loans for which she had used her stock holdings as collateral. The Clintons—both the former president and his newly elected senator wife—held fundraisers for Cantwell, as did other prominent Democrats. "This is a very hard time for her," Sen. Dianne Feinstein told Roll Call, the Capital Hill newspaper. Despite their efforts, Cantwell still owed $3.8 million at the start of 2002. Opponents opened an Internet site (http://www.cantwellscash.com), which mocks the freshman senator's campaign claim that she would shun contributions from special interests.

Cantwell's debt cast a shadow on a shining moment in Washington state's political history when it became the third state, after Maine and California, to elect two women to the Senate. Cantwell won not just because Gorton was vulnerable after forty years in politics, but because the state is gender blind politically. The numbers tell part of the story. In Washington state in 2002, women held 23 of the 49 Senate seats and outnumbered men, 17 to 8 in the majority Democratic caucus. They held 34 of the 98 House seats. The attorney general and the chief state education official were women.

The United States was slow to admit women to the voting booth and to political office, but Washington was one of the first states to give women a chance. In 1912, the first year women were eligible to serve in the legislature, two women were elected. When one of them, Frances C. Axtell, got confused in her first session and voted for the opponent of the man she supported for speaker of the house, the press mocked her for behaving "just like a woman." The first woman to serve in the Washington senate was Reba Hurn, a lawyer and Spokane Republican, who was elected in 1922, two years after women got the right to vote. *The Women Lawmakers*, a book by Kathryn M. Hinsch, reports some responses from a statewide poll taken that year on whether women were qualified to run for office: "I'll never vote for a woman." "The Bible says we shouldn't." "I don't think it's nice for women to sit in halls where men smoke and drink and swear."

Vestiges of that kind of thinking remained a half-century later, in 1995, when Darlene Fairley was asked by a Democratic party official if she could recommend "a young man with good ideas" to run for a state senate seat that had become vacant. Fairley was working at the time as a victims' advocate with the Seattle Police Department. "What would be wrong with a middle-aged woman with good ideas?" she shot back. "I have something to offer that young guys don't. Young guys haven't lived a life, and there are certain things that come from living. I've been through a war. I've been disabled. I've had many things happen to me, and you learn from everything that happens to you. A young guy who's never gone through life's experiences I don't think has much to offer." Fairley won the seat that year.

Most male politicians of the baby-boomer generation cannot boast of having combat experience. But Fairley says, "I've been through a war. I've been shot at. I've gone down in a plane crash." Fairley and her husband are Quakers. They met in Vietnam, where she served from 1966 to 1970. She went there as an English teacher. When bombs destroyed her school, she trained to become a medic. "I would go into insecure areas where doctors couldn't go," she said. "I speak Vietnamese. I'd ask what was going on, who was sick, then tell the doctors. They'd tell me what to do and I'd go back and treat them. A lot died, a lot lived. You know, your life's experiences help you to understand other people. I've been through a lot."

In 1977, Fairley was driving on Interstate 90 with her three-month-old son when, she says, her car was "mashed by a drunk driver." Doctors told her husband they would both die, but they defied the odds. Fairley was told she would not walk again, but she proved that forecast wrong too. Her son, Andrew, graduated from college in May 1999 with a degree in computer science and Fairley manages with a wheelchair and crutches.

Women understand more about what average families face because they've had to deal with more, Fairley says. "We're more tied to what it takes to buy a house if you're starting out, what it takes to feed a family, what it takes just to keep everything together on a certain salary," she says. "As a woman, I know household budgets. I know what it takes to make sure that you have enough to keep two cars running and how much a teenager eats and what shoes cost. I know how much a kid costs these days. I'm closer to it. I pay the household expenses and handle it when there isn't enough to buy what the kid wants. . . . In the legislature, we women speak to what people care about: their house, their kids, their ability to make a living, their jobs."

Fairley thinks voters across the country are beginning to realize that female officeholders are "closer to them, more sympathetic, more truthful." Raising children is good training for politics, she says, because it keeps you honest. "Kids catch on when you're lying," she says.

Children come up frequently when women in the Washington legislature talk about what motivates them. Representative Ida Ballasiotes got into politics in 1988 after her daughter was stalked and murdered by a sex offender on a work-release program. She turned her grief into action, first by joining a citizens group to pressure the government for tougher anti-stalker laws, then by getting elected to the statehouse and working her way up to chair the Criminal Justice Committee. Ballasiotes' efforts became the prototype for Megan's Law and other laws throughout the country calling for the registration of sex offenders and public notification when they come out of prison into neighborhoods. She ran for office to deal with a problem, not, as with many of her male colleagues, to pursue a career.

Because women like Ballasiotes get into politics to do something rather than be someone, partisanship does not come naturally to them. Typically, the first women in the Washington legislature would decide to run and only later decide which party they belonged to. Ballasiotes is a Republican, but she says, "I don't see Republican bills and

Democratic bills. They're either issues that are good public policy or they're not. I work across the aisle all the time."

The high priority given to violence against children, spouses, and the elderly stands out in interviews with female legislators in Washington. "It's hard for a lot of men to understand the unequal power struggle that takes place in domestic violence because a lot of men have never been afraid or powerless or had no place to go," said Senator Pat Hale, a Republican. Hale sponsored a law that protects domestic violence victims from having an insurance claim denied when an angry spouse destroys a jointly owned house or car. She acted after hearing the story of a woman whose home-owner's claim was rejected because her estranged husband, co-insured on the policy, burned down the family home to keep her from getting it in a divorce. Another female-generated bill that passed in Washington State in 1999 increases protection for domestic violence victims by enabling them to route their mail through the secretary of state's office so that estranged husbands or boyfriends cannot trace them to a new address.

The anecdotal evidence of how women govern mirrors findings of a study of state legislators conducted by the Center for the American Woman and Politics at Rutgers University. "Elected women are working to make the agendas of legislative institutions more responsive to women's demands for equal rights . . . and more reflective of women's concerns stemming from their roles as caregivers," the study found. In Washington State, proof of this came with the first bill introduced by the first female legislator in 1912. It was a proposal to improve standards for women's working conditions.

Recently, female legislators in Washington have marshaled their girl power, as Senator Jeri Costa put it, behind such issues as breast-feeding rights for working women, health insurance coverage for contraceptives, and allowing licensed midwives at childbirth. All three passed in the senate, where women control the majority Democratic caucus, but stalled in the house. The sponsors vowed to keep pressing for passage. One of the first bills the female bloc pushed through removed sales tax from birth control pills, which had been the only taxed prescription drug in Washington. "A couple of years ago we tried to take sales tax off diapers and feminine hygiene products," Costa said. "The men laughed at us and voted it down. But we're not giving up."

Many women in politics maintain that their conciliatory style frequently makes the difference between success and failure of legislation. Kari-Lynn Frank, a lobbyist for the Puyallup Indian Tribe in

Washington State, said women "tend to tell you why they voted the way they did if they didn't vote with you. The female chairmen that I've worked with try to make the best of the legislation. It's fair and even-handed, even though it doesn't always go my client's way. They go out of their way to try to give everybody a horse to ride home on."

Public opinion polls show that people think women tell it like it is and are less likely to engage in political double-speak. That proved true in April 1999 when Washington senator Rosemary McAuliffe spoke with a group of teachers from her district who were among several thousand teachers demonstrating outside the capitol in Olympia, demanding a 15 percent pay raise. "I could have told them how wonderful they all are and left it at that," McAuliffe said. "But I told them the truth. It's true they are 15 percent behind in their pay. But that didn't happen in one session and it can't be fixed in one session. They didn't like that. . . . They taught my six children. Do I not believe they work hard? I know they work hard. I not only value them, I owe them a lot. I wanted them to hear the straight story."

For her efforts, McAuliffe was pictured on the front page of the Olympia paper being heckled by teachers. In the end, however, she helped the legislature craft an increase of roughly 13 percent for new teachers and 6 percent for experienced teachers.

Then there was the way Senator Valoria Loveland, chair of the Ways and Means Committee, handled the drafting of the Washington State budget. Loveland's committee produced a budget that sailed through the senate and passed the politically divided house with only technical changes—the first time anyone can remember such an occurrence without huge fights and many amendments. "She spent many, many hours listening to everybody and what they wanted," said legislative aide Kate Sandboe. "She gave everybody what they said they needed, and if she couldn't, she made sure they understood why."

Loveland, a Democrat, compared the budgeting process to keeping peace in a household. "When two kids are fighting over a toy, you either get two toys just alike or you divert their attention and take them both away from the toy and find something else for them to do that they would enjoy," she said. "Women traditionally have had to settle disputes with our children. We certainly don't want to make one mad and one happy."

Showing the confidence that comes with their growing numbers, female lawmakers, lobbyists, and staff members created a tongue-in-cheek secret society called the "Mean Old Bitches." The idea came from a woman working in one of the government agencies who overheard a male colleague say, "You don't have to listen to her. She's just a mean old bitch." Soon, women all over the capitol were sporting pins showing a blonde, brunette, and redhead and the acronym M.O.B. Fairley said wearing the pin signifies that a woman is "someone who will say it like it is, won't sugarcoat it, and won't back off. We have some arrogant, mean types, and they're not members. There are some real sweethearts, and they're not members. It's for women you can trust to do what they say they're going to do."

Not all women in the Washington legislature put the sisterhood ahead of politics. Senator Pam Roach, a Republican, said, "I vote my constituents, not my gender. To decide that all women think the same is demeaning, because they don't." Roach dismissed the proposal for a bipartisan women's caucus as divisive. "Sure, there are things we can all agree on," she said. "But when it comes down to the hard-core issues, it's right or wrong, yes or no. Confrontation is the lifeblood of politics. If that bothers you, you better get into something more sheltered."

Senator Karen Schmidt, another Republican, agreed, saying, "I didn't come down here to be a woman in the legislature. I came here to work on issues that are important to my district." Schmidt described the legislature as a rough-and-tumble place where women have to learn to play the game. "You have to play by the rules," she said. "And if you think you're going to win just because you're a woman or just because you think you're right or just because you can cry, that's not going to get you your issues." In a whiny voice, Schmidt mocked a female colleague saying, "Oh, please . . ." "That kind of argument doesn't go very far around here," she said. As for a women's caucus, she says, "I belong to one caucus—the Republican caucus. I don't need another one."

On one point the sexes agree. Women have changed the culture of the capitol. The first thing a visitor to either the senate or house chamber notices are the flowers on the legislators' desks. Lobbyists who once presented bottles of liquor with their calling cards now send roses. Some of the women bring flowers from their home gardens to brighten their desktops. "Liquor used to play a big role in what went on here," said Senator Val Stevens, a Republican. "There even used to be a bar set up on the premises. That went by the wayside several years ago."

Democratic male senators, finding themselves unexpectedly in the minority, have taken it in good humor, at least for public consumption. Senate majority leader Sid Snyder, whose legislative career spans four decades, recalled that in 1969 there were forty-nine men in the senate and no women. Then, as now, there was a no-smoking rule. But at the start of each day's session, it was the first rule suspended, followed immediately by dozens of senators lighting up cigars. "Change is good for us," Snyder says, without much conviction.

The youngest member of the Washington State Senate, Calvin Goings, a Democrat who was twenty-four when he was elected in 1996, said, "I'm used to having a few extra mothers around. I get mothered quite a bit." Goings is of a generation that takes power sharing for granted. At his two-year community college, he was vice president of the student body both years. The president each year was a woman. Goings said he was amused when the women achieved a majority in the Democratic caucus and promptly converted a male senator's large office to a women's lounge. The men's lounge was transformed into an office for one of the women.

The eight male Democratic senators put a happy face on their situation by forming the Last Man's Club. Goings said the club has purchased "a bottle of sparkling apple cider" and stashed it at a member's house. If the day ever comes, it will be opened to toast the senate's last male survivor. Goings did not wait for the inevitable. He left his seat to run for local office.

EIGHT

The Governor Gap

Given the results of recent elections, many analysts believe a likely source of presidential material is the state house. Four of our last five presidents have been governors, a signal that voters prefer people with executive experience to lead the country. John F. Kennedy is the last president to have gone directly from the U.S. Senate to the presidency. This is a problem for women candidates because it is almost as hard for women to get elected governor as it is for a woman to be taken seriously as a presidential contender. Polls show that voters by a wide margin have more confidence in men as decisive leaders. They think women can hold their own in debating and crafting legislation, but when it comes to executive command, men have the edge. "There's a different dynamic running for executive office," says Ellen Malcolm, founder of Emily's List. "You have to convince the voters of many things—that you can take care of the budget, and that you're tough enough to manage the bureaucracy and deal with issues like crime." The ability to project leadership is key, and that's where campaign ads can help. A White House Project study of executive leadership is researching the advertising used by female candidates— what worked and what didn't work, and why. They expect to have a data bank of some 700–800 spots from 60–70 candidates going back 25 years.

Women bring a different life experience, for better or worse, to the electoral arena. Some of those differences are generational, and over time will be erased. Others reflect powerful societal forces that ebb and flow, and that shape who we are, and who we elect. The elevation of Sandra Day O'Connor from the Arizona legislature to a seat on the U.S. Supreme Court is one woman's story, but it is also a tale of the times and the obstacles women have had to overcome.

Emma Jordan had gained prominence as a member of Anita Hill's defense team, but she was an anonymous special assistant in Ronald Reagan's Justice Department in 1981 when the résumé of a little-known Arizona state judge and legislator landed on her desk. "When I first read Sandra Day O'Connor's résumé, I said, 'No way,'" recalls Jordan. "She had never practiced with a major law firm. There were gaps in her background where she clearly had been at home having babies. She had never held a national position. Under awards, she had something like Phoenix Ad Woman of the Year. Excuse me," Jordan remembers thinking, "this is *not* Supreme Court material."

Jordan noticed something else unusual. Not a single man's name appeared in the briefing book that she was handling of potential Supreme Court nominees. "That was clearly an affirmative action seat," she says. A closet Democrat who had put aside her politics for the opportunity to serve in government, Jordan couldn't believe what was unfolding. Kenneth Starr, a promising young jurist who would later become the independent counsel investigating President Clinton, had hired her. Starr had traveled to Arizona to conduct the background check on O'Connor. President Reagan wanted to name the first woman to the Supreme Court.

As Jordan examined the credentials of the handful of names in the briefing book, she thought that the women appeared underqualified. O'Connor stood out from the others primarily because of her sponsor, Arizona senator Barry Goldwater, the former presidential candidate and the spiritual godfather of modern conservatism. Goldwater vouched for O'Connor, and that counted a lot with the Reaganites.

Conservatives hate to admit it, but Justice O'Connor was an affirmative action product. If Reagan had chosen purely on the weight of a résumé, he would have found her wanting, just as Jordan did at the time. "That's because I'm in the next generation down from her and didn't encounter the blatant career discrimination that she faced," Jordan says. "Her résumé was shaped by that discrimination. But she's done just fine. I have no problem with her."

Born in 1930, O'Connor faced the kind of gender barriers that were commonplace throughout most of the twentieth century. She graduated third in her class from Stanford Law School, but few private law firms would hire a woman. Many educated women put aside their degrees and returned home, raising children and working as volunteers. The silver-haired women who today might be governing states and chairing congressional committees are absent with cause.

O'Connor's appointment as the first female Supreme Court justice was an important step in the political evolution of women. Before the century was out, President Clinton would name a woman secretary of state and attorney general, shrinking the number of top jobs never held by a woman. President Bush continued the progress, naming Condoleezza Rice, an African-American woman, national security advisor. Seeing these women in these high-profile jobs makes it easier for voters to imagine a woman as vice president, or even as president, and for young women to see themselves choosing a career in politics. Asked if she regarded herself as a role model, O'Connor said, "I was quite conscious of not wanting to be the first and last."

Albright was the most hawkish member of Clinton's foreign policy team, and was the driving force behind Clinton's risky but successful military intervention in the Balkans. She worked with a male defense secretary and national security adviser and it has been said that she was the only man among them. She broke stereotypes about women and war, and helped neutralize the commander in chief hurdle faced by any woman running for president. Reno was at the core of controversy several times, but survived to become the longest-serving attorney general of the century. Women activists push hard for cabinet appointments, seeing them as a route to power that is more accessible than elective office.

Appointing women to the Supreme Court and to cabinet posts is a laudable attempt to carve out new pathways to power. Someday a female justice or cabinet secretary will run for president or be nominated for vice president. But for now, the clearest route to the nation's top executive jobs is climbing the ladder of elective political office. Over the last two decades, no position has offered a better stepping-off point to the White House than governor. Georgia's Jimmy Carter, California's Reagan, and Arkansas' Clinton all advanced to the top rung that way. And after the 2000 election, Texas's George W. Bush joined their ranks. Here, women who aspire to become president have a problem. In the history of the United States only twenty-three women have served as governors. Of these, sixteen were elected in their own right, not as replacements for a deceased husband or surrogates for husbands who could not run for reelection. At the start of the twenty-first century, only five women—two Democrats, Jeanne Shaheen in New Hampshire and Ruth Ann Minner in Delaware; and three Republicans, Jane Dee Hull in Arizona, Jane Swift in Massachusetts, and Judy Martz in Montana—held governorships. These officeholders are almost half of all the women who have been elected governor on their own. The numbers are dismal, but Malcolm says they sound worse than they are. If you account for the fact there are half as many governors' seats (50) as Senate seats (100), the representation of women in each body is about the same, nothing to brag about but slowly inching upward.

There is no affirmative action program for a woman who wants to be governor. If there were, surely Mary Sue Terry would have become the first female governor of Virginia.

When she ran for the office in 1993, Terry seemed to be an ideal candidate to become Virginia's first female governor. For starters, she had a Lincoln-like life story. She was born in the town of Critz (population fifteen) in rural, conservative, southern Virginia. For the first seven years of her life, Terry and her two younger sisters lived with their parents in an apartment above the auditorium at Hardin-Reynolds Memorial School. "The school was so small," she says, "they had to teach driver education and sex education in the same car." Later, her family moved to a farm. "We raised pigs," she says. "I cleaned out the pig houses. I got up corn." When she went off to Westhampton College, she told her parents that her classmates mocked her as "a hick from the sticks." But her determination and persistence overcame her lack of academic and social skills. She was elected president of her freshman class. She went on to get a master's degree in government in 1970 and a law degree in 1973 from the University of Virginia.

Terry did not set out to carve a career in politics. Her ambition after law school was to be a country lawyer. But politics was in her blood. Her father had been a Democratic county chairman and, as a girl, she would ride into town with him on Saturday afternoons. While he presided at a political meeting, she would go to the drugstore and drink cherry Cokes with town girls. As a teenager, she went to the meetings with her father and passed out campaign balloons and pencils at county fairs. Still, when she was approached in 1977 to run for the Virginia House of Delegates, she hesitated. "I asked myself, 'OK, Mary Sue, why is this not attractive to you?' Being comfortable with my life as it was and afraid to try something new were not good reasons." She ran and won.

Almost from the day Terry arrived in Richmond, Democratic leaders encouraged her to run for attorney general. No woman had been elected to statewide office, but Terry fit the profile of someone who could break that barrier. In 1985, she did. She was reelected easily in 1989. In seven years as attorney general, she compiled a "solid record," says a *Washington Post* profile. She reduced the blood-alcohol level required to prove drunken driving, gave police additional tools to prosecute drug dealers, increased penalties for sexual assaults, made stalking a crime, forced Ford Motor Co. to withdraw unsafe ambulances across the country, and joined federal officials in prosecuting Lyndon H. LaRouche, Jr. Many thought she was ready to become the state's first female governor in 1989, but she yielded to fellow Democrat Douglas Wilder, who became the state's first African-American governor.

In 1993 it was Terry's turn, but the political climate for a Democratic candidate was perilous. By then, Democrats had governed Virginia for twelve straight years, and the state's top two Democrats, Wilder and Senator Charles Robb, had been feuding bitterly in public for two years. At the national level, Clinton had stumbled in his first year in office and the Democratic-controlled Congress was in its death throes after almost forty years in power. Even in this environment, Terry started substantially ahead in the polls over her Republican opponent, George F. Allen, who had served in the state assembly and for one term in Congress but was widely considered a political lightweight. His biggest claim on the public's affection was that he was the son and namesake of the highly successful Washington Redskins' football coach. At age forty-five, Terry was at the peak of her political powers. She had never lost an election and there seemed no reason to start now.

One measure of Terry's ability is an offer conveyed by the Clinton White House in December 1992, before the campaign for governor got into gear. She was at a holiday party when she got an urgent message to phone Warren M. Christopher, who was heading Clinton's transition team. He asked Terry whether she would like to be considered for U.S. attorney general. She would be the first woman to hold the job. "I was very flattered," Terry told the *Washington Post*, but she asked Christopher to take her name off the list. "The timing just wasn't right. . . . My response was that my course has been set here in Virginia." The attorney general's job eventually went to Janet Reno.

Looking back on a campaign that ended in November 1993 with Terry losing, 58 to 41 percent, many reasons can be put forth for one of the most lopsided defeats in Virginia history. It was, in fact, the beginning of a bad period for all Democrats. (The next year would see the Republicans seize control of both the House and Senate.) The bad blood between Robb and Wilder spilled over to Terry's candidacy. It didn't help that Terry got into her own feud with Wilder, which hurt her among African Americans, a core Democratic constituency. Allen was fuzzy on issues, but he had an affable, homespun, Reagan-esque personality. He presented himself as the alternative to the divisiveness of "Robb-Wilder-Terry," as he referred to his opponent. At one point, Terry said, a poll by her campaign showed that 49 percent of Virginians would not vote for a Democrat for any office.

Terry's decorous demeanor was a contrast to Allen's aw-shucks persona. With her feathered haircut, compelling blue eyes, and bright smile, she could convey warmth and openness. More often, she was unsmiling and studious-looking—"a humorless policy wonk," as one profile described her. In endorsing her candidacy, the *Washington Post* said, "The other way of saying the same thing is that Ms. Terry is a serious student of how state government works and how it can be improved."

But voters based their impressions mostly on her TV ads, which portrayed her as a sophisticated professional woman. Focus groups commissioned by Emily's List said the impression they got from watching her ads was that she was rich. "She wore pearls and she was pictured in an antebellum Virginia setting," said Ellen Malcolm. "People thought of her as a Virginia lady." Mary Beth Cahill, the political director for Emily's List at the time, said women, more so than men, have to be careful how they are pictured. "Voters react badly, for instance, against women who stand by a computer in a suit or wear high heels and a hard hat at a construction site. They don't think it's realistic. It's not anything she would do in real life. So the focus groups concluded that Mary Sue Terry, who had pulled herself up by the bootstraps in a remarkable way, had been born rich. They made all kinds of assumptions based on the way she was dressed."

There were other problems, ranging from Terry's health to her conduct of the campaign. Terry started the year by undergoing a hysterectomy in January 1993. The operation's lingering side effects caused her moods to swing up and down, a campaign aide said. "She was short-tempered," the aide said. "She would lose focus. She became more autocratic in running the campaign. She was hard on the staff. It was a very difficult time." At a crucial point in her campaign she agreed, against her better judgment, to run negative ads against Allen. They backfired. Over the single weekend when the ads ran, she slipped behind in the polls, never to recover. Although Terry had built a reputation as a tough-on-crime attorney general, it was Allen who seized the issue with the simple (some might say simplistic) theme of eliminating parole for criminals and putting more cops on the street. Bumper stickers saying "No Parole!" made more of an impact than Terry's more tailored approach, highlighted by a proposal for a five-day waiting period to buy a gun. She could hardly have adopted Allen's no-parole tactic even if she had wanted to without offending blacks, who comprise a disproportionate percent of the prison population.

But Terry's biggest problem may have been one shared by many women candidates. She was unmarried. The issue was raised publicly by Oliver North, who gained notoriety for his role in the Iran-contra affair during Reagan's presidency. In endorsing Allen's candidacy, North spoke of how the "pitter-patter of little feet" was a welcome sound in the governor's mansion and that it was appropriate for a married man and his family to occupy that house. Allen repudiated North's remarks, then added, coyly, that he meant no criticism of the single and childless Terry when he said having a wife and two small children made him "more understanding of the challenges facing the families of Virginia." When one of Terry's supporters defended her by saying Terry would be "free to give all her energies to the duties of office," Allen accused Terry of exploiting the issue for her benefit.

There was worse. Less than a month before the election, a Roanoke, Virginia, psychiatrist whose license was revoked after Terry's office produced evidence that he had engaged in inappropriate sexual relationships with at least four young male patients struck back. The psychiatrist, William G. Gray, claimed that from 1982 to 1990 he had treated a woman who claimed to be Terry's lover. The patient had committed suicide, Gray said. Reporters confronted Terry as she prepared for a televised debate with Allen in Richmond on October 7. She denounced the charge, saying it was ridiculous and untrue, and asserted she had never had a homosexual relationship. "Unfortunately, this is what women are subject to when they enter politics," she said. But the damage had been done. The *Washington Post* could not independently verify the doctor's charges and did not print a story. But newspapers in the central and southern parts of Virginia published the accusation and Terry's denial and local TV stations broadcast the story as a "bombshell" in the governor's race. One station interviewed people on the street, asking them if they would vote for a lesbian for governor. After a day or two, the story disappeared, but the innuendoes, jokes, and double entendres persisted.

Terry's campaign team was torn over how to respond. "The women wanted to deal with it straight up, but the men said nothing negative was showing up in the polling and that we should ignore it," Terry said. "So we ended up doing nothing." Campaign consultant Tom King recalled, "It was a strategic decision. The Allen campaign was spreading the rumor in a subtle way and it would have been hard to prove a negative. I stood beside her when the reporters asked the questions and, seeing her face, I knew she couldn't go through that for a whole campaign. She was too fragile. I told the others, if we make this the battle royal, that's all she'll be remembered for. We decided to stick with an approach that was heavy on her knowledge of the issues. As a woman candidate, she had to be perceived as very competent." In the end, King conceded, the unfounded charge of lesbianism hurt Terry badly politically in the rural, conservative regions of Virginia.

Not until the last week of the campaign did Terry come out swinging against the malicious charges. Her campaign ran this ad:

ANNOUNCER: The bad guys are ganging up on Mary Sue Terry. The LaRouches assault her because she stopped their rip-offs. The gun lobby riddles her with attack mailings. Ollie North ridicules her for not having children. And her defense of a woman's right to choose brings the right wing down on her head.

TERRY: You have to admit, I have all the right enemies. My opponent has even tried to change my name—from Mary Sue Terry to Robb-Wilder-Terry. But I'm still the same Mary Sue. So he can have his friends. What I need is you.

After interviewing Terry, columnist Mary McGrory wrote, "She says it is not what she did but what was done to her that accounts for the wretched state of her fortunes. She sees herself as the victim of right-wing smears." On October 26, exactly a week before the election, Terry went public with her feelings, telling McGrory, "I'm heterosexual. So we begin with that proposition. But I am single. Early on, the Republicans put in a 900 number. They said they wanted to collect information, but it was pretty clear the phone line was used to collect dirt and sleaze. . . . Ollie North has been going around Virginia for months saying I am less qualified because I haven't had any children. The religious right has been handing out flyers showing me with Hitler in a Nazi salute—for my position on gun control."

In a series of interviews with us in 1998 and 1999, there was still an edge of bitterness in Terry's voice as she spoke about the governor's election more than five years earlier. "Every state has its dark side," she said. "Virginia in its first vote in 1861 voted against seceding from the union. The newspaper in Richmond went on a rampage, editorializing against that vote. There was a second vote, and Virginia seceded. We're a state that should have known better, a state of enormous attainment, educational facilities, the mother of presidents. . . . We never adopted the amendment that gave women the right to vote. It went into the Constitution without Virginia ever voting. Then there was massive resistance. We're an extraordinary state, but there's a malevolent element here, and they were after me. . . . The only way to defeat me was to destroy me."

What would Terry have done differently if she could turn back the clock? "I would have dealt with the issue of being single at the outset," she said. "I would have said, 'Let's make sure this issue doesn't cause anybody any confusion. I'm a single woman and I'm heterosexual. If anybody has anything to say about that, speak up. If not, let's get on with this campaign.' That's what I would have done."

Terry, who now teaches leadership classes for women at the University of Richmond, is young enough to try again for political office, but King doubts that she will. "She's been underground too long," he says. "It's too bad. She would have been a good governor. She's very inclusive. She brings people together."

Another woman who seemed to have what it takes to become governor is Barbara Kennelly. Her résumé was strong and she had impeccable family credentials when she gave up a safe seat in Congress to run for governor in Connecticut. When she announced her candidacy in September 1997, polls showed her running even or ahead of the incumbent governor by four or five points. She seemed a natural for the job. She had served with distinction in the Congress for seventeen years, rising to become one of the few women in the male-dominated Democratic party hierarchy. She was a savvy inside player, using her seat on the powerful Ways and Means Committee to benefit her state and to make her mark legislatively.

Kennelly's constituents loved her. They reelected her every two years by wide margins. And she loved her work on Capitol Hill. Why tamper with a good thing? She admits that the polls that showed she could win were intoxicating. But more than numbers enticed her into the governor's race. In her early sixties, Kennelly craved a new challenge. "My children were grown, my husband was dead. I had one more opportunity to help somebody out and I wanted to do it for Connecticut. Boy, what a fatal error," she says with a hearty laugh.

We talked with Kennelly in December 1998, a month after she lost her bid for governor by the lopsided margin of 63 to 35 percent. It was a blow for Kennelly, who has deep political roots in Connecticut.

Her father, John Bailey, chaired the state Democratic party from 1947 to 1970, and served as national chairman for the Democrats during the turbulent sixties. Adlai Stevenson, twice the Democratic presidential nominee, was a frequent houseguest when Barbara Bailey was growing up. Yet there was no expectation that she or her brother would enter politics. "My father was the politician," she says. Her brother ran for Congress but lost, and any further aspirations he might have had were cut short by his premature death.

Like other women of her generation, Kennelly put off her own plans for the sake of her husband and family. After graduating from Trinity College and getting a master's degree in business from Radcliffe, she got married and gave birth to four children. Her husband rose to become speaker of the Connecticut assembly. Kennelly found fulfillment outside the home in unpaid community activity. "I volunteered with a vengeance," she says. But Kennelly had told her husband that when their last child reached first grade, she was going to work. By then she had been knocking on the door of City Hall for so long in her role as community activist that the idea of running for the city council seemed a natural step. Her father was ill and dying at the time. When she told him she planned to run, he was not enthusiastic. "Oh, Bobbi, city politics is tough," he said.

Despite her father's misgivings, Kennelly ran and won. Tough or not, city politics beat staying at home. "Oh God, I loved it," she said. When the roof of the Hartford Coliseum collapsed, Kennelly headed the commission that investigated the disaster. Her competent handling of the probe gained Kennelly positive publicity and positioned her to run for secretary of state in 1978. Her announcement angered Governor Ella Grasso. It wasn't personal. Grasso liked Kennelly, but she wanted to name a Jewish woman to replace the Jewish woman who was leaving the job. Grasso reminded Kennelly that her father, John Bailey, had always taken into account ethnic and geographic balance in putting together a ticket.

"If your father were alive, what would he think?" she asked Kennelly.

"If he were alive, I wouldn't give any thought whatsoever to running," Kennelly replied. She won the election.

When a congressional seat opened up in 1982, Kennelly didn't hesitate to go for it. She was forty-five when she arrived in Washington as a freshman legislator. Ronald Reagan was president, but Democratic control of the House appeared secure.

Women members were so outnumbered in the House that they volunteered to campaign for other women trying to join their ranks.

Democrat Pat Schroeder, who co-chaired the Congressional Wo-men's Caucus, asked Geraldine Ferraro to fill in for her as a favor and campaign with Kennelly. "Geraldine thought it was Kennelly with a *C*, so she was happy to campaign for a nice Italian. She got in the car with a friend thinking Connecticut was just over the line from New York. She kept driving and driving and driving. She didn't realize how far Hartford was," Kennelly recalls with a laugh. "Anyway, we just hit it off and became good friends."

Two years later, Kennelly nominated Ferraro for vice president at the 1984 Democratic National Convention. When Ferraro left for the campaign trail, she turned over her apartment to Kennelly. "She just walked out the door," Kennelly says. "She left food in the refrig-erator." Part of the deal Kennelly struck to get the apartment was to promise that Barbara Mikulski, one of Ferraro's pals in the House, could crash on the couch whenever the Congress ran late and she needed to stay in Washington. Pictures of Kennelly, Ferraro, Mikul-ski, and Madeleine Albright, arms linked and smiling, adorn Mikul-ski's Senate office. One picture taken some time ago has them all dressed in red. Was the color choice a legacy of Nancy Reagan, whose favorite color was red? "No," says Mikulski, "it's the legacy of televi-sion. Every woman in the House, even before Mrs. Reagan came, learned to show up in red for the president's State of the Union ad-dress so that your constituents would know you were there."

The four women have stayed friends through the years, attending each other's children's weddings, crying together over the deaths of their parents, and sometimes vacationing together. They were all raised as Catholics and educated by nuns in all-girls schools. They're all about the same age (mid-sixties) though Mikulski relishes the fact that Ferraro is a year older. They trust each other with their secrets without fear of being quoted. Before Kennelly ran for governor, she talked it over with her girlfriends. She needed to figure out whether she could handle defeat. "If I lost, would I be terribly disappointed I was out of the game? Could I handle that?"

Looking back, Kennelly thinks the extensive self-analysis was mis-placed. What she should have paid attention to were the campaign re-sources available to her in Connecticut. The state Democratic party structure had atrophied since her father's heyday. She couldn't count on it for organization or money. If she was going to put together a campaign and raise money, she would have to do it herself. The money part proved formidable. Her friends in Congress told her not to worry. "The first million, lobbyists will give to you," they assured her.

But few lobbyists gave to Kennelly. She said that her opponent, Connecticut governor John Rowland, had put out the word that his administration wouldn't tolerate the time-honored practice of big donors hedging their bets and giving to rival candidates. In a debate, she accused the governor of telling lobbyists, "This election, you don't give to both candidates. You give to me, or forget it." Rowland did not dispute the charge, but an aide later said it was false.

Contributions from friends and relatives got her started, but she was unable to crack the bigger givers. Representative Loretta Sanchez of California, a feisty, thirty-something freshman, gave Kennelly pep talks on raising money. Sanchez had a reputation as a giant-killer, having defeated the bombastic Bob Dornan. "There's only one thing standing between you and the governor's office, and that's money," she told Kennelly. "When it's tough to get money, you've just got to get tough." Before coming to Congress, Sanchez put together million-dollar deals for Booz Allen, the financial consultants, and she wasn't shy about asking people for money. Except for members of the Democratic leadership, she was on her way to raising more money than any other Democrat in the House.

Sanchez met Kennelly when she sat next to her at a welcoming dinner for incoming freshmen after the 1996 election. Sanchez had won by only 984 votes out of 102,000 votes cast, and her victory was in doubt. Kennelly offered to share her apartment until the Dornan investigation was over and Sanchez was assured a seat. Sanchez was thrilled to sleep on the couch in an apartment that once belonged to Geraldine Ferraro.

Listening to Kennelly pitching for money, Sanchez couldn't believe how soft sell she sounded. "Hi, I'm Barbara, I need to raise . . ." Sanchez advised her to flatter the people she calls. "Tell them, 'You're the Big Cheese in town. You're the one who can raise money. I know I can count on you to raise $30,000.' Then they gasp. By law, they can only give $1,000. You say that's all you want, and they're relieved. You'd be amazed how fast you can max people out with this line."

Hard sell was not Kennelly's style. "My modus operandi is that I'm a nice person," she says. As the margin widened between her and the incumbent governor, Kennelly's media adviser proposed a negative campaign. She had authorized opposition research, the polite term for digging up dirt on an opponent, but refused to give the go-ahead after screening one of the ads. She felt a negative campaign was counter to her image and would backfire. More practically, she said,

"If you're going to go negative, you have to do it heavy and hard. I didn't have a lot of money."

Kennelly had never catered to the organized women's groups, but she shared their agenda and expected their support. Rowland, a moderate Republican, stressed his commitment to improving education and preserving the environment. The National Abortion and Reproduction Rights Action League (NARAL), anxious to be with a winner and to support a pro-choice Republican, endorsed both Rowland and Kennelly even though she had been stauncher in her support and, as a Catholic, had summoned the political and moral courage to vote against a late-term-abortion ban. Disappointed in the lukewarm support she got from women's groups, Kennelly said, "They've become just like every other special-interest group. The National Women's Political Caucus, the Women's Campaign Fund—who heads them? You don't know, and I don't know." The exception was Emily's List. She praised Ellen Malcolm ("the only good campaign operative we have") and credited Emily's List "for every Democratic woman here."

Even if the sisterhood had been in her corner, Kennelly could not have overcome Rowland's huge advantage. What particularly galled her was Rowland's million-dollar "Come to Connecticut" ad campaign, paid for by the taxpayers. The ads ran in Connecticut and featured Rowland and his attractive wife extolling the virtues of their state. The impact on Kennelly's campaign was devastating. Democrats in the state legislature tried to pass a bill prohibiting such self-promotion with tax dollars, but their hearts weren't in it. Rowland had begun addressing many of the issues they cared about, and Kennelly's poll numbers were dropping fast.

After sixteen years in the House, she was not prepared for a modern campaign. For one thing, she had not employed a press secretary for years. In Congress, she was an inside player, working the power grid among the members, crafting compromises, and putting together deals. She didn't court the media and rarely appeared on the Sunday TV talk shows. She fielded her own press calls. "To start a campaign without a crackerjack press secretary was stupid," she says. Instead of having a buffer against the media's relentless questioning, she defended herself, acting curt with reporters, and generally making a mess of things.

Despite her family's political roots, Kennelly did not enjoy statewide recognition. Former Republican congresswoman Lynn Martin, who tried for the Senate as a House member and failed, had warned her, "Barbara, don't think the whole state knows who you are."

Having the right friends is important. Kennelly had plenty of warmhearted, well-meaning women volunteers. Many were lifelong friends, the wives and widows of prosperous men. "A lot of my friends never had to work," she said. Kennelly could not have waged a campaign without them, but they had their limitations. Campaigning for other Democrats around the country, Kennelly had seen what a network of well-connected friends could accomplish. When the campaign of a colleague in the Midwest was falling apart, the partners in his law firm literally moved into his headquarters and took over. "When you have trouble, if you have professional friends—I don't mean necessarily lawyers, but businesspeople who can come in and surround you and hold you up until you get going again—that's very helpful," she says.

Kennelly's volunteers handled the mail, sent thank-you notes, and answered the phone expertly. But the atmosphere was more like a tea party than a combative campaign. Kennelly came to rely on one younger woman volunteer who had run a business of her own and had connections and confidence. "If I had had five of her, things might have been different," says Kennelly. "I would advise any woman running to get a kitchen cabinet going before she announces, and to make sure it will be there through the good and the bad."

A lifetime of winning had not prepared Kennelly for losing. "I had won since I was president of the student government in high school, all the way through—city council, secretary of state, primaries, and general elections. I always won," she says. Former Texas governor Ann Richards, who had lost her bid for reelection, tried to buck up Kennelly's spirits. "Don't read the newspapers; they'll only make you feel bad," she said. "Keep yourself sunny by having positive people around."

Kennelly brushed away the one previous exception to her winning record, a failed run for chairman of the Democratic Caucus in 1989. That was different, she says, because she didn't expect to win, and ran mainly to make a point about the need for women in leadership positions. She lost the race to popular Maryland Democrat Steny Hoyer, but got her wish to serve in the leadership. Speaker Tom Foley, bowing to pressure from Democratic women members, appointed Kennelly chief deputy whip, a newly created position in the party's operation. "You had the guts to run," he told her.

Drawing attention to her gender had not been Kennelly's style. "I never believed in the women's vote," she says. "Women vote on the economy, just like everybody else." But she became convinced the Democrats could have better handled the scandal that brought down Speaker Jim Wright in 1989 on charges of corruption if a woman had been in the backroom strategy sessions. Kennelly thinks women's top priority should be getting into the room with the decision-makers. Women members dwell too much on equalizing amenities. "The 'poor me' phase is over," she says. "There's no bathroom on the same floor, you walk up one floor. Just make sure you're in the Ways and Means room." Kennelly had a reputation as one of the guys. She courted Ways and Means Committee chairman Dan Rostenkowski, who ruled for years with the authority of a Mafia don, strongarming legislators to do his and his party's bidding. Kennelly played golf with Rosty, a rare honor accorded a woman. That relationship helped her get legislation passed.

Rostenkowski was eventually tripped up when a Justice Department investigation accused him of putting ghost employees on his payroll and converting postage vouchers to cash. He lost his bid for reelection in 1994 and later served several months in a federal prison. After he was released, and after her defeat for governor, Kennelly met her former mentor for lunch and sought his advice about her next career move. She told him that a friend had suggested she model herself after Lynn Martin, the former Republican congresswoman and labor secretary who had landed spots on corporate boards eager for women. "That was then," Rosty replied with a dismissive wave of his hand. "Nobody cares about that anymore."

The pressure once felt in corporate America and elsewhere to promote women has lessened, in part because of the progress women have made. A woman rising to CEO of a big company is no longer news. A woman running for governor in Connecticut, the state that elected Grasso, the country's first woman governor in her own right, is not news either. "The media used to write about women because they were a novelty," says Kennelly. "It's not a story anymore."

Women have such a poor record running for governor, it is tempting to blame it on gender discrimination. Martin doesn't buy it. "I don't think you can assume that every time a woman loses it is because of gender," she says. "You know, you don't get over being a woman, you don't get over being black, you don't get over being a male. There are all sorts of things that you are. They're not the sum total of your existence. There are lots of other things going on."

Mikulski thinks women's chances of achieving the highest offices in the land depend on the value society places on those offices. Women have fared better on the lower rungs of politics, Mikulski says, because term limits, lower pay, and media scrutiny have made these jobs less desirable to men, thus creating more openings. "Somebody said to me, 'When do you think a woman will be president?'" Mikulski says. "I said, 'When America starts running out of money.' When we have no more money, when whoever is president will have to pay for her own housekeeper, send out for Chinese food, and maybe even pay for her own security, then they'll let us do it—when there's a demise in power."

Top executive jobs in government continue to be prized, however, and even highly qualified women find them hard to get. A case in point is the 1998 race by three-term House member Jane Harman for governor of California. She didn't survive the Democratic primary.

On June 2, 1998, the day of the primary, pollster Geoff Garin did not have to monitor the returns. He knew that Harman would be lucky to finish second in the race. (She finished third behind Gray Davis and Al Checchi. Davis went on to win the governorship.)

When Harman announced she would run for governor, her prospects seemed promising. Women comprise 57 percent of the Democratic vote in California, which would seem to give a woman candidate an advantage. A Harman victory would have put her on the short list of prospects for the national ticket, if not in 2000, then 2004. Besides her gender, Harman had a winning political profile—conservative on fiscal issues, progressive on social issues—and family money that she and her husband were prepared to spend on the campaign.

Garin explained why Harman had gone from sure winner to big loser in less than a year. He said women have a hard time being seriously considered for governor unless they have executive experience. "Six years in Congress doesn't do it," he said. Harman surged at the start of her campaign after paid ads showcased her combination of government and private sector experience as a lawyer. But Garin's polling showed voters had concerns about her qualifications to be governor. Davis ran as the experienced hand in the race. Voters found his persona, gray as his name, reassuringly bland. Checchi, a former Northwest Airlines executive, assumed Harman would be his chief opponent and targeted her in a barrage of negative advertising. One ad said she had voted to increase taxes on social security; another called her Republican House Speaker Newt Gingrich's best friend.

As with most negative advertising, there was a crumb of truth baked in a loaf of innuendo. The tax increase was part of President Clinton's 1993 budget, which passed without a single Republican vote, and which many economists credit with setting the nation on a sound fiscal course. Harman's alleged friendship with Gingrich, a despised figure among hard-core Democrats, was based on her voting record, which leaned enough to the right for the ambitious Checchi to cast aspersions. Never mind that Harman was reelected in 1994 by only eight hundred votes, and Gingrich spent the next year trying to prove fraudulent voting in a vain effort to kick her out of Congress.

Harman's strategy was to exploit her advantage against two male opponents by focusing on women's concerns. The strategy backfired early in the campaign in a telephone conference call from Washington with California reporters. They pressed her to comment on state and local issues. Harman, who hadn't spent much time pondering California issues while she was in the House, said she would get into specifics later. The response was interpreted as an indication that she wanted to avoid controversial issues and coast to victory on the strength of her appeal to women. The press reduced her campaign theme to the Helen Reddy song "I Am Woman."

Jane Harman's picture hangs on the wall of the Lindy Boggs Reading Room in the U.S. Capitol, along with other current and former women members of the House. The suite of rooms is named after the former representative who took her husband's seat after he disappeared and was presumed dead in a plane crash in 1972. It provides a quiet getaway for female members in both political parties. After her losing race for governor, Kennelly retreated there for our interview rather than sit among the depressing stacks of packed boxes in her congressional office. Pointing out her favorite women among the portraits, Kennelly stopped at the picture of Harman, her role model in defeat. "She spent all that money [$4.7 million of her own funds, plus $740,000 from others] and got 12 percent of the vote," said Kennelly. "But she came back here and acted like a million dollars."

Harman was interviewed in her office, where she served for six months after her defeat in the primary. Propped against one wall was a bright yellow surfboard, a gift from her staff and a symbol of the free time she would have as an ex-member of Congress. A rock on her desk was etched with the phrase "Never Never Quit." She was to host a fund-raiser in her home that evening for Davis, who had trounced her in the primary. "Good manners," she said tightly. The personal fallout from the campaign was substantial. Democratic consultant Robert Shrum, a law school classmate of Harman's and a friend for thirty years, ran the Checchi campaign, which said that Harman's record showed she was untrustworthy. Shrum had handled Harman's three congressional campaigns. He knew where she was vulnerable. "The friendship will not be repaired," Harman said.

Shrum insists he did not rely on any poll or research he had done for Harman's congressional campaigns, and is clearly anguished over their ruptured friendship. Before he signed on with Checchi, he checked with Harman to see if she planned to run and she said no. Harman got into the race after Checchi had been on the air for months with television spots, and only after Dianne Feinstein bowed out right before the filing deadline. By then, Shrum says, "I felt obliged to represent the person who hired me, and who had been paying me for a year." The most damage he did to her campaign, he believes, was inflicted by a spot filmed at one of Harman's public events, which the Checchi campaign attended with a camera. It was the week before she announced, and in emphasizing her centrist views, she said she was the best Republican in the Democratic party. It was a devastating comment for a candidate running in a Democratic primary, where the people who vote tend to take their partisanship seriously.

If there's a lesson, says Shrum, it's that in big, serious races, you can't jump in at the last minute. You have to think them through.

Eighteen months after her defeat, Harman announced she would run again for her congressional seat. It seemed an odd choice to try to recapture her old life, but the Democrats, within striking distance of regaining control of the House, had offered her an inducement she couldn't refuse. If she ran, and if she won, she would chair the Intelligence Committee. No woman had ever had that assignment, and she really liked meaty issues.

Harman took back her seat in the 2000 election, narrowly defeating Republican Steven Kuykendall, who had only served a single term. It took more than a week of counting absentee ballots before Harman's victory was assured. The Democrats fell short in their bid to win back the House majority so Harman didn't get her chairmanship and had to settle for being a member of the Intelligence Committee. But Democratic leader Dick Gephardt belatedly made good on his promise to Harman by naming her the ranking Democrat on a new Homeland Security task force created after the September 11 attacks, a challenge that Harman took on with gusto.

Harman remains sensitive about the charge that in her governor's race she skirted issues and ran a gender-based campaign. She had gotten into politics because she cared about issues and had made the traditionally male area of military spending and national security her specialty. Harman did so much for the defense contractors in her district she was known as "G.I. Jane." At home in California, she went running at 6:30 many mornings with a group of guys, all rabid Republicans, who support her. The notion of her as a fuzzy candidate dodging specifics struck her as preposterous. But first impressions are hard to overcome, and the bar is set high for a woman seeking to be governor of a major state like California. Kathleen Brown had demonstrated that point in the 1994 governor's race. Her father and brother had both been two-term governors of the state and Kathleen was a popular state treasurer. She took an early lead in the polls, but saw it evaporate, losing eventually to Republican governor Pete Wilson, 55 to 41 percent.

Like any beginning job applicant frustrated by an employer's demand for experience, women have had to cope with the requirement for executive experience when trying for governor and other state offices. Ann Richards and Christine Todd Whitman were exceptions, and until recently, women have been elected governor only in small states. It can be argued that they were special cases. Richards had been state treasurer of Texas and was a bona fide national figure after her 1988 speech at the Democratic Convention mocking George Bush for being born with a silver foot in his mouth. Whitman unseated incumbent governor James Florio in New Jersey. He had broken his promise not to raise taxes and, so, was unelected more than she was elected.

After Grasso was elected in 1974, Madeleine Kunin followed in Vermont, and, much later, Jeanne Shaheen in New Hampshire—all small states. Peter Hart, Garin's partner, did the polling for Grasso's campaign. Grasso's biggest problem was with middle-aged women like herself. They knew how men treated them. In focus groups, they said, "Men wouldn't listen to me. Why would they listen to her?" The campaign addressed this concern with ads that showed Grasso giving orders to men.

Anxiety about whether a woman is a credible commander in chief surfaces in governor's races. The 1979 governor's race in Mississippi pitted William Winter against Evelyn Gandy, then the lieutenant governor. Democratic consultant Robert Squier produced an ad for Winter that said, "One of the most important responsibilities of the governor is commander of the state national guard." Squier had his candidate ride around in a tank firing guns, which defined the job as one only a man could do. It worked for Winter, who was elected.

From Connecticut to California, the failure of promising women candidates to win gubernatorial races prompted a new round of soul-searching by women political activists. "Is there more that we could be doing to enhance these women's ability to be leaders?" asks Joanne Howes, a member of Team A, which pushed for Ferraro in 1984. "How can we have women better prepared? It's a burden women still carry. People are less sure we are prepared to govern. We saw it with Gerry. Women as voters are willing to embrace Clinton knowing he's not perfect. We didn't give that to Gerry. Maybe she wasn't ready to be vice president. Women are still afraid that we're going to fail, and if a woman fails, that says something about all of us."

Happily for the evolution of the political species, for every woman like Mary Sue Terry who has left the battlefield beaten and discouraged, there is a newcomer brimming with confidence and competence to take her place. Two years after Terry lost her race for governor of Virginia, Emily Couric burst onto the scene by upsetting an incumbent in November 1995 to win a seat in the Virginia State Senate. Couric won in the Charlottesville district that is home to George Allen, the man who defeated Terry for governor. As they had done with Terry after her 1977 election to the legislature, the media immediately singled out Couric as a woman to watch. Maybe she would succeed where Terry had failed in winning her way to the governor's mansion.

Couric had not yet been sworn into office when she got a phone call from Marjorie Margolies Mezvinsky, head of the Women's Campaign Fund. "Do they have you running for governor yet?" Mezvinsky asked jovially.

"Me?" Couric asked assuming Mezvinsky had her confused with another legislator. "I just got elected for the first time. I'm not thinking of anything else."

Mezvinsky laughed. She, too, had been a golden girl once. Elected to Congress in 1992, when women's political fortunes appeared to be rising rapidly, she daydreamed about future possibilities in the Senate or beyond. But just two years later her dreams were dashed by the Republican sweep of 1994. "Everybody told me I was going to be vice president," Mezvinsky said.

Overnight, the look-alike older sister of Katie Couric, co-host of NBC's "Today Show," became the most celebrated local officeholder in the country. *People* magazine and the *Wall Street Journal* wrote about her. Phil Donahue invited her to appear on his TV show. Just two days after her election, the *Washington Post* and the *Richmond Times-Dispatch* listed Emily Couric as a possible Democratic lieutenant governor candidate in the next election. Virginia Democrats, eager to regain the governorship after two straight losses, said Couric, with her amazing ability to raise campaign funds and appeal to voters of all political ideologies, could go all the way to become the state's first female governor.

Born in Atlanta in 1947, Emily Couric grew up with three younger siblings in the Washington, D.C., suburb of Arlington, Virginia. Despite her proximity to the nation's capital, Couric never envisioned herself in politics. After graduating magna cum laude from Smith College in 1969 with a degree in botany, she taught high school biology for two years in Cambridge, Massachusetts, before heading with her husband to Alaska, where she worked for the Fish and Wildlife Service of the U.S. Department of the Interior. Returning to Virginia in 1974, she took a job as a public information specialist in the U.S. Department of Labor. In 1979, she put her interest in environmental law to work as a reporter for *Legal Times*.

Couric's first marriage ended in divorce and left her with custody of two sons. In 1981, she married Dr. George Beller, head of cardiology at the University of Virginia Medical Center, and moved to Charlottesville, too far from Washington to continue commuting. She tried her hand at freelance writing and authored two books on law, *The Trial Lawyers* and *Divorce Lawyers*. She balanced the solitary life of an at-home writer with community service. Her first taste of politics came as an appointed member of the Charlottesville School Board. She served on the board for six years, the last two as chairman.

When an editor with whom Couric worked suggested that she run for public office, she responded without giving it a moment's thought: "Are you crazy?" Later, however, she wondered whether she might be underestimating herself. Working on the school board, on the local planning commission, and on a board dealing with the problems of aging taught her that she was good at dealing with people and their problems. What's more, she liked doing it.

Her hesitancy about running for office, she said later, was the product of growing up in a generation of women who put their responsibilities as homemakers and mothers ahead of any professional ambition, at least until their children were grown. "I had raised two children successfully, I had a happy marriage, a wonderful community, and lots of friends," she said. "I was experiencing the freedom of not having children at home. I was comfortable. I wondered whether I had the confidence to risk running and losing."

Couric's husband encouraged her to run. His career was demanding and involved a lot of travel. He liked the idea of his wife pursuing her own calling. "He's the perfect political spouse," Couric said. Democratic party leaders were less enthusiastic. They didn't think a first-time candidate could defeat the Republican incumbent, former FBI agent Edgar S. Robb. No other Democrat wanted to run against Robb, so Couric got the party's blessing.

Working from makeshift campaign headquarters in her Victorian-style home in Charlottesville, Couric began by consulting everybody she could think of for advice. She wrote thank-you notes to everyone she talked with ("Doesn't that sound so feminine?" she said), building a database of six hundred names. Many of them became recruits in her army of volunteers. As the campaign progressed, stacks of campaign literature, bumper stickers, lawn signs, voter rolls, and miscellaneous papers covered the dining room table and spilled over into the front hall. "Your campaign's metastasizing," her physician husband groused good-naturedly. Couric had never had more fun.

No woman had been elected in the Charlottesville district, comprised of a university community with upscale, progressive voters and conservative rural areas. When she campaigned in the rural areas, Couric brought her husband along "so people could see I was normal," she said. Couric stressed her commitment to improving education in Virginia. Robb had been a junior high and high school teacher, but he emphasized his law enforcement credentials in running a tough-on-crime campaign, as Allen had done against Terry in the 1993 governor's race.

The stakes were raised in the Couric-Robb race because it was one of the pivotal contests to decide which party would control the forty-member Senate. The district was split about evenly between Democrats and Republicans. The candidates matched each other dollar for dollar, raising over $250,000 each in the most expensive legislative race in the state. As election day drew near, polls showed the race was too close to call. It was then that Couric, the newcomer, got her first taste of the seamy side of politics.

Years later, Couric recalled how the blood drained from her face and her breathing became labored when aides showed her a flyer being circulated by the Robb forces in the campaign's final days. It attacked Couric's record as a member of the school board with a poignant photograph of a sad-eyed child with the caption "She didn't take care of me." A checklist of Couric's votes on the board left the impression that she alone bore the blame for lower test scores in the state. "I was shocked to see something that ugly about me," Couric said.

The Republicans saved one trick for the final weekend of the campaign. On orders from J. Scott Leake, director of the Joint Republican Legislative Caucus, six thousand postcards were distributed in the district with the return address of a phony political committee, "Dems 4 Day." The postcards urged a vote for Donal B. Day, a liberal activist running as an independent. Leake, who later apologized for the ethical breach, had hoped enough Democrats would vote for Day to deny Couric the victory.

Couric won the election with 50 percent of the vote to 45 percent for Robb and 4 percent for Day. Couric successfully appealed to progressive-minded voters in and around Charlottesville without alienating the more conservative voters in rural areas of the district. Underlying her victory was the intangible value of "the Katie factor," the glow of celebrity that surrounded her because of her famous sister.

From the day she started campaigning, Emily Couric's broad smile and huskily sweet voice reminded "Today Show" fans of her younger sister. Since Katie Couric enjoys a reputation as a wholesome girl-next-door, the comparison was not unwelcome. Couric's campaign polling showed that a large percentage of people knew she was Katie's sister, but that they would not necessarily vote for her because of it. "It helped them spell my name," Couric shrugged, adding in Katie-like language, "She has oodles of fans."

In late August 1995, an Associated Press reporter captured a telling scene on a dusty street outside the Court Square luncheonette in Stanardsville, Virginia. Emily Couric pressed a piece of campaign literature into the hand of a gray-haired woman and asked for her vote in November.

"You're Katie's sister, right, hon?" the woman trilled. "I watch your sister on TV every morning. You look a whole lot alike. . . . Well, you're both good people."

"We have the same parents," Couric deadpanned.

When Katie came to the district to campaign for Emily, she drew large crowds and a mob of media. When asked, Katie discounted her influence, saying that Emily, who is ten years older, established her own reputation as a writer and community activist before Katie achieved TV fame.

As is typical of firstborn children, Emily was more serious-minded than her younger sister. Katie favors casual clothing, whereas most of Emily's wardrobe came from Talbots, which specializes in tailored businesswear. On the day of our interview, she wore a slate blue dress with matching shoes. Emily went through a phase when "I dressed kind of funky and had big hair—scrunchy, curly out to here," she said, holding her hands several inches out from her then close-cropped hairstyle. When she decided to run for office, a male adviser told her to tone down her hair. "You don't want to give people an extra reason to criticize you," he said.

The Couric sisters' niceness and likableness caused them to be underestimated. Katie initially was discounted as a serious interviewer until critics realized that asking pointed questions could be done graciously and with a smile. Emily thought being underestimated was an asset. "You have to let people get used to you so you're nonthreatening," she said. "You need a more personal touch."

Couric needed all the feminine guile she could muster in a senate dominated, thirty-two to eight, by men. The Virginia legislature has only been coed since 1980. The atmosphere in the statehouse has been likened to the raucous fraternity life in the film *Animal House*. While debating legislation affecting Native Americans, male lawmakers drummed on their desks like tom-toms. Taking up a bill on animal rights, they filled the chamber with barking sounds and meows.

Couric said what bothered her most is not the occasional sexist comment but the condescension shown by a male colleague who takes her by the arm and, in a gentle, syrupy voice, says, "There, there," as if comforting a daughter. "It makes me want to slug him," she said. Once, in a rare display of anger, she told a male senator, "Take your hand off me. You have no right to be stroking me." He recoiled, throwing his arms back in a display of mock horror. Couric felt she had made her point. The patronizing treatment of women legislators was a sign that they were not to be treated as equals, and it had to stop.

Another measure of the unequal power balance is committee assignments. Only a few women have enough seniority to chair committees, and they get the committees the men regard as peripheral. In the senate, a woman headed the Rehabilitation and Social Services Committee; in the house, women headed the Militia and Police and the Privileges and Elections Committees. Of the seventeen members on the powerful Senate Finance Committee, not one was a woman while Couric held office.

The November 1999 election saw Republicans sweep both houses in Virginia after nearly a century of Democratic rule. Yet Couric easily won reelection with 66% of the vote, putting her on the fast track to become governor, when tragedy struck. Couric announced in a press conference in July 2000 that she had been diagnosed with pancreatic cancer, and would have to drop out of the lieutenant governor's race. Her running mate, Democrat Mark Warner, went on to win the governor's race in November 2001.

Couric died a few weeks before the election, on October 18, 2001. She was fifty-four years old. Katie Couric, who had lost her husband to colon cancer in 1998, said, "Pancreatic cancer is not, as my sister says, the cancer of choice."

With their party firmly in charge of the legislature, Republican women decided it was time to assert themselves. They held a news conference to announce that the historic "Gentleman's Lounge" just off the floor of the House of Delegates was getting a name change. It would be called the "Members Lounge," and a ladies room had been added so women lawmakers would have the same convenient restroom facilities as the men. "It's kind of been a good old boys' place for many years," said Majority Whip Jeannemarie Devolites, who spearheaded the press conference and is the first Republican woman elected to a House leadership post. None of the Democratic women were present, evidence of the breakdown in their relations with the newly emboldened Republican women. Devolites announced the formation of a Republican Women's Caucus, and said her goal was to change voters' misperception that Democrats do a better job of representing women. Democratic women retaliated by calling their Republican sisters "Johnny-come-latelies," and pointing out Democrats had broken the gender barrier seventy-eight years ago in the House and twenty-two years ago in the Senate.

Women from the two parties used to meet weekly to help boost each other and find common ground on legislation in the male-dominated Virginia legislature. But as more Republican women got elected, partisan differences grew more intense and the bipartisan women's caucus disbanded.

Complaints about sexual harassment weren't so easily dismissed as women increased their presence in the Capitol working as lawmakers, lobbyists and legislative aides. Symbolizing the changing times, Republican House Speaker S. Vance Wilkins, Jr., was forced to resign in June 2002 after acknowledging that he had paid $100,000 to settle a woman's claim that he had fondled her against her will and tried to use his position in government to intimidate her. The incident is a reminder that the good old boy network is alive and well in state government, but that it is slowly giving way to more progressive attitudes.

In the run-up to the 2002 elections, ten women in nine states secured their party's nomination for governor, including two women in

Hawaii. Four women went on to win in November, the most in any election cycle, yet hardly a dramatic breakthrough. There would now be six women governors (up from five). Most of the media attention centered on Jennifer Granholm, who won in Michigan, a Midwestern battleground state, proving that women need not be relegated to serving only in smaller states. As Michigan's attorney general, Granholm had proved her toughness and when she held "coffee talks" around the state, voters were receptive because they knew she was somebody who could deliver. She handled questions about her personal life with humor, suggesting her husband be called "First Hunk." Campaign professionals raved about her skills as an orator, her centrist message, and her striking appearance, wishing only that she hadn't been born in Canada so that she could someday compete for the presidency.

Democrats had misgivings about Janet Reno as their potential standard bearer in Florida against President Bush's younger brother, Governor Jeb Bush. But Reno refused to heed calls to leave the race despite her worsening Parkinson's disease and a fainting spell in public. The voters had the last word, narrowly choosing moderate businessman Bill McBride over the more liberal Reno to oppose Bush, who won reelection by a large margin.

The women with the best chance of winning had already been elected statewide, and were using those posts as a stepping stone to the governor's mansion. In Kansas, Democratic state Insurance Commissioner Kathleen Sebelius benefited from the last-minute decision to get out of the race by Republican Attorney General Carla Stovall, who said she lacked "the passion required to run and serve." Analysts speculated that Stovall's "new love interest," a wealthy radio-network owner, was the real reason for her sudden loss of zest for government, and the prospect of these two highly respected and competent women facing off against each other was averted. In Arizona, Attorney General Janet Napolitano easily captured the Democratic nomination for governor while her colleague in state government, Secretary of State Betsy Bayless, lost her bid on the Republican side. They said it would have been no big deal if they had run against each other. Coming from a state where the top five elected officials have been women, how can gender be an issue? Napolitano won with a tough-on-crime campaign. Hawaii elected its first woman governor. The race between Republican Linda Lingle and Democrat Mazie Hirono would be a novelty. But not for long. As more women enter the arena and take their partisan corners, the phenomenon of women competing against each other will one day become commonplace.

In Ohio, history was made with the first African American woman to break through as lieutenant governor. Both incumbent Governor Bob Taft and his challenger, Democrat Tim Hagen, selected a black female running mate, sending a powerful signal of positive change in a state where only 11.4 percent of the population is African American. Taft and his running mate, Jenette Bradley, won easily.

NINE

The Un-Kennedy

Men do not surrender power without a fight. Massachusetts is perhaps the most liberal, progressive state in the union, but it hasn't sent a woman to Congress since Republican Margaret Heckler was defeated in 1982 by Democrat Barney Frank. Massachusetts is home to Wellesley, Smith, and Radcliffe, all premiere women's colleges. Women are starting businesses in record numbers in the state, as they are throughout the country, but politics remains largely a man's game. Until Lieutenant Governor Jane Swift was elevated to governor because of happenstance (her predecessor was named ambassador to Canada), avoiding a campaign she probably could not have won on her own, no woman had gotten that high in the state's political structure. The biggest players, of course, are the Kennedys—past, present and future, from Jack and Bobby to Ted and Patrick (who represents a district in neighboring Rhode Island), the only father and son team in Congress. The lone female Kennedy to seek elective office chose to pursue her political hopes in Maryland, where the climate for women candidates is more hospitable, and where she could better bear the weight of her family's legacy.

Kathleen Kennedy Townsend, the oldest of Robert F. Kennedy's eleven children, thinks there are so few women in politics in Massachusetts because politics matters there in a way it doesn't matter in other states. Rather than compete on the Kennedy clan's own turf, where the family did not encourage her political ambition, Townsend moved to Maryland where she carved a reputation of her own, serving two terms as lieutenant governor and positioning herself as the heavy favorite for governor going into the 2002 election. "And if she's governor—what the hell!" exclaims Frank Manciewicz, who was her father's press secretary. That's shorthand for saying KKT, as she's known, could go all the way to the White House. Until his tragic death at sea in July 1999, John F. Kennedy, Jr., was the most direct heir to Camelot. Now media attention has shifted to the unassuming Kathleen as the Kennedy best positioned to move up the career ladder to the presidency.

It is midafternoon, and an aide brings Townsend a Ben & Jerry's chocolate milk shake. "Instead of lunch, I presume," says a startled male visitor. "Oh, no, I had lunch," replies Townsend matter-of-factly. "I get hungry." The man takes in her slender frame with renewed interest, shakes his head in wonderment, and says he wishes he could put away milk shakes and stay thin. Townsend's brown eyes crinkle up the way her father's used to, and she laughs heartily as she shares her dieting secret: "You become lieutenant governor and have four kids."

Anybody with even a passing acquaintance with Robert Kennedy from television or photographs will recognize Townsend as her father's daughter. She has his restless energy, toothy smile, and passion for public service, which was instilled at an early age. Growing up, Kathleen and her siblings were grilled each evening at the dinner table about what they did to help the less fortunate that day. But there is nothing in the Kennedy tradition where women take center stage. As Kathleen notes wryly, her uncle Jack, when he was president, named his brother-in-law to run the Peace Corps, not his sister. "Growing up we were taught the importance of getting involved," she says. "But there was never a sense that women could run for public office. It wouldn't have occurred to me. If you asked my mother, she'd say it never would have occurred to her either."

That may have been a gift in the sense that it freed Kathleen from expectations. She could pursue her dreams and, come what may, she was never going to let anyone down. The Kennedy men were groomed to carry the torch; the women to bear life's vicissitudes.

Townsend's office is like a Kennedy museum. Photographs of her father and other family members occupy every side table, end table, and spare shelf. RFK is pictured with Martin Luther King, Jr., the civil rights leader, and in Poland in 1964, with Kathleen at his side, reaching out to the adoring crowd. Her uncle Ted Kennedy's watercolors of New England coastal scenes adorn the walls, evoking admiring comments from visitors who hadn't realized Kennedy had artistic talent. There are framed portraits of Abraham Lincoln, Franklin Roosevelt, George Washington, and Golda Meir, a recent acquisition and the only non-American in the honored group of leaders. "I needed a woman," says Townsend in her typically forthright manner.

"She founded a country. That was impressive. She deserved the recognition."

Kathleen was twelve when President Kennedy was assassinated, an event that taught her early how to cope with tragedy. "Dear Kathleen," her father wrote on that sad occasion. "You seem to understand that Jack died and was buried today. As the oldest of the Kennedy grandchildren, you have a particular responsibility now—a special responsibility to John and Joe. Be kind to others and work for your country. Love, Daddy." The framed letter hangs in a prominent place in Townsend's home in the Baltimore suburbs. John was John Kennedy, Jr., and Joe, Kathleen's younger brother, Joseph, then eleven. Adhering to the partriarchal tradition in the Kennedy family, there is no mention of Kathleen's numerous younger siblings, or of Caroline Kennedy, the surviving female heir of the dead president.

Five years later, when a lone gunman cut short her own father's life, Kathleen bore the additional responsibilities with apparent aplomb. As the eldest in a raucous family of ten—and her mother pregnant with the eleventh—she stood out as an oasis of calm. For a while, she considered becoming a nun, and took on the countenance of someone who had given up worldly pleasures in the service of something more important. She left her hair untended, scorned makeup and fine clothes, as if looking drab could distract the world from noticing she was a Kennedy. "So earnest," says a friend, "you know she's up to good." Some of her siblings still call her "the nun."

With some members of the Kennedy family, success and scandal have competed for the media's attention. That is not the case with Kathleen. Married to the same man for almost thirty years, there is not a hint of scandal in the life she has led. She is known variously as the "Un-Kennedy," the "Quiet Kennedy," and "Clean Kathleen." Though unmistakably a Kennedy, she does not light up a room in the sense of being an electrifying presence in the manner of her father, or late cousin, JFK, Jr., and she is reluctant to press the advantage of her birthright. Journalist Michael Barone recalls once meeting Townsend for lunch in a Washington restaurant and being ushered to a less than desirable table. When he lightheartedly observed that she would have gotten a better table if the maître d' had known who she was, Townsend brushed aside the suggestion with a groan and a dismissive wave of her hand.

Townsend is a hardworking public servant, brimming with ideas about how to energize democracy. She is known nationally for her innovative approaches to crime fighting, her emphasis on volunteerism, and her unabashed embrace of "character education" in the public schools. When an aide says her office functions like a think tank, she makes a face. "No, this is a *do tank*," she says, not some intellectual exercise.

How far can she go in politics? Charlie Peters, publisher of the influential *Washington Monthly* magazine, has been on record for years predicting Townsend would be the first female president. In the early 1980s, she wrote a series of essays for his magazine about virtue, morality, and volunteerism, themes that, at the time, made traditional liberals uneasy. This was the heyday of Ronald Reagan, and liberals feared that adopting values associated with the political right would yield ground to conservatives who wanted to replace government assistance with more personal responsibility. Peters saw in Kathleen the same mix of qualities that marked her father's career, a steady moral compass combined with a willingness to defy liberal dogma and be tough on those who fall short. Her determination to make government work for the less fortunate comes across as more pragmatic than sentimental.

Yet questions persist about whether KKT has what it takes to make it in the combative, celebrity-driven environment of modern politics. A woman friend once despaired over the way Townsend, a slight figure to start with, seemed to shrink in the limelight. "She does less to push herself into good issues than any politician I've ever seen," said the friend. "When Clinton was in Baltimore, he was surrounded by all these goofy males from the legislature, and you could hardly see her."

Townsend is aware of the doubts, and is taking concrete steps to erase them. She will never be a megawattage Kennedy, but she is learning the value of charisma, and how to find it within herself. Where once she thought nothing of dashing out in public with her hair disheveled and her hands stained blue from leaky pens, she now takes greater care with her appearance. At a February 1999 luncheon hosted by Women Executives in State Government, Townsend appeared simultaneously authoritative and feminine in a dark pants suit with a bright scarf around her neck. Complimented on her new look, she confessed that she had an image consultant go through her closet. "She threw everything out. She said nothing worked. She got me a few basics that last and told me how to accessorize. I'm not very good at it, but I'm getting better. I hate shopping. My feeling is if you don't like it and you're no good at it, why not hire somebody to do it for you?"

Townsend also worked at turning her stream-of-consciousness thinking into organized public presentations. She kept her trademark intensity, but worked to develop a substantive framework so her thoughts tracked for reporters searching for a news story. The stylistic discipline helped dispel early whisperings that she had too much of a scattershot approach to public policy, and that she was an intellectual lightweight.

A turning point in Townsend's image occurred during the fall of 1998 when she took over Governor Parris Glendening's floundering reelection campaign. It was an extraordinary step for the junior partner in the enterprise to assert control, and it sent a message that Townsend was not somebody to trifle with. Going into the race, Glendening had been ranked as the nation's least popular governor. Quirky, emotionally distant from the voters, and plagued by political mistakes, he faced an uphill battle for reelection even among hardcore Democrats. The campaign's research showed that Townsend had established enough of her own identity to remain popular despite the dissatisfaction with Glendening, and that she could add much-needed votes.

Tension over the way Glendening was conducting the campaign, and how best to exploit Townsend's popularity, came to a head after Glendening refused to appear at a campaign event in Maryland with President Clinton. The snub angered Democrats who believed the impeachment proceedings under way in the Congress against Clinton were politically motivated, and that Clinton's behavior with a young White House intern, however distasteful, was not grounds for impeachment. Glendening dropped ten points in the polls. Black voters in Maryland defected in droves, telling pollsters they would rather stay home on election day than vote for a turncoat.

For a time, it looked as though Maryland might elect its first woman governor, Republican Ellen Sauerbrey. The daughter of a steamfitter, she came across as real and natural in her television ads. She softened her conservative position on guns and abortion rights, and ran as a centrist. She had nearly beaten Glendening four years earlier and for weeks refused to concede, charging the Democrats with voter fraud. Editorial writers dubbed her Ellen Sauergrapes. For the rerun, she underwent a total makeover. Gone was the bulldog of 1994. Democratic media adviser Frank Greer fretted that Sauerbrey had transformed herself into a clone of New Jersey's moderate Republican governor Christine Todd Whitman in appearance and on issues.

Glendening had descended into denial. He didn't like hearing bad news and seemed incapable of making the changes necessary to avoid defeat. With her career on the line, Townsend took charge. It was an uncharacteristic assertion of power, one that months later Townsend still seemed amazed at having engineered. "I realized in September that if nothing changed, we would lose—and I didn't want to lose," she said. "I did take charge. I don't like to put it that way," she smiles nervously. "But the governor's been terrific. Most people don't like to share power."

Townsend proved she could be bold and coldly calculating. She fired Frank Greer as the campaign's media consultant when the television commercials he produced weren't hard-hitting enough. Greer was furious at what he saw as her betrayal. A soft-spoken southerner, he was the one who urged Glendening to select her as lieutenant governor in the first place, and then fought to get her on the ticket. Townsend brought in family friend Bob Shrum, a talented wordsmith with a taste for hardball politics. In one swoop, she sacrificed her professional and personal relationship with Greer, one of her biggest fans and promoters, and injected herself into the campaign in a way that could alienate voters. Greer's ads showed Townsend, but as a sidekick, with Glendening the featured figure. Shrum's first spot opened with Townsend speaking directly into the camera, offering a warm testimonial to Glendening. Subsequent ads showed the two together, but Townsend had clearly emerged from the shadows. Shrum was showcasing her as an equal partner, and Democrats were counting on her skirt-tails to carry the ticket across the finish line. The one unanswered question: Would voters object to their lieutenant governor elbowing aside the governor?

By aligning herself with Shrum, Townsend sent the message that she would do what it takes to win. Shrum focused selectively on Sauerbrey's voting record in the Maryland legislature, deftly creating the impression that she was a foe of civil rights. His ad undermined Sauerbrey's claim to moderation. The tactic energized blacks and other core Democrats and helped produce the large voter turnout that returned Glendening and Townsend to office with 56 percent of the vote for a second four-year term. Political analysts gave Townsend much of the credit for Glendening's come-from-behind victory, citing her help with two pivotal voting blocs—blacks and women.

Kathleen is the dutiful eldest daughter. Born on July 4, 1951, her father named her after his beloved sister Kathleen, who died in a 1948 plane crash. Robert Kennedy made it a condition of his daughter's naming that nobody call her "Kick," the nickname that his sister was known by because of her ebullience. Any resentment she might have felt about having to share her parents' attention with a succession of siblings was assuaged by her status as the trusted firstborn. In the late sixties, at the height of the drug culture, her father reluctantly agreed to allow her to leave the tightly restricted all-girls Catholic school she'd been attending in Maryland to enroll at the progressive Putney School in Vermont. Kathleen was attracted to the earthy, back-to-nature side of the hippie movement, which flourished at the coed, counterculture academy. Her father only half-jokingly called the place "Potney," but believed his eldest daughter was immune to the darker side of the sixties. In 1969, with the Vietnam War raging and President Lyndon Johnson in disrepute among young people, students at Putney argued over whether a woman could be president. "Some people thought it was possible; some didn't. You know, the classic question: Do women have the right temperament? Where was I?" she asks with a sheepish smile that gives away the punch line. "I was on the wrong side." Kathleen, at seventeen, couldn't imagine a woman president any more than she could a political future for herself.

It was a turbulent time, with women beginning to question their secondary role in society and pushing to expand the boundaries of what was possible. When Kathleen entered Harvard in the fall of 1969, her dorm was all women; by spring, it was coed, a sign as small and yet as insistent as the first crocus signaling a new season. Reflecting on that period, Townsend says, "I think there were the inklings of a women's movement making its way into Harvard, but it didn't make its way to me very clearly." She can't remember having a single woman professor at Harvard, but it was of no concern to her. She didn't become actively interested in issues of women's equality until years later, when she attended law school. At Harvard, it was the war in Vietnam that captured her attention. Far more noteworthy than the introduction of male students into her dorm were the antiwar protests that shut down the university. Her father's zeal for social change and civil rights also burned within her. She marched on Washington. She took a semester off to work with the United Farm Workers.

She also set her sights on a young teaching assistant at Harvard named David Townsend. "I had a crush on him, but he was going out with somebody else," she recalls. "So I had an idea how to get him away from his girlfriend. We had been studying American literature and Mark Twain, so I thought we should build a raft and float down the Mississippi." Kathleen enlisted her mother, Ethel Kennedy, to research the venture. Mrs. Kennedy called Mississippi senator James Eastland, who warned of dangerous currents and river rats. "Well, my daughter is strong," she replied. "She can just bop them over the head with an oar." Townsend loved the idea, and he and Kathleen and three friends spent ten days constructing an elaborate wooden raft with a roof, and rigging it underneath with twelve fifty-five-gallon oil drums for flotation. Townsend's girlfriend was not the outdoorsy type and stayed behind just as Kathleen had calculated.

Capturing Townsend's heart was her primary motive in designing the trip, but Kathleen had other worthy goals as well. Learning about the Mississippi firsthand rather than by reading about it in books appealed to her sense of adventure, as well as her intellectual curiosity. She also liked the idea of defying all those who questioned her ability to pull off such a stunt, a trait that would appear throughout her life as she rose in elective office after being initially underestimated. Kathleen wrote about the trip in the February 1973 issue of *Ladies' Home Journal*. The piece was accompanied by a prominent picture of a grinning Kathleen with her hair tied in two pigtails, along with photos of the raft, dubbed *Snopes*, after William Faulkner's trilogy about a southern family of that name, and her crewmates, including the long-haired and very serious-looking Townsend. Kathleen tells about being hauled into jail early in the voyage by a river patrol officer, and how she would have been booked along with the others except she had conveniently forgotten her wallet, and nobody knew who she was. The local officials were mollified once the out-of-towners forked over the requisite fee. At a stop in Oxford, Mississippi, the scene of riots in 1962 over James Meredith's enrollment as the first black at the University of Mississippi, she was no longer anonymous. "According to my host, I was visiting the scene of a crime where my father, then attorney general, had been guilty of misunderstanding and destruction. I was held guilty as well," Kathleen wrote. "These people of the South had suffered during those times and resented the intrusion of freedom fighters, Northern liberals, and all that they stood for. They were happy to tell me so."

Over the course of floating five hundred miles down the Mississippi, Kathleen and David got to know each other, and David forgot all about the girlfriend at Harvard. The two married in November 1973 and moved to Santa Fe, New Mexico, which by East Coast Kennedy standards was a form of dropping out. Kathleen's wedding gift from her bridesmaids was a potter's wheel. The couple's holistic approach to life was evident in Kathleen's insistence on delivering her children at home by natural childbirth. Assisting in the first birth, David followed a procedure he learned from a police emergency manual, biting open the amniotic sac with his teeth. The couple then buried the placenta in their yard and planted a piñon tree above it, a ritual that is traditional in New Mexico. Kathleen reveled in her earth mother role, but also managed to earn a law degree from the University of New Mexico. Inequities of all kinds stirred her passion, and politics was in her blood.

A quiet and unpretentious intellectual, David Townsend enjoyed his time at home, and had no hang-ups about helping out with domestic chores. As Kathleen's political life took hold, he would eventually take over more of the family cooking and carpooling. Profiles tend to make him seem saintlike, and he may well be. But these arrangements are never as simple as they appear. The lieutenant governor of Maryland's press secretary emphasizes that his boss still does laundry and drives her children places. But who's counting? The Kennedy-Townsend marriage has endured as their careers and children flourish. Yet in the balancing of lives, it should be noted that most of the nine moves the couple made in the first ten years of their marriage were generated by opportunities for Townsend to further his academic career. A teaching job at the western campus of St. John's College prompted the move to Santa Fe; the chance to earn a law degree at Yale and then a job in the U.S. Attorney's Office in Boston brought them back East. Kathleen was never idle during this period. In addition to her growing family, she kept up her pottery, wrote freelance articles, worked in Santa Fe as an investigator for the state's Human Rights Commission, in Boston as a lawyer, and of course answered the call to work on Ted Kennedy's failed 1980 presidential campaign.

When her uncle asked her to manage his 1982 reelection race for the Senate, she leapt at the chance. The Townsends by then were living in Boston, and after the election, Kathleen got hired as a policy aide to Massachusetts governor Michael Dukakis. Managing Ted Kennedy's successful reelection campaign whetted Kathleen's appetite to plunge into politics on her own. She thought about running for Congress from Massachusetts, but except for attending college in Boston, she had not put down real roots in the state. Her younger brother Joe had the same aspiration, and he got first dibs at the family franchise. The year was 1986, and Kathleen's husband had gotten a job teaching Greek and philosophy at St. John's College in Maryland. The Democrats in Maryland needed a candidate to challenge incumbent Republican representative Helen Bentley, a populist Republican with a blue-collar background. "I thought, 'Great, I should try,' " recalls Kathleen. Her family was not thrilled. There was no tradition in the family of a woman running. Some family members pointedly asked who would care for her young children. They gave lip service to her candidacy, but they didn't turn over family lists of donors. For her part, Townsend was disappointed but not surprised. She realized she was taking a huge risk with the family name in what ultimately turned out to be a lark, and a losing one at that. She hadn't been raised with the same expectations as her brothers and male cousins, and didn't think enough of her potential as a political figure to feel rejected. She didn't seem to understand or appreciate the value of her maiden name, dropping it from billboards and bumper stickers, and running as Kathleen Townsend.

Her 42 percent of the vote stuck her with the dubious distinction of being the only Kennedy to lose an election, except for Ted Kennedy's failed attempt to wrest the Democratic presidential nomination from President Carter in 1980. "I learned that you can actually figure out whether races are winnable or not," she says with a laugh. A Democrat had represented the district for twenty-two years, but his defeat two years earlier signaled the new Republican majority that had emerged. Townsend declined a rematch, knowing she would lose again. She remains proud of the energy and idealism her campaign unleashed among young people. At a tenth reunion of the campaign in 1996, former staffers wore T-shirts that said "I walked with Kathleen." Five of the young men who worked in the campaign subsequently ran for political office, but none of the women, an outcome that Townsend attributes to differences in ambition. "The women worked for me because they liked me, and they liked the issues," she says. "The men may have liked me, and they may have liked the issues. But mainly they wanted to learn politics."

Townsend recalls asking an intern whether she planned to run for office. "Oh, no, that would be too ambitious," the young woman replied. "It's okay to be ambitious," Townsend told women students in a seminar on politics at Wellesley College. "I have a daughter at Harvard. When she was a senior in high school, she was asked how she would like to be remembered. 'I want to be the fastest runner, the best math student, and the best science student.' Her teacher said, 'You're only going to be disappointed.' My daughter protested. She *wanted* to set her standards high. This was an all-girls school where you're supposed to be remembered as kind and shy. We've got to teach our girls to feel good about ambition.

"I'm the oldest of eleven children. My youngest sister was born sixteen years later. She does not have that same challenge of ambition. She's a documentary filmmaker. She did a documentary on drug-addicted homeless women, and when a doctor testifying in a hearing on Capitol Hill asked her about the film, my sister said it was the most gripping film and the best film she'd ever seen. You've got to believe in yourself, believe that you can do great things.

"I attended a seminar at Radcliffe," Townsend went on. "The message was that politics is dirty, and that there should be campaign finance reform. This idea that until politics changes, women shouldn't run is another way that we make decisions. Politics is an alternative to battles. Our deepest fights about what we believe take place in politics. Don't be ambitious for yourself. Find out what issue moves you, what great idea inspires you, because if you think that way, you'll be in for the long haul."

After her losing congressional race, Townsend kept her name in circulation. She founded the Maryland Student Service Alliance, an organization dedicated to getting kids involved in community service, and in 1988 she received the second highest number of votes statewide running as a Dukakis delegate to the Democratic National Convention. In 1992, she was a Clinton delegate, which led to her appointment as a deputy attorney general in the Clinton administration. Despite the important-sounding title, it was a job with no visibility. There she labored with no obvious political future until Glendening selected her as his running mate.

In the 1990s, coed leadership in the statehouses became a national trend. At the start of the decade, only four states had female lieutenant governors. By the end of the decade, there were eighteen women serving as lieutenant governors—eleven Republicans, seven Democrats, and one Reform party. Running with a woman helped Republican men soften their stereotypical image. At the same time, Democratic men facing a rising tide of Republican conservatism turned to women as running mates to boost the turnout of women voters essential to their electoral success.

Preparing for his gubernatorial race in 1994, Glendening had narrowed his choices to four finalists for lieutenant governor. All were women. His selection of Townsend initially seemed a marriage of convenience. She had the name and the political connections to raise the money that the colorless Glendening needed to wage a competitive race. But after they took office, it became clear that something of seismic proportions had taken place. Instead of being consigned to ceremonial duties the way past lieutenant governors had been, Townsend was granted extraordinary authority. Three cabinet secretaries reported directly to her, and she oversaw spending for public safety. She seized the opportunity to champion a number of innovative crime-fighting and crime-prevention programs, and it wasn't long before she became known as the state's crime czar. Asked what kind of power-sharing deal she struck with Glendening, she says in her disarmingly straightforward manner, "I wasn't going to do it unless I could do something."

Townsend's credentials as a crime-buster were tarnished in December 1999 when the *Baltimore Sun* published a four-part series exposing what one critic described as "institutionalized child abuse" at the state's three boot camps for juveniles. Glendening was away at the time, but when he returned he immediately ordered a task force to investigate the newspaper's findings. When the task force confirmed the alleged brutality by guards at the boot camps, a Baltimore judge ordered all the city's youth moved out and the camps closed. Responding to the task force's findings, Townsend said the administrator in charge of juvenile detention had misled her.

The *Sun* quoted Townsend as saying that she began promoting boot camps in 1996 after touring one in Cleveland. The newspaper noted that a U.S. Justice Department study in October 1999 reported that Cleveland's camp graduates had a higher recidivism rate than teens released from juvenile jails. The camp in Cleveland was one of several in Ohio ordered closed after officials determined they were less effective than other, cheaper methods of incarceration and rehabilitation. In August 1999, a *Sun* reporter told Townsend about violence he had witnessed in the camps. She said she reported it to department officials who subsequently assured her that the abuse had stopped.

Just as Townsend had stepped in to soften criticism of Glendening during the campaign, the governor shielded his running mate from most of the blame for the badly supervised boot camps. When Glendening asked for and received the resignations of four top juvenile justice officials and fired a fifth, he let Townsend make the announcement. "There was a complete breakdown in the [juvenile justice] department's chain of command," she told the press, and the guards had engaged in "unconscionable abuse of authority." Even so, she had given her rivals for the governorship in 2002 an issue to use against her.

As her advocacy for boot camps and other tough anticrime measures shows, Townsend may be a bleeding heart, but she's no liberal. She has distanced herself from her uncle Teddy's politics of largesse and is firmly planted in the New Democrat camp. She is passionate about volunteerism and community service, which she sees as a way to teach young people they can make a difference. "I think that's the greatest thing I learned from my family," she says. "I don't think there's any way that you can be happier than feeling that you can make an impact. That's the epitome of life. And I thought there were too many kids who didn't feel that way." She took on the education bureaucracy in Maryland to win approval of a mandatory student-service program that requires seventy-five hours of community service from high school students before they can get their diplomas. The program was initially opposed by twenty-two of twenty-four local boards of education, the PTA, and both teachers' unions. One union head likened the mandatory aspect of the program to slavery and said it was a violation of the Thirteenth Amendment. Townsend persevered, and between the combination of her evident sincerity and the changing climate of the times eventually won over her critics.

A crusader on the theme of personal responsibility, Townsend established the first statewide Office of Character Education, which is dedicated to incorporating into the regular academic curriculum the teaching of such universally accepted values as honesty, fairness, courage, respect, and responsibility. The office provides advice and suggested lessons, but exactly how to implement them is left up to local school systems. Townsend's emphasis on values wins her support among voters who normally would not gravitate toward a Kennedy. Liberals who might otherwise harbor concerns about heavy-handed moralizing trust the curriculum because of its Kennedy bloodlines.

Townsend has launched a variety of anticrime measures, from a Police Corps program to recruit promising college students to her HotSpots campaign, which puts more police in high-crime areas. Since 53 percent of crimes in Maryland occur in 3 percent of neighborhoods, she reasoned that focusing on the most vulnerable neighborhoods would reduce crime. Additional police are coupled with grants that encourage community involvement. "Where I'm coming from is to make democracy work, which means getting citizens involved," she says.

Townsend developed the HotSpot idea as a pilot program in a Baltimore neighborhood while she was working at the Justice

Department in the early 1990s, and took it statewide after she was elected lieutenant governor. She rarely misses an opportunity in a public forum or interview to credit HotSpots for a fall in crime numbers. The program has had a mostly positive effect, and prompts police to work more closely with local citizens in fighting a variety of problems, from drugs to juvenile delinquency. But critics say that by targeting one neighborhood, the crime gets pushed elsewhere, and that Townsend's community grants are little more than payoffs to political friends, or "social pork," in the words of Baltimore Mayor Martin O'Malley, who for a while toyed with challenging Townsend for governor.

Townsend supports the death penalty. When she talks about violent crime, she often manages to work in the fact that her family has suffered irreparable tragedy because of gunfire. She oversees the state's efforts to trace illegal firearms seized by police. While she is never maudlin about the Kennedy family's travails, she does cite her brother David Kennedy's death by drug overdose in 1989 as an event that spurs her determination to curb heroin use in Maryland.

Ordinary people and political professionals who encounter Townsend voice the opinion that she is "too nice" for today's politics. Her idealism about public service, her reluctance to press her family advantage, and her unassuming personal demeanor lead people to mistakenly take her measure as somebody who can be rolled. This is a criticism frequently leveled at women, but rarely, if ever, at men. Asked her reaction, Townsend feigns surprise, says she's never heard that before, then musters a rare but stinging sarcasm. "But thank you, I'm really touched," she says. Her perceived niceness is a sensitive subject for KKT, and she keeps returning to it. She's irritated at the lack of attention the media pay her in comparison to her brothers when she is doing the work of government. "Ask the people in Baltimore about my tough-on-crime image," she says. "They'll know, but they won't know in Washington, where they rely on the *Washington Post*, which doesn't cover me."

Major media have put more focus on the misdeeds of some of her brothers (five of them after the deaths of David and Michael) than on good works by Townsend and her three sisters. Townsend is still smarting over a 1997 *Newsweek* cover, "The Young Kennedys: A Dynasty in Decline." It featured six Kennedy males (including Kathleen's brother Max, who had never run for office), but excluded her. "I think there are different expectations for women than for men," she says. "There are women in my family who are doing terrific things.

They didn't make the cover. Boys make the cover for doing bad things. If the three girls had gotten in trouble, I bet it would not have made the cover."

The backbone Townsend shows by pursuing a political career was put into perspective in November 1999 when her brother Chris chose the opposite course. Democratic leaders in Illinois had urged Chris Kennedy to run for the seat of retiring representative John Edward Porter, a Republican, in Chicago's northern suburbs. Chris, an executive with the Merchandise Mart in Chicago, wrote to the state's Democratic chairman declining the offer. "I have come to believe that the bullet that kills a father wounds his children," Kennedy said. "There were a lot of wounded children when I grew up, and extending the difficulties of a single-parent household to another generation would violate the promise I made to myself a thousand times when I was a child."

With four daughters of her own, Townsend confronts daily what she calls the "internal war" between work and family responsibilities. "We're struggling to keep all the balls in the air, and each passing day they seem to be heavier and heavier," she told a Solutions Summit that she convened in 1998 to promote, among other ideas, state funds to provide after-school supervision for middle school children.

Part of the reason Townsend is able to have a political career is because her husband takes an active role in raising their children and running their household. She points out that as a professor, he gets the summers off and has a more flexible schedule. Part of the reason the couple's move to Maryland appealed to Kathleen was the expectation that she would begin a career in public life, and that David and his parents, who live close by, could provide the support system that would keep the family strong. Kathleen would never say anything negative about the Kennedys, but she gravitated to the simpler, more stable life that the Townsend family represented. David's father was a public school teacher and principal, and his mother worked as a secretary. His childhood was a far cry from what Kathleen or any Kennedy experienced, and the couple agreed that it was important they give their children an upbringing where they would have the freedom to be ordinary people. Townsend couldn't handle the demands of political life if she didn't have a husband willing to take over duties normally associated with the woman of the house. Her personal situation aside, Townsend recognizes that institutions have to change if future generations are to do a better job of balancing work and family.

Women now comprise 29 percent of the Maryland legislature and are making an impact. "We're getting through our domestic violence legislation, our child care, in a way that they literally laughed off ten years ago," says Townsend. When the Budget Committee tried to cut back on the social spending that Townsend oversees, all it took was one phone call from her to trigger a response from a network of women supporters. "Stop this campaign," the committee chairman pleaded. Deluged with calls and letters, the lawmakers restored the funds. "There is this network that says, 'Don't touch Kathleen,' " said an aide.

The example is instructive. If women are to make a difference, they need to achieve critical mass. "If we're supposed to change politics, we have to make it fit our lives rather than fit into anybody else's lives," says Townsend. "I think one of the saddest stories I ever heard was from [former representative] Lynn Martin, who said when she went into Congress she had to leave behind who she was. She was a teacher and a mother, but she concentrated on defense and economic policy. She told me, 'There was part of my heart that died.'"

When Martin served in Congress and as a cabinet secretary in the Bush administration, she was one of only a few women. They felt compelled to play by the men's rules. "It's hard to make a difference by yourself," Townsend said. "But if you're part of a group, then you can concentrate on issues of more concern to women. But you can't do it alone."

Getting an assist from men helps. Glendening has come to regard electing Townsend governor as part of his legacy. Squiring Townsend at a political event, Glendening told his supporters, "You helped me, now help her." Glendening also expanded Townsend's portfolio, making her the point person on the state's economic development efforts, a key perch to woo support from the business community for her gubernatorial run. Townsend was popular in Maryland though there were some doubts about her effectiveness. Her ability to tap into a national network to raise money made her a formidable candidate. Because of her family's deep political roots, she had more donors in New York and Massachusetts than in her home state of Maryland.

It had become conventional wisdom that no candidate in either major political party could match Townsend in fundraising. As the campaign season got underway, and Townsend reported raising some $6 million dollars before the curtain even opened on 2002. Baltimore Mayor O'Malley, a brash and ambitious Irish-American who reminded Townsend of her brothers, kept making noises about running but polls showed his constituents, a large chunk of the state's voters,

liked him as mayor and would resent his moving on before complet-
ing even one term. Townsend was convinced that in the end the
charismatic O'Malley would see her as a member of the family, and
not take her on and she proved right. The Republican candidate, Rep.
Robert Ehrlich, entered the race late by modern standards, announcing on March 25 from the front stoop of his childhood home in a
working-class suburb of Baltimore. He had hesitated, not wanting to
sacrifice his House seat for a race that had such long odds for him.
Registered Democrats outnumber Republicans 2-to-1 in Maryland,
and the GOP hadn't captured the statehouse since Spiro Agnew was
elected in 1966.

Still, there were qualms about Townsend's ability to win the top
job. She had never run on her own, and would have to create an
identity separate from Glendening while still taking credit for the accomplishments of the previous eight years. It was a balancing act that
faces every junior partner in a political enterprise. Townsend's first
test came before she had even officially announced when Glendening
submitted a budget to the legislature that called for rescinding a
promised tax cut to make up for lost revenue during the economic
slowdown. The alternative, he said, would be to cut spending on
popular education, health and criminal justice programs. Townsend
backed the governor but refused to say publicly whether she agreed
with his priorities, and declined to be drawn into the budget machina-
tions with the legislature.

Though the tax cut under discussion amounted to about $75 a
year for the average Maryland family, its symbolism was far greater
than its dollar value. Whichever position Townsend took would cost
her support; yet not taking any position raised questions about her
leadership. The *Washington Post* in a news story on Feburary 24, 2002,
observed that Townsend's style of governing, with its emphasis on volunteerism and inclusiveness, was not well suited to playing hardball
politics. "She is so focused on getting people involved that she sometimes seems reluctant to burden anyone with her own opinions," the
story concluded. The *Baltimore Sun* on February 3, 2002 questioned
whether Townsend, even after an eight-year apprenticeship, was ready
for prime time. "She is still learning to talk under pressure. Sometimes
she seems to be riffling through file cards in her head for just the right
cliché. Sometimes her enthusiasm leaves her tongue-tied. She's a
smart woman who sometimes sounds as if she is not."

The 44-year-old Ehrlich, a popular, pro-choice member of Congress with deep roots in Maryland, represented the GOP's best hope
for ending Democratic dominance in the state. A *Washington Post* edi-

torial predicted a lively campaign and advised the Townsend camp to "stash any plans for a coronation." The race was expected to turn on local issues—a hotly debated highway connecting two populous counties that Ehrlich strongly supports and Townsend sort of supports, and whether slot machines should be permitted in the state, which Ehrlich wants while Townsend rules them out as a way to raise revenue.

The race was hardly underway when it became apparent that Townsend was struggling. The Kennedy name was losing its allure among Democrats, yet Republicans were able to capitalize on anti-Kennedy sentiment by raising the prospect of Townsend as a prospective president. A GOP fundraising appeal described Ehrlich as "literally the one Republican standing in the way" of the Kennedys putting another family member in the oval office. But as a campaigner, KKT lacked her father's people skills and seemed unable to connect with the audiences who yearned to recreate Camelot.

Ehrlich, by contrast, seemed to have discovered the magic formula. He combined a friendly, guy-next-door demeanor with a platform that was fiscally conservative but socially unthreatening. Ehrlich reached out to black voters and soccer moms, campaigning aggressively in the city of Baltimore and the liberal Washington suburbs thought to be Townsend's territory. When a pair of snipers began a killing spree in Maryland that terrorized the Washington area for three weeks, many analysts thought Townsend would benefit because of her long history of championing gun control.

But when she talked about the need for stricter gun laws, Ehrlich accused her of exploiting the tragedy. Townsend's slide in the polls continued. Republicans, sensing victory, poured so much money into the race that Ehrlich overtook Townsend in the one area where everybody thought she was unassailable. He raised three times as much money in the final two weeks of the race, some of it from gambling interests eager to take advantage of his support for slot machines and get a foothold in the state. The financial windfall enabled Ehrlich to aggressively advertise on television and radio, and to wage an intense get-out-the-vote effort. The race was by far the most expensive in Maryland's history with Ehrlich coming in at $10.4 million and Townsend with $8.5 million.

Townsend lost to Ehrlich by 52 to 48 percent, a result that stunned Democrats and spelled the end of Townsend's prospects as a presidential candidate. She was not alone in her loss; not a single lieutenant governor running across the country (and there were several) managed to win. Townsend was weighed down by Glendening's baggage—a huge budget deficit and a quirky personal style that voters had tired of after eight years. The episode with the snipers underscored voter concerns about personal safety, and sent many women voters who should have been with Townsend to Ehrlich, who they perceived as the stronger candidate. Townsend lost white married women by a large margin. Townsend did not rule out running again, but recovering from a race she had been expected to win easily would be a long-shot.

Reports that Townsend was overly scripted and unwilling to move beyond vague generalities furthered a negative stereotype that she was relying on her family name to get elected. Her choice of a conservative white male, retired Admiral Charles Larson, a registered Republican, as her running mate, angered black voters, the core of her support and whose enthusiastic turnout was crucial to her election. Ehrlich responded by putting an African American, Michael Steele, the GOP's state chairman, on his ticket. Townsend had hoped to win over moderates and Independents with her choice. Instead it was Ehrlich who attracted crossover votes, and whose running mate made history as the first black elected statewide in Maryland.

TEN

Governor Swift:
A Cautionary Tale

On average, women enter politics ten years later than men. They wait for children to grow up, for husbands to become secure in their careers, for the restlessness of middle age to prod them to seek satisfaction outside the home. Jane Swift's generation—the Y generation, demographers call it—is the first where women in substantial numbers are plunging into politics even as they cope with the responsibilities of marriage and motherhood. "In my early twenties, I thought I could do it all—be a mommy, have a family, have a great career," Swift says. "In my early thirties, I began to hear the biological clock ticking. I was in politics, and it occurred to me that I had to make choices. The big factor in elective politics is the time. You have to prioritize your professional life or prioritize your family."

Swift's story is instructive for other young women who whet their appetites for politics by working in someone else's campaign, but fear they can't run for office themselves without giving up the equally compelling drive to be a wife and mother. Swift was thirty-three in October of 1998 when she gave birth to a baby daughter less than three weeks before the voters of Massachusetts elected her their lieutenant governor. As a pregnant woman running for office, she got national attention and helped Republican Paul Cellucci win the governorship. Not long after Swift took office, a *Boston Globe* headline writer dubbed her "Lieutenant Mom." She is a test case for women who dare to mix motherhood and elective office.

Swift's time in office has been marked by sharp ups and downs, personally and professionally. As lieutenant governor, she had a tin ear for what were permissible perks for a public servant and drew criticism for a variety of minor ethical lapses, including using state employees as babysitters in a pinch. By December of 2000, her approval rating had sunk to 17% in a *Boston Herald* newspaper poll. There seemed to be no way back from political purgatory. Then President Bush named Governor Celluci ambassador to Canada, and Swift was elevated to governor. It was April 2001, and she was due to give birth to twins in May. As the nation's first pregnant governor, she drafted contingency plans to conduct state business from her hospital room, declaring that she didn't believe giving birth "results in incapacitation." Some of her male political rivals questioned the validity of meetings held by speakerphone, and the ensuing controversy generated enormous sympathy for Swift. Her critics looked petty and sexist, and her supporters delighted in reminding voters that a former governor and Boston mayor, James Michael Curley, had once conducted official business from jail, where he was being held on charges of mail fraud.

The arrival of Swift's two new daughters vaulted her once again into the ranks of celebrity. She was the first governor to give birth in office, and questions about how she would juggle the growing demands of her work life and her family dominated the media's coverage of Swift. "How do you do it?" asked Betty Sperling, whose husband was moderating a breakfast interview with Swift in late October 2001. It was rare for Betty to venture a question at a "Sperling Breakfast," a Washington institution her husband had presided over for several decades. Swift talked about how she uses commuting time in the car to read briefing materials. She said a friend told her that if she were a lawyer, those would be billable hours. Massachusetts doesn't provide a governor's residence, and the 130-mile trip back to her farm in the western part of the state takes just under three hours each way, more if there's traffic or snow. She conceded that life is "sometimes mind-boggling," but she reminds herself how lucky she is to have three happy, healthy children and a job she loves that is meaningful. "And they sleep through the night," she added with a bright smile.

Swift has an appealing, direct manner. She looked more glamorous than when we caught up with her on the campaign trail three years earlier. She is thinner; her black hair is sleekly bobbed; there is an American flag pin in the lapel of her dark power suit. Two of the hijacked planes seized by terrorists on 9/11 had taken off from Boston's Logan Airport, and Swift was in Washington promoting the idea of federalizing airport security. The events of 9/11 had changed her job dramatically. She said she spends one-quarter to one-half of her time on security and safety issues. When host Budge Sperling asked mid-way through the hour-long interview session whether she wanted more coffee, Swift said yes, gratefully. "That's the real answer to your wife's question," she said, "lots of coffee."

If she can balance her family responsibilities with the duties of the highest office in a major state, maybe others can too. If she can't, her experience will discourage women just now reaching adulthood who grew up believing they, not just their brothers, could rise to become a senator, governor, even president. Swift eventually decided she couldn't do it all, and in a tearful press conference in Boston on March 19, 2002, she announced that she would not seek election in the fall. "I am sure there isn't a working parent in America who hasn't faced the same issues," she said. "When the demands of the tasks you take on increase substantially, something has to give."

Yet just days before, she seemed up for the challenge. It was only when Republican superstar Mitt Romney, fresh from a triumphal tour chairing the winter Olympics, declared his intention to take on Swift in the GOP primary, that she bowed to the obvious. Polls showed Romney leading Swift 75 percent to 12 percent. "I'm not just a Republican. I'm also a realist," she said. If those numbers had been reversed, Swift might not have found her family obligations quite so onerous. Sometimes citing the conflicts of parenthood is a way of saving face.

Swift got an early start in politics. When she was six, her father, who ran a plumbing and heating business, took her with him to political meetings in western Massachusetts. He was the campaign manager for the man who held the state senate seat that Jane eventually would claim as her own. After graduating from Trinity College in Hartford, Connecticut, Swift was hired as a management trainer for a major department store. But when she was asked a year later to work for Peter C. Webber, the Massachusetts state senator from her hometown of North Adams, she accepted. "I thought two years of politics would be a great way to figure out what I wanted to do with my life," she recalls. Before the two years were up, Webber announced he would not seek reelection in 1990. At age twenty-four, Swift decided she would run for the seat. "I was too young to know how daunting it would be," she says. "It became very obvious that the fact that I was a woman made a difference in the way I was treated."

Reporters asked Swift questions they didn't ask her male opponent. She cites the hardened political reporter who asked whether she was married. When she answered no, he followed up: "Do you have a boyfriend?" She said yes. "Well, how serious are you?" he asked. "Are you going to get married?"

"I don't think a man my age would have been asked about his dating status," Swift says. "The implication was that if I were married I certainly wouldn't want to do this job." The media commented regularly on her hairstyle, the color of her stockings, and the length of her skirts. Her age became an issue. Questions were raised about her maturity, although the man she succeeded had been only a year and a half older when he was elected.

As it turned out, Swift says, the fact that she was a woman—and a young woman at that—may have worked to her advantage in 1990, when voters seemed to want a change from the status quo. "My face on a billboard said change more strongly than any cute commercial message I could have run," she says. Her opponent inadvertently helped her by running an ad comparing his résumé to hers. In the ad, he referred to her as a department store clerk. "That was an insult not only to me but to all the store clerks in a pretty service-oriented district. They figured they couldn't have messed up the state much more than all those lawyers on Beacon Hill who couldn't balance a budget."

Swift won, becoming the youngest woman elected to the state senate. At a welcome lunch for new female legislators, the sturdy, outgoing woman with a reputation for fearlessness found herself unexpectedly intimidated. A book containing the biographies of all the women who had served in the Massachusetts Senate was to be distributed, and Swift worried that her brief life story would not measure up to those of the long list women she assumed had preceded her. As dessert was served, the chairwoman instructed the guests to look under their plates. Beneath the china was a booklet so slender it might have escaped detection if no one had pointed it out. Swift and another woman elected that year were the thirteenth and fourteenth women in the state senate. Being the youngest in history no longer struck Swift as special. "I had to beat out thirteen people," she says, laughing.

Although it is considered a liberal state, Massachusetts has one of the poorest records in the country when it comes to electing women. Before 1998, only one woman, Evelyn Murphy, a Democrat who served two terms as lieutenant governor under Governor Michael Dukakis, had been elected to statewide office. Only three women had represented Massachusetts in Congress, the last of whom, Margaret Heckler, was defeated for reelection in 1982.

Writing in the *Boston Globe*, Don Aucoin describes Massachusetts as a state with "a political culture strangely inhospitable to women at the highest levels." The article portrays the state's political machine as dominated by "white Irish guys" rooted in the patriarchy of Catholicism. That has begun to change in recent years as women have asserted the power of their majority vote behind men and women candidates who speak to their issues.

Swift thinks the Democratic dominance in the state perpetuated an old boys pecking order with a long waiting list for every office. She said many competent women hesitated to give up their privacy to participate in the rough-and-tumble of Massachusetts politics. "When I got involved, I didn't have a family, I didn't have responsibilities," she said. "I had only the good family—the parents, sisters, cousins, and aunts who stuffed envelopes and put up lawn signs. But if I didn't show up for dinner twelve nights in a row, nobody cared."

After six years in the state senate, Swift reached higher. In 1996, she challenged U.S. representative John W. Oliver, a two-term Democrat. At age thirty-one, Swift was a tireless campaigner. She began the campaign almost fifty points behind, and although she was outspent by $300,000, she came surprisingly close before losing, 53 to 47 percent. Republican governor William Weld rewarded Swift by appointing her coordinator of regional airports at the Massachusetts Port Authority. When Weld left office for a promised ambassadorship that was rejected by the U.S. Senate, Cellucci, Weld's lieutenant governor, became governor. Cellucci named Swift state director of consumer affairs, a job she held only six weeks before Cellucci picked her to run for lieutenant governor.

Swift learned that she was pregnant two weeks after formally announcing her bid for lieutenant governor. She had warned Cellucci when he asked her to run that she intended to press ahead in her efforts to conceive. But she didn't expect the two events to collide the way they did. "You can't always sequence these things like you want to," she says. "I mean I'm hardly the first woman who decided to focus her personal life on having a baby who had the professional opportunity of a lifetime dropped in her lap."

With the baby due two weeks before election day, Swift's pregnancy became an issue. Some political professionals declared the pregnancy would wrap up the family-values vote for the Cellucci ticket. Social conservatives, however, criticized Swift's decision to remain a candidate. Evelyn Reilly, executive director of the Massachusetts Christian Coalition, said, "My first reaction was, 'Thank God she's not having an abortion,' and my second reaction was, 'I hope she'll have enough time to spend with the child.' This is a good opportunity for us to discuss the broader issue, which is: Does institutional day care compare with a parent caring for the child in the home?"

Radio talk-show host Dan Yorke in Springfield, Massachusetts, called Swift's decision to run "selfish," and urged her to set an example and declare "enough's enough. The chase for the brass ring has got to stop in favor of parenting." Yorke claimed that professional women phoned the station in droves to express regret they had not taken his advice when they had the chance. One radio caller wanted to know whether Swift planned to breast or bottle feed. When she declined to answer, the caller persisted, justifying his question as a taxpayer's right to know how much time away from her duties this baby would require. "I have one word for you," Swift retorted, "pump." She giggled when she repeated the story.

Swift refused throughout the campaign to answer questions about what child care arrangements she planned if she were elected. "Every candidate needs a thirty-second sound bite that says, 'None of your business'," she says. Swift and her husband, Charles Hunt III, had decided that initially he would be the primary caregiver. As the owner of an excavation contracting company in a rural part of the state, he had more flexibility. But sharing this kind of information would only invite more questions and criticism. "If you want to maintain some privacy, the more you answer every single private question, the farther the questions go," she says.

Swift's pregnancy pitted career women against stay-at-home advocates. The Republican-leaning *Boston Herald* weighed in, saying, "Look, folks, she's running for lieutenant governor. There couldn't be a less demanding job for a new mother. The heaviest thing she'll have to lift is her paycheck." This was no comfort to Swift. She bristled at the notion that she was Cellucci's token woman. Hers would be a policymaking role, she said. She would function as a full partner to the governor. If she did her job well, she would be positioned to run for governor. "Chuck and I wouldn't have chosen to make the sacrifices that we're making, personally, to do nothing," she said. "There may come a day when I'll want a cushy job where you can just sit and smile and have people take your picture and attend dinners. But I think like most women I'm motivated to make the sacrifices to be in politics to make a difference on issues that matter."

Publicly, Swift asserted she could be successful as a mother and a politician. Privately, she questioned whether she was doing the right thing. "I don't think there's a professional woman who has a family who hasn't had those internal conflicts," she said. "Am I being fair to my husband? Am I being fair to this baby? Any mother feels those things. Having to justify it publicly is difficult." At the childbirth class she attended, she felt out of it when other mothers worried about Winnie the Pooh versus Noah's Ark wallpaper. Talking to women enrolled at Harvard's Kennedy School of Public Policy, Swift said, "I told my mother that this baby will come home in a shoe box, that I really am an evil person."

The young women, who will face similar choices soon enough, listened intently as Swift told them there is no right answer. She talked about a friend of hers who had been Weld's campaign manager but quit her job when she became a mother. "Her anxiety is no less than mine," Swift said. "She feels just as guilty about being home and slowing down as I feel about giving up the opportunity to be a full-time mom, and doing this." Whether it was the pregnancy or just the fact that she was a woman, Swift found that the hardest people to win over were other women. "As a voting bloc, women are the most skeptical, and hold women to a higher level of performance," she said.

Much of the media criticism of Swift came from female columnists and reporters who covered her every move. *Boston Globe* columnist Eileen McNamara wrote that Cellucci had engaged in "tokenism" by naming Swift as his running mate, adding that men frequently "choose inexperienced women eager to play the supporting, subservient role." Swift, she wrote, "no doubt has a promising political future in the Republican party when she grows up." Proof of her immaturity, the columnist said, was her willingness to change her opinions overnight on assault weapons and capital punishment to align her more liberal views with Cellucci's conservative positions.

On October 16, 1998, five days before her due date, Swift gave birth to Elizabeth Ruth Hunt—seven pounds, six ounces, nineteen inches—by caesarean section. She returned to the campaign trail with baby in tow. Nineteen days after the much publicized birth, the voters of Massachusetts elected Cellucci their governor and Swift their lieutenant governor with just over 50 percent of the vote. On election night, Cellucci referred to Swift as his co-governor and said he would make her a full partner in his decisions. He made good starting the next day by appointing Swift to head his transition team.

How big a role did Swift's candidacy play in Cellucci's election? Swift agreed with pundits who said that without her pregnancy she would have been just another anonymous lieutenant governor candidate. But being pregnant got her a lot of publicity, most of it favorable. Swift's story made the Republican ticket more appealing to the key voting bloc of working women. One measure of Swift's impact was the simple fact that the GOP duo won. Democratic candidates dominated the 1998 elections nationally and even more so in Massachusetts. Cellucci and Swift were the only Republicans to win statewide in an election that saw Democrats sweep all ten congressional seats and increase their majorities in the state legislature. Like Maryland's governor Parris Glendening, whose reelection was aided immeasurably by running mate Kathleen Kennedy Townsend, Cellucci may have owed his job to the popularity of his lieutenant governor.

Before long, capital sources were telling reporters that Swift enjoyed extraordinary influence in the administration. One early sign was her role in the appointment of a new public safety commissioner. The governor's top choice was a Democratic state senator who had crossed party lines to support Cellucci. But Swift recommended Inspector Jane Perlov, the chief of detectives in New York, whom she had met at the Harvard conference where she and Perlov both addressed women studying public policy. Perlov was well-qualified, Swift said, and the new administration needed more female faces in the cabinet. Cellucci agreed and appointed Perlov.

The attention Swift got during the campaign for bearing a child continued after she took office. At her first postelection news conference, the questions centered on how she would juggle her job, marriage, and motherhood. Swift said she and her husband planned to sell their home in North Adams and rent an apartment in Boston. Dad and baby Elizabeth Ruth would spend weekdays in the city and weekends at Swift's parents' home in western Massachusetts. She would go with them on the weekends as her schedule allowed. There would be no crib in the statehouse. Like many career women with families, Swift was torn between her responsibilities at home and at work. "The conundrum now is that here I am with the biggest professional challenge of my life and I can't cope with it the way I always have, which is work, work, work, work, work," she told a reporter.

Swift's lifestyle—with a stay-at-home husband, state-provided driver, and flexible hours—drew criticism when the Cellucci administration cut less-fortunate women from the welfare rolls. "Not to be harsh about it, but the reality of having children is that you have to accept a level of responsibility," she said. And for those who disapproved of a new mother continuing to work when she could afford to stay at home, she said they might get their comeuppance when their own children grow up. "This somewhat ambitious person who thinks she can do everything was nurtured by a stay-at-home mom," Swift said. "All those stay-at-home moms who disapprove of what I do are probably going to raise someone like me, an independent, ambitious person."

Midway through her first year in office, Swift's power-sharing relationship with Cellucci matched the one Cellucci had had as Weld's lieutenant governor. Her duties went far beyond the lieutenant governor's only official function, presiding over the weekly Governor's Council meetings. She was a kind of co-governor with prime responsibility for the Department of Social Services. John Barrett III, the Democratic mayor of North Adams, Swift's hometown, was quoted as saying, "Mark my words. Within two years, Jane Swift will be the most powerful and influential person in state government." Weld's campaign manager said that Swift "has the stuff to become the first female governor—no question about it."

With the notoriety came intense scrutiny. Swift, who had taken a $3,000 pay cut in the lieutenant governor's job, made unwanted headlines for signing on to teach a two-and-a-half-hour course one night a week at state-run Suffolk University for the unusually large stipend of $25,000 a year. That boosted her $75,000 lieutenant governor's salary by 33 percent. Adjunct professors typically are paid between $6,000 and $10,000 a year, and some have to supplement their income with welfare benefits. The Boston papers portrayed Swift's arrangement as a sweetheart deal, technically legal but ethically questionable. Reporters digging into Swift's past also discovered she had been compensated for health care expenses when she was a consultant at the Massachusetts Port Authority. Paid health care was unusual, if not unique, for a contract employee.

By all accounts, Swift is an attentive and typically guilt-ridden mother. Her child care arrangements sometimes break down, and when she's in a pinch, she seems to have a blind spot when it comes to the ethics of being a working mother. The women she works with, and many men too, sympathize with the difficulty she faces in juggling work and family. But state workers resent being used as a family support network. "Working mother Swift relies on free help from her aides," declared a *Boston Globe* story on January 5, 2000. Swift did not deny allegations that she repeatedly asked her colleagues to baby-sit for her fourteen-month-old daughter, explaining that many were friends whom she knew before she was elected, and that she would return the favor if asked. "I try to hold it together the best I can," Swift told the *Globe* reporter while her daughter could be heard crying in the background. Swift's husband put his construction business on hold to care for the child. But on days when Swift worked more than ten hours, their deal was that he brought the baby to the statehouse for an hour or so to give him some relief. Young Elizabeth was a familiar figure in the office, and state workers told the *Globe* of dozens of instances where Swift turned to them for help when she had to dash off to a meeting or take a phone call. Governor Cellucci stood by his lieutenant governor, saying that he enjoyed it when Elizabeth visits, and that Swift is an "outstanding role model" for working mothers.

Criticism of Swift's private dealings was offset by praise for her professionalism as Cellucci's right-hand woman. The governor was on vacation when the administration's first real crisis erupted. Massachusetts Port Authority director Peter Blute was forced to resign after newspaper reports—with pictures—of a four-hour party cruise on a charter boat paid for with funds from his agency. Cellucci opted not to return early, saying that Swift could handle things. And she proved she could. After conferring with Cellucci, she announced Blute's resignation. A source close to Cellucci was quoted as saying, "I think it was a fortunate coincidence that the female lieutenant governor was the public face on this crisis, given that the crisis involved ill-behaving, white, middle-aged men."

With Swift's urging, the old boys network at the statehouse began making room for women. Cellucci appointed a woman to replace the port authority director and another to fill a vacancy on the State Supreme Court. Over the objections of Cardinal Bernard Law, a powerful political force in the state, the governor nominated Supreme Judicial Court Justice Margaret Marshall to be chief justice. Cardinal Law accused Marshall of anti-Catholic bias, but Cellucci and Swift lobbied for her among members of the Governor's Council, who had veto power over the nomination. Swift was prepared to cast a tie-breaking vote in Marshall's favor if it came to that, but the nomination was confirmed, 6–3. Marshall became the first woman to head a branch of Massachusetts government.

Swift had much to be proud of, but few people believed she could win an election on her own. In addition to the personal foibles that regularly made headlines, economic good times had given way to a recession and the state faced a budget crunch. Swift was making new enemies by the day with draconian cuts in social services, and her poll numbers were once again in free fall. Two potential running mates turned her down before she settled on an openly gay former mayor and state legislator, thirty-three-year-old Patrick Guerriero, as her lieutenant governor. The choice seemed to signal defiance. If she isn't progressive enough for Massachusetts, who is?

Republicans made no secret of their displeasure with Swift. Eager to hold the seat for their party, they openly courted Mitt Romney, the telegenic head of the Salt Lake Olympic organizing committee who was being credited for staging the most successful winter games ever. Anybody who watched him on television during the seventeen days of the games wondered why he wasn't in politics. He had tried, challenging Ted Kennedy for the Senate in 1994, but taking on the Kennedy dynasty in Massachusetts proved impossible. Moving Swift aside would be easy by comparison, and Romney would have a competitive edge against whoever the Democrats chose as their candidate.

Swift struck back, charging that "powerful men" were seeking to drive her from the governor's race. She had spoken from her heart, not her head, and her advisors warned her against going head-to-head with the party's leadership over gender. If she could survive the challenge within her party, Swift believed she would be in better shape for the general election than people thought. She had never had support from the base of the Republican Party, which she privately referred to as "knuckle draggers." But in the end, she decided to cut her losses. Her fundraising had fallen off, her poll numbers were dismal, and the party had ganged up on her. She faced the very real possibility that she might not even muster the 15 percent support needed to win a place on the ballot for the September primary. It was time for a graceful exit.

For a state that has been inhospitable to women running for high political office, the rise of Democrat Shannon O'Brien offered a glimpse of what might be. The same year that Swift was elected lieutenant governor, O'Brien captured the state treasurer's job with an impressive 63 percent majority. At age thirty-nine, she was the first woman elected to statewide office in Massachusetts without being part of a ticket or running in a special election. She made a good first impression on the voters by exposing and cleaning up the fiscal mess left by her predecessor. By winning the 2002 Democratic primary, O'Brien was positioned to become the first woman elected governor of the state in her own right.

Early hopes soon gave way to reality. O'Brien was criticized for being overly aggressive in a debate. Romney called her behavior "unbecoming." O'Brien's defenders complained about a double standard, but the voters had the last word. Romney won the race, and the feminization of Massachusetts politics would have to wait.

ELEVEN

Careful and Cautious

For women who aspire to a life in politics, there are lessons to be learned—positive and negative—from the experiences of others. One classroom is the state of New Hampshire. The women there with lessons to teach are Jeanne Shaheen and Arnie Arnesen. They are alike in some ways. Both are Democrats, wives, and mothers. Both are ambitious, energetic, and capable. Both ran for governor of the state. Shaheen won and put herself on the track for national office. Arnesen lost and found herself on the sidelines.

Oil paintings of prominent male politicians line the walls of the New Hampshire statehouse. Emerging from her office in the historic chamber to greet a visitor, Governor Jeanne Shaheen seems suddenly aware that the state's decorating scheme is not politically correct. "We have lots of pictures of white men around here," she says, sheepishly. "Maybe I should take them down."

Actually, that would be too revolutionary a step for Shaheen, a cautious centrist who became New Hampshire's governor by playing it safe and smart. A Democrat with roots in the progressive wing of the party, she nevertheless took "The Pledge," a conservative mantra against new taxes in tax-phobic New Hampshire. She stuck to it in the midst of a school financing crisis that pitted her against the State Supreme Court, elite editorial opinion, and many fellow Democrats. The issue has almost religious overtones in the state, and Shaheen knew better than to challenge people's religious beliefs.

For a time, the impasse appeared disastrous for Shaheen. She suggested funding the schools by installing slot machines at horse and dog tracks, a scheme ridiculed as "slots for tots." The court ruled that her Advancing Better Schools (ABC) plan did not rectify the inequality in funding between school districts, which had prompted the court to intervene in the first place. Because the schools are funded by property taxes, wealthier districts can afford the latest computers and air-conditioned gymnasiums while schools in poorer neighborhoods make do with outdated equipment and deteriorating buildings. Seeing no other solution, many lawmakers set aside their traditional opposition to taxes and prepared to send a state income tax bill to Shaheen's desk. Her signature on the legislation would reverse more than two hundred years of tax tradition in the state with the motto "Live Free or Die." Good-government types hailed Shaheen as a leader with the credibility to bring the state out of the dark ages. No doubt she had political capital to spend, having won reelection in November 1998 with 66 percent of the vote, sweeping in the first Democratic state senate since 1912.

For Shaheen, vetoing the measure was unthinkable, yet breaking her campaign pledge by signing into law the state's first income tax surely would end her political career. She had her eye on running for the U.S. Senate in 2002, and didn't want to foreclose that option. She had also been talked about as a possible running mate for Al Gore in 2000.

How she balanced her own interests against those of the state demonstrates her skill as a politician. She worked quietly behind the scenes to avert a veto by persuading Democrats who initially supported the legislation to reverse themselves. When twenty Democrats defected, the measure failed, and Shaheen was spared the embarrassment of a veto.

But that was not the end of it. Under the law, Shaheen had to find an equitable method of financing the public schools. The solution that she devised relied on a statewide property tax combined with increased cigarette taxes. The *Concord Monitor*, a liberal voice in the conservative state, lambasted Shaheen as "a play-it-safe, poll-driven politician who would rather nibble at problems than chew on the real solutions." Granted, the plan lacked boldness, but it preserved Shaheen's future electability. And it fit nicely with her politics of conciliation and consensus. "For those local and national geniuses who crowed that Jeanne Shaheen, after this mess, would never be considered for national office by Al Gore or Bill Bradley, let's drag out those two words one last time—wrong again," declared *Boston Globe* columnist Thomas Oliphant.

A governor from New Hampshire would not normally be on anybody's vice presidential list because it's a small state with only four electoral votes. But Shaheen offers an interesting mix of issues. She has fought for lower electric rates, championed insurance reform, and promoted small business. Her record is strong on protecting children from abuse, improving education, expanding kindergarten, and combating domestic violence. She operates with a nebulous ideology. That's a résumé that could be useful to a presidential candidate reaching out to independent voters. In the fall of 1999, months before the New Hampshire primary, an aide to Vice President Gore confided that Gore's short list for vice president almost certainly would include Shaheen. Shaheen's husband, Bill, signed on as Gore's campaign manager in New Hampshire. Shaheen herself stayed neutral for a while, but everybody knew she was in Gore's camp. Seeking to make a good impression on her, the vice president freed up some of his own staffers in 1998 to assist in Shaheen's reelection.

As she edged toward the announcement that she would seek another term as governor, Shaheen was coy about her allegiance to "The Pledge." When asked about it in early February 2000 on New Hampshire Public Radio's "The Exchange," Shaheen said, "I haven't, at this point, made a decision if I'm going to run again, and so I'm not going to be addressing 'The Pledge.' " Shaheen's reelection bid hinged on finding a solution to the school-funding problem that a majority of voters would find acceptable.

Potential Republican rivals, headed by former U.S. Senator Gordon Humphrey, lined up for the opportunity to run against Shaheen. State senator Mary Brown, a conservative Republican, said she might enter the race as an independent running on an income-tax platform. "This is [politically] a huge risk for me," Brown said. "But I want to explain: I don't care. I don't care if I'm ever in politics. I don't care if I ever hold office. If I can help solve this, then it's all worth it, and I don't need to do anything else."

Shaheen appeared to be running out of solutions for the school-funding problem. New Hampshire house speaker Donna Sytek, a Republican, said the ten-cent increase in the cigarette tax proposed by Shaheen would fill only half the $38 million hole in the state's budget. Besides, she said, the state was not collecting as much as expected from the most recent tobacco tax increase. Shaheen gave her support to a package of two proposed constitutional amendments that would shift the burden of deciding on an income tax to the voters.

As a couple, the Shaheens complement each other. Jeanne Shaheen is aloof and cerebral while her husband is a natural politician who revels in the game. Bill Shaheen gave up the district judgeship he had held for sixteen years to campaign for his wife when she ran in 1996, and jokes about becoming the "First Hunk" if she becomes president.

The Shaheens met in the summer of 1969 while she was on break from college working as a waitress in York Beach, Maine. Six weeks later, he asked her to marry him, and she said yes, an impulsive act that she describes as "completely out of character."

A *Boston Globe* profile describes Shaheen as "a volleyball mom in flats, a woman so thorough she wipes the silverware before she eats, a woman so methodical she rearranges the dishes in the dishwasher if it is packed by someone else." Her homespun manner has earned her the nickname "Betty Crocker," after the cheerily bland housewife who produces perfect three-layer chocolate cakes without smudging her apron. She is a former high school prom queen, raised in a staunchly Republican household in Missouri. She voted for Richard Nixon in 1968, but became a Democrat after Nixon bombed Cambodia and plunged into the Watergate scandal. "She's so centrist she could be reelected in either party," says Frank Manciewicz, the late Robert Kennedy's press secretary. An example of Shaheen's middle-of-the-road approach is her handling of a campaign promise to mandate statewide kindergarten. Once in office, she stopped short of making kindergarten mandatory, instead settling for tax incentives to communities to encourage them to begin a kindergarten program.

Given New Hampshire's conservative roots, women hold a surprisingly large share of political power. Females comprise one-third of the New Hampshire legislature and Donna Sytek was speaker of the House until she retired in 2001. When a man succeeded her, it sparked talk that "the boys are back." But women are still very much in evidence especially in the governor's office where women held 9 of the top 10 jobs. By the time Shaheen was elected to her third two-year term, 70 percent of her staff was female. An analysis of staff salaries revealed that men earned on average less than the women did, though Shaheen's chief of staff is a man, and he had the highest salary. The conservative newspaper, *The Union Leader*, harrumphed, "If we were less broad-minded about gender, we would be advising New Hampshire men to burn their boxers on the steps of the Statehouse to protest the wage gap in Gov. Jeanne Shaheen's office." Still, the editorial concluded Shaheen was within her rights to hire who she pleased, wishing only that men could do the same without fearing charges of gender discrimination. A hidden factor in the willingness of New Hampshire men to share power is that legislators are volunteers, receiving a token $100 a year in compensation. The women take their work seriously. Shaheen says she and the Republican women leaders joke that women take work home with them every night while men leave empty-handed. "Women want to be very well prepared before talking about an issue," she says. But the camaraderie hasn't made reaching a compromise on tough topics like school financing any easier. "The issues don't break along gender lines, but party lines," Shaheen says.

Shaheen annoyed her supporters by advocating a tougher death penalty in New Hampshire, a state that has not executed anyone in sixty years. In her January 1998 State of the State address, she said, "Views of the death penalty are deeply held, and I respect the right of each of you to vote your conscience on this issue. But I believe that there are murders so heinous that the ultimate penalty is warranted, and I believe our laws should cover them." The Republican speaker of the house agreed with her and backed a bill to expand the kinds of crimes that warranted capital punishment. But the GOP-controlled house dealt both women a setback when it refused to hear the bill.

Shaheen, whose work experience ranged from teaching to managing a retail business, got her start in politics working in Jimmy Carter's 1976 presidential campaign. She was Gary Hart's campaign manager in New Hampshire in 1984 when he beat front-runner Walter Mondale in the primary. Dotty Lynch, who worked in the Hart campaign, recalls how the media wrote off Hart, assuming the contest for the nomination was between Mondale and Senator John Glenn, the former astronaut. "We'd go to the campaign headquarters at eight o'clock on a weeknight, and she'd have volunteers lined up," Lynch said. "We'd joke about it, 'Don't they read? Don't they know we're out of it?' " When Hart did better than expected in the Iowa caucuses the week before the New Hampshire primary, Shaheen's preparations paid off. The volunteer canvassing to identify and get out Hart voters played a big role in the upset.

Shaheen learned a valuable lesson from the Carter and Hart campaigns: If you want to get elected, you've got to really want it. "With Carter, if there was one more person on the street that he hadn't met, he would go up and introduce himself," she said. "With Hart it was, 'Do I have to talk to that person?' "

Shaheen applied what she had learned to win a seat in the state senate in 1990. If she didn't aspire to higher office from the start, she at least protected her prospects by avoiding anything that could be construed as a pro-tax vote, even in committee, where most members are less vigilant. When Republican governor Steve Merrill decided not to run for reelection in 1996, Shaheen felt that it was her year. She called a family council to share her plans. Steffany, at twenty-two the oldest of the Shaheens' three daughters, volunteered to postpone her final college semester to campaign for her mother. Stacey, eighteen, the middle daughter, also pitched in and wrote in her application essay for college that the campaign taught her "I could become anything I wanted to, even if I was a girl." But ten-year-old Molly wanted nothing to do with politics. "She can't remember a time when I wasn't in politics," Shaheen says. "Sometimes she would like to be doing other things."

Shaheen projects the quiet efficiency of a staff person, which is what she was for a long time. Like any other working mother, she tries to get home at a reasonable hour each evening. "There's something very real about going home at night and cleaning up the dishes, putting my daughter to bed, and getting up in the morning and feeding the cat and doing those real-life activities that everyone has to deal with," she says. To those who suggest that household chores undermine her image as a chief executive, she says, "What's more presidential than being with your family?"

Shaheen has ambition or she would not be where she is. But does she have what it takes for the next level of politics? After Shaheen's reelection in 1998, "Gore-Shaheen" buttons and bumper stickers sprouted in New Hampshire. But not everyone thought Shaheen was qualified for the second spot on the ticket. "She's a really nice woman, but she doesn't project power," said a female Democratic consultant. "She used to be a staffer, and she's accustomed to being in the background. Her speaking style is kind of mousy." Democratic activist Arnie Arnesen ridiculed a Gore-Shaheen ticket as "two wooden Indians." Nancy Snow, who teaches political science at New England College, concurs. "It would be a fire hazard," she says.

When it comes to assessing Shaheen, Arnesen is not a disinterested analyst. She is, by her own description, the "other woman" in New Hampshire Democratic politics. In 1992, she was the first woman ever to run for governor of the state. It was a good year for Democrats—Clinton was elected president and even carried New Hampshire by 1.2 percent—but Arnesen ran on a pro-tax platform and lost. Even so, her candidacy shattered stereotypes about women politicians and created an opening for Shaheen's successful bid in 1996.

Arnesen accepted an invitation to Shaheen's swearing-in ceremony. "We actually do *not* get along, but she had to invite me because I paved the way," Arnesen said. She sat in the balcony next to a reporter from the *Union Leader*, the conservative newspaper that has shaped the state's politics for decades. Arnesen knew she was under scrutiny and that her reaction would be chronicled for the newspaper's readers. She tried to keep a tight hold on her emotions, telling herself, "Don't emote, Arnie, don't emote."

At the conclusion of the ceremony, the reporter asked, "How difficult was it, Arnie?" She looked at him, and despite her best intentions, tears flowed along with her words. She had run and lost twice—for governor and for a seat in Congress—in grueling campaigns where Democrats and Republicans alike attacked her policies and her character. And here was Shaheen, literally walking into the governor's office with no primary fight and not much of a general election contest. "I've learned a lot," Arnesen told the reporter. "Politics is a lot like life. The person who opens the door isn't necessarily the one who gets to walk through it."

Dark-haired and intense, Arnesen radiates heat. She would never be confused with the soft-spoken Shaheen in style or substance. Having grown up in Brooklyn, New York, she retains the fast-talking ethnic energy of the borough. Not surprisingly, the two women clash. Arnesen publicly opposed Shaheen's plan to fund the schools with revenue from slot machines. She wrote a scathing tract for a newspaper that mocked Shaheen by saying, "A spine is a terrible thing to waste."

Arnesen has never lacked spine, which has been both her biggest asset and largest liability in politics. The 1981 graduate of the Vermont Law School had just turned thirty when she won a seat in the state legislature in 1984. Sizing up her colleagues, she quickly determined there were three kinds of women serving in the legislature: those who inherited their seats from a deceased husband; those protecting their husband's business interests; and reformers who wanted to make changes. She was one of the reformers.

Despite the high percentage of women in the volunteer legislature, men still run the place. "I've always described it as made up of the rich, the retired, and the remunerated," says Arnesen. "Because of that, there tend to be lots of old men. Old men don't know what the new workplace is like. They all are retired on pensions. They had the same job for forty years. Women bring to the table a very different work perspective and a very different family perspective. It's not that the older men don't care. They've never experienced it. Again, it's important to have us because we bring information of value."

Arnesen illustrates her point by analyzing the designation "part-time worker," and how the phrase evokes different images for men and women based on their own experiences. "A male hears, 'Oh, I don't have to pay them benefits. They're cheaper, they're more flexible.' When a woman thinks part-time worker, she, too, thinks no benefits. But she also thinks low pay, no esteem, and no possibility of moving up the corporate ladder. It's the same part-time worker, but men and women translate it to very different economic realities."

Arnesen was sworn in with a baby in her arms, the second of her two daughters, born just before the 1984 election. "Baby Nursed, Versed in Politics," said the headline in the local newspaper. A male legislator, asked how he felt about Arnesen nursing her baby during committee sessions, retorted, "At least I know the kid gets a warm bottle." Arnesen recalls bringing the infant to a hearing only to have male lawmakers scold her for not being at home with her child. "Two minutes later, they were complaining about welfare mothers at the government, pardon me, teat. I said, 'You told me I was an important role model, and, in the next breath, someone not as affluent and a different color is irresponsible for staying home. Isn't that a double standard?' What a wonderful opportunity to reeducate," she says, savoring the moment.

Arnesen was thirty-eight years old and in her fourth term as a state representative when she ran for governor in 1992. She got in the race after former five-term congressman Norman D'Amours, a personal friend of Arnesen's, took the antitax pledge. "That's immoral," she protested. "Don't be naive," he told her. They fought about it for weeks until one day Arnesen told him that if he took the pledge, she would run against him. He didn't back down. When she announced she was running for governor, her mother didn't talk to her for three months because she was afraid her daughter would embarrass the family. "My mother wanted me to be a great secretary," says Arnesen without a trace of irony. "She was mortified that I was running."

Arnesen entered the race in March 1992, hoping to pressure D'Amours to reverse himself, and then she could withdraw her candidacy. Six months later, she was not only still in the race, but she had won the Democratic nomination. She got 48 percent of the vote, easily beating D'Amours (27 percent) and a third Democrat, Edgar Helms (23 percent). Like Arnesen, Helms had proposed an income tax as a means of lowering the local property tax.

Two weeks before the November general election, polls showed Arnesen in a dead heat with affable Republican Steve Merrill. The numbers unnerved the Republican establishment in and out of the state. Losing the White House to Clinton would be bad enough, but losing New Hampshire, the nerve center of conservative Republicanism, would be catastrophic. "An incredible amount of money poured into the state," says Arnesen. "They could not let a liberal female tax-raiser win in New Hampshire." Whether it was the influx of campaign cash or the antitax history of the state reasserting itself, Arnesen got only 40 percent of the vote.

In pursuing her political ambition, Arnesen paid close attention to the wishes of her husband, attorney Thomas Trunzoto, and their daughters, Melissa and Kirsten. After losing the governor's race, Arnesen probed the girls for their reaction. Were they angry that she had lost? "Oh, no, Mommy, I'm not mad at you for that," said Kirsten, the younger one. "You left me when I was six and came home when I was eight." The words stung, and Arnesen wasn't sure she would ever run again.

Four years later, in 1996, she was back in the political arena, this time running for a congressional seat against a Republican incumbent. Her opponent, Representative Charles Bass, portrayed her as a tool of labor union bosses even though she had supported NAFTA, a trade agreement opposed by the unions. Bass created unease about her values and her mental stability by stringing together snippets from some of the provocative positions she had taken over the years. "Think of something that would scare you, and he found the phrase to do it," she says. There was plenty of material; since the early eighties Arnesen had been a regular on AM talk radio, a medium that prizes shock value. "I'm funny and I'm self-deprecating and I'm obnoxious," she says. "He took all my stuff, cut and pasted it together, and turned it into radio ads that were outrageous." The ads ran repeatedly during the last four weeks of the campaign, prompting her children's classmates to say hurtful things like "Your mom is crazy" and "Your mom is evil."

Polls showed that people liked the name Arnie, which is Arnesen's middle name, and the name she has gone by for years, so Bass addressed her as Deborah, the first name on her birth certificate. "The only people who call me Deborah are my mother and the congressman who ran against me," says Arnesen, who countered with radio ads about "the real Arnie Arnesen." They featured the sounds of kids playing baseball in the background, and ended with a male announcer saying, "When you do good politics, it makes the world better for your kids." The ads evoked a positive emotional response from listeners, but not enough to change the outcome. Bass defeated Arnesen, 51 to 43 percent.

It wasn't only Republicans who found Arnesen an inviting target. Shaheen, waging her first race for governor, assured voters she was "not the liberal Arnie." The contrast allowed Shaheen to position herself between Arnesen on the left and her conservative Republican opponent, lawyer Ovid Lamontagne. A fundamentalist Roman Catholic with strong views against abortion rights, Ovid was too far right even for New Hampshire. Mainstream Republicans went into mourning the day Lamontagne won the primary because they knew he couldn't win statewide. The combination of a weak opponent and a strong showing by Clinton running for reelection created the conditions for Shaheen to make history by becoming the state's first female governor. "It's timing, timing, timing in politics," says Arnesen. "She had the best of times, and the worst of candidates running against her."

Arnesen was the "Bulworth" of New Hampshire politics. Like the no-holds–barred candidate portrayed in the film by Warren Beatty, Arnesen confronted voters with straight talk they were unaccustomed to hearing from politicians. "I did all the fence-busting that had to happen," she says. "I said I can raise as much money, and I did. I said I was as intelligent, and I was. I was so tough that Jeanne could run against me in 1996 as the kinder, gentler Arnie. Because of me, she could be Betty Crocker. She could be sweet, kind, and gentle because I had hammered away at all those things they said women couldn't do. Do I understand why she ran against me? Probably yes. Not that I sanctioned it, but I understand it. That's what she felt she needed to do. The sad thing about politics is you have to do what you have to do to win."

Arnesen wonders how Shaheen will handle the so-called wedge issues—the emotionally charged disputes that divide the public—if and when she ventures onto the national stage. "She doesn't go near the gun-control issue," Arnesen says. "You will never hear her open her mouth on guns." Gun violence is not a big issue in New Hampshire, where the right to own a gun is paramount. But if Shaheen has to appeal to a bigger constituency against the parochial druthers of New Hampshire, she will sacrifice some of her prized centrism.

It wasn't until she was facing reelection for a third term as governor that Shaheen realized she could no longer run away from the school financing issue. She appointed a blue-ribbon commission to come up with a plan, and announced that she was no longer taking the pledge to oppose a state income tax, or any other broad-based tax. She had a tough primary race. Liberal Democrats thought she had dilly-dallied too long on the issue, and didn't like her support for the death penalty. Her Republican opponent, former Senator Gordon

Humphrey, noting that the commission was conveniently timed to report after the election, papered the state with signs that said, "What's your plan, Governor?" Shaheen survived with 49 percent of the vote, a far cry from the 66 percent acclimation she had won two years earlier.

Shaheen got to where she is by being careful. As a state senator, she was adept at avoiding controversy. Arnesen deplores middle-of-the-road politics while grudgingly acknowledging that it works. "The only time she took up an issue was when it was 98.9 percent decided," says Arnesen. "She waited on health care reform until the bill was on the verge of passing, then she attached her name to it. When the bill passed, she took credit for it. The next year, when they gutted the bill, she didn't open her mouth. What she cared about was the pluses, not the minuses. But then again, I'm a naive politician." Arnesen pauses for effect. "I'm actually not naive," she says. "I've made a conscious choice to be this way. But she won and I didn't. That's a difficult lesson to learn."

Arnesen could be generous with political foes. Once, when she appeared with other candidates before a southern New Hampshire Jewish men's group, she intervened when New Hampshire senator Bob Smith, a Republican, was put on the spot by a question from the audience. "How many blacks, Jews, and gays do you have on your staff?" the questioner demanded. Taken aback, Smith replied haltingly, "Uh, uh, I don't know. I think my campaign manager is Jewish." Arnesen leaped to her feet to defend Smith. "I'm proud that my U.S. senator doesn't know how many blacks, Jews, and gays are on his staff because he's not supposed to," she declared with characteristic verve. "The point is the integrity of their résumé, not where they come from or what their ethnic background is."

Smith later thanked her for defending him "in front of your people." Arnesen realized from his choice of words that he thought she was Jewish. After the election, she saw him and said, "Bob, I hate to break it to you, but I'm not Jewish. I'm Italian." Remembering the look on Smith's face, Arnesen laughs. "He was blown away. He said, 'Why didn't you tell people in New Hampshire that you were Italian? You would have gotten more votes."

Arnesen's campaigns illustrated difficulties that a married woman with children faces when running for office that a male candidate doesn't. Arnesen's husband insisted that she not subject their daughters to the campaign trail and he himself rarely accompanied her. "Not only didn't I gain any value from being a family person, but my opponent was able to distort who I was. He could cart his own kids around on his hip. He could create the illusion with these portable kids that he was Mr. Family. Because my husband chose to keep his daughters protected and away from the campaign, I became a loner. I suddenly was perceived not to be a mother. The irony is that I am the mom. I did math homework on the phone every night with my kids." It is a rare marriage where the male spouse is both a willing companion and an asset on the campaign trail, giving rise to Dianne Feinstein's observation that "in the end, women always campaign alone."

Shaheen grew bolder in her efforts to resolve New Hampshire's school financing crisis. The fact that she was reelected despite her refusal to take the no-new-taxes pledge was a triumph in itself. No candidate had been elected in the state without taking the pledge since 1970. Still, she and the legislature were at loggerheads over what to do. Shaheen proposed a modest sales tax that the House rejected. She also tried to revive her plan to install video slot machines at racetracks. It went nowhere. Some of the pressure to find a solution was relieved when the state supreme court upheld as constitutional a statewide property tax that Shaheen had long supported. The plan that became law relies on a combination of the new property tax and a hodgepodge of business taxes. It is not perfect, and faces continued court challenges from the five poor towns that brought the original case against the state.

Controversy over school financing had dogged her entire gubernatorial career, and Shaheen believed she had taken the issue as far as she could. Her thoughts were elsewhere. She was now a candidate for the U.S. Senate, running against Congressman John Sununu, who had won the Republican nomination by defeating incumbent Sen. Bob Smith, the first sitting senator in a decade to lose in a primary. Smith had abandoned his party briefly to run for president as an independent in 2000, saying the GOP wasn't far enough to the right. Sununu was younger, more personable, and carried no political baggage. He could be tough to beat. With majority control of the U.S. Senate ready to turn with a single seat, Shaheen's vaunted ability to play it safe would get its toughest test yet.

Shaheen was counting on the state's libertarian instincts to come through for her. Sununu opposes abortion rights, and New Hampshire, while fiercely conservative, has always been pro-choice. But her efforts to portray the genial Sununu as an extremist failed. He won handily.

TWELVE

Women in the House

Two constituencies determine the role women play in U.S. politics. One is the electorate, comprised of a majority of women who support female candidates in greater numbers than male voters. The second is the elected members of the House and Senate, mostly men, who vote on the leadership positions for each party and make the rules for committee chairmanships. Here, men have been reluctant to yield power even as the number of female legislators has increased.

One example illustrates the extreme hostility sometimes displayed toward women penetrating their once all-male domain. Former representative Patricia Schroeder tells the story of the unfriendly welcome she received from the House Armed Services Committee chairman, a fellow Democrat named F. Edward Hebert, when she reported as a new member of his committee in 1973. The seventy-two-year-old Hebert, one of the last of the old-style committee barons, did not want Schroeder on his committee, but had to yield to the demands of his superiors in the party.

"Although I was on the committee, I did not get a seat," Schroeder says. "Hebert was patronizingly contemptuous of women in politics. He also objected to the appointment of Ron Dellums [a Democrat from California]. Ron had been in the House only one term when it was decided that it was time for an African American to be on the Armed Services Committee. Hebert didn't appreciate the idea of a girl and a black forced on him. . . . He announced that while he might not be able to control the makeup of the committee, he could damn well control the number of chairs in the hearing room. . . . He said that women and blacks were worth only half of one 'regular' member, so he added only one seat to the committee room and made Ron and me share it."

Over the next quarter century, the male members of Congress smoothed the sharp edges of their antifemale attitude, but the determination to keep women in their place did not diminish. It has been hard enough for women to get a place at the table in Congress, but getting a place at or near the head of the table has been next to impossible. Which is why the election by her peers of California Rep. Nancy Pelosi as Democratic Whip in the fall of 2001 made history. As the first woman in either party to break into the top leadership, her victory was hugely symbolic. More than that she had entered the top ranks of her party and won a coveted position that carries real power. What the Congress does is determined by the leaders of the House and Senate and by the committee chairmen. Until Pelosi won a voice for herself and by implication the women in Congress, today's female representatives and senators had almost no say in which bills get taken up and which die without a hearing. Except for the Speaker of the House and the Senate Majority Leader, congressional leadership positions have little public recognition, but wield a great deal of clout on Capitol Hill.

In the House, besides the speaker, the key leadership jobs are majority and minority leader, majority and minority whip, along with another half dozen or so positions on each side, only a few of which are elected. Others are appointed by the leadership. Until Pelosi's breakthrough, a woman had never won a contested election for a leadership job. Naming women to appointive posts is even a relatively recent phenomenon as the parties recognized the symbolic importance of making women members more visible. Rep. Nita Lowey of New York, a feisty grandmother, became the first woman to head the Democratic Congressional Campaign Committee when she was appointed after the 2000 election to spearhead Democratic efforts to regain the House in 2002. Perhaps it was coincidental, but heading into the 2002 election, each party had exactly two women in its leadership roster: Ohio's Deborah Pryce and Wyoming's Barbara Cubin for the GOP; Lowey and California's Maxine Waters for the Democrats.

In the Senate, the top jobs on the Republican side are leader, whip, conference chairman and vice chairman, policy committee chairman, and campaign chairman. The top Democratic jobs are leader, whip, policy co-chairman, campaign chairman and vice chairman, conference secretary and steering committee chairman. Senator Patty Murray of Washington state cracked the leadership ceiling on the Democratic side when she was named campaign committee vice chairman in the 2000 election. When Democrats gained enough seats in 2000 to tie the Republicans 50-50 in the 100-seat Senate, Murray moved up to chair the Democratic Senate Campaign Committee (DSCC) for the 2002 election. Two other women held leadership posts: Maryland Senator Barbara Mikulski as Democratic conference secretary and Texas Senator Kay Bailey Hutchison as Republican conference vice chairman.

Much of the legislative power is in the hands of the House and Senate committee chairmen. Of the twenty chairmanships in the House and the additional twenty chairmanships in the Senate, none are occupied by a woman. When power shifted suddenly between the parties in the narrowly divided Senate, where Democrats held a one-seat majority going into the 2002 election, Maine Senator Susan Collins was next in line to chair the Governmental Affairs Committee. With the voters interested in reform (and the scandals that produce reform), chairing the committee could boost Collins' visibility and national reputation. In the House, if the Democrats had regained the majority, New York's Nydia Velasquez would take the reins of the Small Business Committee. California Representative Jane Harman returned to Congress in 2000 after a hiatus of several years, only after Democratic leader Richard Gephardt restored her seniority and promised to smooth the way for her to chair the Intelligence Committee, should the Democrats take control of the House.

Men are mindful of the potential power of their female colleagues. When women in Congress huddle on a policy matter or even walk out of a room together, male lawmakers exchange glances, wondering what the sisterhood might be up to. Democratic women once planted themselves around the podium on the floor of the House until Republican leaders agreed to an amendment assuring money for international family planning. "Just don't gloat," warned the GOP leader who conveyed his party's change of heart to the women. Caving on the issue was bad enough, the GOP didn't want to lose face with C-SPAN viewers.

Men in both parties are uneasy about the growing importance of women. They need their involvement, but power-sharing does not come easily on Capitol Hill. And women have been reticent about challenging the male dominion. Rep. Jennifer Dunn's bid to become majority leader after the 1998 election was at the time the highest any woman of either party had ever reached, and she seemed ambivalent about it. After signaling she would run, Dunn hesitated before making the commitment. Commenting on her halting start, *New York Times* columnist William Safire asked, "Why isn't Jennifer Dunn more ambitious?"

Oh, but she is. Earlier in 1998, she had spoken confidently about her qualifications for the top job in the House. While downplaying speculation that her real aim was to become the first female Speaker of the House, Dunn told the Capitol Hill newspaper *Roll Call*, "I think a lot of people could do the job. I've been in politics for a long time, and I have very good instincts." Dunn lost the majority leader's race, coming in a distant third in a three-way race but her ambition is intact. She is still regarded as a possible future speaker, and she is a long-shot candidate for vice president on the Republican ticket. "She's capable of playing in the big leagues," says Larry Sabato, a professor of political science at the University of Virginia. "She's got a great image."

In the political gender wars, Republicans have relied heavily on the votes of angry white men. After the Democrats gained seats and nearly took back the Congress in 1998, the GOP decided that diversity has its place. Dunn was one of the first women put on display as proof of the party's open-door policy toward women. Dunn, fifty-eight at the time, is not the stereotypical helpmate the GOP once put forward as its ideal woman. Divorced with two grown sons (one named Reagan after the former president), Dunn epitomizes single motherhood, a status previously pitied by the party of family values.

Dunn eagerly accepted the role previously held by Susan Molinari of New York as cheerleader for the GOP's "big tent" philosophy. *Slate*, the on-line magazine published by Microsoft, awarded a prize for "the most peculiar utterance of the day" to Dunn for her explanation to a CNN audience of how she and Representative Steve Largent of Oklahoma, a former NFL star, represent the Republicans heterogeneity. "Steve has been a famous football player and I'm a single mother," she said. "We're an example of the diversity that we want to see in our party." *Slate* dubbed the GOP "The Party of Lincoln, Madonna, and Namath."

The daughter of a staunch, outspoken conservative, the late John Charles Blackburn, Jennifer inherited her father's pugnaciousness. Her older brother, John, told the *Washington Post* that Jennifer was always "whupping him good—outboxing him and outfishing him and just generally being the larger-than-life presence that loves and is loved by success." She played tennis and softball, skied and water-skied, and won a trout-fishing competition when she was in elementary school. Her father taught her how to shoot a .22 rifle. Her brother was athletic too, but when their father bought boxing gloves for them, "she knocked me all over the room," he recalled. In sixth grade, she was the first girl in her school elected student body leader.

"She feels she's had to fight for just about everything she got," John Blackburn said in his interview with the *Post*.

After graduating from Stanford University with a bachelor's degree in English literature, she worked as a systems engineer for IBM in the 1960s, then stayed home to raise her children. Her ex-husband, Dennis Dunn, whom she divorced in 1977, was the Republican chairman in Washington's King County, the state's largest. Dunn herself was active in party politics and was the first woman Republican chairman in Washington in 1981. She held the post for eleven years until her election to Congress in 1992. She is pro-choice on the abortion issue and perceived as a moderate although she rates nearly 100 percent from the American Conservative Union and the Chamber of Commerce. A stylish dresser with white-blond hair and patrician bearing, Dunn turns heads when she enters a room. When she served as vice chair of the Republican conference, her task was to put a friendlier face on her party.

Whenever there's a camera nearby, Republicans thrust Dunn forward, exploiting her gender to put their party in a better light. Early in 1998, Dunn was the first woman in sixteen years selected by the GOP leadership to appear on the Sunday TV talk show "This Week with Cokie Roberts and Sam Donaldson." She took the opportunity to lambaste President Clinton over his sexual affair with White House intern Monica Lewinsky. "If the president is not willing to tell the truth, a whole nation of children are being taught to lie, and that's a terrible situation," she said on the show. Later, to dramatize her call for women to be part of the committee investigating Clinton, Dunn reported an "unnerving" incident that had occurred five years earlier in which she allegedly was kissed on the lips by a Republican congressman on an elevator. Dunn said she didn't say anything about the incident when it happened because the congressman was retiring.

Dunn's icy bearing sets her apart from backslapping colleagues and underscores how difficult it is for a woman to find her place in the fraternal order of Congress. Dunn took up golf to try to be one of the boys, but one profile of her pointed out that her solitary hobby of gardening reveals her true personality. As pleased as they are to have Dunn as a front woman on the gender gap, male Republicans hint privately that she has risen as far as she has because she is a woman, not in spite of it. They say she is the creation of former House Speaker Newt Gingrich, who saw to it that she got a spot on the House Ways and Means Committee and installed her as vice chair of the GOP conference. They say she has neither the breadth nor depth of understanding on issues to rise to the top ranks of House leadership. As for Dunn's surfacing of a five-year-old accusation against a kissing colleague, one fellow Republican said, "Yeah, right."

What she lacks in interpersonal skills, Dunn has tried to make up for with her extraordinary fund-raising skills, always an asset in politics. Besides raising more than $1.1 million in 1996 and almost $1.5 million in 1998 for her own campaigns, she raised and contributed tens of thousands of dollars to fellow Republicans. But money could not buy her love in her own party.

Dunn's effort to narrow her party's gender gap amounts to the medium as the message. As a single mother, she has instant rapport with similarly situated women, but her fiscal conservatism has little appeal for many of these women who depend on government for their survival. Dunn's support of abortion rights also puts her in the female mainstream, but she cannot escape the fact that she is a pro-choice woman in a pro-life party. One woman, or even a handful of women, cannot alter the public's impression that the Republican-controlled House is a male bastion.

If further proof is needed that women are the handmaids of the GOP, consider the vote count in Dunn's effort to win the majority leader's position. Out of 221 votes cast by secret ballot, Dunn got 45.

Having defeated Dunn's bid for majority leader, Republican House members awarded women in their ranks a consolation prize by electing Florida Rep. Tillie Fowler to succeed Dunn as vice chair of the Republican conference, the fifth-ranked leadership slot. Fowler beat Kentucky's Ann Northrup for the position that has become the GOP's sop to women. The party that rails against affirmative action to counter racial and gender bias saw to it that J. C. Watts of Oklahoma, the only congressional African-American Republican, and Fowler, one of only seventeen Republican women, got lower-rung leadership titles. Being able to present a black and a woman on the TV talk shows gave the GOP the veneer of diversity in an age of multiculturalism. (Watts declined to run again in 2002.)

Fowler's story is a cautionary tale for women who aspire to a career in politics. The moral of the tale is that a dream deferred is a dream denied. Fowler fits the profile of many women in politics who get off to a promising start only to sidetrack their careers by dropping out to marry and raise a family. When they return—if they return at all—the years lost cannot be made up easily.

Fowler was born into politics. There is a picture of her as a little girl with her father, Culver Kidd, and legendary Georgia governor Herman Talmadge. Six-year-old Tillie is standing on Talmadge's desk and appears to be lecturing him while her father looks on indulgently. Fowler's father, a druggist, was a state representative from Milledgeville, Georgia, where Tillie was born. He served forty years in the legislature before he was defeated in 1992 at the age of seventy-eight. His full head of white hair and cunning in the political arena earned him the nickname "Silver Fox."

After getting a bachelor's and law degree from Emory University, Fowler embarked on her own career in politics. From 1967 to 1970, she was a legislative assistant to U.S. Representative Robert Stephens of Georgia, who, like her father, was a conservative Democrat. Then, for a little over a year, she worked in the White House Office of Consumer Affairs under President Nixon. She worked with Elizabeth Hanford, another law school graduate and a Democrat at the time who was testing the political waters. Years later, Fowler would name her second daughter Elizabeth after Elizabeth Hanford, the baby's godmother, who went on to marry Senator Bob Dole and pursue the presidency. Tillie married Buck Fowler. The couple moved to Florida, where they raised their family.

The move to Jacksonville derailed Fowler's political ambitions for fourteen years. As the wife of a well-to-do tax lawyer and the mother of two small children, she was expected to set aside her own career and devote herself to enriching leisure-time activities. "I was climbing walls," she says. "I'm not a bridge player. I'm not a garden clubber. So I got involved in the volunteer community." Her girls were ten and twelve when Fowler's friends pressed her to run for the Jacksonville, City Council as a reform candidate. Before agreeing, she consulted her pediatrician and her preacher. "I worried about the impact my running would have on my children."

When she told her father she wanted to run for office, he was not concerned that she would be at a disadvantage as a woman in a man's game. "There were five women in my Emory Law School class, and only three of us graduated," says Fowler. "It was due to his encouraging me that I was one of them. When I was little, he used to say that I could argue with a fence post. So, it was only natural that I would go to law school. He never said, 'You can't do this because you're a woman.' The only question the Silver Fox asked was, 'Are you sure you want to run as a Republican?' The lifelong Democrat lived to see his daughter sworn in as a member of Congress, but he was never reconciled to her conversion to the other party.

Fowler, like many other female candidates, found that the greatest resistance to her running in 1985 came from senior women. They couldn't picture themselves running for office and so found it hard to take Fowler's candidacy seriously. However, her southern manners and her patient explanation about why it was important for a woman to run persuaded many of the elderly women to give her a chance. Fowler won and went on to become the first woman elected president of the city council. Another woman would not be elected until 1999.

As a candidate for council and later for Congress, Fowler made term limits her signature issue. When council members balked at limiting their terms, she helped lead a petition drive that forced term limits onto the Florida ballot in 1991. The voters approved the measure, and its effects continue to ripple across state politics. In 1999, twelve of the nineteen members of the council where Fowler launched her political career were barred from running for reelection. Term limits caught fire as a national issue in the early nineties. The Democrats had controlled Congress for forty straight years and had outworn their welcome in much of the country. Fowler, the term-limits crusader, was the ideal candidate to run against Charles Bennett, the Democratic congressman whose forty-four years in office symbolized his party's immutability.

Redistricting after the 1990 census put more Republicans and independents into Bennett's district, increasing the odds of defeating him. Fowler spent six months analyzing her chances and consulting with people whose advice she trusted. Her deliberate approach frustrated her older daughter, who thought the decision was a no-brainer. "Mom, you should have done it before now," she said. Fowler's husband was also supportive. Fowler, still worried about abandoning her family, flew to Washington to hear firsthand from other female members that it is possible to balance a career in Congress with responsibilities as a wife and mother. "For women, the timing has to be right," she says. "I probably wouldn't have run if my younger daughter hadn't gone off to boarding school. My older daughter was in college." Finally, she decided that 1992 was the right year for her to run.

Fowler cleared the field by employing a variation of Ronald Reagan's approach to ending the cold war by outspending the Soviet Union into submission. She persuaded fifty leaders in the district to serve on her finance committee. She announced her candidacy on a

Wednesday and followed the announcement by publishing an advertisement in the Jacksonville paper three days later listing her prominent backers. A third of them were Democrats. The day after she announced, Bennett, who was eighty-two, announced his retirement. "That finance committee got me elected," Fowler says. "Women have to show they can raise money."

Fowler raised money by drawing on the contacts she had made as a volunteer in the community. She had been president of the Junior League and had been "a bleeding heart on lots of social service boards," she says. The men she served with often were the heads of banks and corporations. When the time came to run for Congress, she could turn to them for financial support. "I tell women, if you think you want to run, get to know the people in your community," she says.

Capitalizing on the term-limits fever, Fowler campaigned with the slogan "Eight Is Enough," promising to resign voluntarily after no more than four terms. She defeated Mattox Hair, a former legislator and judge, 56 to 44 percent. Fowler quickly won over her constituents in the once-Democratic district and in the next three elections ran unopposed. Jeb Bush, making his second run for governor of Florida in 1998, asked Fowler to be his running mate. She turned him down. Fowler was honored, but never seriously considered the invitation. Bush went on to win the governorship, but Fowler has no regrets. "If I ever do run statewide, I can do it on my own," she says.

Fowler, who turned fifty-seven in December 1999, must have felt a little like Cinderella. Just when she was starting to have fun at the ball, the clock struck midnight and her coach was about to turn into a pumpkin. She decided against running for the Senate seat vacated by fellow Republican Connie Mack and put off until the first days of 2000 her decision on whether to run for a fifth term in the House. Term-limit advocates ran thirty-second television commercials in the Jacksonville market portraying Fowler as "Slick Tillie," a play on the "Slick Willie" moniker hung on President Clinton. Bowing to her own "Eight is Enough" promise to serve no more than four terms, Fowler announced on January 4 that she would retire. "I've always believed that with hard work, determination, and the help of people here at home, you can accomplish a lot in a short period of time, and together we have," she said in a prepared statement.

Fowler's decision to retire was spurred by other reasons as well. Her eyesight had worsened because of a detached retina, and her brother's near-fatal motorcycle accident the previous fall made spending huge chunks of time in Washington more problematical. She had proved herself in Congress, and maybe it was time to do something else. There was always the possibility of an administration appointment should George W. Bush win the White House. Republican leaders did little to dissuade Fowler from leaving because her district is safely Republican, and there was little danger a Democrat would replace her.

In the days following her resignation, Fowler spent $160,000 on television ads that her office said were intended to explain that she had accomplished her goals and that eight years representing the Fourth Congressional District were enough. Neither her resignation speech nor the ads mentioned the television campaign run by U.S. Term Limits taunting her for even thinking about breaking her pledge, but there was speculation that she wanted to cement her political legacy and erase the memory of those negative spots.

Prim and proper with dark, coiffed hair and oversized glasses, Fowler looks like the Junior League president she once was. There is nothing about her that says "feminist" or "women's libber" or "troublemaker." She comes across sweet and southern. Yet she is an unabashed cheerleader for women in politics, no matter which party they come from. "I just want to get more women on the state and local level to run," she says. "Whenever I speak to women's groups, I encourage them to run for the school board, the city council—anything." Typically, Fowler says, the women she tries to encourage express fears about negative campaigns being run against them and exposing their private lives to public inspection. Fowler sympathizes. When she ran for city council in 1985, financial disclosure was required. Her husband protested, "Do we really have to do that?"

Were it not for the fourteen-year interlude between her apprenticeship on Capitol Hill and her first race for political office, Fowler might have risen higher. She is moderate on some issues and conservative on others and combines team play with a stubborn individuality. She voted for Clinton's impeachment, and when the GOP leadership needed a woman's voice on the issue, she volunteered. After Clinton ordered the bombing of Iraq during the impeachment proceedings, Fowler said, "I think this president is shameless in what he would do to stay in office."

Fowler's mother was dying of lung cancer, so Fowler accepted no money from the tobacco industry as a way of honoring her mother. She also rejected contributions from the National Rifle Association, another major backer of GOP officeholders. She supports abortion rights, a position more typical of Democrats, and is one of the few Republican women who took an active role in the congressional women's caucus, where she became friendly with a number of her Democratic counterparts. She refused to campaign against House incumbents, saying, "I can't sit next to them one day and campaign against them the next. If I'm your friend, then I'm your friend."

Fowler's reasons for wanting more women in Congress are practical ones. First, women would tolerate fewer night sessions of the House, "where both sides stay just to prove they're macho," she says. Women are more likely to say, "We think clearer in the morning. Let's stop at 8 P.M. instead of midnight." Second, she thinks a truly representative body in a democracy should reflect the diversity of the country. Women are a majority of the population but were less than 13 percent of the House during the time Fowler served. When the army was charged with sexual harassment, Fowler, then the only Republican woman on the Armed Services Committee, teamed with Democrat Jane Harman of California and Republican Steve Buyer of Indiana to investigate. After visiting several army installations, Fowler said she was surprised there weren't *more* problems between the sexes in the 86 percent male army.

Congress, like the military, has pockets of resistance to the expanding role of women. Instances of sexism that used to be commonplace on Capitol Hill have diminished, but not disappeared. When Fowler and other Republican women held a news conference before the 1998 election to discuss Clinton's impeachment, *Roll Call*, a Capitol Hill newspaper, covered it with a photograph showing only the women's legs, down to their sensible black pumps. The caption was "Sole Sisters." Fowler pointed out the implicit sexism, asking whether the next time men held a news conference "are we going to be looking at whether they were wearing penny loafers, wing tips, or lace-ups?"

Women had never been on the leadership track in the House, but that didn't stop Rep. Nancy Pelosi from thinking she might be the first. Her bold bid, launched two years before the votes would be counted, was the equivalent of crashing what former Rep. Pat Schroeder calls "the tree house with the sign that says, 'No Girls Allowed'." Among those gathered to celebrate Pelosi's success at a reception at the National Museum of Women in the Arts on November 6, 2001 was Geraldine Ferraro. "When I look around this room, I feel I've died and gone to heaven," said Ferraro, a former member of Congress and the first woman named to a major party presidential ticket. "No, that's not a comment on my health," she hastily added. (Ferraro had recently announced she was suffering from multiple myeloma, a blood cancer.) "I expect to be around until there's a woman president or my hair turns gray, whichever happens last. I have a great relationship with my hairdresser, so I can put that off for quite some time."

Ferraro is often asked why there hasn't been a woman on the ticket since 1984—"as though it's my fault!" she exclaimed. "Women are smart enough and women are tough enough, but there aren't enough women in that universe," she explained. "There are now ten Democratic women in the Senate; there were none when I was a member of Congress. And there are forty-four Democratic women in the House—many more than when I was there, and I remember how hard we tried to get women on Ways and Means and Appropriations (the committees that decide tax policy and control the purse strings). Where our voices were once ignored, we are now speaking up and leading the discussion."

As Whip, Pelosi's principal duty is to "whip" the Democratic members into line for House votes so the party can present a unified front. With ideological and regional differences splitting the party, the task is not unlike herding cats. Pelosi signaled early her intent to play an activist role in setting the party's message, and getting it out to the media. With congressional elections looming, she knew she would be judged by her ability to formulate a winning message for Democrats desperate to regain the majority control they had lost in 1994. Democrats found it hard to be heard in a nation still recovering from terrorist attacks and preoccupied by wartime concerns. Pelosi ruffled some feathers within her party by instituting a regular Tuesday meeting, when many members were just returning from their districts to Washington. The Democratic Caucus normally meets once a week on Thursday, but Pelosi feels that in today's fast-paced political and media environment, a more rigorous schedule is needed. She tried to make amends to stressed-out lawmakers by having food available. "I'm Italian," she exclaims. "First we eat."

Even before she was officially sworn in, Texas Rep. Martin Frost, a savvy inside player on Capitol Hill and chairman of the Democratic Caucus signaled that he would challenge Pelosi after the November 2002 election. The stakes were too high to let her, or anyone for that matter, have such a choice position without a fight. If the Democrats regained the majority, and if the current leader, Rep. Dick Gephardt, left Congress to run for president, as was widely anticipated, Pelosi would be in contention to become Speaker of the House. The fabled post had been held by among others the legendary towering Texan

Sam Rayburn, the earthy Boston Irish pol, Thomas P. ("Tip") O'Neill, and the fiery revolutionary, Georgia's Newt Gingrich. Pelosi had fought hard to get where she was; remaining in power would be a battle of at least equal proportion. Pelosi's district covers four-fifths of San Francisco. It is one of the most liberal and Democratic districts in the country, and Pelosi is routinely reelected with 85 percent or more of the vote. When Pelosi arrived on Capitol Hill in 1987, she was one of only two women in the California delegation. In 2002, there were seventeen women in the state's fifty-two-member House delegation, and the state's two senators are women (Dianne Feinstein and Barbara Boxer). The Democratic party has grown so dependent on the support of women voters that some commentators call it "the mommy party," yet no woman before Pelosi ever held one of the party's top elected positions in Congress.

Although she is sometimes included on long lists of vice presidential prospects, based on her proven vote-getting and money-raising talents, Pelosi invariably is discounted as too liberal for national politics. But among Democrats in the House, where liberalism is the majority sentiment, her bleeding-heart activism is not a detriment. Pelosi announced in the summer of 1999 that she was running for whip. The job was held by Rep. David Bonior, who was planning to step down to run for governor in Michigan, his home state. Her early declaration dismayed some Democrats, especially two male colleagues who were angling for the same job. One of them, Georgia representative John Lewis, an African-American veteran of the civil rights movement who *Time* magazine described as "a living saint," sent a letter to fellow Democrats urging a moratorium on campaigning until a more "appropriate" time. "The Book of Ecclesiastes reminds us that for everything there is a season," Lewis wrote. Pelosi brushed aside the criticism. "In order to buck two hundred years of history, if I have to start earlier than someone else, so be it," she said.

Bright-eyed and youthful at sixty-one the year she made history, Pelosi's meticulous networking has built her a mini-fiefdom in the House. Democrats of all ideological stripes respect her ability to round up votes. "She can snap her fingers and get a hundred votes for anything," says Loretta Sanchez of California. Pelosi is generous with her time and money, so her colleagues are more likely to respond favorably when she asks for their vote. She won over Sanchez by arranging three fund-raisers to help her fend off a second challenge from Republican Bob Dornan. Leading up to the 1998 election, Pelosi raised tens of thousands of dollars for Democratic campaign committees and distributed more than $300,000 from her own campaign funds to fellow Democrats, a display of largesse that paved the way for her leadership bid. In 2001, Pelosi's political action committee, "PAC to the Future," contributed $500,000 to congressional candidates, many of whom returned the favor by backing Pelosi for Whip. "I have an incredible financial base," she says matter-of-factly. Her base consists of the old wealth of San Francisco and the new money of Silicon Valley in a Democrat-friendly environment.

The youngest child and the only girl after six boys, Pelosi grew up "protected from every harsh thing that could ever come my way." She was born in Baltimore in March 1940. Her father, Tommy D'Alesandro, was a member of Congress, the capstone of his long political career. She has pictures on the wall of her Capitol Hill office that show her father listening to Winston Churchill addressing Congress and to Eleanor Roosevelt testifying about the shocking conditions she found in welfare institutions in the District of Columbia. Pausing to comment on the photograph of FDR's First Lady wearing a hat and a velvet dress, Pelosi tells her visitors, "Look how beautiful she looks. Her nails are all manicured."

Politics was a way of life for the D'Alesandro family. "I was christened in the Democratic party and in the Catholic Church," says Pelosi. "I don't know in which order." D'Alesandro served in a succession of local and statewide elected positions before he ran for Congress, and he was later elected mayor of Baltimore. From the time Pelosi was in the first grade until she went to college, her father reigned as mayor, a kind of local FDR. The front hall of their house overflowed with campaign paraphernalia for D'Alesandro and every Democrat he supported. The phone rang constantly with constituents seeking answers or favors. As a little girl, Pelosi says, "I knew how to get people into the city hospital, on relief, out of jail. I would say, 'This is the person you need to call,' or 'I'll tell Mommy.' I would answer the door and sometimes the people standing there didn't have anything to eat. My brother said that when we were really little, you never knew how many people would be at the table. Mother would just fit them in."

Pelosi always knew which side she was on. "I loved the Democrats, and I thought that was the right place to be, but I had no personal ambition to be a candidate myself," she says. The issues that would later draw her into politics—the environment and abortion rights—were not yet on the horizon. Economic issues separated the two major political parties, and Pelosi was taught from a young age that Democrats were the party of the people, while Republicans represented the wealthy. "And that's the way it was," she says. Leading up to the 1952 election of Dwight Eisenhower, her mother told her that if a Republican becomes president, he would bring back the Great Depression. When Eisenhower won, Pelosi, who was twelve, took the money out of her piggy bank and spent it on paper, pencils, and crayons for school. When her mother asked why, she replied, "Because we're never going to have any money and I've got to buy all my supplies now."

President Reagan, running for reelection in 1984, was scheduled to visit the Italian section of Baltimore to dedicate a statue of Christopher Columbus. When the White House called to invite the former mayor, D'Alesandro, to the ceremony, his wife rejected the invitation with such threatening language that the Secret Service investigated. Pelosi quoted her mother as telling the Reagan White House, "If you know what's good for you, don't come anywhere near our house. After what he's done to the poor people of our country, we're not going anyplace with him." On the day of the event, Mrs. D'Alesandro pulled down the shades and put Mondale signs in the window.

Like her parents, Pelosi is a partisan Democrat and proud of it. She is pro-choice, has a strong interest in protecting the environment, and wants to raise the minimum wage. "And if that's described as being too liberal, then you wonder what does this party stand for," she says. "Isn't that what we are about as a party?"

Pelosi's path into politics was typical for women of her generation. As a young mother, she had marched against the Vietnam War and gone door-to-door for a variety of causes, often with a baby carriage or a child or two in tow. Since moving to San Francisco with her husband in 1969, she had been immersed in politics. She managed Jerry Brown's upset victory in the Maryland Democratic primary in 1976, and before long was chair of the Democratic party in California. In 1984, she ran for national party chairman and lost, but her spirited race positioned her for the job of finance chair for the Democratic Senate Campaign Committee. She raised a lot of money, and shared in the credit when the Democrats regained control of the Senate in 1986.

Pelosi was frequently mentioned as a possible candidate for Congress. But it was the mid-eighties, she was the mother of five teenagers, and a political career of her own seemed out of the question. Then, in January 1987, California representative Sala Burton, who had just been reelected, phoned to say she was too ill to attend her own swearing-in in Washington. She would take the oath at her bedside, and she wanted Pelosi there. Burton surprised Pelosi by saying she intended to endorse her as her chosen successor.

"I've never even talked about running for office," Pelosi protested.

"I don't feel well," Burton said evenly. "It will make me feel better if you will allow me to announce that I am supporting you. Are you prepared to accept my endorsement?"

Three weeks later, on February 1, Burton died of colon cancer. The Burton machine had dominated California politics for a generation. The widowed Sala had taken the seat when her husband, Phil, died. Between Phil and his brother John, one or another Burton had been Pelosi's representative in Congress. Pelosi was personally close to Sala, as she had been to her husband and brother-in-law. They were soul mates, the result of years of shared political struggle and triumph. Sala's endorsement put Pelosi over the top with 39 percent of the vote in a crowded primary with thirteen candidates. It was rare for a woman to be the heir apparent, but Pelosi had paid her dues, and this, after all, was San Francisco.

Pelosi's bone-deep partisanship made her a controversial choice for the Democrats as they gathered after the 2002 elections to select a new leader. Democrats had failed to take back the House, and had lost control of the Senate. Gephardt was stepping down, and the party was divided over whether to move left or right to better compete with the GOP. Republicans salivated over the prospect of Pelosi as leader. Liberals were not popular in much of the country, and she was a card-carrying liberal. But Pelosi had more than enough votes to win. Texas Rep. Martin Frost dropped out of the race. Tennessee Rep. Harold Ford, a 32-year-old centrist and an African American, launched a last-minute effort to overtake Pelosi, arguing she was the wrong face for mainstream America. Pelosi won the November election easily, but confessed she feels she's getting served up like a Thanksgiving meal. "Everybody oohs and ah's. . . . We have a woman leader in the party . . . and then they begin to carve you up like the Thanksgiving turkey." Pelosi would be the most prominent Democrat to create and convey the Democratic message, at least until the 2004 presidential contenders emerged.

Pelosi carried the Black Caucus, which is more than a third women. Their numbers have grown since 1970, when there was only one black woman in the House, Cardiss Collins of Illinois, to fourteen in 2002. David Bositis, who analyzes African-American voting patterns for the Joint Center for Political and Economic Studies, cited several reasons for the rise of black women: They are more likely to have college and advanced degrees than black men; roughly one-third of black men are incarcerated, on parole, or have felony records making it impossible for them to hold office or even vote; white voters are more likely to vote for black women than men because women are less threatening. "It's not a random phenomenon that a third of black elected officials are women," Bositis said.

Shirley Chisholm of New York and Barbara Jordan of Texas achieved national prominence, but no black woman reached the Senate until Carol Moseley-Braun was elected from Illinois in 1992. She got the Democratic nomination partly because two white males destroyed each other's chances in the primary, Bositis said, and won on the coattails of Clinton. She was defeated after one term. Noting that most African Americans in Congress, male and female, won in majority-black districts, Bositis said none of the women is realistically in a position to move up to senator or governor in statewide elections.

Most of the women currently serving in Congress came up through the ranks of local politics. Their résumés tell the story. They ran for the PTA, then the city council, then the statehouse, and then the leadership of the statehouse before they dared to attempt a run for Congress. Ellen Tauscher is an exception, first elected to Congress in 1996 from California, Tauscher is the prototype for a generation of women to rise in policies through what she calls "parallel or alternative credentialing." Tauscher had never run for public office before she defeated a two-term Republican. But she had held a seat on the New York Stock Exchange and had created her own business in California. These accomplishments gave her credibility in the political arena. "Nobody believed I was lying on a chaise lounge eating bonbons," she says.

Tauscher arrived in a chauffeured car for the first day of orientation for Democratic freshmen, another touch of credentialing in the status-conscious political world. A survey of the personal wealth of members done at the time rated Tauscher as the eighth richest member of the House. Her husband, William, had owned ComputerLand, a string of computer discount stores, and transformed it into the highly successful Vanstar Corp., with operations in forty countries. The couple's net worth was estimated at upwards of $30 million. She and her husband poured $1.7 million of their own money into her $2.6 million campaign; her opponent spent $1.4 million, making it one of the most expensive congressional races in the country.

Tauscher's blue-chip background smoothed her entrée into the cliquish world of Capitol Hill. When the stock market took a sudden downturn, Democrats turned to Tauscher, then only a freshman, to brief them about the economic implications. She was an expert on "guy issues" like computer encryption and export controls, and her grasp of e-life and on-line communications left her elders gasping for air. "It's a little disappointing when I talk about a server and half my colleagues think it's the person who handed them their lunch," she says, laughing.

As Tauscher herself says, you can't miss her when she walks into a room. At five-foot-ten with a buxom frame, bright blond hair, and a broad, toothy smile, she is physically imposing. And she doesn't hide in basic blacks and demure navy blues. She wore a fuchsia dress for her swearing-in ceremony. On the day we interviewed her, she had on a tangerine orange suit with a short skirt and oversized gold earrings. She talks fast, walks fast, and thinks fast. In the gray and colorless world of official Washington, she is an exotic creature.

A portrait of a blue dog hangs on the wall in Tauscher's office as a whimsical symbol of her pro-business fiscal conservatism. Why a blue dog? Democratic loyalists in the South, so the story goes, would vote for any Democrat, even if it was a "yellow dog." The two dozen self-styled "Blue Dogs" in Congress got their name when one of their leaders vowed to vote his conscience "even if the Democratic leadership beats us till we're blue."

Tauscher's name comes up as a likely heir apparent for Dianne Feinstein should she choose not to run again The two women are friends, and Tauscher served as co-chair of Feinstein's campaign for the Senate in both 1992 and 1994. It is generally assumed that when Feinstein leaves the Senate, for whatever reason, Tauscher would run for her seat. "It would be like the starting gun at the Boston Marathon," says Tauscher, who anticipates a stampede among Democrats to succeed Feinstein (or Barbara Boxer for that matter, California's other Democratic senator). Though Feinstein is not one to fawn over anybody, let alone a possible rival, Tauscher comes closer than anyone else to being Feinstein's protégée.

"I have a life experience that is relevant for this time," says Tauscher, who grew up in a working-class community in Hudson County, New Jersey, across the river from Manhattan. It was the kind of neighborhood where "the dead vote Democratic," she says. Her Irish immigrant grandparents worked as a janitor and cleaning lady at night and lived upstairs in the two-family house they shared with her parents. Her father ran a grocery store for forty years until he was forced to retire after two varicose vein operations. He was active in the community and served as a local councilman and volunteer fire chief. Her mother volunteered on bingo night at Holy Cross School and worked in the local library. As much as young Ellen admired her parents and grandparents, she figured out at an early age that life would have been easier and filled with more opportunities if they had more money.

Tauscher was quoted saying that she always wanted to be wealthy. Asked about that, she laughs and rephrases the sentiment. "I didn't always want to be rich. I wanted to be independent and I assume, rightfully so, that it comes with financial independence." But when Tauscher graduated from Seton Hall University in 1973 with a degree in early-childhood education, teaching jobs were scarce. A baby bust had followed on the heels of the large baby-boom generation, and elementary schools were closing because of the lack of students. Tauscher had student loans to pay back, and she had promised to help her parents with the tuition of a younger sister, who was in college. She needed a job.

Tauscher knew where Wall Street was, and what it stood for. As a teenager, she had watched the World Trade Center being built as she walked to high school. She decided that was where she wanted to work. Armed with nothing but her education degree and a lot of chutzpah, she got a job at an investment firm and was soon trading municipal bonds. "I walked fast and I talked fast, and I weaseled my way onto the trading desk," she says. "I was like a monkey with a machine gun. I couldn't make a mistake." Next to her on the trading desk was a young man who wasn't nearly as productive but was earning considerably more money. Once she realized the disparity, she promptly quit and got a job at another firm for twice the money she had been making.

Tauscher saw job-hopping as a way to get ahead. Not happy with her progress at her new company, Tauscher again resigned. She was summoned to a meeting with the firm's top executives. "We want you to go to the New York Stock Exchange," one of them told her. "Why today, and why me?" Taucher asked, suspicious of the sudden burst of generosity. The executives told her that more women were investing in the stock market, that the firm's women clients had increased in number, and that they needed her and valued her and didn't want her to leave. Flattering as it was, Tauscher was still skeptical.

Tauscher assessed her credentials. She was twenty-five years old and a newcomer to Wall Street. "OK, why me and why now?" she asked again.

"Well," said one, "you know that our firm is number two in the world."

"Yes," Tauscher said.

"And Merrill Lynch is number one."

Tauscher nodded.

"Merrill Lynch is putting a woman on the floor in six weeks and you're going to beat her to it," the executive said. "You're going Monday."

This was not the first time that something good had happened to her, but not for the right reasons, Tauscher thought. But why quibble? It was 1977. The women's movement was in full swing. She was about to represent the venerable Bache Securities on the New York Stock Exchange, the youngest woman ever accorded the honor.

Throughout the fourteen years she lived in Manhattan, Tauscher was in demand. Being a successful young woman in a man's world gave her star status and produced numerous invitations to sit on corporate boards, which she accepted. This was the era of the token woman, and Tauscher was often the lone woman at the conference table. She dabbled in politics on the side, serving as a co-chair of the 1980 Democratic National Convention in New York City. "It was a social thing, going to parties, more than anything else," she says.

In 1989, she married and moved with her husband to the San Francisco Bay area of California. She was thirty-seven, an age when most people settle down, and here she was starting over. "I went to the Safeway, and didn't know anybody," she says. "Then I went to a lunch and met some people, and I went other places and met more people. Within a year, I was co-chairing Dianne Feinsten's Senate campaign. I just kind of made the most of what I was doing."

Tauscher says she was "a good corporate wife," but that was not enough. When she investigated child-care options for her preschool-aged daughter, she was not happy with the choices. "There was not a testosterone solution to be found," she recalls thinking. "Women had to figure this out." She founded the ChildCare Registry, a company that created the first national background check for child care workers and provided parents with detailed information about child care providers. She wrote the *Child Care Sourcebook* and coupled it with a software disc.

In the midst of starting her business, she was approached to run for Congress in 1994. In addition, her daughter, Katherine, born in 1991 three months prematurely, was still undergoing painful rehabilitation for a congenital hip malformation. "I laughed at the guy who called me about running," she said. "I said to my husband, 'Why would I want to do that?' "

Tauscher had struggled hard to become a mother. During her first pregnancy, she suspected something was wrong when the technician doing the sonogram left to find her doctor. Forty long minutes later, he hadn't returned, and Tauscher couldn't bear not knowing any longer. She had taken two sonogram companies public while on Wall Street, and knew how the equipment worked. She performed the test on herself and saw that the fetus was not developing properly. After an early labor that lasted eighteen hours, she gave birth to a boy who died moments later. She told an interviewer that it was "the first bad thing that ever happened to me." A second pregnancy ended when Tauscher developed an infection from a diagnostic test and miscarried. She was almost thirty-nine when she became pregnant with Katherine, and spent the last sixteen weeks of the pregnancy confined to bed.

Politics was not on her mind in the winter of 1995 when she returned to her Manhattan hotel after taking Katherine to the Christmas show at Rockefeller Center. She and a friend from her childhood had gotten orchestra seats so close to the stage they could almost touch the performers. The two women had tears in their eyes remembering how as kids they had sat in the nosebleed section. Their children shot them sidelong glances. Tauscher was still glowing when the hotel concierge interrupted her reverie to say in somber tones that several calls had come for her, including two from members of Congress. She couldn't imagine why the congressmen had tracked her down in New York.

Figuring the congressmen would be hard to reach, Tauscher called Judi Kanter of Emily's List, who had also left a message. Kanter reported that with ten days to go before the filing date, the Democratic candidate in Tauscher's district had dropped out of the race. Finding a replacement was urgent. Tauscher figured that Kanter wanted her help to persuade a prospect to get in the race. "Judi hits 'em high, I hit 'em low, and we get this person on the ballot," she thought.

"Judi, is this about me calling some person?" Tauscher asked. "Who is it?"

"No, you don't have to call anybody," Kanter replied. "It's you."

"Is this my reward for going out of town?" Tauscher replied with some irritation. "Did you all meet and I wasn't there so I got the short straw?"

Kanter said as soothingly as she could, "No. We've all decided it's you."

"I'm not doing this. No way," Tauscher said emphatically.

"You have to," Kanter pleaded.

Tauscher agreed to talk it over with her husband, who she assumed would veto the idea. "Somebody important in California die?" Bill Tauscher quipped when he came in and saw her call list. "Not yet," Tauscher replied. She waited until later in the evening when they were alone having a drink to spring the surprise on him. She recited the facts dispassionately, that the Democratic candidate in their district had dropped out, and she was being pressed to run. The incumbent, Republican Bill Baker, was a sharp-tongued social conservative whom the Democrats believed could be beat. "We don't like him," she said. Then she waited for her husband's response. When he didn't immediately say anything, she rushed to fill the void. "You don't want me to do this," she said.

"Let's think about this," he said. "I don't know whether it was the sixties or the seventies, but people like us stopped going to Congress and that's why we've got people like Bill Baker. And unless people like us go back, we deserve what we get. I think you need to do this." Bill Tauscher is a Republican, and his invocation of "people like us" reflected the frustration of mainstream Republicans with the far right's success in capturing the party. Getting permission from her husband freed Tauscher to think vicariously about what it would be like if she ran. She kept telling herself that in the end she probably wouldn't do it. So what's the harm in dreaming? Twenty-four hours later, she had practically mapped out a campaign. By thinking about it, she says, "we thought ourselves completely into it."

She and her husband would later divorce. Looking back, Tauscher said her husband may have encouraged her to run "out of an understanding that he had made some choices outside the marriage. At some level, he had abandoned the relationship, and my finding a new interest gave him running room."

Tauscher ran an aggressive campaign that portrayed Baker as a Gingrich clone whose right-wing views were out of step in the prosperous district. "It's where Silicon Valley sleeps," she says, describing the bedroom communities, places with idyllic names like Danville and Walnut Creek, that are home to a disproportionate number of college graduates and "socket moms," women who work in the high-tech industry. Tauscher was relatively new to the district, but so was practically everybody else. Fifty-three percent of voters had lived in the district less than twenty years and 35 percent less than ten years. "These people want an independent, moderate, fiscal conservative who is going to work for them. They don't care if you're a Democrat, a Republican, or a three-headed giraffe—as long as that doesn't interfere," says Tauscher.

The tenth district of California is one of fifty "swing districts" in the country where a majority is not aligned with either party. With only a handful of seats separating the parties, it is in such districts where control of the House is decided. Baker accused Tauscher of using her personal wealth to try to buy a seat in Congress, and Tauscher barely beat him with 49 percent of the vote to 47 percent for Baker and 4 percent split among others. Defending her seat in 1998, she defeated Republican Charles Ball, 53 to 43 percent. For the 2000 race, it was the Republicans' turn to have trouble finding a candidate willing to take on Tauscher. With her pro-business views and her connections in Silicon Valley, she has tapped into a vein of gold for the Democrats. In August 1999, the Democrats made her the head of a newly formed Democratic Business Forum that caters to $10,000 donors, offering them special entrée to members and issue briefings in return for their financial support.

On the surface, Tauscher seemed to have it all. Unlike many of her colleagues who live like nomads in Washington, bunking dormitory-style or renting an efficiency apartment, Tauscher and her husband bought a house in the city and enrolled their daughter in a prestigious private school. Katherine adjusted so well that twelve of her first-grade classmates asked to sit next to her in second grade. "Isn't that terrific!" Bill Tauscher marveled when one of the teachers passed along the compliment. Ellen Tauscher reacted like a politician who had just been handed a poll of the twenty pupils. "What about the seven other knuckleheads?" she asked. "What's wrong with those seven other people?" Tauscher laughs at this telling commentary about the drive she brings to everything she does.

That moment of levity was one of the last for the Tauscher family. In December 1998, seven weeks after Tauscher was reelected, she filed for divorce from her husband. News accounts said Bill Tauscher had admitted having an affair with another woman. There had been rumors of an affair during Tauscher's first race in 1996, but she assumed they were just part of the dirty tricks of a campaign. "My attitude was he couldn't be this stupid," she says, laughing. A year later, she found a picture of her husband and his girlfriend taken at New York's Rainbow Room, where the Tauschers were married. She confronted him. He asked for another chance, and she agreed. The Tauschers celebrated their ninth anniversary in August 1998 with a fund-raiser for her campaign amid rumors that the marriage was on the rocks. After the election, Ellen Tauscher received an anonymous e-mail at her congressional office telling her it was common knowledge that her husband was having an affair with an employee at his company. This time, Ellen Tauscher wasted little time filing for divorce.

"I think it's humanizing," Tauscher says. "Up to then, people would look at me and think that other than a bad hair day, I had everything. I was rich, successful. For a lot of people, I had too much." When details of the split became public, Tauscher tried not to let it affect her public performance. She did not miss a roll-call vote. "What happened to me happens in many families," she says. She went about her business and made sure her daughter went to school every day, but inside she was crushed. "I had this feeling of disappearing," she says. "When someone puts so little value on you, no matter how strong you are, there's this drip, drip, drip."

Tauscher found refuge in her child and in her new life in politics. Late in 1999, the Republicans still had not found a candidate willing to challenge her. Then one day before the filing deadline, Claude Hutchison, a local party activist, entered the race. Unlike how she handled her previous opponents, Tauscher could not assail Hutchison, a pro-choice moderate, for having views that are out of touch with the district. Still, she won with 53 percent of the vote. While that is not an overwhelming margin, Tauscher looked secure enough by 2002 that the Republicans didn't bother to field a candidate against her. Except for a minor challenge from a Libertarian candidate, Tauscher ran unopposed in 2002. But there could be trouble brewing ahead for Tauscher. She had gone public with her belief that Nancy Pelosi—in retaliation for Tauscher backing her opponent for Democratic Whip—had used her influence against Tauscher in redistricting. On its face, it was a hard charge to prove. Tauscher's new district had 5 percent more Democrats, and she had no serious opposition. But those additional Democrats are rural, working-class people while the bulk of the district is upper class. The new voters are wary of Tauscher, who was one of only thirteen Democrats to vote for President Bush's tax cut, which heavily favored wealthier taxpayers. So Tauscher, while safe for now from Republicans, could be susceptible in the future to a primary challenge from a more populist Democrat.

Continued friction with Pelosi seemed inevitable as Tauscher signaled she would support Texas Rep. Martin Frost in any head-to-head contest with Pelosi, whom she thinks is too identified with the left of the party at a time when centrist politics are on the rise. In an interview for this book Tauscher talked about how her Blue Dog, mainstream politics suited not only her district but the country as a whole. She said she would consider seeking higher office if the opportunity presented itself. "I think there's a place for centrists," she said. "It takes more courage to take a stand on principle than it does to see where the leadership is going and vote with them. I've got a high labor score and a high environmental score, but I also got an award from the Chamber of Commerce."

The idea that her "alternative credentialing" could be a model for other women getting into politics pleases Tauscher. "There's something very life-changing about standing in front of voters," she says. "It's not a job, it's a life. You have to share yourself with a lot of people, and you're asked to do things that are awesome and ridiculous at the same time. You have to know who you are and what your priorities are."

Tauscher thinks women get too comfortable with "starter jobs" in politics. "We have so many women, especially Democrats, who are stuck at a certain level," she says. "In California, we run things at the county level, and the same is true around the country. But when it comes to pulling triggers, and red buttons and red phones, and the really big money, we're not at the table. We've got to be able to say, 'Look, I know more about this than you do.' Frankly, on a lot of issues, certainly about computers and software, I know more than most of my colleagues in Congress do."

Tauscher talks about "resetting expectations" for women. She thinks women are ready for greater achievements in politics, and that society is ready for women. As for her own aspirations to move up, she says, "I love my job . . . but if the timing is right and the opportunity presents itself, I will be ready."

Another ambitious Californian who came to Congress with business-world credentials is Loretta Sanchez. In 1992, Sanchez was a financial analyst with a nationally known investment firm, earning big bucks for putting together business deals. She had an MBA from American University and was in the vanguard of women making it in the new, high-flying economy. Like most of her neighbors in conservative Orange County, she was a registered Republican.

That summer, Sanchez had a political awakening. Watching the Republican National Convention on television, Sanchez was outraged by her party's mean-spirited message, especially with regard to immigrants. The daughter of Mexican immigrants, she had experienced prejudice. As a child growing up in Anaheim, which was then heavily German and Catholic, she could swim in the neighborhood pool only on Friday evenings when Mexican children were allowed in. On Saturdays, workers changed the water. Sanchez listened with alarm as conservative commentator Pat Buchanan urged Americans to take back their neighborhood street by street with M-16 rifles if necessary. That week, she changed her party registration from Republican to Democratic.

Sanchez's congressman was Bob Dornan, a bombastic right-winger who had represented the district for twenty years. Known as "B-1 Bob" for his hawkish views on defense spending, Dornan was a skilled provocateur, and often filled in for Rush Limbaugh on his radio show. Nobody, it seemed, could dislodge Dornan, whose strong anti-abortion views resonated in the heavily Catholic and Christian fundamentalist district. Even voters who disagreed with him found his flamboyant style entertaining.

At first, the newly registered Democrat wrote checks supporting Democratic candidates seeking to unseat Dornan. When that didn't work, she decided almost on a whim to take on Dornan herself in the 1996 election. Her only previous electoral experience was a failed 1994 run for the city council in Anaheim, but she had learned from her mistakes. The biggest one was using her married name, Brixey. Besides being hard to remember, it signaled no ethnic identification. Anaheim had undergone a demographic transformation since Sanchez, as a child, was barred from the local swimming pool. An influx of Hispanics and Vietnamese had created an ethnically mixed district in which whites were the minority. In such a district, the surname Sanchez was an asset.

Raising money would be difficult because Democratic backers would not want to risk money on an unknown with little chance of winning. Sanchez paid for her primary campaign with the $57,000 proceeds from a condominium that she sold. Emily's List contributed $5,000 for the general election but did not put Sanchez on its mailing list, which would have brought her contributions from women all over the country. Her family became the core of her campaign team. Between her parents, her husband, and her six siblings, they visited more than sixty thousand households over the course of a year. "My sisters and brothers going to someone's house is about the same as me," she said. "They know how I think, and they know the issues. They have had experience with the school system, then and now. And they giggle the same way."

Dornan barely took notice when Sanchez won the Democratic primary. He was off on a quixotic run for the presidency, taking for granted that he would be reelected to his House seat. After handily defeating a Latino opponent four years earlier, he assumed his support in that community was solid. For past races, he had raised as much as $2 million. This time, he didn't bother to break $1 million. He relied on his son and surrogate, Mark Dornan, to keep an eye on the Sanchez campaign, an assignment he took literally. About midnight one evening, the younger Dornan spotted Sanchez's husband, securities trader Stephen Brixey, replacing Dornan campaign signs with Sanchez signs. He made a citizen's arrest. Sanchez's husband was prosecuted and fined $640.

While Dornan was busy pursuing his presidential pipe dream and playing call-in radio host, his district had undergone a cultural and political upheaval. The Hispanic vote had jumped from 14 percent in the previous election to 20 percent, and Sanchez was the beneficiary. Her shoestring campaign had gained momentum when the Democratic establishment realized that they had a chance to win. Sanchez outspent Dornan, $811,000 to $742,000, and beat him by a scant 984 votes out of 102,500 votes cast.

Dornan refused to accept defeat. He accused Sanchez and her supporters of fraud and appealed to the Republican Congress to overturn the election results. After months of examining ballots and questioning witnesses under oath, Dornan was able to substantiate several hundred suspect ballots, but not enough to invalidate the election. The contentious process consumed all of 1997 and dragged on into 1998 before the GOP finally ended the investigation.

In Washington, Sanchez was hailed as a giant-killer. Even some Republicans privately cheered the departure of Dornan, whose intemperate remarks on hot-button issues like abortion and affirmative action they found embarrassing. Sanchez loved the limelight, but nearly buckled under the strain of beating back Dornan's challenge while simultaneously trying to establish herself in her job and raise money for the next election. For newly elected representatives, the first election after the freshman term is the hardest. In that first term, the steep learning curve is coupled with a need to prove to the voters that they elected the right person. Sanchez, after all, had won by only a single percentage point. Months after the election, with Dornan's claim still pending, a California colleague casually asked how she was getting along. Sanchez broke down. "I can't do it" she wailed. "I'm going to lose the seat."

Sanchez poured out her tale of woe. She said Democratic leaders had assured her Dornan's case would fizzle, and had promised to help pay her legal bills. But the cloud still hung over her election and her party had done almost nothing to help her raise the $500,000 she owed her lawyers. The Democratic Congressional Campaign Caucus (DCCC) had contributed a measly $5,000. It was five in the afternoon when Sanchez confided her problems to her fellow Californian, Representative Lucille Roybal-Allard. Just two hours later, Roybal-Allard assembled thirty of the thirty-eight Democratic women in the House dining room. "I want you to tell them what you just told me," Roybal-Allard said by way of introduction. Sanchez ran down her list of broken promises. She told the women she felt abandoned and alone, and didn't know where to turn. "I'll be right back—you all stay here," announced Rosa DeLauro of Connecticut.

Minutes later, DeLauro returned with Dick Gephardt, the Democrats' leader in the House, trailed by Martin Frost of Texas, chairman of the DCCC. At DeLauro's request, Sanchez retold her story of promises not kept by her own party. Turning to Gephardt and Frost, DeLauro asked, "Is what she's saying correct or not?" Neither man contested Sanchez's version of events.

To make amends, Frost turned over the DCCC's proprietary list of ten thousand major donors in California, including several Hollywood celebrities. Provided with the addresses, Sanchez sent a letter to each of them pleading for help to rebuff Dornan's challenge. But when she asked Frost for phone numbers so that she could follow up with personal calls, he said no. "Thanks, Martin," she said sarcastically. "Out of the ten thousand letters I sent out, I'm lucky if I get sixty responses." Actually, she got only fifty replies. Again, she called upon her female colleagues, who divided the list of names, looked up the phone numbers, and made calls on Sanchez's behalf. The group effort raised enough money to pay off most of Sanchez's legal bills.

For Sanchez, the support of the other women came as a surprise. "This is the first industry I've been in where the women really stick together and help each other," she said. "I think the reason they do is the environment is so hard. In the business world, you don't find women helping other women. It's like every woman's on her own in a lot of ways—at least it was at the financial institution that I came from. In the House, women are really tight."

An oppressed minority has a greater stake in sticking together. Women Democrats in a Republican-controlled House are a double minority, outnumbered and often outmaneuvered by the Democratic men who control their party's leadership, and by the Republicans, who control the agenda. A full year after her election, when the

House had not yet settled Dornan's compliant, four congresswomen linked arms with Sanchez and marched on House Speaker Newt Gingrich's office in the Capitol to demand an end to the lengthy probe. The Capitol Hill newspaper *Roll Call* published a front-page photograph of the women looking determined and exuberant under the headline "Another March on Washington."

The long investigation of Sanchez's narrow election victory produced an unexpected dividend. It gave Sanchez a measure of fame rarely accorded junior members of Congress. Democratic National Committee polling discovered that the case had gotten so much attention on Univision and Telemundo, two Spanish-speaking television networks, that Sanchez was the third most recognized Hispanic elected official, after Henry Cisneros, the former housing secretary, and Federico Peña, the former energy secretary.

The fact that Dornan sought a rematch in 1998 only added to Sanchez's aura. Dornan billed himself as the "true Hispanic" in the race, reminding the strongly Catholic community that Sanchez had voted against a ban on a type of late-term abortions known as partial-birth abortion. When Dornan said Sanchez wasn't a good Catholic, she began wearing a pin with a three-dimensional picture of Jesus. "I'm wearing my Jesus on my chest," she declared. When the local Catholic bishop decried her practice of visiting different churches, synagogues, and even a Buddhist temple, saying she was more interested in politics than religion, Sanchez said she would continue the visits.

With her bouncy shoulder-length brown hair and dimples, Sanchez projects the improbable combination of innocence and street smarts. In a business that requires a bottomless supply of bonhomie, she has a sharp tongue and can be abrasive. She topped the "Freshman Flop" list in *Washingtonian* magazine's July 1998 poll of Capitol Hill staff, a result determined by the high number of negative comments about her lodged mostly by Republican staffers who regard her as an irritant because of her wiseacre partisan style. The runner-up was another former Republican turned Democrat, New York representative Carolyn McCarthy, who switched parties and ran for office after her husband was killed and her son grievously injured by a deranged gunman on the Long Island Railroad. McCarthy has a much softer style than Sanchez, but her insistence on bringing up gun control, an issue that divides Republicans, won her the enmity of GOP staffers.

Sanchez's voting record reflects the economic interests of her constituents, sometimes against her better judgment. When the White

House scrounged for votes for a free-trade initiative that would have given President Clinton more leeway in negotiating trade deals, Sanchez stood firm against entreaties from Vice President Gore, Treasury Secretary Robert Rubin, White House Chief of Staff Erskine Bowles, and, finally, Clinton himself. "You don't have to tell me about the merits of the thing. I understand," she told them. As a former financial analyst, she realized that granting the president so-called fast-track authority would benefit the nation and the wealthier areas that ring her district. But she represents Anaheim, where Disneyland is located, a district that is home to the men and women, many of them Mexican immigrants, who change the beds and bus the tables for the tourist community. They're the ones who are left behind in the rush toward globalized trade, and unless President Clinton could sweeten the deal with promises of job training, she planned to vote no.

When Gore called trying to change her mind, she said coquettishly, "For you, I might think about it." That tiny opening prompted a phone call from Clinton, followed by an urgent invitation from the White House to meet personally with the president that afternoon. It was raining, she had votes to attend to in the House; and she did not intend to reverse her position. But you don't say no to the president. So she headed to the White House, where she was ushered into the Oval Office and took a seat as far from where Clinton sat as possible. "Why are you sitting so far away?" he asked genially. "It's easier to say no," she quipped. Turning to Bowles, the tight-lipped chief of staff, Sanchez smiled sweetly. "Erskine, what part of 'no' didn't you know how to tell him?" Bowles whitened a bit before sputtering, "You told the vice president that you might change your mind."

Sanchez acknowledged that she sympathized with the administration on the substantive merits of the trade issue, but she concluded, "Mr. President, I'd love to, but I just can't. Ask a Democrat who's got an easy election." Then her pager sounded. There was an important vote on the Hill. She left in a hurry.

The House was still in session at 2 A.M. when Gore reached Sanchez in the cloakroom off the House floor. "Al, what are you doing calling me at two in the morning?" she teased. "I'm trying to find votes," he replied glumly. "Al, I told you and I told the president no," Sanchez replied. "Oh, come on," Gore pressed. Sanchez could feel herself weakening. This was her party. Some analysts credited her narrow victory to a late campaign visit by Clinton to the district. She told Gore that if her vote made the difference between winning and losing, she would vote with the White House. "Otherwise, don't bother me," she said. "How many are you short?" When Gore said only four votes, she didn't believe him. Conversations with her colleagues and news accounts suggested a much larger deficit. "You're lying to me," she said to the vice president. "You've got to be short at least ten."

She ticked off several Democrats she thought were gettable. The GOP leadership had warned the White House that it would not deliver its members if the Democrats fell short. "Get off the phone and go call them," Sanchez declared, her impatience showing. Gore was exasperated too. "You know, Loretta, I'd rather sit here talking to you because there are no more votes to be found." Sanchez started laughing at the absurdity of the vice president begging for her vote when victory was out of reach. "It sounds to me like you don't have fast track then," she said. That proved to be the case. Knowing it could not win and wanting to avoid a humiliating defeat, the White House decided not to bring the measure to a vote.

Sanchez is a less reliable barometer of her district on social issues. Pro-choice and progressive, she is often at odds with religious conservatives. Some battles are worth fighting, like preserving abortion rights; others, she sidesteps. She voted with conservatives to allow the display of the Ten Commandments in some public places, for instance, a vote that a majority in her district approved of, although it went against her personal preference. "Part of my being a leader is pushing my constituents in a direction where I believe they are better off in the long run," she says. "I just can't lead on everything all the time because at some point they would say, 'This woman doesn't match anything we believe in.' So it's picking and choosing where you want to expand their world. . . . I didn't want to stand up and explain why I voted against the Ten Commandments. It's not easy, particularly in my district. It was symbolic, and I'm not going to let my political opponents do that to me."

When Sanchez first ran, she encountered the strongest resistance from women. Three weeks before the election, a poll showed that Clinton had an eighteen-point gender gap in his favor in her district, whereas Sanchez had a zero gap; women were not especially inclined to vote for her. After she took office, her gender gap soared to 36 percent positive, a phenomenal rise that Sanchez attributes to a prominent story in the *Los Angeles Times* about how she was sewing her own gown for the inaugural ball. "Women thought, 'She's like me—she sews,'" says Sanchez.

Sanchez's sewing was no affectation. Her father had entered the United States legally when he was twenty-five and single. He spoke no English, had only a seventh-grade education, and got a job in a plastics factory. Her mother emigrated separately. She had a third-grade education and worked at an office job in the same factory. They met and married, and for the next twenty years, Mrs. Sanchez stayed home "doing all the things a mom of the lower middle class does," says Sanchez. "She sewed our clothes. That's how I learned to sew. I would sew for my younger sister so my mom would have more time to sew for me." After her children were grown, Mrs. Sanchez went back to school. She now teaches the third grade in public school. Sanchez's parents applied for U.S. citizenship after Proposition 187 passed in California, curtailing the access of noncitizens to social services.

Sanchez's reelection in 1998 was emblematic of the growing political power of Hispanics in the district, the state, and the country. Between 1971 and 1992, the voting age population of Hispanics in the United States grew 162 percent, compared to 56 percent for African Americans and 30 percent for whites.

Unable to comprehend why his district rejected him two years earlier, Dornan spent five times as much ($3,864,920) in a vain effort to regain his seat. He sent out flyers decrying abortion with a picture of Our Lady of Guadalupe, the patron saint of Mexico, on the cover. He repeatedly proclaimed himself the "true Latino" in the race. He called Sanchez a "giggling airhead," and when she refused to debate him, he followed her to a grocery store where she was meeting with constituents. An altercation followed, and eyewitnesses say it was Sanchez who landed the most elbows. With plenty of willing backers this time, she raised more than $2.5 million and coasted to victory with 56 percent of the vote.

With Dornan finally out of the picture, Republicans united behind the candidacy of Gloria Matta Tuchman, a public school teacher. Tuchman was a co-author of proposition 227, which in 1998 ended bilingual education in California. Tuchman also is Hispanic. If imitation is the sincerest form of flattery, the Republicans found their Sanchez. But Tuchman was no match for Sanchez, garnering only 35 percent of the vote and posing no serious challenge.

Sanchez is not slowing her pace. She remains one of the most prodigious fund-raisers in the House, commuting home every weekend when Congress is in session to tend to her constituents, and raise money. At Gore's urging, the Democratic National Committee in January 1999 named her a general co-chair with the responsibility of leading a get-out-the-vote effort among Hispanics. Gore evidently enjoyed jousting with Sanchez, and figured his presidential campaign could benefit from the extraordinary drive that she brings to the political arena.

Between the demands of her district and the DNC, her friends worry that Sanchez won't have the time to develop expertise on issues, that she'll be running around the country raising money. There are whispers that she isn't substantive enough, and that her high-voltage personality generates more heat than light. Sanchez turned forty in January 2000, a birthday that invites reflection. She has despaired over not fitting in, and worries that the skills she honed in the business world have atrophied in the hothouse of politics. She gave up carrying her laptop computer on the long flights between the coasts because it took too long to go through security, and she was always running late. "All I'll know how to do is shake hands, smile, and pose for pictures," she frets. "I worry about getting my hair done, and my makeup done."

Sanchez spends Mondays in California raising money, then takes the overnight flight back to Washington, landing at 6 A.M. She says she wears black, which makes her look thinner, to help fool herself into thinking she'll sleep if she fits more neatly into the seat. By seven, she is in the House gym working out. In her freshman term, she regularly encountered House Speaker Newt Gingrich, then in one of his periodic slimming-down periods. She remembers telling him, "I eat nails for breakfast, Newt. If you run someone against me, remember that."

The congressional lifestyle has been hard on her marriage. Stephen Brixey, Sanchez's husband, is registered in the securities industry. He has a high-stress job, but when he leaves the office, he leaves the stresses and strains behind. She describes him as "kind of a homebody," and says she rarely insists that he accompany her to political events. On those occasions that she feels it is mandatory to have an escort, she lets him know well in advance to lessen his complaints about politics invading his personal space. Sanchez puts the best face on Brixey's disinterest. "It's great for me," she says brightly. "It's not like we're competing against each other."

It's fair to ask whether this merry-go-round life is worth it. Sanchez's answer is yes. How many people can point as she can to authoring a school construction bill that would free federal funds to begin the massive overhaul of the nation's aging public schools? Fighting the good fight is what attracted her to politics in the first place, and it's what keeps her in the game.

With her own seat safe for 2002, Sanchez turned her attention to helping her younger sister (by ten years) win the Democratic primary in a newly created Hispanic-majority district in the Los Angeles area. Linda Sanchez is an attorney and labor activist who moved into the district with an eye toward running. Thanks to Loretta's efforts, Linda was by far the best-financed candidate in the race and easily won the March primary, making her a shoo-in for the seat in November. There have been brother acts on Capitol Hill, but Loretta and Linda Sanchez will be the first sisters to serve together in the Congress.

The growing political clout of Hispanic voters in California bodes well for Loretta Sanchez's future. She makes no secret of her interest in running statewide should a Senate seat become available. Her ability to raise money combined with her family's strong appeal to traditional, immigrant values could be a powerful combination. "My daughters know that education is a key to success," their mother, Maria Marcias Sanchez declared in a thirty-second, Spanish-language television spot for Linda's race. "How do I know? Because I taught them."

California, a pacesetter in American culture, has sent more women to Congress than any other state—twenty-nine to date—and may well be the state that produces the first female president or vice president. In the spring of 1998, with President Clinton embroiled in a sex scandal, news analysts talked about the prospect of a woman as president. A woman at least would be more discreet in her sexual behavior than Clinton had been. "This whole scandal will create more sympathy for putting a woman in the White House," said Robert Dallek, a Boston University historian. When Bob Dole touted his wife, Elizabeth, for the presidency, the *Patriot-News* in Harrisburg, Pennsylvania, editorialized in favor of a female president. The April 20 editorial pointed out that "both major parties would have to confront the problem of the all-male presidential club sooner rather than later." Among several "interesting comers," the paper listed California representative Zoe Lofgren.

Lofgren's press secretary immediately whipped up a press release headlined "President Lofgren?" and sent it to a number of media outlets. Lofgren, then a two-term member of Congress unknown outside of her district, seemed an unlikely presidential contender. Mentioning Lofgren said more about the dearth of realistic women contenders than it did about her.

Lofgren has since become better known, though she is not yet on anybody's short list for president or vice president. A lawyer and member of the House Judiciary Committee, she got a lot of airtime as a defender of Clinton during the impeachment proceedings. "If they [the Republicans] had come up with a case that the president engaged in behavior that threatens our constitutional form of government, he would be in trouble with me," she said in an interview. "But you can't afford to cause this kind of disruption over which body parts he touched. That is not what George Mason [one of the framers of the Constitution] had in mind."

A moderate Democrat, Lofgren was elected in 1994, the year of the Republican sweep, and demonstrated her staying power in the next two elections. Her seat is now rated safe. She is no political novice, having worked in Democratic politics since graduating in 1970 from Stanford University, first as a staffer on Capitol Hill, then as an elected member of her local board of supervisors. She attracted national attention when local officials barred her from describing herself as "county supervisor/mother" when she filed the papers for her candidacy for Congress. California law allows only the listing of an occupation. The resulting uproar gave Lofgren a platform to defend the unpaid work by women in the home, and provided the momentum for a campaign based on bettering the lives of women and children.

The daughter of a truck driver and a secretary, Lofgren speaks to and for the middle class. Yet the notion that she is a potential presidential candidate drew snickers and raised eyebrows on Capitol Hill. The newspaper *Roll Call* advised against printing bumper stickers just yet. But that didn't stop Lofgren, then fifty-two and in her prime, from handing out to supporters a color photo of her standing next to Vice President Gore on the steps of *Air Force Two*. She is waving and smiling, and, critics be damned, she looks like a credible running mate.

The role that serendipity plays in political life should not be underestimated. The 2000 presidential campaign spilled over into Florida with a disputed vote count and charges of favoritism, if not nepotism, in how the state tallied the election results. At the center of the debate was Katherine Harris, Florida's Secretary of State, who acting on her own authority ended the recount before it was complete, handing Bush an advantage, or so it seemed, in the state where his brother, Jeb Bush, was governor. Harris was vilified by Gore supporters, praised by Republican partisans, and caricatured on Saturday Night Live for her heavy makeup. The publicity boosted her name recognition and made her an appealing candidate for Congress in the heavily Republican Gulf Coast town of Sarasota that is home to wealthy retirees from the upscale suburbs of northern cities. The outgoing Republican, Dan Miller, is a pro-choice moderate on cultural issues with a conservative economic voting record, a mix that is popular in the district. Miller pledged to term-limit himself after five terms, and Harris conveniently found herself waiting in the wings. Her election in November 2002 promised to be a lot smoother than the one she presided over. She raised more than $2 million from admirers around the country, and easily defeated her Democratic opponent, who had trouble breaking $700,000. Her fairytale story continued when she became the luckiest member of the 2002 freshman class by drawing No. 1 in the office lottery, entitling her to first pick of space among the 52 new members of the House.

THIRTEEN

Hurrying History

Barbara Lee never holds a dinner party without a program, some-thing important to talk about. On a chilly evening in early December 1997, the topic for discussion was "Why Not a Woman?" Lee, a Boston philanthropist, had just given half a million dollars to pro-mote the idea of a woman president by 2008. The seventy guests in her Brookline mansion had come to discuss the merits of a ten-year public-relations campaign to get the nation comfortable with the no-tion of a "Madam President." It was an eclectic group of academics, members of the media, political activists, and feminists, including sev-eral potential funders of the project.

The mood was festive. During the cocktail hour, Lee's teenage son, Robbie, and his jazz band played background music as the invited guests admired Lee's art collection, ranging from old masters to mod-ern. Later, they examined Madison Avenue–style storyboards with prototypes of ads[1] for the campaign to stimulate interest in electing a woman as president. One display pictured President Nixon, President Clinton, and House Speaker Gingrich with the caption "Heels in of-fice." The flip side had a pair of women's shoes with the same caption. Another showed a series of pictures: a child getting vaccinated with red letters saying "There will never be a cure for polio"; a portrait of President Kennedy with red letters saying "There will never be an Irish Catholic president"; lastly, a blank frame with red letters saying "There will never be a woman president. . . . Why not a woman pres-ident?" Another mockup featured a photograph of Eleanor Roosevelt

---

[1] The ads were compiled by Dorit Byrne, the CEO of FashionBug, a women's cloth-ing manufacturer, and creator of the highly successful "The Softer Side of Sears" ad campaign.

accompanied by a list of her accomplishments as First Lady with the punch line "Imagine what she could have done as president."

Over a sumptuous meal of glazed filet of salmon, the guests, three-quarters of them women, took turns identifying themselves and telling something about their backgrounds. When it was her turn, Lee confessed sheepishly that she had been a cheerleader in high school. Several other women giggled with relief as they unburdened themselves of the same secret, then concluded that, contrary to conventional thinking in the women's liberation movement, the cheerleader credential must be a sign of early feminist inclinations. George Stephanopoulos, the former Clinton aide turned pundit, chimed in with a fact not listed in his résumé: As a teenager, he had declared himself a Republican.

After dessert, the guests voted on the names of possible female candidates. Not wanting to appear partisan, the dinner organizers had left Hillary Rodham Clinton's name off the ballot. Enough people wrote her in that the First Lady was the winner.

People change, and so do the times. A poll commissioned for the White House Project, as it eventually came to be known, found that 76 percent of the public would vote for a woman as president, but, Lee says, "I don't trust the numbers." She suspects at least some of the people who tell pollsters they would vote for a woman do so only because they do not want to appear sexist. A similar phenomenon exists for African-American candidates, who regularly poll higher than their actual votes.

Even if a substantial majority would consider voting for a woman as president, the question is, which woman? Focus groups conducted in the spring of 1998 surfaced only three names: Elizabeth Dole, Hillary Clinton, and talk show host Oprah Winfrey. "We figured that no one knew the names of anybody else," says Lee. Women without college educations were the most responsive to the idea of a woman president. But when asked to list the names of women they'd like to see as president, they were stymied, and it embarrassed them. They wanted to know choices.

Introducing the public to a rich variety of accomplished women—not only in politics but also in business, medicine, education, and the military—became the goal of the newly named White House Project. The original slogan "Why Not a Woman?" was discarded after it tested badly in focus groups. The breezy phrase made gender stand out more as a negative, and voters found it confusing. Public relations is about positive thinking, and Barbara Lee wanted very much for her life, and her money, to make a difference. "Boston was the start of the

American Revolution," she says. "The second American Revolution started in my living room."

Lee is not a woman given to modesty, either about herself or her beliefs. Wispy thin with blond hair and delicate bangs, she is as intense about her mission as the early suffragists were about theirs. Her family practiced "righteous giving" according to Jewish religious tenets, and ingrained in her at an early age an impulse for social change. A nasty divorce in mid-life left her more intent than ever on making her mark in the world, and with the financial resources to do it. The agreement Lee reached in 1995 with her husband of twenty-seven years, the leveraged buyout king Thomas Lee, left her with $200 million plus a continued stake in the company they had built together. Barbara and Thomas Lee had always decided together which social and cultural causes would be the beneficiaries of their generosity. After they separated in 1992, Barbara Lee started making gifts on her own. When her alma mater, the all-women Simmons College, asked for money to build a new gymnasium, the former cheerleader turned them down. She offered instead to fund an Institute for Leadership and Change with programs dedicated to advancing women. In this and other gifts she would make, she wanted her money to empower people to change society.

Until the divorce forced her to take charge of her life, Lee had been a traditional wife with feminist yearnings. When her contemporaries protested in the streets over the Vietnam War, she was already married. Eighty percent of her 1967 class at Simmons married and had children within two years of graduation. Lee's first child, a son, was born in 1971. Struggling with the stresses and strains of motherhood, she had what she calls "an epiphany" when she spotted an advertising insert announcing a new publication, *Ms.* magazine, with an article headlined "I Want a Wife." On her son's first birthday in 1972, instead of handing out party favors to the babies, who were too young to appreciate them anyway, she bought every mother a copy of the premiere issue of *Ms.* "That was mine and their introduction to the women's movement," she says proudly. Despite her qualms about motherhood, Lee was ecstatic when, after several miscarriages, a pregnancy "took," and her second son was born in 1981.

In the argument that became the foundation of her divorce settlement, Lee claimed she had been beside her husband every step of the journey from lending officer at a bank to financial entrepreneur. She credited her college roommate's husband with generating the idea in 1974 for a leveraged buyout business, which uses borrowed funds to buy up businesses, then sells them at a profit. Her husband did the spreadsheets, and she did "the people work," which included sizing up everything from prospective employees to potential deals. They struck it rich in several lucrative leveraged buyouts, most notably General Nutrition, Playtex, and Snapple Beverage. In his twenty-fifth reunion report for Harvard in 1990, Tom Lee described his wife and two sons as "great personal acquistions" in a lifetime of acquiring "lots of companies, houses, cars, boats and planes." Foreshadowing the discontent that would eventually end his marriage, Lee said that he yearned for a simpler life where he would need "just one key."

The marriage had not been idyllic for some time. Barbara Lee had quietly filed for divorce in 1987, only to drop the proceeding in 1989. If her husband concentrated on acquisitions, her refuge was activity. A human dynamo, she had days so jam-packed that when she gave up having a paid job, her family couldn't tell the difference. She remembers filling out a form for one of her sons to attend a private school. In the space for profession, she was going to write "Homemaker." Her sons laughed at the notion of their mother as a homemaker. They suggested a better label was "Arts and Social Justice Activist," a description Lee happily adopted.

Lee had given money over the years to the Ms. Foundation, an independently funded spinoff of *Ms.* magazine, and she credits executive director Marie Wilson with the idea for the White House Project. Wilson in turn drew on research done by Laura Liswood, a Harvard Business School graduate and founder of the Council of Women World Leaders. Liswood traveled to fifteen countries, spending mostly her own money, to interview women presidents and prime ministers to document women's leadership around the globe. When Liswood shows a video of her interviews to American women, their reaction is often one of anger that the U.S. system is so far behind in promoting women as leaders. Liswood's research, Lee's money, and Wilson's nose for publicity combined to launch the White House Project at a press conference on June 11, 1998, at the National Press Club. Wilson had spearheaded the highly successful Take Our Daughters to Work Day in 1992, and is known as somebody who is good at making a media splash. She had taken over the Ms. Foundation fourteen years earlier and had built the endowment from $450,000 to $15 million. Take Our Daughters to Work Day had been a smash hit that few people connected to Ms. or the feminist movement. "If you put out something the public sees as really important, they're not going to be as interested in tracking down its feminist roots," says Wilson.

The White House Project created a ballot listing twenty women[2] with various occupations who exhibit leadership skills and are plausible presidential candidates. The ballots were inserted in major national magazines like *Parade* and *Glamour*, posted on the Internet, and handed out at locations as diverse as housing projects and Wall Street. The twenty women were chosen to demonstrate the diversity in women's accomplishments, not their political ambition or their prospects as a candidate. In that sense, the ballot ranged from the real to the surreal. It included three women from the U.S. Senate, a sitting governor (Whitman of New Jersey), the dean of Ohio State University's College of Medicine, a former astronaut, the president of Maxwell House Coffee, the first female three-star general in the U.S. Army, and the former chief of the Cherokee Nation.

Lee remembers her first call-in radio show to promote the project. She had not done much public speaking, aside from events at her son's school or at Simmons, and she had been assured that the interviewer would be friendly. He introduced her by saying, "This group wants to elect a woman president. I don't know if that's good idea or not." Lee sensed she could be in for a rough ride. "Are you the National Organization for Witches?" the first caller wanted to know. Lee stuck to the script. The group was bipartisan, Republican men and women, and Democratic men and women. She was so sincere the caller, a man, had no response. The second caller was a woman, who said, "Great idea. I'd like to run." By the end of the show, the host concluded his grandmother would have made a good president.

The ballot project is like chicken soup for the sisters. It probably won't hurt. But why would the Ms. Foundation, the cradle of the fem-

---

[2] The twenty women: Carol Bellamy, head of UNICEF, former Peace Corps director; Carol Browner, administrator of the Environmental Protection Agency; Linda Chavez-Thompson, vice president of the AFL-CIO Executive Council; Hillary Rodham Clinton, First Lady of the United States; Elizabeth Hanford Dole, former president of the American Red Cross, former secretary of labor and transportation; Maria Echaveste, White House deputy chief of staff; Marian Wright Edelman, founder and president of the Children's Defense Fund; Dianne Feinstein, U.S. senator from California; Ann Fudge, president of Maxwell House, Bernadine Healy, dean of Ohio State University's College of Medicine; Kay Bailey Hutchison, U.S. senator from Texas; Mae C. Jemison, physician and engineer, first black woman astronaut in space; Claudia Kennedy, U.S. Army's first female three-star general; Mary Landrieu, U.S. senator from Louisiana; Wilma Mankiller, former head of the Cherokee Nation; Angela Oh, attorney, member of the advisory board of President Clinton's Initiative on Race; Judith Rodin, president of the University of Pennsylvania; Donna Shalala, secretary of health and human services; Olympia Snowe, U.S. senator from Maine; Christine Todd Whitman, governor of New Jersey.

inist movement, promote women for the highest office who, in the privacy of a voting booth, feminists would never support? Gloria Steinem, the founder of *Ms.* magazine, was one of the guests at Lee's dinner party when the idea was introduced. Minutes taken by feminist writer Letty Cottin Pogrebin quote Steinem warning against elevating "someone who looks like us but acts like them." The skeptics were in the minority. Pogrebin writes that most of the conferees seemed motivated "by some deep private yearning, a vision fueled by a lifetime of dreams. They seemed to share the belief that on the day that a woman is elected president of the United States, women's voices will break the sound barrier and little girls will hear new music and both will know that from then on, anything they imagine for themselves can become a reality."

Wilson's goal is not to identify Ms. Right, or to find the female version of the founding fathers, but to get the public used to seeing the kinds of women who could someday be president. Wilson grew up in the racially segregated South, and her activism is fueled by her life experience. After graduating from the University of Delaware in 1964 with a degree in philosophy, she fashioned a "civil rights ministry" to work with poor African-American girls at the Presbyterian church where her husband was choral director. By 1968, when the couple moved to Des Moines, Iowa, Wilson had given birth to four children in three years. A fifth child, an African-American boy with cerebral palsy, was adopted later. Wilson taught preschool and got into politics because she was concerned about the lack of decent child care for low- and middle-income working mothers. She was the first woman elected to the Des Moines City Council, but, frustrated by the glacial pace of politics, served for only one year.

Wilson has seen the power of mass-marketing techniques, and believes if that approach was applied to politics, a climate of acceptance for a woman president could be achieved, much the way consumers are enticed to receive a new product.

Claudia Kennedy returned to her Pentagon office late one afternoon in the spring of 1998 to find a message from Marie Wilson of the Ms. Foundation. "The message said something about names," Kennedy recalls. As the army's first female three-star general, Kennedy assumed Wilson wanted her to recommend promising women in defense and national security. By the time she returned the call the next day, Kennedy had compiled a list of some two dozen women. To her surprise, she was told her help wasn't needed. The call was simply to inform her that she would be one of the twenty women on the White House Project ballot, and that a press release was being prepared. "I don't know what they would have said if I didn't want to do it," she says. "I thought it was a great honor. I am myself a feminist. I think it's a great label. I'm very proud of my service in the army. I think thirty-one years in the army is exactly what a feminist ought to be doing."

When the ballots were tallied at the end of the year, Kennedy finished in the top five, the only unknown to score that high with the public. The other winners—Hillary Rodham Clinton, Elizabeth Dole, Christine Whitman, and Dianne Feinstein—all benefited from high name recognition. Kennedy thinks her showing has to do with "respect for the way the military chooses its leaders." In an era when less than 7 percent of the public has ever served in the military, people still look to the military for heroes, and get their impressions of women in military life from movies like *Private Benjamin* and *G.I. Jane.*

A female lieutenant from the army's public information office escorted us through the Pentagon, punching in a security code at the door to enter Kennedy's suite of offices. Desks with uniformed personnel lined each side of the corridor leading to her spacious office. Paperwork is organized into neat piles on Kennedy's executive-sized desk. A high-speed computer purrs nearby. A painting that depicts American colonists battling the British hangs on one wall. Kennedy has a round and friendly face framed by soft blond hair. Three white stars outlined in gold braid glimmer on her shoulder. She is wearing a light green shirt under a darker, army-green V-neck sweater. It is mid-morning, and she is sipping a Diet Coke without caffeine from the can.

As the army's deputy chief of staff for intelligence, Kennedy was charged with projecting future threats out to about 2020 or 2025, determining who are the likely enemies (or "peer competitors," as Kennedy calls them) and what resources will be needed to combat them. She was one of only forty-five three-star generals in the army. Her chances of being promoted to four-star general were "very slim," she told us, because there are only a dozen of them, and a suitable slot would have to open up. Still, she held out hope of becoming the first woman to achieve the top rank. Instead, Kennedy was told that her current assignment, due to end in May 2000, would be her last job. Then it was revealed that Kennedy had filed a sexual harassment complaint against a fellow general. In an interview on the March day in 2000 the story broke, Kennedy insisted her retirement is "totally unconnected" and praised the army for its handling of the matter. "No matter how senior you get, you can be subject to sexual harassment," she said. The incident of alleged unwanted touching occurred in 1996, and Kennedy, then a two-star general, complained informally to her superiors. She took the additional step of lodging a formal complaint in late 1999 when she learned of the offending general's impending advancement.

"This is not a man-woman thing," she says. "This is about people who behave appropriately in the workplace, and those who don't." Kennedy's rise through the ranks had been a matter of pride for the male-dominated army. But there was tension. News accounts reported "Pentagon insiders" griping about Kennedy's competence and credentials. She was said to be "Hillary Rodham Clinton's favorite general." One sergeant said that she "giggled, much like a little girl." Kennedy was not surprised by the attacks. In the past, she had counseled senior women to deal with sexual harassment quietly, "because you will face damage to your credibility and authority for saying it aloud because a bunch of people won't believe you." The *Washington Post* noted, "The high-profile confrontation appears likely to bring a sour note to the end" of Kennedy's thirty-two–year career. "I'm at peace with this," says Kennedy. Once the facts are aired, she believes, her critics "will look like idiots . . . because we are on very solid ground."

The case was resolved when the accused, Army Maj. Gen. Larry Smith, retired soon after, in September 2000, with a reprimand for conduct "unbecoming an officer and a gentleman." A decorated veteran with three tours in Vietnam, Smith, then fifty-five, had been nominated to be the Army's deputy inspector general. The job would have involved overseeing investigations into a variety of alleged misconduct, including sexual harassment. Kennedy felt she could no longer remain silent if it meant elevating Smith to such a sensitive position.

Kennedy never thought about a political career before, but making the cover of *Parade* magazine as a potential presidential candidate got her attention. It also caught Ann Richards' eye. The former Texas governor invited Kennedy to come see her in her Washington office. Nurturing new political talent is Richards' avocation. In her colorful way, Richards tried to size up Kennedy's interest and potential. If you run for political office, she told her, you either tell the voters what you're going to do for them in the future, create fear about your opponent, or simply say, "This is who I am and what I stand for." The last, she confided, is the least preferable way, and it's the approach she took when George W. Bush challenged her for governor in Texas. "I thought I had done a wonderful job, and I said so." She lost the election.

Kennedy describes herself as a military brat. She was born in Germany, where her father was stationed while in the army, and like most military families, the Kennedys moved a lot. "I grew up everywhere," she says. Her father was conservative politically, but his mother had worked, and he encouraged his daughter to pursue a profession, although he never suggested that she follow in his footsteps. She remembers coming home one day in the seventh grade and declaring she wanted to be a nurse. "Why not be a doctor?" he said. That meant taking algebra a year early and Latin rather than Spanish. She happily complied, and did well until eleventh-grade biology when she couldn't bring herself to kill and dissect a rabbit.

Kennedy remembers being intrigued from an early age by the world of work, whether it was her grandmother's real estate office in Memphis, or the television images of Eve Arden, the star of "Our Miss Brooks," who portrayed a feisty high school teacher running circles around a hapless male principal. But it took Kennedy a while to come into her own when she was in college during the turbulent sixties. She majored in philosophy at Southwestern, a small liberal arts school in Memphis that is now Rhodes College. Her grandfather had taught math there and also coached football. Kennedy was not a leader in college. She joined a sorority and had a few good friends. But it was a confusing time for her because of the campus protests against Vietnam. Her father was in Vietnam at the time. "I wasn't about to break ranks with my family," she says. "Although I wasn't sure about the war itself, I did know that if my country is at war, I serve my country."

In the spring of Kennedy's senior year of college, she had to make a decision about her future. Respect among young people for the military was at an all-time low. But an army recruiting coupon in *Cosmopolitan*, a savvy woman's magazine, caught her eye. The ad featured a female soldier with an attractive man, and promised prospective recruits foreign adventure. Kennedy filled out the coupon, and mailed it in. While her male classmates scrambled to avoid military service, Kennedy enlisted in the Women's Army Corps. "If you are a feminist and you believe you're an equal citizen, then you also have equal obligation to serve your country," she says. "Is a boy's life less valuable than a girl's? And what do you say to girls, 'We're in a fight for national survival, but you'll have to just stay back'? That's excluding women as adults."

Kennedy figured she'd spend two years in the military, but the role of women in society was undergoing a transformation and the military was no exception. The opportunities offered her were too good to pass up. By 1978, the Women's Army Corps had been phased out, and most of the female officers were given their choice of assignment in the regular army. Kennedy chose intelligence. She says it helped her gain acceptance among her male peers when she finished fourth or fifth out of seventy in the two-mile run. "It meant everything to me—and to them," she says. "I trained hard for it, and men trained me. There weren't any other women."

At first she wasn't ambitious enough to say she wanted anything beyond battalion command. Once she accomplished that, she said she would retire with a smile on her face. But the battalion command came and went, and soon she was competing to command a brigade, the last step in the narrowing pyramid to become a general. She kept getting promoted ahead of her peers, men in most instances. In 1993, she was named a general officer and got her first star. Acceptance became less of a problem with each promotion. "We wear our rank right here," she says, pointing to the three stars on her shoulder.

When allegations of sexual harassment at the army's Aberdeen training facility surfaced in 1996, Kennedy served on the task force that did the investigation. A hotline installed by the army for women to report abuse recorded more than 8,000 calls and resulted in 341 criminal investigations. Some of the charges were forty years old. Kennedy knew that sexual harassment had been pervasive in the past, but the volume of calls indicated the problem was still widespread. "I was very surprised by the numbers," she says. Unlike the navy, which dragged its feet investigating sexual misconduct at a "Tailhook" convention, the army got high marks for taking the explosive allegations seriously and disciplining the offending officers.

Residual resentment of Kennedy surfaced in early 1999 when a presentation she made about diversity to a group of senior noncommissioned officers drew negative publicity in the *Richmond Times Dispatch*. The Consideration of Others program, or COO, was started by the commandant of cadets at West Point and expanded throughout the army to help people of different backgrounds (and gender) work comfortably with each other. An article with anonymous quotes and then an editorial ridiculed the teaching of political correctness in a training regimen preparing warriors for combat, and pointed out that Kennedy "has never seen nor ever will see the face of battle." Her height or lack thereof (she's five-foot-four) was also cited. "Like it has anything to do with anything," she flares. "Let's just point out that height has nothing to do with courage, candor, commitment, competence." She suspects her critics never served with women colleagues and are out of touch with today's army, which is 15 percent female. After defending the COO program at some length, she concludes that the critics don't merit an answer. "They are terminally insecure about their own manhood," she says.

Asked how women and men differ as military leaders, she relates a favorite anecdote, warning, "Be careful how you write it. It can really inflame people." She said that when she visited a military installation and needed directions at the gate, the female MP (military police) at the guard post was courteous but vague, leaving Kennedy more confused, whereas the male MP offered precise instructions. Kennedy observed that the woman did not focus her full attention on giving directions, but continued to wave through other cars while checking their identification, and detaining a driver who could not immediately produce an ID. "She was multitasking," says Kennedy. "And the man? Saddam Hussein could have walked through with a stinger missile on his shoulder, and he wouldn't have known it. And I say to people, 'Who would you rather have at the gate?' Before they give me their answer, I say, 'You want both.' You want someone who can be focused and direct and get closure. You also want someone with a broader view who can juggle multiple tasks and make a quick decision about what's important."

Generalizing broadly, she thinks women are better at the balancing act. But she can point to women leaders who fit the male model, and men who do not practice command-and-control leadership. In the end, she thinks the role of gender in leadership is exaggerated. Women can do the job. The long audition should be over. "I'm single. I don't have children," she says. "The real pioneer will be the lieutenant general who comes in here next and does this job with a husband and children, who brings all the same things that a man does." There were thirty-seven women serving as active-duty generals or admirals during Kennedy's time in the military. The army, Kennedy points out, had yet to promote a mother to general while she was there. The navy had promoted three mothers to admiral, but all were in the special medical or support branches, presumably less taxing from a military standpoint. The air force had one mother who was a general. The difficulty of blending work and family is that much harder for women in the military, where the combination of rigid work schedules, unpredictable travel demands, and constant uprooting deter all but the most committed.

Kennedy watched the army transform itself after the Vietnam War into an institution that commands respect the world over. She sees no reason why that same concerted effort shouldn't be applied to the country's problems. She cites two issues that she wishes she could spend the next forty years dealing with. One is "getting children fed and loved and educated." The other is shoring up failing nation-states, the root of disorder and violent ethnic clashes that she anticipates will spread in the next century. "We don't recognize a way to rewrite boundaries in any way other than through force," she says. "We can see these situations developing. But we wait until we are absolutely with our backs up against the wall, then we use the military. We ought to look ahead five years, and get things in place. But most people currently in office don't expect to be there five years from now."

When told she has the makings of a campaign speech, she responds with a hearty laugh. "I'm very tempted," she says. After her picture appeared on *Parade's* cover, she got several probing phone calls from emissaries for the political parties trying to gauge her interest in running for office. One person in particular laid it on the line. He had run for office himself, and he told her, "The first order of business is to raise money. Forget substantive issues, they're about the last thing you deal with." The caller followed with a description of what it is like to raise money: The candidate sits by a phone with a list of names and phone numbers and starts at the top. "Hello, Joe," she says, mimicking a candidate's cadence. "As you know, I'm running for Congress in such and such a district. I'm trying to raise the money, and I wonder if I can put you down for $1,000." After a little back and forth, the candidate closes the sale: "Good, Joe, thank you so much. I'm going to put you down for that. In fact, let me transfer you to Susan. She's sitting right here. She'll give you some specific information." Then the candidate picks up the phone and dials the next number. "If you don't have the stomach for that, forget it," says Kennedy.

Soon after Kennedy's June 2000 retirement ceremony, the buzz began that she would challenge Virginia Sen. John Warner. Democrats thought he might be vulnerable, and if she didn't succeed in unseating him, she could position herself as the heir apparent. Warner, seventy-five, is well regarded in the state, but he can't serve forever. Kennedy's military credentials would neutralize some of the advantage he held as a former Secretary of the Navy and the ranking Republican on the Senate Armed Services Committee. Kennedy had just gotten her exploratory committee up and running when the terrorist attacks of 9/11 occurred. The plane that plunged into the Pentagon destroyed her old office, and Kennedy was one of the few women who appeared on television news shows offering expert commentary after the attacks.

Politics seemed peripheral for a time after 9/11 as the nation sought to recover from the devastating attacks. Kennedy found it hard to raise money, and she didn't have the stomach for a partisan race. She suspended her exploratory committee and quietly ended her Senate challenge.

Kennedy is no Colin Powell in the sense of evoking a clamor for her candidacy. The former head of the Joint Chiefs of Staff had the nation enthralled with the idea of his running for president until he took himself out of the 1996 race. But the response Kennedy generated suggests the kind of female candidates who could do well if coaxed into the arena.

As ideas go, promoting women from different walks of life as potential presidents is nice, but not terribly realistic, and the White House Project fell into some disrepair. Barbara Lee felt she had been relegated to the role of donor, and abruptly resigned from the board. Wilson was overheard at Gloria Steinem's sixty-fifth birthday party on March 25, 1999, explaining that Lee's departure was both good news and bad news. The tension was over, but so was the financial support that Lee had provided. A lot of the breakup centered on control and authority. Wilson is a self-admitted control freak, and Lee understandably wanted her own work and her own voice after subsidizing others for most of her life. Lee created her own family foundation, which in the spring of 2001 produce "keys to the Governor's office," a guide for women who want to run that offers practical advice on everything from demonstrating leadership to handling family matters.

The White House Project pressed ahead with its goal of a woman president by focusing on the vice-presidential sweepstakes for 2004. It had publicized fifteen women as potential running mates for the 2000 candidates. With a few notable exceptions such as the army's Claudia Kennedy, Elizabeth Dole, and then Stanford professor Condoleezza Rice, who had served on the first President Bush's national security staff, the women who made the list all held public office, the likeliest place for a president to look for a running mate.[3]

The vice presidency is a gateway to the presidency, but a woman hasn't appeared on a major party ticket since 1984. Former Rep. Pat Schroeder, speaking at a "Madam President" symposium at the Uni-

---

[3] The 2000 Vice Presidential Ballot in alphabetical order: Elizabeth Dole, Jennifer Dunn, Dianne Feinstein, Jane Hull, Kay Bailey Hutchison, Claudia Kennedy, Mary Landrieu, Patsy Mink, Gloria Molina, Condoleezza Rice, Jeanne Shaheen, Olympia Snowe, Kathleen Kennedy Townsend, Maxine Waters, Christine Todd Whitman.

versity of Missouri, Kansas City in March 2002, said she is not optimistic about the prospects for a woman president. Asked when the ultimate glass ceiling might be shattered, Schroeder predicted 2020 "at the earliest," which would be one hundred years after women got the right to vote. There were groans from the mostly female audience. With one exception, she went on to say, and that is if President Bush decides to put Condoleezza Rice on the ticket in 2004. The groans changed to oohs and ahs, as though the skies had parted and there had been a revelation from above. Marie Wilson noted that Rice, Bush's national security advisor, while competent and authoritative and the first female and African-American to hold the job, was not "warm as toast," which voters demand from women politicians. Still, nobody could question her toughness. And if the war against terrorism went reasonably well, she could claim her share of credit.

The glacial pace of progress for women in politics frustrates Schroeder. "I thought surely by the twenty-first century we'd have more than sixty-two women in the House and thirteen senators," she says. "This is evolving, and I guess I'm a revolutionary." Since women make up more than half of the voting population, and women's votes are courted by politicians, why is it, Schroeder wondered, women haven't demanded their fair share of political power? "Women don't feel entitled, and until we do, we're not going to do much about it," she said. "If women spent half what they spent on make-up last year on a candidate, we could have a woman in the White House."

Four years of heading the White House Project challenged many of Marie Wilson's assumptions. She came away from a focus group testing candidate ads shaken by the voters' insistence that a woman running for office immediately take a firm stand, especially if the woman is older. "And let's face it, a woman who is going to be governor is mostly an older woman. The dials would plummet the minute she hit the screen unless she said something like, 'I told my party. . .' " These voter reactions echoed what Wilson was hearing from the Sunday talk-show producers and bookers when a White House Project survey revealed how few women appear as guests. The bookers, who are mostly young women, said they look for interview subjects who will take a stand, who have "juice." They complain that women officeholders are always "on message" and less likely to say what they really think, which makes for a boring interview. Male politicians are also carefully scripted, Wilson points out. The subtle double standard determines whether women are seen and how often and whether they are portrayed with authority.

Women have to show they're effective but still appealing. Some of the ads the professionals raved about landed with a thud in American living rooms. One showed a candidate playing pool, a scene designed to convey her ability to play a man's game with nuance and finesse. But voters doubted she really played pool, and they found the image unappealing. She lost the race. "You can't step over the appeal line," says Wilson. "There is some fine line we're asking women to walk where they're competent and in charge but they're saying 'I'm all girl.'"

A believer in the power of cultural images, Wilson is counting on Hollywood to help change the climate for women's leadership. If Martin Sheen in his role as president on the popular drama, "West Wing," were to put his national security advisor, played by Anna Deavere Smith, on the ticket as vice president, that would send a powerful message about what's possible. "Seeing women in these cultural settings makes an enormous difference for people in conveying who's important, who we can trust, and who's a hero," says Wilson.

Ninety percent of men who run for office do so because they are asked to run compared to only 30 percent of women, a disparity that colors women's expectations about political life. Karen Strickler, the founder of Fifty Plus One, an organization that trains pro-choice women in campaign skills, remembers how angry she was when 1992 became the "year of the woman" because six women were elected to the U.S. Senate. "When women still are there in such shockingly small numbers, it was hard for me to understand why that was such a big deal," she says. "I wondered why we weren't aiming higher."

Strickler, in her mid-forties, is a handsome woman, tall, blond, and earnest in manner. She brushes a stray lock of hair out of her eyes with the air of an Olympic swimmer readying for the competition. As an adolescent growing up on a farm in Carroll County, Maryland, Strickler was only vaguely aware of the women's movement. Her father was a father-knows-best conservative, and her mother an awakening feminist, a combination typical of the era. Brought up on farm chores and a philosophy of self-reliance, "I caught the spirit," she says of her mother's early feminism.

Lecturing students in early 1999 at Hood College for women in Frederick, Maryland, Strickler labored hard to generate a response. "Do you realize that my mother's generation is the first generation born with the right to vote?" she said, practically shouting. The young women sat slumped in their seats. "Doesn't that make you angry?" she pressed. The students looked glazed. She talked about how women are stuck in the status of "petitioners," depending on men to protect their right to an abortion rather than making that decision themselves. She could see that she might have offended some antiabortion women in the audience, but she was trying to find issues they could relate to on a personal level. "Unless more women run for office, we'll have to rely on men to pass the Equal Rights Amendment," she declared with all the fire she could muster. The puzzled looks on the women's faces were answer enough. "Equal rights? What equal rights? They didn't know what I was talking about. They slumped down farther in their chairs. I think they were very happy to see me go," she says.

Strickler comes out of a tradition of progressive politics, beginning in 1986, when she worked in the Maryland office of NARAL (National Abortion Rights Action League), and then became director of the National Endangered Species Coalition. She noticed a pattern that women were generally more progressive then men, but few women got elected or even ran for office. "When I began looking at the numbers, I was startled and appalled," she says. "I wondered whether politics would be different if there were a higher percentage of women." Women as a rule seemed more likely to share her priorities of issues relating to children and families, abortion rights, pay equity, and protecting the environment.

A turning point for Strickler came in 1990 during an eight-day filibuster over abortion rights on the floor of the Maryland State Senate. Maryland is a pro-choice state, and she believed that the anti-choice legislators who were acting as obstructionists could be defeated in the next election. She told an aide to the Democratic president of the senate that she intended to defeat three of the lawmakers, all Democrats. He told Strickler she had about as much chance of succeeding as she would winning the presidency of the United States.

Strickler recruited candidates from the Maryland House of Delegates to challenge incumbent senators in the Democratic primary. She had done grassroots politicking and knew how to get out the vote. She wrote campaign plans and helped implement them. She sat on the steering committee of each campaign. All three of her candidates won, ending the careers of the three incumbents she had targeted.

The experience convinced Strickler that running an effective campaign is not difficult, and that she could teach the skill to other women. One of the first people she approached to serve on the advisory board of Fifty Plus One was Kathleen Kennedy Townsend, who said yes so fast that Strickler almost didn't know how to respond. She needn't have worried because the positive mood didn't last long. When Strickler pointed out that the organization would be bipartisan, Townsend said, "Forget it." She wasn't interested in helping to elect Republican women.

An experienced fund-raiser, Strickler thought that foundations and women's groups would line up to back a training program for female candidates. But she found that raising money to train "beginner women" in politics was harder than anything she'd done before professionally. The established women's groups viewed Strickler as an upstart threatening their turf. The head of one group chided her for "errors" in her initial query letter. "They're not errors," Strickler countered. "They're differences in opinion." What rattled the founding mothers was Strickler's blunt assessment of the scanty number of women in Congress. By failing to pay homage to the early, hard-won gains, Strickler seemed to be criticizing the women's movement. At a public forum at American University, NOW president Patricia Ireland responded to a question from Strickler about promoting more women for office, "I don't want someone just because they wear a skirt." Strickler discovered that feminists were reluctant to push too hard for women in public office because they were afraid of electing the wrong women. Betty Friedan, the godmother of the women's movement, agreed to give the keynote address at one of Strickler's two-day training sessions. Strickler was thrilled until the famously cranky Friedan began her remarks saying, "Fifty Plus One, that's a lot of crap."

Strickler started Fifty Plus One in 1994 when conservatism was on the upswing. It is generally easier to generate funds for grassroots activism when the political climate is hostile. Usually that's when foundations are eager to fund progressive causes. But Strickler fared no better in the foundation community. They told her she didn't have enough of a track record, and that other women's organizations were doing training. She finds it ironic that the U.S. government provides money for groups like hers to train women in foreign countries to run for office.

A study by the National Women's Political Caucus shows that when women run, they win in percentages as high as men. "The next question," says Strickler, "is what does it take to get them to run? My answer is training, technical support, and the money to win. Unless those resources are there, women won't run."

Strickler has trained women in three states: her native Maryland; Massachusetts, where few women hold office; and Virginia, where conservatism has taken hold. Her curriculum is straightforward: (1) message development and delivery (who you are, how you tell people about your candidacy, how to develop a message); (2) grass-roots organization and connecting with voters; and (3) fund-raising. She has trained five hundred women over four years, and knows of only six who have actually run for office. Five of those won, all in minor offices. There may be others she doesn't know about, but it's a long, lonely slog for teacher and pupils. Strickler asked on the first day, "How many of you are thinking about running for office?" Of the thirty women enrolled in her opening session, only one raised her hand. Strickler was beside herself trying to figure out what was going on. Why did these women sign up for campaign training if they had no intention of running? At the end of the second day, she asked the same question. This time, almost three-quarters of the women raised their hands. The pattern repeated itself in subsequent training sessions. "Women want to make sure they know everything they need to know before they're willing to say they're even considering a run for public office," she says.

The reluctance to commit also has to do with the seasons of life. Women in their reproductive and family-raising years are wary of getting involved in public life because of the demands. Strickler, who is married and has a young child, is asked all the time whether she would run herself. She used to duck the question by saying that what she does affects more women than just herself. But she finally reevaluated that position and decided that if she was to continue encouraging other women to run, she should try it herself. Strickler didn't overreach, stuck close to home, and won election as treasurer of the Wyngate Citizens Association, her neighborhood organization. "I defeated an incumbent," she says proudly.

Relative to running for Congress, the stakes were small, almost laughably so, but the lessons learned universal. "I'm perceived as someone who is good at self-promotion," says Strickler. "But it made my stomach do an absolute flip." At the same time, her opponent, knowing Strickler's focus on electing women to public office, accused her of wanting to use the treasurer's post as a springboard to run for the U.S. Senate—or even the presidency. It is a well-worn tactic to paint a woman with the dark brush of careerism when a man's ambition is taken for granted and not subject to scrutiny. A woman seeking power is still enough of an oddity that she must surely have some ulterior motive.

Would she do it again? "Not especially," says Strickler. "I know how to run, how to raise money, how to go door-to-door, and how to communicate with people. But it's so hard to get out there and say, 'Hi, vote for me because I'm special.'"

Winning the election as treasurer of the Wyngate Citizens Association puts Strickler one up on Jean Elliott Brown, whose first political race was a run for Congress in Florida. Enticing consumers to try new products is how she earns her living. A public relations and marketing consultant living in south Florida, Brown introduced the country to Post Waffle Crisp and to General Foods International Kahlua Coffee flavor. She used some of the same techniques to introduce her candidacy for Congress. "I always did my PR with a little bit of hoke," she says, laughing. "I come from nowhere. I have no background in politics. I have no money. In order to be taken seriously, I have to create a buzz."

Brown ran against Mark Foley, a three-term Republican congressman who a year before the election had already raised $1 million. When Brown informed the head of the West Palm Beach Democratic party of her intentions, he was underwhelmed. Mimicking his reaction, Brown checks her watch and says, "Excuse me, get me a real candidate. I don't have time for you." His tone was one of disdain. How could she contemplate going to Congress when she'd never even run for dog-catcher?

Brown's political activism began during the impeachment fight in 1998 when she supported a petition effort to persuade Congress to censure President Clinton for his behavior, and go back to doing the nation's business. Names were collected over the Internet, and Brown carried the "MoveOn.org" petitions to Foley's office. The *Palm Beach Post* published a front-page story and photograph of Brown with her words highlighted in bold letters: "The politicians just aren't listening. This e-mail protest has grown into something they won't be able to ignore." The photograph shows her with a broad smile, leaning on her computer as if she were communicating over the back fence. Her brown curly hair is cut short, and her gaze is direct and unflinching. She looks earnest and reliable, like someone you could trust with your life, or at least your vote. Early on the morning the story was published, her telephone started to ring. Republicans, Democrats, and independents applauded her stand and urged her to run for Congress.

"I've been a PR and marketing person for the last sixteen years," she says. "I thought, hmmm, there's something here."

Brown's background is in theater, which is good grounding for politics in the media age. While attending Sarah Lawrence, an elite women's college in upstate New York, she performed at Café La Mama in the East Village of Manhattan. She could sing, dance, and act—"a triple threat" in theater slang. She appeared in the cutting-edge musical *Oh! Calcutta!*, which opened at the Coconut Grove in 1976 and then moved to Broadway. The performers were mostly nude. "My mother nearly had a cow," says Brown, who adds, "I kept my clothes on the most." A scene in the movie *Taxi Driver*, with Robert DeNiro, and a cameo with Elliott Gould in *Over the Brooklyn Bridge* expanded her repertoire but didn't earn her enough money to live on. Between gigs, she worked as a legal secretary. Briefly married to and then divorced from a stagehand, she was receptive to changing careers when a friend invited her to join a public relations firm he was starting. Seven years later, she was a partner handling prestigious accounts, including General Foods, Lipton, and Dannon Yogurt. Her success prompted Slim Fast, the liquid diet formula, to woo her away. It was the year that Los Angeles Dodgers manager Tommy Lasorda was competing to lose weight. She saturated the market so that even people who were not sports enthusiasts knew about Lasorda's battle with a bulging waistline.

Brown met her husband at Slim Fast, where he was a vice president. The company relocated to Florida in 1994, and they moved with it. Bill Brown was laid off soon after, and is now a management consultant. When Jean expressed an interest in running for the seat in Florida's sixteenth congressional district, her husband analyzed her chances to make sure his wife wasn't embarking on a hopeless quest. The odds were against her, he concluded, but not insurmountable. The reaction from their Democratic friends was unanimous. They all thought the district was not winnable for a Democrat and that she would be foolish to try. But Brown was not deterred.

There is good reason why everyone from the party chairman to Brown's close friends felt skeptical about her chances. Foley, a former Democrat with moderate leanings, was swept into office with the Republican tide in 1994. He outspent his opponent by almost four to one and got 58 percent of the vote, just short of the 60 percent generally considered a landslide. In 1996, he outspent his opponent by more than seven to one and was reelected with 64 percent of the vote. When Brown interviewed the two Democrats who had run, one told her that he found the campaign such a painful experience that only going to war could be worse. In 1998, the Democrats gave up and Foley ran unopposed.

Brown makes the case that the district is not as Republican as Foley's easy victories make it look. She notes that President Clinton carried the district in 1996, with 47 percent to Bob Dole's 42 percent and Independent Ross Perot's 11 percent. In her mind, the biggest obstacle she faced was not Foley but the attitude—among people who ordinarily contribute money to Democrats—that neither she nor any other Democrat can win in the district. "People assume I can't raise enough money, so they don't give me money because I'm going to lose, and then I lose," She says. "So we're going to shake the tree and see what happens. It's Palm Beach for goodness sakes!"

The first call Brown made was to Emily's List. She spoke to a young man named Jonathan Parker, and he and others have been "mentoring me, advising, assisting, and offering emotional support." After a pregnant pause in which she appears to be deciding whether to mention it or not, she adds that Emily's List has not endorsed her. Why? "Because I'm running against a third-term incumbent with a million dollars," she says, and Emily's List does not take on hopeless causes. Brown needs credibility as a candidate. Her husband's bar charts analyzing the district's voting patterns help, but whether she can raise the money to compete is key.

The second call Brown made was to Wes Boyd in California, who together with his wife had created the MoveOn.org website. "I'm running for Congress, and it's all your fault!" exclaimed Brown, who talks in sentences that demand exclamation points. Her words tumbled out so fast that Boyd barely knew what hit him. Now that he had created her, she seemed to be saying, he had an obligation to share with her his list of the 500,000 people who joined MoveOn.org. "It's only fair!" she said. Boyd was sympathetic to Brown's plea, but told her that he was committed to protecting the privacy of the people who had logged on to his petition drive.

Brown didn't give up. Every couple of weeks, she "hocked" him— Yiddish, she says, for nagging. She'd call up with various suggestions of how he might plug her into his list without compromising people's privacy. Finally, after months of prodding, Boyd developed a letter that passed legal muster and allowed interested cybercitizens to contribute money to five candidates featured on the site who were running for Congress, including Brown. Boyd posted the letter on the website at 1 P.M. on Friday, June 25, 1999. Six minutes later, Brown got her first contribution. Throughout that first night, her computer beeped away, signaling every several minutes that she had mail. Brown was so excited that she got up at 3 A.M. to check her e-mail. The deadline for candidates to report how much money they had raised was June 30, only five days away. The merits of her candidacy would be evaluated based on her bottom line. By the filing deadline, she was able to report $65,000 raised on her own, plus another $40,000 that had come from the Internet.

The third call Brown made in the early days of her fledging candidacy was to Karin Johanson, a former political director for Emily's List. A talented organizer and activist, Johanson had gone over to the Democratic Congressional Campaign Committee (DCCC) to implement the Democrats' program for winning back the House in the 2000 elections. Johanson agreed to meet with Brown in Washington in February. The gist of what she said, as Brown remembers it, was: "I'm sure your philosophy is wonderful. Where are you going to get your money? Call us back if you can raise a hundred grand by June 30." Watching the money flow in over the Internet, Brown was giddy at having confounded the skeptics. "I felt like I came back with the wicked witch's broomstick," she laughs. "They gave me an impossible task, and I did it."

Armed with her fund-raising report, Brown came to Washington in mid-September 1999 to meet with the head of the DCCC, Congressman Patrick Kennedy, and with representatives of several political action committees (PACs) from women's groups that should be her natural allies. She had met Kennedy before, when she happened to be seated one row ahead of him during a performance of *The Iceman Cometh* that the actor Kevin Spacey had dedicated as a fundraiser for the Democratic party. She and Kennedy had gotten acquainted during intermissions in the four-hour play, and he had arranged for her to get into a reception afterward with President Clinton that cost paying guests $25,000 a ticket.

Brown came away from her meeting with Kennedy believing he would help her reach her goal to raise another $100,000 by December 31, 1999, the cutoff date for another report to the Federal Election Commission. These periodic financial reports are like EKG tests that monitor the health of a campaign. "Whether you can do the job is a distant second to whether you can raise the money," she says. "The fact that I am able to do this job, that I understand the issues, and can connect with people, is only a coincidence. Ability is nothing next to the weight of money." After money, the professionals in

Washington want to know which pollster, media adviser, and direct-mail expert the candidate has hired. If a poll has been taken, they want to see the numbers. All this goes into assessing whether the candidate is worth an investment of time and money.

Hurricane Floyd was making its way up the East Coast on the Thursday in September that Brown was scheduled to meet with the PAC representatives in Washington. The public schools in Washington were closed and Congress had recessed for the day because of the storm warnings. Only a few hardy souls showed up to meet with Brown. They were with the National Women's Political Caucus, the Business and Professional Women, the National Organization for Women, and the Women's Campaign Fund. They were more interested in her stands on issues than the other professionals with whom she had met. Their seeming enthusiasm for her candidacy, however, was not matched by their checkbooks. "I inelegantly asked them, 'How much do you guys give?'" Brown says. The answer was not much. The Women's Campaign Fund, for instance, might write a check for $2,500. But there would be other benefits from an endorsement. The fund would feature her at events in the fund-raising meccas of California and New York, and even put her name on the invitations. They would help create the buzz that a candidate needs.

With more than a year until the election, Brown was getting traction. A prominent labor union, the Florida AFL-CIO, approved an early endorsement of her candidacy. And the head of the local Democratic party was more receptive to her candidacy. "I wouldn't call him enthusiastic. He could raise more money like this," she says, snapping her fingers. "But he's come along." Charles Cook, a political analyst who handicaps congressional races, changed his forecast for incumbent Foley in the 2000 election from "Safe" to "Leaning Republican." Rattled by his upstart opponent, Foley tried to make an issue out of Brown relying on "out-of-state political activists" to bankroll her campaign. He pointed out that over seventeen hundred people in fifty states had sent her money. The *Palm Beach Post* called Foley's bluff, pointing out that he had collected substantially more than Brown from individuals living outside of Florida. An editorial in the newspaper on Sunday, September 12, 1999, had the headline "Foley Not a Local Talent."

Brown's persistence was paying off, and she was having fun. She loved to tell the story of how she had gotten the backing of music star Jimmy Buffett. "It should be a TV movie!" she says. She had cold-faxed him after her husband tracked down his agent in California.

Knowing Buffett lives in Palm Beach, and that he's an environmental-ist, she appealed for his help to defeat Foley. Protecting the Ever-glades is a priority for Florida environmentalists. The state's powerful sugar interests, whose industry runoff degrades the Everglades, back Foley. Buffett agreed to meet Brown for breakfast on June 10 at the Ritz-Carlton Hotel in Washington. He was accompanied by Sun-shine, his business partner of twenty-five years. Asked what Buffett had for breakfast, Brown hesitates, says she can't remember, then blurts out, "Fruit. Say fruit. I'm safe with fruit." Not wanting to evoke unnecessary controversy is a good political instinct.

At the end of a genial meal and light conversation, Buffett got seri-ous. "What can I do for you?" he asked. "Be on my steering commit-tee," Brown replied. "Yes," he nodded. "Contribute personally," she said. "Yes," he nodded again. "Raise money," she said. "Yes," he said again. Brown could scarcely believe her good fortune when the enter-tainer brought her down to earth. "No offense, Jean," he said. "But anybody who ran against Mark Foley, I would support." True to his word, Buffett set aside a hundred tickets to his December 9 concert in Florida for Brown to offer to supporters in exchange for contribu-tions of $375, $500, or $1,000, minus the actual cost of the seats. By December 31, 1999, Brown had raised almost $400,000, enough to demonstrate her staying power as a serious candidate. She figured her opponent would raise $2 million, and that while she doesn't have to match him dollar for dollar, she would need a million to be competi-tive. "When I meet with people in Washington, they don't say, 'What's your position on choice and what will you do for working families?' They want to know where I'll get the money."

Brown's success at fund-raising, modest though it was, jolted Foley from his complacency. In a November 30 letter to supporters, Foley said he was facing a well-organized opponent who was well on her way to raising a million dollars. To underscore the threat he faced, Foley enclosed a copy of what Brown calls her "sell sheet," a one-page summation of all her assets that is titled "Why will Jean Elliott Brown win?" It touts everything from her appearance on "Good Morning America" to the support she has gotten from labor, and concludes, "Jean's campaign is the buzz in Washington." On a December fund-raising trip to Washington, Jean handed out copies of Foley's mailing to potential backers. "Who sent this out?" asked a representative of the National Education Association. "My opponent," Brown replied. "You've got to be kidding," the NEA rep exclaimed. "Who's advising him?"

Brown's issue profile is mainstream Democrat. She opposes school vouchers, supports reproductive choice, stronger gun-control measures, and a bright line separating church and state. "I thought that was handled in the Scopes trial," she says in a sardonic reference to the reemergence of the battle between religion and science sparked by a Kansas state school board decision to sanction the teaching of creationism. She doesn't like what she refers to as "the general intolerance spewed by the Republican Congress." On abortion rights in particular she feels strongly that the Republican-led Congress in embracing measures like a ban on certain types of late-term abortions is meddling in areas that should be left between a woman and her doctor. She had a second-trimester abortion when a test revealed the fetus she was carrying had an extra chromosome. While she could have gone to term and given birth, the genetic disorder meant that her baby's organs could not survive outside of the womb, and the outcome would be certain death. She didn't hesitate to have an abortion, and recoils against rhetoric from politicians suggesting women have late-term abortions on a whim. "I don't find these concepts particularly liberal," she says. "I think they're reasonable."

Early in the campaign, Brown seized an issue that works to the disadvantage of some female candidates and tried to turn it to her advantage. In a television interview with a leading local political journalist, Brown said that Foley, who is unmarried, does not relate as well to the district because he hasn't had to think about day care or schedule dentist appointments for a child. "There's just a certain reality that he hasn't experienced," she explained. Asked about the exchange and what point she was trying to make, Brown squirms. She says she doesn't mean that you can't understand people's problems if you haven't been there, but she thinks she brings a richer life experience to politics because she is married and working and raising a child. Lifestyle is a loaded issue that has frequently been used by married, family men against single women in politics. "You can say 'I'm working class and he's rich,' but can you say, 'I'm a family person and he's not'? I don't know whether that's kosher or not," says Brown, clearly troubled about whether she crossed some line and ambivalent about how to proceed.

Sometimes the candidate raising the issue is the one who suffers. In Montana's congressional race, two-term incumbent Rick Hill dropped out of the race after a severe backlash to comments he made about his challenger's lifestyle. Hill had sought to make an issue of the fact that his opponent, Nancy Keenan, is forty-one and single in contrast to his own rich marital record. At fifty-two, Hill had been married twice and had three children. He told the Capitol Hill newspaper *Roll Call*, "I'm a family man. I'm a grandparent. I'm a small-business man. Nancy has never been married and obviously has no children. If you haven't been there, you don't know what it's like, that lifestyle. She's basically been working for the government all of her life."

Keenan's counteroffensive was brilliant. She explained that she had always wanted to have children but couldn't because, for health reasons, she had undergone a hysterectomy. After that "devastating" experience, she said she adopted 150,000 children, referring to her twenty-five years as a teacher and state superintendent of schools. Asked by reporters if she feared something might come out about her background that she wished to hide, Keenan replied, "I'm a single woman. Period." Again turning the tables on her opponent, Keenan pledged she would not delve into Hill's past, which includes reports that he left his first wife for a cocktail waitress and fought for eight years with his ex-wife over child support.

The state's major newspapers took Keenan's side. "Hill's opening salvo sinks to the bottom of the barrel," said the *Billings Gazette*. The *Great Falls Tribune* accused him of "smearing his likely opponent with irrelevant innuendo." And the *Missoulian* pointed out that "Hill's personal life doesn't exactly bear close scrutiny, and the last thing he ought to be doing is suggesting that his lifestyle and life choices form the basis for his reelection. Trust us, Rick, you don't want to go down that road."

Jean Elliott Brown followed the events in Montana with interest because Keenan was another of the five candidates featured on the MoveOn website. What happened to Hill when he tried to turn the race into a contest about private lives is instructive to Brown, who was moved to run in the first place by the zealotry of the Republican-led Congress in blurring the line between Clinton's public and private conduct. Friends said she is unlikely to talk much more about Foley's marital status. In the heat of battle, however, women are not necessarily more restrained than their male opponents. They just haven't had as many opportunities.

The *Free Press*, an alternative Palm Beach newspaper, asked Brown, "If the campaign gets dirty, is there anything they're going to be able to dig up on you?" The Democratic screening committee had previously raised the same question in sizing up her potential as a candidate. Brown said that being an actress for twelve years had gotten her used to rejection. Were there any skeletons in her closet? "I have hundreds of skeletons," she said, "only they're not in the closet. I was in *Oh! Calcutta!* on Broadway. Am I gonna hide that?" She hinted that there might be more, but that she didn't mind if the media or her opponent tried to make something of it. "I'm a prototypical candidate of my generation," she said. "I'm forty-eight years old. I did everything that everybody did, and I'm not gonna say I'm sorry. That's part of life."

As 1999 drew to a close, Brown felt good about how far she had come. Seeking outside confirmation, she phoned Russell Hemenway, the executive director of the New York–based National Committee for an Effective Congress (NCEC). "How am I doing?" she asked.

"Aside from the fact that everybody loves you, you're a Three," he replied amiably.

"A Three?" Brown shrieked. "Why am I only a Three?"

"It's a Republican district," he replied calmly.

"No it's not," Brown replied, making the argument for what seemed the thousandth time that the district is not solidly Republican. She recited the numbers: 44 percent Republican, 40 percent Democrat, and 16 percent Independent. "What do you say to people about my chances?" she pressed.

By now Hemenway was squirming a bit. "I'd say you have a shot," he said. "Okay, a real shot."

Brown maintained her enthusiasm until Election Day, borrowing from her IRA to keep her campaign afloat. But when the votes were tallied, she got only 37 percent of the vote, proving the experts right that the 16th district of Florida is safely Republican.

The previous year she was a volunteer in an Internet petition drive. She got Jimmy Buffett to sing for her, and Barbara Boxer sent out a fund-raising letter for her candidacy to the U.S. Congress. Her web page won the grand prize award for civic excellence in online campaigning from George Washington University. "I'm in PR," says Brown, flashing her megawatt smile. "It's a good story."

Every campaign season brings new stories and new hopes and dreams. Alabama State Auditor Susan Parker made history when she won the Democratic nomination for the U.S. Senate. Though the state has elected women statewide, no woman has ever run for the top of the ticket. The race took a nasty turn when her opponent, lawyer Julian McPhillips, declared himself the better candidate for families because Parker, who is forty-five and married, doesn't have children. When Parker responded that she had been unable to bear a child, McPhillips wondered why she hadn't adopted, pointing out that his youngest child is adopted. Women voters in particular found the remarks grossly insensitive, and McPhillips eventually issued a public apology. The controversy enabled Parker to overcome a huge fund-raising disadvantage and pull just ahead of McPhillips in the initial Democratic primary vote and then decisively beat him in a run-off election three weeks later.

Parker hoped to beat the odds again in November. She faced an uphill fight against freshman Republican Sen. Jeff Sessions, who had all the advantages of incumbency and was considered vulnerable only because he is a first-termer and untested. The major newspapers in the state agree that Parker has been the best state auditor in history, and her reputation for fiscal probity is the bedrock of her campaign. "You cannot have that liberal Democratic image in Alabama," she says. "Stopping fraud and abuse and getting more money into the taxpayers' pocket are good things to run on." Parker's life story is testimony to her determination to succeed. She was born on a small farm in Alabama and picked cotton until she was sixteen and got a job as a file clerk at a local community college. For the next thirteen years, she worked full time during the day and went to school at night, eventually earning four degrees, including a doctorate. Asked whether being a woman hurts her in this Deep South state, Parker cites polling that shows a substantial number of voters prefer to vote for women "because they think we're more honest and we work together in a more bipartisan way." Parker didn't have the money or the backing to prevail in an election that turned heavily on issues of national security and support for President Bush. Women voters turned out for Parker in the primary because they didn't like a male candidate lording it over a woman on something so personal as childbearing. Voters care about where a politician stands on the issues, but it is not unusual for a side issue that nobody anticipated, and that reveals a previously hidden side of a candidate, to decide an election.

A How-to for Women

Imagine that it is the summer of 2008, and for the first time, one of the two major parties has nominated a woman for president. Polls show her running neck-and-neck with her male opponent, and political analysts agree that she has a real chance to win the election. Voters are impressed with her command of the issues and the way she stands up to the onslaught of questions about her private life. ABC commentator George Stephanopoulos remarks that he hasn't seen such a resilient campaigner since Bill "Comeback Kid" Clinton. The husband-and-wife team of James Carville and Mary Matalin announce that they will put aside their partisan differences to try to elect the country's first female president. Pollsters predict the election will spark a voter realignment that will affect presidential races far into the future.

Presented with this hypothetical situation, Michael Sheehan, a media training guru, set out to design a campaign for the first woman to head the ticket for a major party. Sheehan, a graduate of Yale Drama School, generally coaches Democrats, including President Clinton and Vice President Gore, but the basics are the same for a woman in either party. The title of Sheehan's seminar on women's leadership sums it up: "Husbands, Hemlines, and Hairdos." Sheehan counsels women running for public office that "things are better than they were, but you don't have as much leeway as you think."

Sheehan, a friendly man with a shock of brown hair that flops in his eyes, can make anybody he's with drop his or her guard. He's the kind of guy people are willing to fail in front of, and to share their deepest anxieties about public speaking with, an experience that ranks with death among humankind's worst fears. Sheehan's empathy with his clients may come from his own experience. He conquered a severe stuttering problem and went on to become a teacher of public speaking.

Sheehan's office in downtown Washington has the technological trappings of a modern television studio, except that nothing video-taped there ever goes on the air. Prominent authors, business executives, and politicians who seek Sheehan's services know their struggle to become more engaging public figures is guarded by a kind of doctor-patient confidentiality. But Sheehan agreed to share his advice for a would-be Madam President:

Do your homework. Learn from other women who have been successful in politics, starting with Margaret Thatcher. The former British prime minister inspired many followers, including women who do not share her conservative politics but admire her pluck. Thatcher had no sympathy for feminist policies, and had almost no women in Parliament to bond with even if she had sought female allies. She became the Conservative party leader with a ploy that capitalized on her disadvantage as the only female candidate in the race. "Vote for me in the first round because I'm not going to win," she urged the men. They complied, and she won. Years after Thatcher, women the world over acknowledge their debt to the Iron Lady. Charles Saatchi, the art collector and co-founder of Saatchi & Saatchi Advertising, credits Thatcher with freeing the entrepreneurial spirit in Britain that produced the radical art that he favors. A Virgin Mary decorated with elephant dung from Saatchi's collection became an issue in Hillary Clinton's New York senatorial race. Twenty years earlier, in 1979, Saatchi masterminded the advertising campaign that helped dislodge the Labour party and elect Thatcher. Saatchi cleverly exploited Britain's high unemployment with the slogan "Labour isn't working," and the image of hundreds of jobless men queued up outside an employment office. Thatcher is as important a symbol for women candidates as the Barbie doll is for Miss America.

Highlight executive experience. Thatcher's rise to power was made easier by Britain's parliamentary system, which rewards party participation. In the United States, it's easier to launch a woman for national office if she's been a governor or a big-city mayor. She can point to her record and say, "I know how to take charge, make decisions, and get things done." The public, on the other hand, sees members of Congress as the embodiment of all talk and no action. Nobody has gone directly from the House to the White House, and John F. Kennedy was the last president who ran successfully as an incumbent senator. A governor can say she cut the budget, cut taxes, increased spending on education, got deadbeat dads to pay child support, and reduced the welfare roles.

Look good. Thatcher made some cosmetic changes that have been well documented. She worked on her voice to bring its pitch down, which lends authority, and she had her teeth fixed for a more pleasing smile. Hillary Rodham Clinton once said she started lightening her hair after reading that Thatcher thought all women benefited from lighter hair as they aged. Female candidates need to get comfortable with the constant scrutiny of their appearance. "It's not sexism," says Deborah Tannen. "Clothes and hair communicate something. There's nothing a woman can wear that doesn't convey a message. There is no neutral costume. The problem comes when what a woman wears is more important than what she says." Pat Schroeder got more mail about her hair than on any issue, much of it from women and all of it critical. She recalls the woman who enclosed a check with the note, "Here, get it dyed on me." Schroeder ignored the unsolicited advice and stuck with her natural color and a hairstyle that suited her. "Does anybody write to Newt Gingrich and say, 'Get it thinned—you look like a chrysanthemum.' What is it that makes women so nervous about seeing women . . . ?" Schroeder wonders. Sheehan thinks the cosmetic challenge is overrated, and that a potential problem in a candidate's image can be overcome with relative ease. "You bring along a makeup artist and a hair stylist and you try it a couple of times until you get it right," he says.

Get a haircut. For women in public life, the price tag is often femininity. "Are there any sexy women lurking in politics—like the Bill Clinton of '92?" asks Steve Zdatny, a history professor at West Virginia University. "I can't think of one." Zdatny suggests only half-jokingly that a woman running for president might campaign on the slogan "Give the Safer Sex a Chance." Zdatny is researching two books about French hairdressers, a historical niche that apparently qualified him to appraise the image of Paula Jones, the Arkansas woman who sued Clinton for making an improper sexual advance. Zdatny told the *Washington Post* that when he looked at the original head of hair on Jones, before her makeover, he saw a lower-middle-class Arkansan. "Hair should be neat and not call too much attention to it. Paula Jones' hair used to screech," he says. The advice for women who want to succeed, whether it's in the courtroom, the corporate world, or politics: Keep it relatively short.

Project a warm, friendly image. Women need family to leaven their image, just as men do. Not all men are willing to play the role of supportive spouse in the background of a wife's political career. Small wonder that many women who are successful in politics are either not married or have grown children. Thatcher's husband, Dennis, played the role so well that Schroeder's husband, Jim, a Washington lawyer, formed what he jokingly called the U.S. chapter of "The Dennis Thatcher Society." Membership was open to the anonymous husbands of celebrated women. Dennis Thatcher's meek image, however, played into the negative stereotype of strong women emasculating their mates. The British puppet show, "Spitting Image," a spoof on the Thatcher regime, had the puppet portraying her using the men's room and standing at a urinal.

Put women in charge. A woman running for president should have a woman as one of her two top campaign managers. "The last thing I want to expose my candidate to is being the puppet of the same old white guys you're trying to get out," says Sheehan.

Highlight your handling of a crisis. A governor or mayor has the advantage here because she can show how she dealt with a challenging situation and reassure voters that she is up to handling any emergency. Quelling a riot, resolving labor strife, or cracking down on crime are opportunities to showcase leadership. A female Republican mayor might stress how she broke a municipal union; a female Democratic governor might boast of forcing a key local industry back to work. "A woman needs something real kick-butt," says Sheehan. Men have traditionally used their experiences in war to bolster their credentials as leaders. Democratic pollster Geoff Garin has discovered that voters respond positively to women who have battled breast cancer.

Listen to focus groups. Breaking new ground requires intensive understanding of voters' attitudes on issues, priorities, and the role that gender plays. Polling is much maligned, but it is a lifeline to the electorate. When the first Bush administration was trying to galvanize support for the Gulf War and Operation Desert Storm, it tested language to sell the policy. Focus groups revealed that the public was most receptive to the argument that Iraqi president Saddam Hussein was a crazed dictator who couldn't be trusted with nuclear weapons and must be stopped. Other reasons like disrupting the flow of oil or disturbing the balance of power in the Middle East did not move voters. Used responsibly, says Sheehan, focus groups help a candidate sharpen her campaign. "The way focus groups work is, 'Here's three issues that I really care about. Which two work better? And of those two, there are five or six different things I could talk about. Which two or three are better?' "

Money talks. By capturing her party's nomination, our hypothetical female candidate has demonstrated her ability to raise money. Good for her because there are few women in politics today (Dianne Feinstein, Hillary Clinton, and Christine Todd Whitman come to mind) who have a national network of supporters on whom they can call to raise the enormous sum it takes to run for president. "The more I've done this, the more I'm amazed at how big and how deep that network has to be," says Sheehan. "In the scheme of things, Emily's List is chump change." Elizabeth Dole, who raised billions of dollars for the Red Cross and had extensive contacts across the country on her own and through her husband, failed to generate the millions she needed to compete in the presidential primaries. Many women (and men) shrink from asking people for money. Ohio representative Marcy Kaptur turned down entreaties from the Democratic party to challenge Republican senator Michael DeWine in 2000. "I didn't come to public life to be a beggar and put the arm on everyone I know, and some I don't know," she said. If DeWine agreed to a $2 million limit on spending, she would run, an offer understandably rejected by the amply funded incumbent.

Come from the right state. A candidate has more control choosing her home state than she has choosing her parents. Dropping out of the 1988 race for the Democratic nomination, Bruce Babbitt lamented the fact that his state had only seven electoral votes, not enough to warrant his consideration for the second spot on the ticket. "In my next life, in my reincarnation, I've decided I'm going to be born . . . in Texas," he quipped. Five months later, Michael Dukakis picked as his running mate Senator Lloyd Bentsen of Texas. Other candidates solve the location issue by claiming any state in which they lived for more than a week. Former president Bush called Texas, Connecticut, and Maine home. Still, Arkansas is not exactly a mega-state, and Clinton managed to get elected and reelected president. Ross Perot, the third-party candidate in both Clinton elections, was fond of saying he had been in Wal-Marts bigger than Arkansas.

Inspire true believers. A candidate needs a core of supporters who are willing to spend four weeks in Iowa in the depths of winter canvassing for votes. Centrists usually don't inspire passion, but they win general elections. The first woman nominee for president ought to be able to convert gender pride into a base that spans differences in ideology. That strategy didn't work for Geraldine Ferraro when she ran for vice president in 1984, but the theory won't be fully tested until a woman who heads her party's ticket seeks to inspire commitment based on gender.

Exude high wattage. Some people have it, most don't. It's the ability to light up a room and stop conversation just by walking in. Feinstein has it; so does former Texas governor Ann Richards. People are drawn to them. You don't have to be an extrovert to capture people's attention. Politicians who maintain some mystery about their persona are often intriguing. Former New Jersey senator Bill Bradley capitalized on this phenomenon in the early stages of his primary challenge to Gore. Despite having served eighteen years in the Senate, Bradley benefited from seeming like a fresh face compared to the vice president, whom the public had tired of without really knowing why.

Family matters. The rule of thumb for a male candidate is: When an opponent attacks anyone in your family, go to town. Show emotion. Look as if you're ready to jump over the lectern and slug it out. Democrat Michael Dukakis lost ground in the 1988 race by displaying no emotion when asked in a debate how he would react if his wife had been raped. A woman also can win over voters defending her family. Sheehan gets dreamy-eyed as he conjures up the image of a mama bear protecting her cubs. A single woman as a candidate is not much different from a single male candidate in today's culture. When Senator Bob Kerrey of Nebraska ran for president in 1992, he concluded that even though he had divorced years earlier and was single, he could not date for the duration of the campaign. Given the media's scrutiny in the search for a candidate's inner character, Kerrey anticipated that reporters and possibly operatives from rival campaigns would stake out his motel if he attempted to see a paramour. The only single president in modern times was actor Michael Douglas in the movie *The American President*, a romantic comedy about the difficulties of dating if you're the most powerful person in the world.

The irrepressible Ann Richards wishes women could shed the pretense that they're good at all of life's roles just because they're running for public office. When asked how she wished to identify herself in an Ann Klein fashion spread photographed by the renowned Annie Leibovitz, Richards insisted that her description be limited to "former governor of Texas." She had agreed to participate, along with other prominent women from different walks of life, because she liked the idea of showcasing working women who are not models, and being photographed by Leibovitz is an honor she would not pass up. But when the advertising campaign's promoters wanted to mention in the copy that she was a grandmother and that she also rode motorcycles, Richards told them she didn't want to be known as any of those other things. "I don't understand why we continue to trivialize ourselves," she says. "We try to feed into this pattern of acceptability that seems to be so important, particularly in running for public office or trying to become the CEO of a corporation. You have still got to make the pretense that you are also being a wife and mother, that you're keeping the house clean, and giving parties—when women have no more time to do all that than men do who fill those jobs. But we still play the game because we think or we hope that we will get some acceptance."

When Richards was presented with questions asking her to recount the battles she had fought and to talk about how she balanced her private life, she responded, "All of this business about a man's world and all that crap—you gotta get above that stuff, I think, because continuing to talk about how women do it *and* raise a family just continues to make those questions seem important. And they're not." Richards makes the point that the mom working as a waitress to support her family is faced with the same tradeoffs, has fewer resources, and gets less return financially and probably psychologically, yet she's out there doing what she has to do. So should women in politics, or corporate life. "Just do it and quit whining," she says.

There aren't many welcome mats in politics, and anything that shakes up the established order invites jokes. Jay Leno and the late-night talk-show crowd will have a grand time with the first campaign around a major party's female nominee. "Why not the broad?" chuckles one male political consultant when invited to propose a slogan. "Or 'I can be just as nasty as you,' " he adds to further his amusement. Only when pressed to get serious does he venture what most analysts believe, that the first woman president will run a campaign that is both mainstream and conventional. Hillary Rodham Clinton's careful approach to her Senate race in New York is the model. As the first First Lady to become a candidate in her own right, she created enough controversy without further challenging the voters with a campaign that is too innovative or unfamiliar. Yet a candidate has to be daring enough to capitalize on opportunities, and to take the risks that are the very heart of good leadership.

In that spirit, the first Madam President will have to reach beyond gender for a campaign that lights a pride among women but gives men a reason to vote for her. Her slogan: "New Leadership for a New America."

Source Notes

For each chapter, we have listed our sources in the order that the information they provided us appears. We also spoke to a number of people who agreed to be interviewed only if we did not identify them by name. Our heartfelt thanks to all those who cooperated.

EPIGRAPH

Allida M. Black, ed., *Courage in a Dangerous World: The Political Writings of Eleanor Roosevelt* (New York: Columbia University Press, 1999).

INTRODUCTION

Sources: Marie Wilson, Anita Perez Ferguson, Hillary Rodham Clinton, Mark Penn, Kathleen Hall Jamieson, Lynn Martin, Governor Christine Todd Whitman, Laura Liswood, Farai Chideya, Shirley Chisholm, Warren Rustand.

[manuscript page 3] "vote for a woman": Karlyn Bowman, "POLLitics," *Roll Call*, January 14, 1999, p. 10.

[6] The number of women: Center for the American Woman and Politics, Eagleton Institute of Politics, Rutgers University Fact Sheet.

[15] "Go Team USA!": "The Girls of Summer," *Wall Street Journal*, July 13, 1999.

[15] "They've broken": Ibid.

[16] The ideal woman: Michael Lollar, "A Female President by 2008?," *Commercial Appeal*, November 1, 1998, p. E-1.

[16] "a little getting used to": "Woman in White House," *Newsday*, November 15, 1988.

[16] A poll conducted: "Women in Elected Office," Poll by DeLoitte & Touche, presented at a press conference in Washington, D.C., January 13, 2000.

CHAPTER 1

Sources: Joanne Howes, Joan McLean, Carol Tucker Foreman, John Reilly, Dotty Lynch, Geraldine Ferraro, Ann Lewis, Michael Berman, Lynn Martin.

[47] "apparent slippage": David Alpern, "A Woman on the Ticket," *Newsweek*, October 7, 1985, p. 70.

[55] The new politics: Norman D. Atkins, "Poll Puts Mondale Even with Reagan," *Washington Post*, July 23, 1984, p. A-3.

[58] "Under pressure": *Time*, September 3, 1984.

[58] "I knew what": Denise M. Bostdorff, "Vice-Presidential Comedy and the

Traditional Female Role: An Examination of the Rhetorical Characteristics of the Vice Presidency," *Western Journal of Speech Communication*, 55 (winter 1991), p. 17.

[62]   "By choosing": Ibid., p. 13.

[62]   "Here she is": Lesley Stahl, *Reporting Live* (New York: Simon & Schuster, 1999), p. 208.

CHAPTER 2

Sources: Ellen Malcolm, Judith Lichtman, Carol Tucker Foreman, Ann Lewis, Senator Barbara Mikulski, Harriett Woods, Arnie Arnesen, Lynn Martin, Ann Richards.

[86]   "if it's inevitable": John Davidson, "Mudslinging, Texas-style, No holds-or-words-barred in governor's race," *Toronto Star*, November 6, 1990, p. A-15.

[88]   "If you're a male": Emily's List Annual Convention, Panel Discussion, Washington, D.C., June 11, 1998.

CHAPTER 3

Sources: Emma Jordan, Senator Dianne Feinstein, Elizabeth Holtzman, Geraldine Ferraro, Amy Walter, Senator Barbara Mikulski, Marjorie Margolies Mezvinsky, Karen Shepherd, Ann Richards, Ellen Malcolm, Tillie Fowler.

[96]   "The sense of rage": Jay Mathews, "Courting Voters with Memories of Thomas; Seeking California's 2 Seats, Feinstein and Boxer Emphasize Senate's Lack of Women," *Washington Post*, December 28, 1991, p. A-12.

[97]   "No matter what": Judy Mann, "Why Women Are So Angry at the Senate," *Washington Post*, October 11, 1991, p. C-3.

[102] "Ladies, ladies . . .": Catherine S. Manegold, "The 1992 Campaign: Women; Holtzman and Ferraro Fought Double Standards as Well as Each Other," *New York Times*, September 16, 1992, p. B-6.

[102] "My opponents": John J. Goldman, "Ferraro, Faced with Tight Race, Defends Herself in Rare TV Ad," *Los Angeles Times*, September 16, 1992, p. A-16.

[110] "I made him": George Stephanopoulos, *All Too Human: A Political Education* (New York: Little, Brown and Company, 1999), p. 179.

[111] "You know what": Ibid., p. 182.

[113] "Marjorie Margolies Mezvinsky": Ronald G. Shafer, "A Special Weekly Report From the Wall Street Journal's Capital Bureau," *Wall Street Journal*, October 20, 1995, p. A-1.

[114] "After evaluating": Debbie Goldberg, "Democratic Power Couple Suddenly Rich in Troubles; Husband's Business Deals Entangle Margolies Mezvinsky," *Washington Post*, February 16, 2000.

[115] "Hard prison time": Paul Duggan, "Despite Bush Stance, Texas Drug Laws Changed Little," *Washington Post*, September 20, 1999, p. A-3.

CHAPTER 4

Sources: Pat Schroeder, Linda DiVall, Lynn Martin, Kathy Bonk, Kim Campbell, Senator Susan Collins, Senator Mary Landrieu, Rich Masters, Celinda Lake.

[120] "crying folder": Eleanor Clift, "The Politicization of Pat Schroeder," *Minnesota*, November/December 1992, p. 16.

[128] "She is our Mrs. Thatcher": Charles Laurence, "Canada's 'Iron Lady' Softens as the Premiership Beckons," *Daily Telegraph*, June 7, 1993, p. I-12.

[129] Born Avril: E. Kaye Fulton, with Hal Quinn, Luke Fisher, and Nancy Wood, "The Rising Star: Kim Campbell Becomes Canada's First Female Defense Minister in an Election-Year Shuffle," *Maclean's*, January 18, 1993.

[130] "I find that extraordinary": Tim Harper, "Her Life in Ottawa Often Lonely, She Says," *Toronto Star*, November 14, 1992, p. A-20.

[131] "Campbell . . . ran a": Russell Watson with Linda Kay, "'Yesterday's Man' Is Back," *Newsweek*, November 8, 1993.

[132] After the election: Frances Bula, "PM's Presence Dominates Papers, TV," *Vancouver Sun*, October 2, 1993.

[132] "The intensity": Tom Van Dusen, "Not Mulroney in a Dress: A Kim Campbell Aide Recalls the Malice and Ineptitude That Dogged Her Doomed Election Campaign," *Vancouver Sun*, November 2, 1994.

[133] "It is a bitter pill": Bruce Wallace, "Playing Gender Politics," *Maclean's*, October 4, 1993.

[134] "They felt it was": Ibid.

[153] "Vice President Pelosi?": Marc Sandalow, "Can Pelosi's Politics Play Well in Peoria?," *San Francisco Chronicle*, March 21, 1999.

[153] "Compared to the": Ibid.

CHAPTER 5

Sources: Linda DiVall, Tom Daffron, Ari Fleischer, Elizabeth Dole, Tillie Fowler, Frank Luntz, Senator Kay Bailey Hutchison, Lynn Martin, Josie Martin, Senator Dianne Feinstein, Carla Hills, Governor Christine Todd Whitman.

[162] "If she had lurking": American Forum, School of Communication, American University, "Here We Go Again: Campaign 2000," Washington, D.C., April 20, 1999.

[164] "even more scary": Maureen Dowd, "No Free War," *New York Times*, March 31, 1999, p. A-29.

[167] "a verbal version": Ceci Connolly, "Resurgent Dole Muffles Stances on Social Issues in N.H. Visit," *Washington Post*, August 17, 1999, p. A-4.

[171] "And after a detailed": Ceci Connolly, "The Dole Mystique," *Washington Post*, April 11, 1999, p. A-1.

[177] "We've never had": "Gender on the Campaign Trail," Panel Discussion, National Press Club, Washington, D.C., October 25, 1999.

[178] "She so blew it": Ibid.

[179] "I'd feel a whole": H. W. Brands, "Taft to Hoover to Dole," *New York Times*, March 17, 1999.

[189] "We must admit": *Lufkin Daily News*, August 19, 1996.

[193] "I'm on my third": "Could a Woman Be President?," *Ladies' Home Journal*, July 1983.

CHAPTER 6

Sources: Hillary Rodham Clinton, Harold Ickes, William Galston, Andrea Camp, Tony Bullock, Lawrence O'Donnell, Deborah Tannen, Tony Blankley, Kathleen Hall Jamieson, Bob Squier.

[198] "My God, I": Pindars Corrier, New York, July 7, 1999.

[201] "I feel very strongly": James Bennet, "The Next Clinton," *New York Times Magazine*, May 30, 1999, p. 24.

[202] Pollster Dick Morris: Dick Morris, *Behind the Oval Office: Getting Re-elected Against All Odds* (New York: Random House, 1997).

[211] A February poll: Adam Nagourney with Marjorie Connelly, "Little Movement for New Yorkers in Senate Choice," *New York Times*, February 25, 2000, p. A-1.

[218] "Everybody wonders": "Perspectives," *Newsweek*, May 4, 1998, p. 25.

[219] "There is no ordained": Sperling Breakfast, Washington, D.C.

[219] "You can't find": "The Final Word," *National Journal*, June 30, 1999.

[221] "Political life": Lunch with reporters, Washington Court Hotel, July 14, 1999.

[222] "Our roles are": CBS Interview, November 1999.

[224] *Newsweek's* "Conventional: "Conventional Wisdom," *Newsweek*, November 22, 1999, p. 4.

[224] In a *New York Times* article: Adam Nagourney with Marjorie Connelly, "Hillary Clinton vs. Giuliani: Poll Finds Few Undecided," *New York Times*, November 1, 1999, p. A-1.

[224] A *New York Times*: Ibid.

[229] dead heat: Adam Nagourney with Marjorie Connelly, "Little Movement for New Yorkers in Senate Choice," *New York Times*, February 25, 2000, p. A-1.

[230] "Empire State Voters": Editorial, "Senator Rodham?," *New York Times*, January 5, 1999, p. A-16.

[233] "If somebody says": Michael Deaver at a lunch with journalists hosted by Godfrey (Budge) Sperling, Washington, D.C., July 23, 1998.

CHAPTER 7

Sources: Betsy Bayless, Governor Jane Hull, Carol Springer, Lisa Graham Keegan, Bruce Merrill, Rose Mofford, Janet Napolitano, Jeff Groscost, Lori Daniels, Christine Gregoire, Maria Cantwell, Darlene Fairley, Pat Hale, Jeri Costa, Kari-Lynn Frank, Rosemary McAuliffe, Kate Sandboe, Valoria Loveland, Pam Roach, Karen Schmidt, Val Stevens, Sid Snyder, Calvin Goings.

Some of the material in this chapter originally appeared in the *Plain Dealer* in two articles by Tom Brazaitis: "Women in Politics Move Beyond Feminist Symbols" and "Men Still Dominate Politics in Ohio, Most Other States," June 20, 1999.

[245] "I finally understood": Martin Kasindorf, "Running Arizona," *USA Today*, October 29, 1999, p. A-1.

[245] "I haven't seen": Chris Moeser, "Hull Ruffles Some Hair," *Arizona Republic*, October 30, 1999, p. A-1.

[246] "There's not a lot": Paul Davenport, "Hull, Groscost Fight Over Curler Quotes May Be Over Without a Handshake," Associated Press, November 2, 1999.

[246] "To be perfectly honest": Grant Smith, "Legislative Profile: From the Ostrich Festival to House Majority Leader," *Arizona Capitol Times*, February 26, 1999, p. 3.

[247] "the strongest among": Bob Partlow, "Gregoire to Say If She'll Run," *Olympian*, April 15, 1999, p. A-1.

[249] "It's something she's": Robert T. Nelson, "Cantwell Announces Run for Senate," *Seattle Times*, January 19, 2000, p. 1.

[249] In five years: Sam Howe Verhovek, "Staging a Comeback," *New York Times*, January 21, 2000, p. A-23.

[254] "Elected women are": Susan J. Carroll, Debra L. Dodson, and Ruth B. Mandel, "The Impact of Women in Public Office: An Overview." Study conducted by the Center for the American Woman and Politics, Rutgers University, 1991, p. 5.

CHAPTER 8

Sources: Emma Jordan, Mary Sue Terry, Mary Beth Cahill, Tom King, Barbara Kennelly, Loretta Sanchez, Lynn Martin, Geoff Garin, Jane Harman, Robert Shrum, Joanne Howes, Emily Couric.

[267] "more understanding": John F. Harris, "Allen Makes Family Ties Issue in Virginia; Married Hopeful Says He's More Qualified," *Washington Post*, August 24, 1993, p. B-1.

[269] "She says it": Mary McGrory, "Virginia Is Unseasonably Cold," *Washington Post*, October 26, 1993, p. A-2.

[274] "This election, you": Jon Lender and Christopher Keating, "Funding Enlivens Debate; Questions About Contributions Create Sparks," *Hartford Courant*, October 20, 1998, p. A-3.

CHAPTER 9

Sources: Kathleen Kennedy Townsend, Michael Barone.

[310] Townsend's credentials: Todd Richissin, "On Graduation Day, an Illusion of Hope; Violence at Boot Camp?" *Baltimore Sun*, December 6, 1999, p. A-1.

[311] "There was a complete": Todd Richissin, "Juvenile Justice Chief, Aides Ousted Over Camp Violence," *Baltimore Sun*, December 16, 1999, p. A-1.

[314] "The Young Kennedys": *Newsweek*, July 14, 1997.

[314] "I have come to believe": "A Reluctant Kennedy Turns Back on Suitors," *New York Times*, November 9, 1999.

[319] "What to expect": Daniel LeDuc, "The Daughter Also Rises," *Washington Post Magazine*, November 28, 1999, p. 6.

CHAPTER 10

Source: Governor Jane Swift.

[326] "a political culture": Don Aucoin, "Beacon Hill's Glass Dome," *Boston Globe Magazine*, November 2, 1997, p. 20.

[327] "My first reaction": Carey Goldberg, "A Pregnant Candidate Discovers She's an Issue," *New York Times*, May 15, 1998, p. A-14.

[328] "Look, folks": Editorial, "Swift's Baby No Problem," *Boston Herald*, May 8, 1998.

[330] "choose inexperienced": Eileen McNamara, "These GOP Guys Just Don't Get It," *Boston Globe*, March 11, 1998, p. B-1.

[331] "The conundrum now": Bella English, "Lieutenant Mom; Fast-Rising Jane Swift Brings Up Baby on Beacon Hill," *Boston Globe*, February 24, 1999, p. F-1.

[331] "Not to be harsh": Ibid.

[332] "Mark my words": Tina Cassidy, "'Snow White' Stands Formidable Behind Cellucci," *Boston Globe*, June 20, 1999, p. B-1.

[332] Swift, who had taken: Frank Phillips, "Suffolk University Paying Swift $25,000 to Teach Class," *Boston Globe*, September 20, 1999, p. A-1.

[332] Reporters digging: Michael Crowley, "Massport Gave Swift Health Care Benefits," *Boston Globe*, September 3, 1999, p. B-4.

[333] "Working mother Swift": Tina Cassidy, "Working Mother Swift Relies on Free Help from Her Aides," *Boston Globe*, January 5, 2000, p. A-1.

[334] "I think it was": Michael Crowley, "Swift Assumes a Higher Profile in Rocky Period," *Boston Globe*, August 26, 1999, p. A-16.

CHAPTER 11

Sources: Jeanne Shaheen, Frank Manciewicz, Dotty Lynch, Arnie Arnesen, Nancy Snow.

[339] "a play-it-safe": Mary McGrory, "The Shaheen Machine," *Washington Post*, April 11, 1999, p. B-1.

[339] "For those local": Thomas Oliphant, "Governor Shaheen's Savvy," *Boston Globe*, May 4, 1999, p. A-21.

[340] "I haven't, at this point": John Toole, "Shaheen Sidesteps Tax, 'Pledge' Questions," *Union Leader* (Manchester, N.H.), February 9, 2000, p. 2.

[340] "This is [politically]": John Toole, "Senator Brown Backs Income Tax Plan to Fund Education," *Union Leader* (Manchester, N.H.), February 15, 2000, p. 1.

[341] "a volleyball mom": Sally Jacobs, "Jeanne Shaheen's Journey," *Boston Globe*, November 14, 1996.

CHAPTER 12

Sources: Patricia Schroeder, Larry Sabato, Tillie Fowler, Nancy Pelosi, Loretta Sanchez, David Bositis, Ellen Tauscher, Loretta Sanchez, Zoe Lofgren.

[357] "Why isn't Jennifer Dunn": William Safire, "New GOP Leaders," *New York Times*, November 9, 1998, p. A-25.

[358] "I think a lot of people": John Bresnahan, "GOP Supporters Wonder Whether First Female Speaker Could Be a Dunn Deal," *Roll Call*, March 30, 1998.

[358] "Steve has been": Slate, www.slate.com, January 1998.

[359] "whupping him good": Libby Ingrid Copeland, "The House's Dunn Dealer," *Washington Post*, November 16, 1998.

[359] "She feels she's had": Ibid.

[360] "If the president": "This Week with Cokie Roberts and Sam Donaldson," March 29, 1999.

[366] In the days following: Chris Scribner, "Cash Still on Hand for Fowler; About $250,000 Left in Her Campaign," *Florida Times-Union* (Jacksonville, Fla.), February 11, 2000, p. B-1, and "Fowler Runs Series of Ads to Reiterate Her Decisions," *Florida Times-Union*, January 7, 2000, p. B-1.

[375] "wants to see a woman": Rebecca Carr, "McKinney Backs Woman for Whip; Californian War Her Choice Before Lewis Announced," *Atlanta Journal and Constitution*, September 22, 1999.

[393] "Another March": *Roll Call*, November 6, 1997.

[401] "both major parties": Editorial, *Patriot-News* (Harrisburg, Penn.), April 20, 1998.

CHAPTER 13

Sources: Barbara Lee, Marie Wilson, Lieutenant General Claudia Kennedy, Karen Strickler, Jean Elliott Brown.

[414] Then it was revealed: Rowan Scarborough, "Female General Accuses Peer of Harassment," *Washington Times*, March 30, 2000, p. A-1.

[414] "The high-profile confrontation": Thomas E. Ricks, "Cohen Confirms Probe into Sex Harassment of General," *Washington Post*, April 1, 2000, p. A-6.

[418] "has never seen": Robert C. Penston, "COO May Be Great, But Not During Combat," *Richmond Times Dispatch*, April 2, 1999, p. A-14.

[430] "The politicians just aren't": Dan Moffett, "500,000 on Net Have 1 Message: Move On," *Palm Beach Post*, January 25, 1999, p. A-1.

[436] "Foley not": Editorial, "Foley Not a Local Talent," *Palm Beach Post*, September 12, 1999, p. E-2.

[439] "I'm a family man": John Mercurio, "Rep. Hill Blasts Challenger's 'Lifestyle,'" *Roll Call*, May 24, 1999.

[439] "Hill's opening salvo": David Von Drehle, "Politics," *Washington Post*, May 30, 1999.

[439] "smearing his likely": Ibid.

[439] "Hill's personal life": Ibid.

[440] "If the campaign": Steve Ellman, "Interview: The Many Shades of Brown," *Free Press*, September 1-4, 1999, p. 9.

CODA

Sources: Michael Sheehan, Deborah Tannen, Steve Zdatny.

[450] "In my next life": David Lauter and Bob Secter, "Babbitt and DuPont Quit Presidential Race," *Los Angeles Times*, February 19, 1988, p. 1.

Index